AMERICAN CLASSICAL FURNITURE 1810–40

AMERICAN CLASSICAL FURNITURE 1810–40

REGIONAL IDENTITIES IN THE SCHRIMSHER COLLECTION

Edited by the Schrimsher Foundation

Foreword by Matthew A. Thurlow

Introduction by Wendy A. Cooper and Kimberly E. Schrimsher

Contributions by Clark Pearce, Peter M. Kenny, Alexandra Alevizatos Kirtley, Gregory R. Weidman, Matthew A. Thurlow, and Christine Thomson

The Schrimsher Foundation, Huntsville, Alabama

in association with D Giles Limited

The Schrimsher Foundation
P.O. Box 41
Huntsville, AL 35804, USA

First published in 2025 by GILES
An imprint of D Giles Limited
66 High Street,
Lewes, BN7 1XG, UK
gilesltd.com

ISBN: (hardcover) 978-1-913875-68-8

For The Schrimsher Foundation:
Chairmen: Randall A. Schrimsher and Kelly C. Schrimsher
Chief Administration Officer: Kelly C. Schrimsher
Project Director: Kimberly E. Schrimsher
Managing Editor: The Schrimsher Foundation
Content Editor: Matthew A. Thurlow
All photographs are by Darius Davis, unless otherwise noted, www.dariusdavis.com

For D Giles Limited:
Copy-edited and proof-read by Jodi Simpson
Designed by Helen Swansbourne
Produced by GILES, an imprint of D Giles Limited
Printed and bound in China

All measurements are in inches

Front cover: *Sofa*, c. 1820 (detail of cat. 27)
Back cover: *Pier Table,* c. 1825 (detail of cat. 47)
Frontispiece: *Pier Table,* c. 1815–1820 (detail of cat. 20)
Page 4: *Side Chair*, 1812–1830 (cat. 63)

Contents

Foreword

"I wouldn't give you a nickel to haul that to the dump."

JAMES ORVILLE SCHRIMSHER (1926–2001)

AFTER RECEIVING SUCH a stirring endorsement of their newfound interest in collecting Classical American furniture, we are thankful that Randall (Randy) A. and Kelly C. Schrimsher (see fig. 4) continued undaunted in their pursuit of the best examples of early-nineteenth-century craftmanship and design they could find made by the most talented artisans for their elite clients. This volume is a credit to their perseverance. Collecting is a passion (often compared to a disease or an addiction), and the Schrimshers' devotion to Classical furniture and enthusiasm for the education they have acquired in the process is paying tremendous dividends through the pages that follow.

Working in the carpentry shop of his father's construction business provided Randy with an appreciation for well-made woodwork at an early stage, and the opportunity to live in a historic house created the stage to start a collection. Randy began antiquing at stores in his native Huntsville, Alabama, shortly after college. An advertisement in *The Magazine Antiques* led him to Camden, South Carolina, in the fall of 1981—during football season, no less—to attend a symposium organized by the Decorative Arts Trust (DAT).

Fig. 1. The parlor in the Schrimsher's house in Huntsville, Alabama, showing a variety of Classical furniture from New York and Philadelphia, including cats. 27, 32, 35a, and 48. Dale Chihuly's *Green Glass Seaform Set* is perched on the center table.

The experience proved transformational, with presentations by Wendell Garrett, Jonathan L. Fairbanks, Joe Kindig, Harold Sack, and Frank Horton offering eye-opening insight into the breadth of material and quality within the Americana field. Dean F. Failey's lecture "Dollars and Sense: Collecting American Furniture" struck a particular chord with Randy's business-minded approach to the hobby. A DAT Symposium in Houston, Texas, the following year created the opportunity to introduce his sweetheart, Kelly, who was living in Austin at the time, to the organization. She was impressed just as much by the experience as by the shared interest in history that she discovered in Randy.

Regrettably, as the Schrimshers began to stoke their growing interest in American antiques, they fell under the influence of a disreputable dealer in Franklin, Tennessee, who sold them eighteenth-century Queen Anne and Rococo furniture for a few years. A fortuitous encounter helped them get back on track. The Schrimshers had the opportunity to welcome Gregory R. Weidman to their home while she was in town to lecture. She suggested that they may want to bring in an outside advisor for an evaluation of their nascent collection. Sumpter Priddy III, Luke Beckerdite, and J. Michael Flanigan, having recently established an antiques partnership, traveled to Huntsville to examine the Schrimshers' purchases. What they discovered, later confirmed by Alan Miller and Deanne D. Levinson, was that the dealer in Franklin was obfuscating the

Fig. 2. *Side Chair*, unknown maker, Sicily, c. 1802–1804, giltwood; replacement upholstery, Schrimsher Collection. Such chairs indicate the spread of French design at the turn of the nineteenth century to far-afield locations, including Sicily, which Napoleon visited in 1799 while traveling to Egypt for his military campaign against the Ottomans.

Fig. 3. The dining room in the Schrimshers' house in Huntsville, Alabama, showing pieces from Philadelphia and Boston from the collection (cats. 6, 12, and 52b)

significant repair and restoration of the furniture that he was selling as untainted.

Undeterred by this setback, Randy and Kelly parted ways with their eighteenth-century wares and turned wholeheartedly toward Classical material when they purchased a Greek Revival house in 1986. While poking through the barn behind the shop of a Philadelphia-area dealer, they happened upon a card table by Deming & Bulkley (cat. 22b) and a pier table attributed to Anthony Gabriel Quervelle (cat. 47). The arrival of these fabulous objects in Huntsville elicited the statement from Randy's father that is quoted above. His objections notwithstanding, Classical material held sway for the Schrimshers given the available range, quality, and quantity of material produced in the major cabinetmaking centers of Boston, New York, Philadelphia, and Baltimore between 1800 and 1840. The vibrancy of design during this era was

equally alluring, and the frequency with which these objects were featured in books and auction catalogues also appealed. Furthermore, the need to place those barn finds in the hands of a skilled conservator provided an introduction to Robert D. Mussey Jr. and the essential role of scientific analysis to understanding the surface treatments harnessed by early-nineteenth-century cabinetmakers.

Although the Schrimshers have never considered their acquisitions as investment opportunities, they do acknowledge that higher price tags warranted more education in the field. Interaction with an increasing range of curators, collectors, dealers, and conservators created new opportunities for firsthand study. Randy and Kelly also began to consider the Classical style more broadly through porcelain, lighting, carpets, and window treatments (fig. 1). The chance to tour Wendy A. Cooper's seminal 1993 exhibition *Classical Taste in America, 1800–1840* at the Baltimore Museum of Art reinforced the need to explore the full range of the Classical interior.

Travel has been an important focal point of Randy and Kelly's search for knowledge and insight. Much of that exploration has been achieved through the DAT's Symposia and Study Trips Abroad. The chance to explore important collections in museums and historic houses stateside as well as key sites of ancient design, such as Greece, Italy, and Egypt, served to expand their appreciation of the origins of Classical motifs and forms. They were even inspired to acquire an example of Classical furniture of European origins, a carved and gilt chair from Sicily (fig. 2), which they visited with the DAT in 2015.

The Schrimsher Collection has expanded and evolved over four decades. Decorative arts have always been part and parcel of their family life, even while raising three children and even with the addition of contemporary studio glass as an area of interest. Although a surprising diversion at first glance, the focus of glass artists on elements such as material, form, color, and technique beautifully complements their Classical furniture (fig. 1). Unlike scholars focused on artisans and designers working two centuries in the past, Randy and Kelly have enjoyed and benefited from the chance to communicate directly with the craftspeople responsible for the work.

Aiming to inspire other prospective students and collectors of Classical furniture, the Schrimshers have embarked on two projects in recent years. First, they have relocated a portion of their collection to a historic house in Charleston, South Carolina, where they plan to live for part of the year, with the hope that the objects can be seen by more visitors who appreciate the scale and accomplishment of their endeavors. They will live in the adjacent carriage house, leaving them the flexibility to install the furniture and accessories in the main house in a more academic fashion. With two houses to furnish, the pace of their collecting has only increased in recent years (fig. 3).

Second, they initiated this publication, gathering together a talented and experienced team of authors to shed new light on the story of Classicism in America and the splendid collection they have assembled. Having faced a steep learning curve when they started this pursuit and having benefited from each new publication on early-nineteenth-century cabinetmakers, they are eager to give back to the field. The bibliography provides a comprehensive list of the primary and secondary resources that fueled this study, but a brief recap of the scholarship that preceded this volume will provide the reader with a beneficial context of the interest in Classical design.

With few exceptions, neither collectors nor institutions paid this era much mind until Berry B. Tracy delivered the ground-breaking exhibition and accompanying catalogue *Classical America, 1815–1845* at the Newark Museum in 1963. After moving to the Metropolitan Museum of Art, he folded Classicism into the full run of design in the 1800s through *19th-Century America: Furniture and Other Decorative Arts*, which accompanied a celebration of the museum's 100th anniversary in 1970. In addition to these exhibitions and publications, Tracy inspired a generation of collectors while maintaining a delicate balance between his roles as both a curator and a dealer. With a growing interest in bringing prominent decorative arts to the White House and the State Department's Diplomatic Reception Rooms, the momentum created by Tracy ensured that objects from the 1810s and 1820s were included in those prominent spaces.[1]

The field had to wait two decades after Tracy's show at Newark for significant advancement, but Classical furniture was included in two general surveys of American furniture in the early 1980s. Cooper's *In Praise of America: American*

Fig. 4. Kelly and Randy Schrimsher

Decorative Arts, 1650–1830 concluded with a chapter titled "The Classical Impulse" that highlighted this era, and in the encyclopedic volume *American Furniture 1620 to the Present*, Elizabeth Bidwell Bates and Jonathan L. Fairbanks devoted considerable attention to the style.[2]

The next major boost for the study of Classicism appeared with the opening of Cooper's aforementioned exhibition *Classical Taste in America, 1800–1840* at the Baltimore Museum of Art in 1993, which was complemented by Gregory R. Weidman's *Classical Maryland, 1815–1845: Fine and Decorative Arts from the Golden Age* at the Maryland Historical Society.[3] This curatorial outreach paralleled the rise of another passionate group of collectors, including the Schrimshers and Jack Warner, a fellow Alabamian who built a vast collection on behalf of the Westervelt Warner Paper Company.

A spate of monographic studies of Classical-era cabinetmakers in New York, Boston, and Philadelphia followed in the wake of the 1993 exhibitions and publications. Peter M. Kenny, Frances F. Bretter, and Ulrich Leben's *Honoré Lannuier, Cabinetmaker from Paris: The Life and Work of a French Ébéniste in Federal New York* opened in 1998. Robert Mussey's *The Furniture Masterworks of John & Thomas Seymour* was released in 2003. Kenny and Bretter worked with Michael K. Brown and Matthew A. Thurlow on *Duncan Phyfe: Master Cabinetmaker in New York*, which appeared in 2011.

Alexandra Alevizatos Kirtley and Peggy A. Olley examined a specific Philadelphia furniture commission that defined the era in their *Classical Splendor: Painted Furniture for a Grand Philadelphia House* in 2016. Mussey and Clark Pearce's *Rather Elegant than Showy: The Classical Furniture of Isaac Vose* appeared in 2018.[4]

A handful of city- and state-specific studies have elaborated on the Classical era. In 1987, Beatrice B. Garvan bridged the gap between Neoclassicism and Classicism in *Federal Philadelphia, 1785–1825: The Athens of the Western World.* Weidman delved into the era in the previously mentioned *Classical Maryland, 1815–1845.* Catherine Hoover Voorsanger and John K. Howat's *Art and the Empire City: New York, 1825–1861* in 2000 considered the full swath of fine and decorative arts during the late Classical period. Mussey and Pearce's study of Vose was spurred by their research for the Four Centuries of Massachusetts Furniture conference at Winterthur in 2013 and the subsequent publication of papers in 2017 by the Colonial Society of Massachusetts, *Boston Furniture, 1700–1900.*[5]

This movement has also benefited from the attention of dealers who focus on Classicism, including Stuart and Elizabeth Feld at Hirschl & Adler, Carswell Rush Berlin, and Charles Clark. The Hirschl & Adler team has been particularly prolific in sharing collections of superlative Classical furniture and decorative arts over the past three decades. Most recently, the Felds published *Very Rich and Handsome: American Neo-Classical Decorative Arts* in 2014 and *Augmenting the Canon: Recent Acquisitions of American Neo-Classical Decorative Arts* in 2018. Berlin's essay on the Philadelphia shop operated by Richard Parkin and Thomas Cook in the 2013 edition of the Chipstone Foundation's *American Furniture* journal brought this important partnership to light.[6]

The Schrimshers, along with the team of authors who have contributed to this catalogue, hope that the objects and information contained within will serve as an essential resource for the future study of Classical furniture. By gaining entry to the canon of publications on this era of decorative arts, this book will provide other scholars and collectors with a leg up while also generating new interest in the period. They also intend to honor all of those who provided advice and encouragement along the way. Their collection and this book serve as an embodiment of the cherished relationships that are formed through long conversations with fellow enthusiasts about great objects and the important stories they tell.

MATTHEW A. THURLOW
Executive Director
Decorative Arts Trust

---

1. William H. Gerdts and Berry B. Tracy, *Classical America, 1815–1845* (Newark, NJ: Newark Museum, 1963); Berry B. Tracy et al., *19th-Century America: Furniture and Other Decorative Arts* (New York: Metropolitan Museum of Art, 1970). Early-twentieth-century publications on New York furniture, for example, often discussed work of the earlier Classical style up through 1820. For example, see Charles Over Cornelius, *Furniture Masterpieces of Duncan Phyfe* (New York: Metropolitan Museum of Art, 1922).
2. Wendy A. Cooper, *In Praise of America: American Decorative Arts, 1650–1830* (New York: Knopf, 1980); Jonathan L. Fairbanks and Elizabeth Bidwell Bates, *American Furniture 1620 to the Present* (New York: Richard Marek Publishers, 1981).
3. Wendy A. Cooper, *Classical Taste in America, 1800–1840* (New York: Abbeville Press for the Baltimore Museum of Art, 1993); Gregory R. Weidman and Jennifer F. Goldsborough, *Classical Maryland, 1815–1845: Fine and Decorative Arts from the Golden Age* (Baltimore: Maryland Historical Society, 1993).
4. Peter M. Kenny, Frances F. Bretter, and Ulrich Leben, *Honoré Lannuier, Cabinetmaker from Paris: The Life and Work of a French Ébéniste in Federal New York* (New York: Metropolitan Museum of Art, 1998); Robert D. Mussey Jr., *The Furniture Masterworks of John & Thomas Seymour* (Salem, MA: Peabody Essex Museum, 2003); Peter M. Kenny, Michael K. Brown, Frances F. Bretter, and Matthew A. Thurlow, *Duncan Phyfe: Master Cabinetmaker in New York* (New York: Metropolitan Museum of Art, 2011); Alexandra Alevizatos Kirtley and Peggy A. Olley, *Classical Splendor: Painted Furniture for a Grand Philadelphia House* (Philadelphia: Philadelphia Museum of Art, 2016); Robert D. Mussey Jr. and Clark Pearce, *Rather Elegant than Showy: The Classical Furniture of Isaac Vose* (Biddeford, ME: David R. Godine, 2018).
5. Beatrice B. Garvan, *Federal Philadelphia, 1785–1825: The Athens of the Western World* (Philadelphia: Philadelphia Museum of Art, 1987); Catherine Hoover Voorsanger and John K. Howat, *Art and the Empire City: New York, 1825–1861* (New York: Metropolitan Museum of Art, 2000); Brock Jobe and Gerald W. R. Ward, eds., *Boston Furniture, 1700–1900* (Charlottesville: University of Virginia Press, 2017).
6. Stuart P. Feld and Elizabeth Feld, *Very Rich and Handsome: American Neo-Classical Decorative Arts* (New York: Hirschl & Adler Galleries, 2014); Stuart P. Feld and Elizabeth Feld, *Augmenting the Canon: Recent Acquisitions of American Neo-Classical Decorative Arts* (New York: Hirschl & Adler Galleries, 2019); Carswell Rush Berlin, "'A Shadow of a Magnitude': The Furniture of Thomas Cook and Richard Parkin," in *American Furniture 2013*, ed. Luke Beckerdite (Milwaukee: Chipstone Foundation, 2013), 156–95.

Acknowledgments

Whatever spark first ignites a collector's desire, the journey becomes one of experiences and relationships. Each acquisition underscores a broader community of dealers, auction houses, shippers, conservators, and scholars and generates inspiring encounters with those who share a deep appreciation for a craftsperson's work.

In the early 1980s, Albert M. Sack and Deanne D. Levison wisely instructed us to purchase the best we could afford. Though our initial acquisitions were modest, Sack's book *The New Fine Points of Furniture: Early American, Good, Better, Best, Superior, Masterpiece* (1993) became dog-eared and our go-to manual for education and aspiration.

After Randy saw a membership advertisement in *The Magazine Antiques* for the Decorative Arts Trust (DAT) in 1981, he promptly joined, and soon we were traveling to symposia and lapping up lectures by Wendell D. Garrett, Jonathan L. Fairbanks, and Dean F. Failey. These gatherings became adventures in Americana and introduced us to historical properties, scholars, and fellow collectors. Through this network, we discovered kindred spirits and forged deep and lasting friendships.

In the days before the internet, we furthered our education by purchasing all the books we could find on American furniture, silver, and ceramics. Nightly rituals included combing through antique magazines, auction catalogues, and scrutinizing the *Maine Antique Digest.* After acquiring and restoring our first Greek Revival house, we fell in love with the Classical period and decided a date range of 1810 to 1840 would focus our collection and interiors.

In the life of any collector, along with the joys and excitement, there are moments of frustration and disappointment. Being a repeat underbidder is one. Buying a fake is another. In the latter, there was a humorous moment during a deposition when a cabinetmaker proudly testified how he altered our bow-front chest to make it appear as if it retained period finishes. Having been exposed, he was more interested in furniture expert Alan Miller's opinion of his work than the consequences of the intentional deception.

There were marital moments, too, when we had to determine mutual terms of agreement about what pieces could be sold when new ones appeared. On more than one occasion, Kelly arrived home from work to find a lamp on the floor and the contents of a chest stuffed into paper sacks. New rules had to be made or forged.

Despite all efforts toward a disciplined and harmonious approach to refine the collection, affection for brown wood comes with pitfalls. Randy purchased two Classical sideboards, with no intent to enhance the collection, because he could not bear to see them pass at auction. Kelly acquired a large plantation grain bin when no other buyer came forth because it had been left outdoors to the elements. When you appreciate antiques, there is a physical ache to resolve unrequited love.

Four decades into this journey, having witnessed the evolving tastes and interests of collectors, we see a pressing need to encourage and support new scholarship in the American decorative arts. The DAT is successfully leading this effort through its Emerging Scholars Program by awarding grants to students and young professionals who contribute new ideas and research as they pursue careers in the field. Proceeds from this publication will help support that effort.

This book would not have been possible without the vision of Matthew A. Thurlow, Decorative Arts Trust Executive Director, and the generous efforts of contributors Wendy A.

Cooper, Peter M. Kenny, Alexandra Alevizatos Kirkley, Clark Pearce, Christine Thomson, and Gregory R. Weidman. We are immensely grateful for your expertise, research, and insights on American Classicism.

To this publication's project director, our daughter and late Medieval and Baroque scholar Kimberly E. Schrimsher, we only dreamed that one day we could refocus your attention on the American Classical period. Thank you for bringing this monumental project to fruition.

Darius Davis, our talented photographer, exhibited enormous grace and good humor in traversing multiple locations to capture the objects depicted in this publication.

Our gratitude extends to the valued leadership and enthusiastic members of the DAT, Mount Vernon and its Connoisseur Society; Colonial Williamsburg; Winterthur Museum, Garden & Library; Monticello; Museum of Early Southern Decorative Art (MESDA), and the many museums and institutions we visited and benefited from their vast holdings and curatorial knowledge.

To the many other friends, dealers, and scholars who joined us on this memorable journey and helped to mentor and shape us, we thank you. It is impossible to name everyone who generously shared their time and expertise, but we have attempted to recognize those, past and present, who along with the authors of this publication played a personal or pivotal role in this adventure. They include Daniel K. Ackermann, Linda Ayres, Luke Beckerdite, Carswell Rush Berlin, Michael K. Brown, Andrew Brunk, Carol Borchert Cadou, Charles Clark, Stiles T. Colwill, Adam T. Erby, Stuart P. Feld, Elizabeth Feld, Donald L. Fennimore, J. Michael Flanigan, Nonie Gadsden, Stefan Gortat, Erik Gronning, Clifford Harvard, Ralph O. Harvard III, John A. Hays, Margize Howell, Penny McCaskill Hunt, John Frazier Hunt, Brock W. Jobe, Gary G. Kingsley, Wenda Kochanowski, Robert A. Leath, Deanne D. Levison, Dean Levy, Frank Levy, David N. Luckham, Alan T. Miller, Robert D. Mussey Jr., Jane C. Nylander, Richard C. Nylander, Bruce Coleman Perkins, Sumpter T. Priddy III, Margaret Beck Pritchard, James C. Rees, Helen Scott Reed, David Robb, Albert M. Sack, J. Thomas Savage, Kim Saul, Jim Schantz, Susan P. Schoelwer, Susan R. Stein, Henry G. Taliaferro, Page Talbott, Charles Vaughn, David B. Warren, Elisabeth Garrett Widmer, and Gail Caskey Winkler.

Ultimately, the dedication of *American Classical Furniture 1810–1840: Regional Identities in the Schrimsher Collection* to the DAT celebrates a lifetime of learning and discovery and honors the contributions of many individuals and institutions who have been integral to this lifelong passion for American Classicism. We hope this publication will serve as a resource for ongoing research and scholarship and inspire future collectors.

KELLY AND RANDY SCHRIMSHER

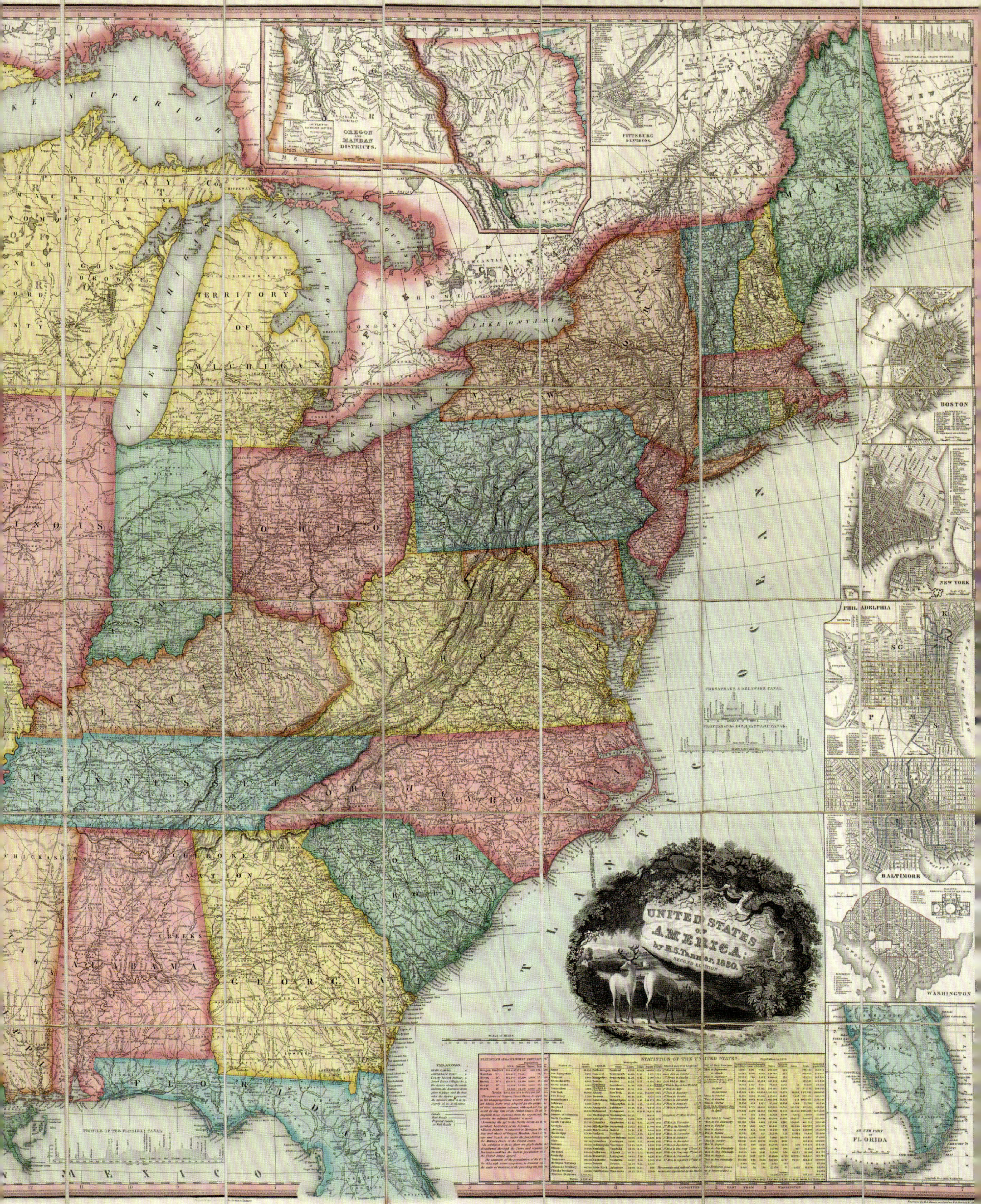
UNITED STATES
OF
AMERICA;
by H.S. Tanner, 1830.
SECOND EDITION
OREGON AND MANDAN DISTRICTS.
PITTSBURG & ENVIRONS.
LAKE SUPERIOR
LAKE MICHIGAN
LAKE HURON
LAKE ONTARIO
TERRITORY OF MICHIGAN
OHIO
GEORGIA
ALABAMA
CHEROKEE NATION
MEXICO
BOSTON
NEW YORK
PHILADELPHIA
BALTIMORE
WASHINGTON
SOUTH PART OF FLORIDA
CHESAPEAKE & DELAWARE CANAL
PROFILE OF THE FLORIDA CANAL
SCALE OF MILES
STATISTICS OF THE UNITED STATES

Introduction

The Rediscovery of the Ancient World and Its Impact on American Taste

WENDY A. COOPER AND KIMBERLY E. SCHRIMSHER

"The poet being an imitator, like a painter or any other artist, must of necessity imitate one of three objects—things as they were or are, things as they are said or thought to be, or things as they ought to be ..."[1]

ARISTOTLE, *POETICS*

THE EIGHTEENTH CENTURY bore witness to two major rediscoveries that would have a profound impact on the visual arts: the Roman cities of Herculaneum and Pompeii. The disastrous eruption of Mt. Vesuvius in 64 CE entombed both cities in volcanic ash and molten rock, the same substances that fortuitously preserved them for posterity. Excavations began in earnest at Herculaneum in 1738, and by 1748 work commenced at Pompeii. The masterpieces unearthed at these sites left European audiences spellbound and ignited a renewed fervor for the classical past.

Henry Schenck Tanner (1786–1858), *Map of the United States of America, Second Edition* (detail), 1830, hand-colored engraving (Courtesy David Rumsey Map Collection, David Rumsey Map Center, Stanford Libraries)

Architects, artists, and amateur enthusiasts alike flocked to the Continent to experience ancient sites firsthand and marvel at the Greco-Roman sculptures, wall paintings, bronzes, and ceramics that now crowded galleries and palaces. The Grand Tour, as it came to be known, functioned as the culmination of an aristocratic education, whereby young men and some women traveled to culturally rich locales, particularly France and Italy. Americans, too, participated in this foreign sojourn but broadened their itineraries to include London and other key locations in Britain. The Grand Tour's impact on the decorative arts, coupled with the copious publications in circulation that chronicled ancient sites, contributed to what are now known as the Neoclassical and Classical styles.

Neoclassicism endured in Britain and the Continent from about 1760 to around 1800. Its forms were linear and light, with delicate carving, inlay, or paint, and festoons, urns, bellflowers, and lyres on their flat surfaces. It was not fully embraced in America until after the Revolution; no doubt the wartime years between 1775 and 1781 contributed to the hiatus in the adoption of this new style. Neoclassicism in America emerged in the Federal era (1790–1830) and waned about 1810 when the Classical style gained momentum.[2] This volume uses the term "Classical" to define the more robust, archaeologically correct style of furniture that came into fashion in the United States about 1810; period documents employ the term "Grecian" or "modern" to describe this fashion. By the 1830s a more streamlined mode referred to as the Grecian Plain style came into vogue as well as the revivalist impulses that dominated the trade in the mid-nineteenth century such as Gothic and Rococo.

The literature on Classical American furniture is robust, but the Schrimsher Collection affords a novel opportunity to explore the genre through the lens of a particular range of regional identities. The essays and catalogue entries in this volume provide context for a vibrant period of evolution in design, specifying the characteristics that connected four urban centers—Boston and nearby Salem, New York, Philadelphia, and Baltimore—and those that divided them. The Schrimshers' decision to focus on these cities does not suggest that high-quality wares were not produced elsewhere in early-nineteenth-century America. Sensing the need to limit the scope of their collection, they oriented themselves to the four most target-rich locales. Washington, D.C., is included in recognition of the early-nineteenth-century geopolitical evolution of the United States and the coastwise movement of furniture to fill the public buildings of the country's third capital (see. p. 14).

Makers in each city had access to an ever-increasing library of design sources from Europe, and that broad selection ensured a variety of unique interpretations of Classicism. These pattern books provided cabinetmakers, upholsterers, and architects alike with drawings of sinuous table legs, swagged drapery designs, and bold furniture forms featuring mythical creatures such as chimera and griffins, to name a few. Artisans on both sides of the Atlantic eagerly embraced these tomes and copied patterns directly. More often, though, American cabinetmakers and craftsmen appropriated elements from multiple patterns within the same book or even sought inspiration from various titles. Through this process of selection, American cabinetmakers produced spectacularly innovative works of art that distinguish their Classical style from its European precedent.

What follows is a brief exploration of the most influential design and pattern books of the Neoclassical and Classical eras. These books circulated in various editions in America, and several are documented in craftsmen's shops or in the libraries of Classical art enthusiasts in every major cabinet-making center. As this volume will demonstrate, despite the reliance on shared source material, regional variations abound in Classical furniture.

Sources for Classical Form and Ornament

The discovery and excavation of Herculaneum and Pompeii encouraged learned antiquarians, architects, and archaeologists to journey to Italy to explore and record the wonders of the ancient classical past. Numerous publications, including impressive engraved folios and travel guidebooks, from the 1750s to the 1820s, would inspire travelers and influence the future of architecture, interior decoration, furniture, and ornament, in both Europe and America.

The first major publication was by German art historian Johann Joachim Winckelmann (1717–1768), who in 1755 published *Gedanken über die Nachahmung der griechischen Werke in der Malerei und Bildhauerkunst* (translated into English in 1765 as *Reflections on the Painting and Sculpture of the Greeks*), which shaped the future reception of antiquities. In this text, Winckelmann famously proclaimed, "there is but one way for the moderns to become great, and perhaps unequalled . . . by imitating the ancients."[3] Winckelmann argued that modern audiences owed the invention of Taste to the Greeks, and he presented the Renaissance as a successful case study of how ancient art could be reinvented for modern audiences. As a product of the Enlightenment, he hoped the Greek aesthetic could serve as a model by which order, reason, balance, and nature could harmoniously conform and broaden the minds of his contemporaries.[4]

Winckelmann had become acquainted with the world of the ancients, and specifically Greek art, as secretary of Count

Fig. 1. Julien-David Le Roy, "Vüe du Temple d'Erechthée à Athenes," (View of the Erechtheion, Athens) plate 5 in *Les Ruines des plus beaux monuments de la Grèce* (Paris, 1758), etching (Courtesy Winterthur Museum, Garden & Library). The angle Le Roy selected strategically captures the temple's Ionic column capitals and famed caryatid porch.

Fig. 2. James Stuart and Nicholas Revett, "The Erechtheum, Athens: Capital, Base, and Entablature of the North Porch," plate 8 in *The Antiquities of Athens*, vol. 2 (London, 1787), etching with engraving (Courtesy Winterthur Museum, Garden & Library). Instead of showing the building in its entirety like Le Roy, Stuart and Revett illustrate the key components of the Erechtheum's Ionic architectural order.

Heinrich von Bunau's 40,000-volume library in Nothnitz, near Dresden. He later moved to Rome, where he continued his study of ancient sculpture and painting. By 1764, he published perhaps his most significant work, *Geschichte der Kunst des Alterthums* (The History of Art in Antiquity), which systematically assessed the arts of the ancient Mediterranean. Throughout the text, Winckelmann unabashedly asserts the superiority of Greek culture and their arts. His publications had widespread influence abroad, and his sentiments on Greece were boldly echoed in architectural treatises and pattern books published well into the nineteenth century.[5]

Working at the same time as Winckelmann, the French architect and archaeologist Julien-David LeRoy (1724–1803) was also captivated by the ancient Greeks and produced measured drawings of the Athenian Acropolis. The scenic renderings in his *Les Ruines des plus beaux monuments de la Grèce* (Ruins of the Most Beautiful Monuments of Greece; Paris, 1758) (fig. 1) tended to be more picturesque and romantic than mathematically accurate, reminiscent of Italian architect and printmaker Giovanni Battista Piranesi (1720–1778). However, LeRoy's engravings were influential in exposing Greek architecture to a broader audience.

Among the earliest British architects to travel abroad were Scotsman James Stuart (1713–1788) and his friend and colleague Englishman Nicholas Revett (1720–1804). In 1751, they were elected to membership of the esteemed Society

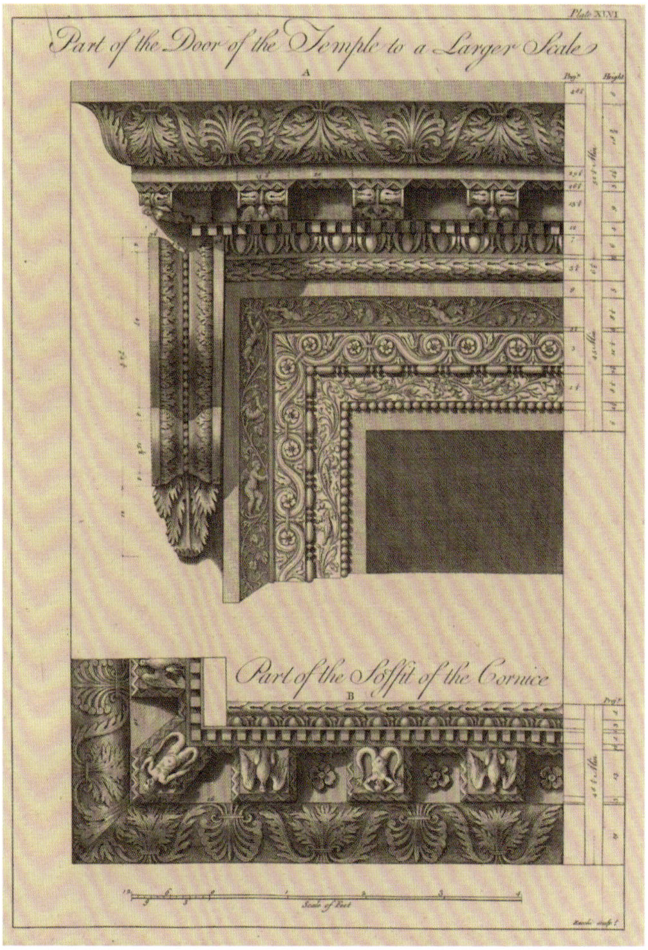

Fig. 3. Francesco Zucchi after Charles-Louis Clérisseau, "Part of the Door of the Temple to a Larger Scale" and "Part of the Soffit of the Cornice," plate 46 in Robert Adam, *Ruins of the Palace of the Emperor Diocletian at Spalatro in Dalmatia* (London, 1764), engraving (Courtesy Winterthur Museum, Garden & Library). Adam recorded ancient motifs such as acanthus leaves, rosettes, egg and darts, ovolo moldings, and eagles that became popular in Neoclassical and Classical designs.

of Dilettanti, an English organization dedicated to the study of the classical arts. As members of this august collective, they were given funds to assist with the publication of their work documenting ancient architecture and statuary during their travels in Italy and Greece. In 1762 they issued the first volume of *The Antiquities of Athens*; three subsequent volumes appeared in 1787, 1794, and 1796. Their focus on Greece rather than Rome underscores Winckelmann's influence; in their preface, the authors exclaim, "Greece was the great mistress of the Arts, and Rome, in this period, no more her disciple."[6] Perhaps in response to the criticism against LeRoy, Stuart and Revett's studies are meticulous in their calculations and offer dissections of the architectural orders for study and contemplation (fig. 2).[7]

Other publications by English and French architects continued to propel the growing desire for knowledge of the ancient world. From 1755 to 1758 Scottish architect Robert Adam (1728–1792) went abroad on his own Grand Tour, and upon his return he established an architectural firm in London with his brother James (1732–1794). By 1764 Robert Adam published *Ruins of the Palace of the Emperor Diocletian at Spalatro in Dalmatia* (fig. 3).[8] His ambitious project served two functions, to record the eroding palace and encourage future study. He wrote,

> The buildings of the Ancients are in Architecture, what the works of Nature are with respect to the other Arts; they serve as models which we should imitate, and as standards by which we ought to judge: for this reason, they who aim at eminence, either in the knowlege [sic] or in practice of Architecture, find it necessary to view with their own eyes the works of the Ancients which remain, that they may catch from them those ideas of grandeur and beauty, which nothing, perhaps, but such an observation can suggest.[9]

Robert Adam heeded his own advice and, with the assistance of his brother James, incorporated Greco-Roman designs in the grand houses they envisioned for England's landed gentry, such as Osterley Park, Kenwood House, Home House, and Syon House.[10] In 1773 they issued the first part of their two-volume *The Works in Architecture of Robert and James Adam* (London, 1773–79), in English and French, to disseminate their architectural designs of interiors and thereby encourage others to emulate them (fig. 4). They confidently claimed, "we flatter ourselves, we have been able to seize, with some degree of success, the beautiful spirit of antiquity, and to transfuse it, with novelty and variety, through all our numerous works."[11] Furniture in the Adam style, as it came to be known, was characterized as light, linear, and fanciful with small-scale ornament such as inlay of festoons, urns, bellflowers, and lyres in flat surfaces; it served as the embodiment of the Neoclassical style in England.

Neoclassicism in America was not fully embraced until after the Revolution concluded in 1781. Prior to the war, the Rococo style of furniture and decoration found favor due in part to English designer and cabinetmaker Thomas Chippendale's (1718–1779) *The Gentleman's and Cabinet-Maker's Director* (first edition, London, 1754). Chippendale's

Fig. 4. Robert and James Adam, "South Elevation of the Wall in the Back Court, House of Sir Watkin Williams Wynn," plate 3 in *The Works in Architecture of Robert and James Adam*, vol. 2 (London, 1773), etching and engraving (Courtesy Winterthur Museum, Garden & Library). This Court reveals the Adams' adept ability to create airy modern spaces predicated on Greco-Roman rules of symmetry.

Fig. 5. Thomas Chippendale, "Library Bookcase," plate 90 in *The Gentleman and Cabinet-Maker's Director* (3rd edition, London, 1762), engraving (Courtesy Winterthur Museum, Garden & Library). The Rococo elements and bulbous proportions of Chippendale's earlier work are not present in this library bookcase created for the third edition of the *Director*.

book focused on interior furnishings and decor, from carpets to silverware to entire room schemes, and his renderings blended aspects of the Gothic Revival, Chinoiserie, and French Rococo styles, begetting heavily carved and florid pieces; later editions comprised a sampling of Neoclassical designs thanks to the pervasive influence of Robert Adam, who regularly commissioned furniture from Chippendale (fig. 5).[12] American cabinetmakers lauded the *Director*, particularly the third edition, but its influence was felt most acutely in Philadelphia.[13]

By the early 1790s more Americans embraced the Neoclassical style with the help of a new influx of British pattern books brought to the continent by immigrant cabinetmakers and patrons. In 1788 *The Cabinet-Maker and Upholsterer's Guide* by London cabinetmaker George Hepplewhite (c. 1727–1786) was published posthumously by his widow Alice. The book comprises roughly three hundred of Hepplewhite's Neoclassical designs with idiosyncratic features such as shield-shaped chair backs, slender tapering legs,

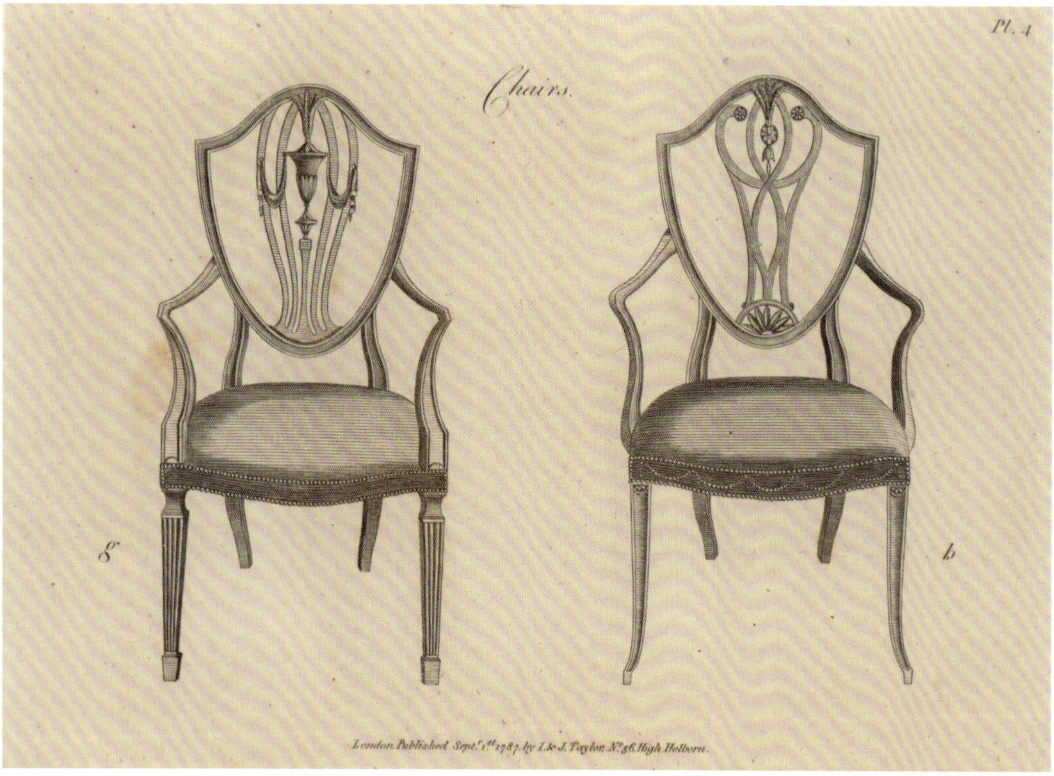

Fig. 6. George Hepplewhite, "Chairs," plate 4 in *The Cabinet-Maker and Upholsterer's Guide* (London, 1788), engraving (Courtesy Winterthur Museum, Garden & Library)

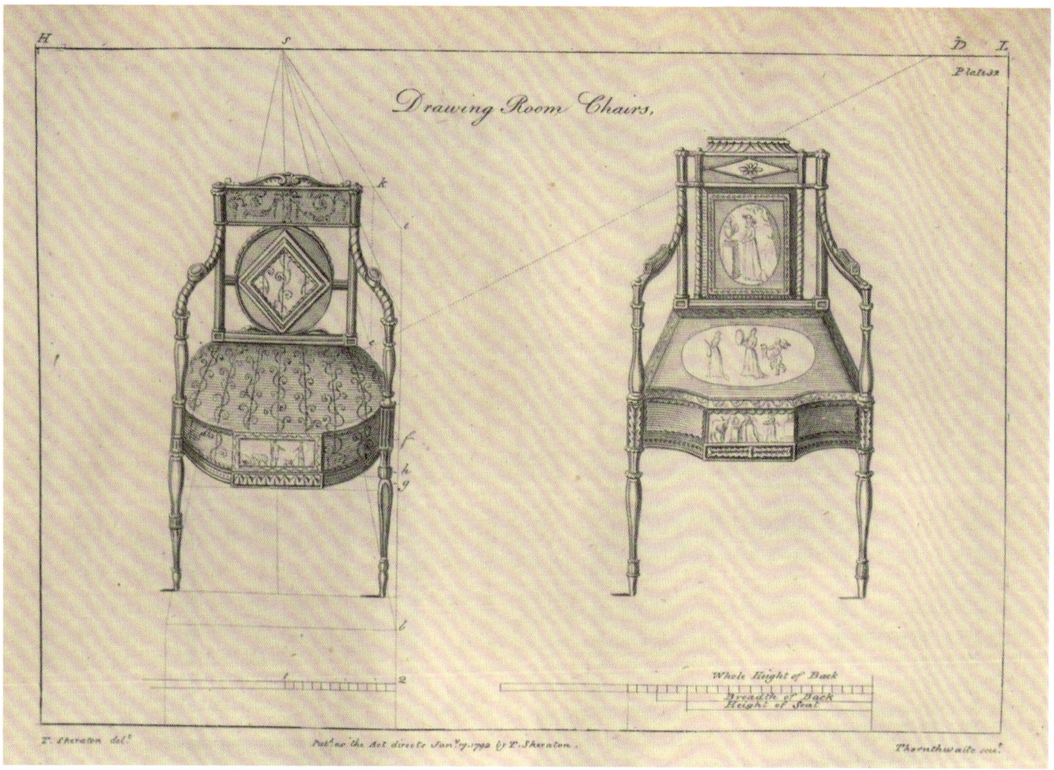

Fig. 7. Thomas Sheraton, "Drawing Room Chairs," plate 32 in *The Cabinet-Maker and Upholsterer's Drawing-Book* (London, 1791–93), engraving (Courtesy Winterthur Museum, Garden & Library)

curvilinear arms, and minimal carving (fig. 6).[14] Furniture could be further embellished by paint or inlay. The text's success in America was widespread and it was documented in Baltimore, Salem, and New York by 1800.[15]

Beginning in 1791, Thomas Sheraton (1751–1806) published *The Cabinet-Maker and Upholsterer's Drawing-Book* (London, 1791–93), which was issued in forty-two biweekly installments.[16] Sheraton, like Hepplewhite, championed the Neoclassical style but favored lighter colored woods and veneers, straighter chair lines, turned legs, and more elaborately painted grotesque decoration (fig. 7). Sheraton's sophisticated work found favor on both sides of the Atlantic. Boston-based cabinetmaker Thomas Seymour (1771–1848) owned one of the few recorded copies of the *Drawing-Book* in America, but evidence of its broad reach appears in furniture produced in Salem, New York, Philadelphia, and Baltimore.[17]

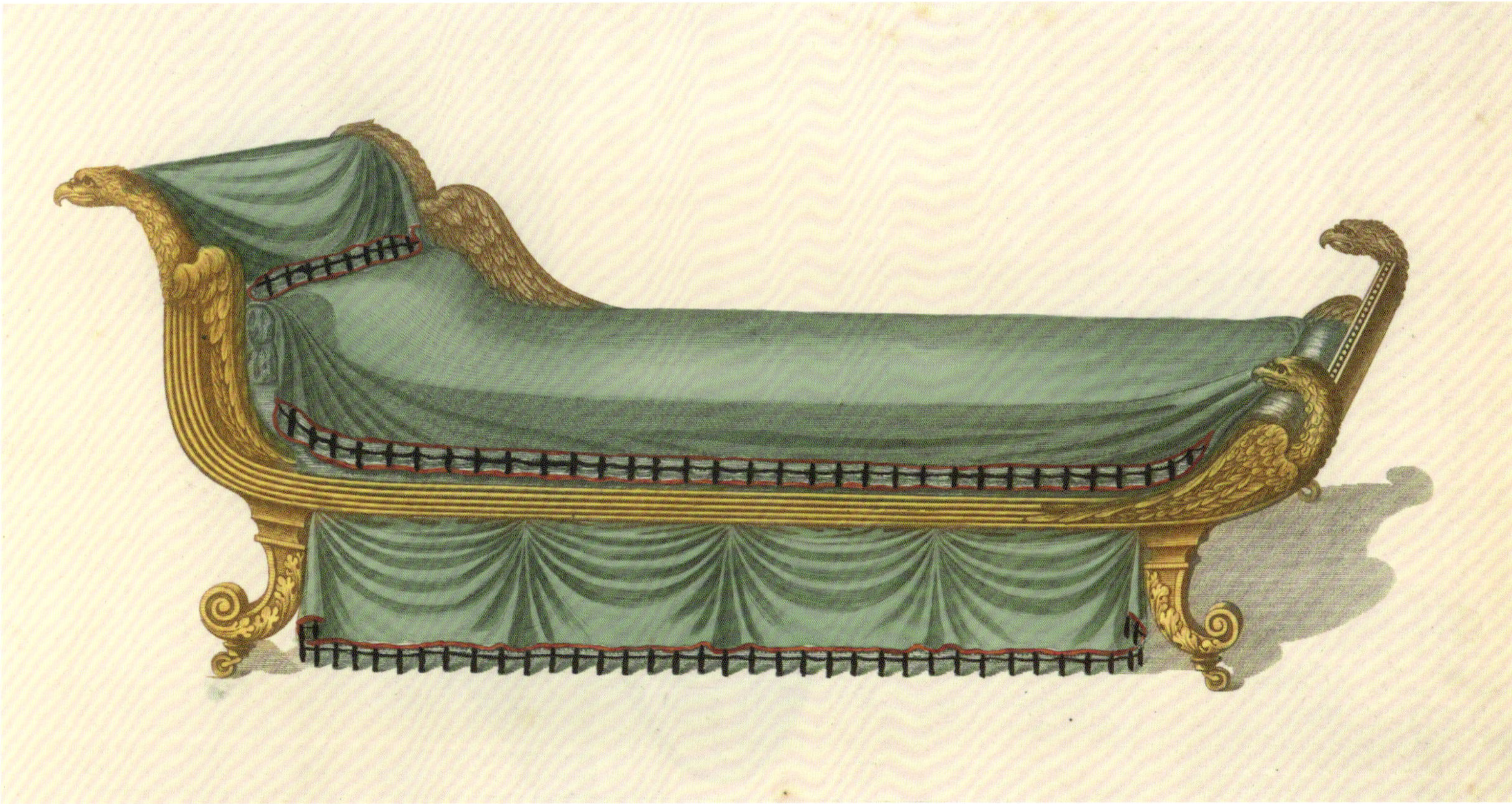

Fig. 8. Thomas Sheraton, Chaise Longue (detail), plate in *The Cabinet Maker, Upholsterer and General Artist's Encyclopaedia* (London, 1804–07), hand-colored engraving, The Miriam and Ira D. Wallach Division of Art, Prints and Photographs: Art & Architecture Collection, b13976291 (Courtesy New York Public Library). Animalia such as lions, griffins, and eagles (as seen here) abound in Sheraton's designs for the *Encyclopaedia*, whereas in the *Drawing-Book* they are completely absent.

Sheraton published two more pattern books in his career: *The Cabinet Dictionary* (2v., London, 1803) and *The Cabinet-Maker, Upholsterer and General Artist's Encyclopaedia* (London, 1804–7), the latter remained unfinished upon his death. Both projects aimed to present an alphabetized list of cabinetmaking terms and techniques with select illustrations. The plates, however, demonstrate more restraint in their designs compared to those in the *Drawing-Book*. Carved decorations such as eagles, lion's heads, and griffins now replace most of the painted festoons and acanthus leaf motifs (fig. 8). Both texts circulated in the major American cabinetmaking centers discussed in this volume.

Sheraton's tomes coupled with Hepplewhite's late work laid the foundation for what is now known as the English Regency style. It was named for George, Prince of Wales (1762–1830), who assumed the throne as Prince Regent in 1811 when his father, George III, became mentally ill. The English Regency style is variant of Neoclassicism and incorporates ancient motifs such as flora and fauna, along with mythological creatures like hippocampi into furniture designs. There was a new desire for rational, geometric forms, especially cylinders, spheres, circles, half circles, sinuous curves, and Ionic scrolls. These shapes gave designs movement, while still conforming to the ancient principles of symmetry and balance. The English Regency style had a profound impact on American furniture, particularly in Boston.[18]

In addition to the influential publications of the architectural remains of Rome and Greece, illustrated compilations of ancient objects encouraged emulation by contemporary artists. Sir William Hamilton (1730–1803), British ambassador to the Kingdom of the Two Sicilies from 1764 to 1800, was an avid collector of Greek vases, among other antiquities. His position enabled him to travel throughout Italy and amass an enormous collection. In 1772 he sold a selection to the British Parliament for the British Museum.[19] A few years later, Pierre-François Hugues, Baron d'Hancarville (1719–1805), an art historian and dealer, published *Collection of Etruscan, Greek, and Roman Antiquities from the Cabinet of the Honble. Wm. Hamilton His Britannick Maiesty's Envoy Extraordinary at the Court of Naples* (Naples, 1766–67) in four handsomely

Fig. 9. Pierre-François Hugues, Baron d'Hancarville, detail of a plate in *Collection of Etruscan, Greek, and Roman Antiquities from the Cabinet of the Honble. Wm. Hamilton, His Britannick Maiesty's Envoy Extraordinary at the Court of Naples*, vol. 2 (Naples, 1766–67) (Courtesy Winterthur Museum, Garden & Library). A klismos chair, like the cushioned example behind the central figure, was one of the many forms Classical cabinetmakers appropriated from ancient Greece.

colored volumes with text in English and French (fig. 9). Hamilton later collaborated with Johann Heinrich Wilhelm Tischbein (1751–1829), director of the Royal Academy of Painting at Naples, to publish Hamilton's remaining vases as line drawings—simplified to facilitate copying by an aspiring artist—with accompanying descriptions of the ancient stories depicted.[20] These works informed the trajectory of French and English decorative arts, particularly a ceramic company established by Josiah Wedgwood, whose products became famous for their classical imagery.[21] The d'Hancarville volumes assisted American craftsmen as well when the Library Company of Philadelphia purchased a set in 1772.[22]

Another influential volume of objects rather than architecture came from the hand of Englishman Charles Heathcote Tatham (1772–1842), who wanted to record ancient ornament across media. A competent draughtsman and budding architect, Tatham went to Rome in the 1790s with the encouragement and financial support of his mentor, English architect Henry Holland (1745–1806). Tatham's focus was on accurately depicting motifs and designs found on various ancient architectural and household forms like friezes, pilasters, altars, candelabra, seats, chairs, and bathing vases.[23] He was most specific in describing (whether correct or not) the varied materials incorporated in these decorative arts, such as Parian marble, alabaster, green basalt, and terracotta.

Upon his return to England, Tatham published *Etchings, Representing the Best Examples of Ancient Ornamental Architecture; Drawn from the Originals in Rome, and Other Parts of Italy, During the Years 1794, 1795, and 1796* (London, 1799) (fig. 10). In his preface, Tatham echoed Winckelmann and Robert Adam:

> ORNAMENT, it is true, with respect to its individual parts, must be originally copied from NATURE; but Nature is a wide field, into which, he who enters without a competent guide, will be in great danger of losing his way. The works of the Ancients are a map to the study of nature; — they teach us what objects we are to select for imitation, and the method in which they may be combined with effect . . . The proper selection and arrangement of all these, is not a matter of wild caprice; it demands indeed the exercise of fertile imagination, but of an imagination corrected by judgment, and ripened by experience.[24]

Tatham rendered his plates as black-and-white line drawings, to facilitate imitation, but some images appear more detailed than others. His depictions reveal an interest in spatial awareness; he often shows the same object or motif from different angles and includes precise measurements. Due to Tatham's skill and honesty in depicting ornament, his work was one of the most influential volumes available to other artists and craftsmen. It was among the numerous publications owned by the English painter and decorator George Bridport (1783–1819), who immigrated to Baltimore in 1808 and promoted Classical design.[25]

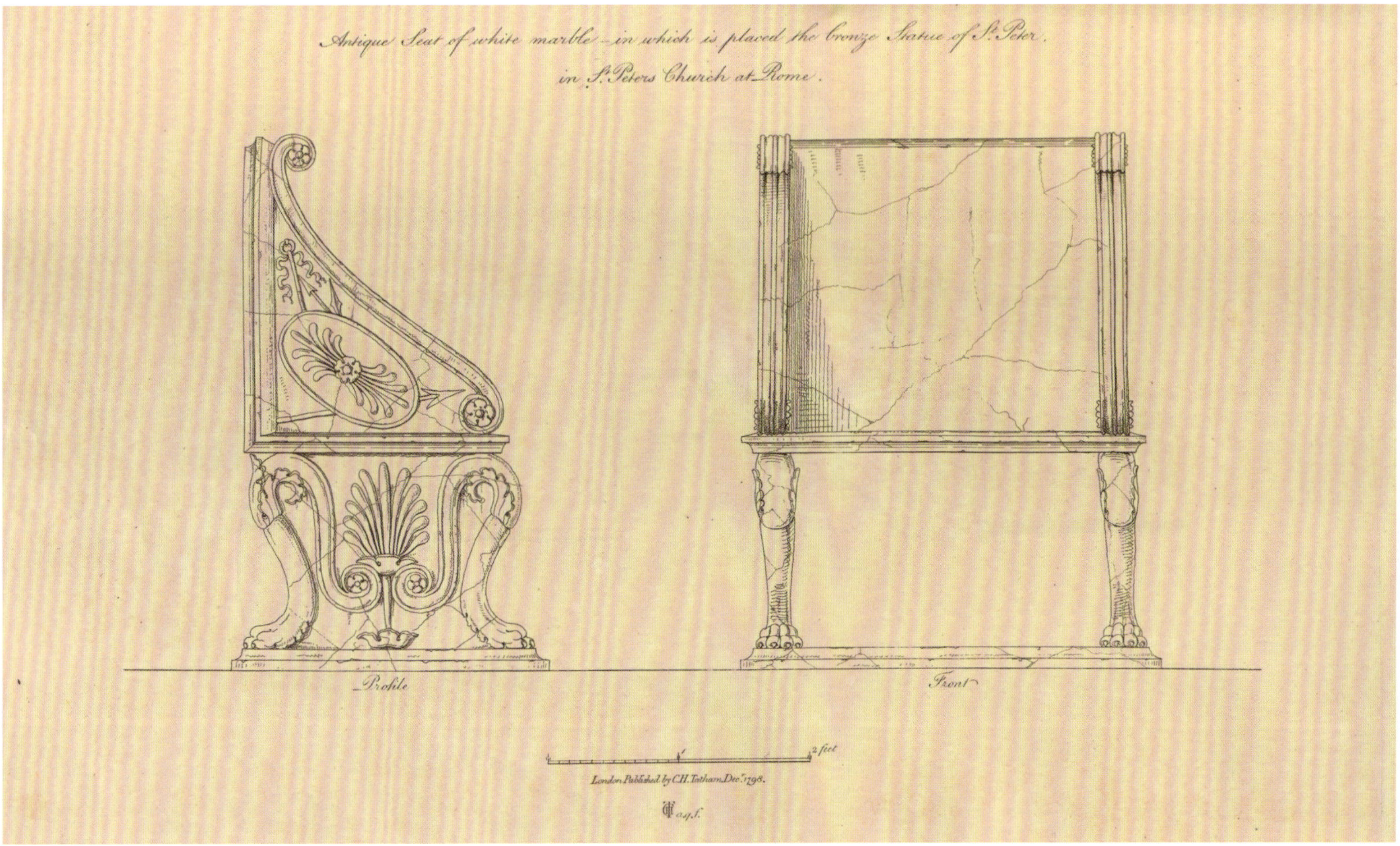

Fig. 10. Charles Heathcote Tatham, "Antique Seat of White Marble in Which Is Placed the Bronze Statue of St. Peter in St. Peter's Church at Rome," in *Etchings, Representing the Best Examples of Ancient Ornamental Architecture; Drawn from the Originals in Rome, and Other Parts of Italy* (London, 1799), engraving (Courtesy Winterthur Museum, Garden & Library). Hairy leg and lion's-paw feet, as seen on this seat, often appear on Classical furniture forms.

Another impetus for Tatham's tome was the rampant looting of art-historical masterpieces by the French general Napoleon Bonaparte (1769–1821). Tatham lamented, "The calamitous events which have lately overwhelmed that beautiful country, and dispersed its treasures over the continent, appear to render such a work at this time particularly necessary for students, who will hereafter find it very difficult, if not impossible, to gain access to many of the originals from which these representations were taken."[26] He was primarily referring to the impact of Napoleon's recent campaigns in Italy.

French interest in antiquity predated Napoleon's rise to power but his military expeditions in Italy, Egypt, and the Near East solidified French favor. Charles Percier (1764–1838) and Pierre-François-Léonard Fontaine (1762–1853) were two French architects and designers who both won the prestigious Grand Prix de Rome to study Italian architecture and antiquities in 1789.[27] In 1798 they published a curated selection of Roman facades and ornaments from antiquity through the Renaissance in *Palais, maisons, et autres édifices modernes, dessinés à Rome* (Palaces, Houses, and Other Modern Buildings, Drawn in Rome; Paris, 1798).[28] Like their English and German predecessors, Percier and Fontaine championed the study of ancient works to enrich and elevate the minds of aspiring artists, stating that an ingenious mind will find inspiration even in the most modest detail.[29] In 1799 Percier and Fontaine began to work exclusively for Napoleon, newly elevated to First Consul of the Republic, and commenced with the redecoration of the Château de Malmaison, Napoleon and his wife Joséphine's official residence. The rooms and objects they designed blended classical and Renaissance aesthetics.

Napoleon's campaign in Egypt and Syria from 1798 to 1801 may have resulted in a military stalemate, but its impact on the arts was transformational. Although the primary aim of his quest was imperial expansion and subjugation of the Mamelukes, Napoleon brought with him 151 artists and scientists representing specialties from musicology to astronomy to explore Egypt.[30] These *savants*, as they were known at the time, painstakingly documented Egyptian flora and fauna, collected ancient Egyptian treasures, and recorded Mameluke culture.[31] Upon their return to France, their drawings and research were published, and physically plundered objects were put on public display. From this body of visual material the Empire style was born and Percier and Fontaine crystallized it in their *Recueil de décorations intérieures* (Collection of Interior Decorations; Paris, 1801–12).

The Empire style derives its name from Napoleon, who was crowned Emperor of France in 1804.[32] Napoleon was instrumental in its formation because he needed a new visual vocabulary that distinguished him from the French monarchy and bolstered his imperial power. The ancient world with its mythological tales of mortal men achieving immortality through deeds alone appealed to the Corsican-born Napoleon, whose family lacked a noble pedigree. Percier and Fontaine worked closely with Napoleon to construct his public image and mined the world of ancient symbols, motifs, and ornament for inspiration; Jupiter's eagle, often shown clutching a thunderbolt, and a bee became Napoleon's primary emblems (fig. 11).[33]

Fig 11. Pierre-Michel Alix (1762–1817) after Jean-François Garnerey (1755–1837), published by Jean Frédéric Osterwald (1773–1850), *Napoléon Ier, Empereur des Français Roi d'Italie* (Napoleon I, Emperor of France and King of Italy, detail), after 1804, hand-colored aquatint, Schrimsher Collection

Percier and Fontaine issued *Recueil* to disseminate the Empire style with the public at large. Beginning shortly after Napoleon's return from Egypt, the plates were published in twelve installments of six between 1801 and 1812. The black-and-white outline engravings depicted interiors and furniture from Napoleon's palaces as well as impressive works for elite Parisian patrons and others around Europe (fig. 12). While the publication presented a regal taste for splendor and show-stopping magnificence, this level of grandeur was never achieved in American interiors. However, *Recueil* functioned as a visual repository for American craftsmen, who appropriated designs from it.

Dominique Vivant, Baron Denon (1747–1825), a French artist, diplomat, and archaeologist, was instrumental in managing Napoleon's public persona. Napoleon invited Denon to accompany him and his team of *savants* to Egypt. Denon's reputation preceded him; aside from his role as a diplomat for Louis XV and Louis XVI, his talents as a draftsman earned him membership in the Royal Academy of Painting and Sculpture in Paris. He also formed a close acquaintance in Naples with Sir William Hamilton, who encouraged him to study and collect ancient art.[34] In 1802 Denon published *Voyage dans la Basse et la Haute Égypte* (Journey in Lower and Upper Egypt) in two volumes chronicling his travels in the form of a daily log. The text is blatantly propagandistic, and he devotes a selection of images to battle scenes underscoring Napoleon's military superiority. The remainder of the plates, however, capture ancient and modern Egypt in its many forms, from Mameluke arms and armor to detailed renderings of ancient Egyptian temples and hieroglyphs (fig. 13).[35] In recognition of this accomplishment, Napoleon appointed Denon to oversee his newly founded Musée Napoleon in the Louvre Palace.[36]

Denon's publication was among the first to bring Egyptian art into European consciousness, and it ignited a continent-wide Egyptomania. Obelisks and pyramids were erected in European capitals, and mummy-unwrapping parties served as aristocratic recreation. The Egyptian Revival style in America did not begin until the 1840s, but elements

Fig. 12. Charles Percier and Pierre-François-Léonard Fontaine, "Lit exécuté à Paris pour Mr. O . . .," plate 25 in *Recueil de décorations intérieures* (Paris, 1801–12), engraving and etching (Courtesy Winterthur Museum, Garden & Library)

Fig. 13. Dominique Vivant, Baron Denon, "Porte intérieure du Temple de Tentyris" and "Vue géométrale du Portoque du Temple de Tenyris," plate 39 in *Voyage dans la Basse et la Haute Egypte* (Paris, 1802), engraving, Royal Academy of Arts, 17/1301 (Courtesy Royal Academy of Arts, London; photographer: Prudence Cuming Associates Limited)

Fig. 14. Pierre de La Mésangère, plate 1 in *Collection de meubles et objets de goût* (Paris, 1799–1831), hand-colored engraving (Courtesy Winterthur Museum, Garden & Library)

of Egyptian design, including pylons, cavetto moldings, and intaglio carving, appear in Classical furniture produced in the major city centers discussed in this volume.

The infusion of Egyptian motifs into the Classical aesthetic is apparent in plates published by French designer Pierre de La Mésangère (1761–1831). La Mésangère was a professor of literature who turned to publishing after the French Revolution.[37] As editor of the periodical *Journal des dames et des modes* (Journal of Women and Fashion) from 1797 to 1831, he commenced his most successful endeavor, *Collection de meubles et objets de goût* (Collection of Furniture and Objects of Taste; Paris, 1799–1831), in 1799. The *Collection* was published annually until 1831 and ultimately totaled some 450 plates detailing a variety of highly ornamented furniture and drapery (fig. 14). Due to the longevity of the project, the images reveal the shifting stylistic tastes following the Bourbon Restoration of 1814.

La Mésangère's influence in America was acute, due in part to the arrival of French *émigré* cabinetmakers. Craftsmen like Charles-Honoré Lannuier (1779–1819), who ventured to New York, and Michel Bouvier (1792–1874), who established himself in Philadelphia, likely brought with them or had access to these impressive designs through colleagues and relatives abroad. American-born cabinetmakers and wealthy Francophiles owned plates from the series, including Henry Hancock of Boston and the Ridgely family of Baltimore.[38]

Despite the political hostilities between France and England, French texts inspired the next wave of British publications on interior decoration. The Dutch-born Thomas Hope (1769–1831) emulated the outline drawings of his French predecessors in his *Household Furniture and Interior Decoration* (London, 1807).[39] Hope had moved to London in 1799 after spending close to a decade traveling Europe and purchased a townhome on Duchess Street designed by Robert Adam.[40] He spent the next several years redecorating and designing furnishings, fusing elements from the Neoclassical and French Empire styles with antiquities he acquired from Greece, Italy, Egypt, and India.[41] Hope preserved his

Fig. 15. Thomas Hope, plate 8 in *Household Furniture and Interior Decoration* (London, 1807) (Courtesy Winterthur Museum, Garden & Library). To complement his collection of Egyptian antiquities, Hope decorated a room in his home in an Egyptian scheme. He appropriated elements from Egyptian wall paintings, papyri, and sarcophagi to produce the furniture and wall designs.

novel interpretation of Classicism in his 1807 book, which reinvigorated the demand for the English Regency style first made popular by Sheraton and Hepplewhite.

Hope had lofty ambitions for his project, as evinced in his introductory remarks. He begins by eschewing the state of furniture making in England and lamenting the use of machinery rather than manual labor.[42] He writes:

> I hoped to contribute my mite not only towards remotely giving new food to the industry of the poor, but new decorum to the expenditure of the rich; not only towards ultimately increasing the welfare and the commerce of the nation, but refining the intellectual and sensible enjoyments of the individual; and thus, through the distant but powerful operation of the new stimuli applied to the human mind.[43]

He conceived of his designs as a medium to engender creativity and thereby produce works that elevate the country's position in the art world; he extols Charles Percier (Fontaine's name is not present) as the French example of this feat.[44] The sixty plates in the book commence with entire room schemes (fig. 15), followed by line drawings of furniture, chandeliers, ornament designs similar to Tatham's, and other decorative objects. How widely this publication was owned in America is not certain, but some of his designs (or portions of them) were modified and adopted by American cabinetmakers.[45]

Following on the heels of Hope's 1807 volume, the English Regency upholsterer and cabinetmaker George Smith (1786–1826) published *A Collection of Designs for Household Furniture and Interior Decoration* (London, 1808). Smith billed himself on the title page as "Upholder to his Royal Highness the Prince of Wales," a lofty title suggesting the success of his shop, but no documented work from him survives. His book's scope was larger than Hope's, with a total of 158 colored plates, although he too wanted English craftsmen and cabinetmakers to ennoble themselves to the level of sophistication achieved by the French.[46]

Smith divided the book into two sections: upholstery and cabinetmakers' work. He did not solely base his designs on the classical past, for he incorporates Gothic and Asian motifs. His Gothic-arched chairs and use of chinoiserie elements such as sweeping roofs, lanterns, and figural renderings are reminiscent of those in the first edition of Chippendale's *Director*.[47] Smith's preference for drapery is evident in the

Fig. 16. George Smith, "Design for a Bed," plate 22 in *A Collection of Designs for Household Furniture and Interior Decoration* (London, 1808), hand-colored engraving (Courtesy Clark Art Institute Library, Mary Ann Beinecke Decorative Art Collection). Hope combined ancient elements in the creation of this bed including torches, wreathes, acanthus leaves, and figures reminiscent of the Greco-Roman goddess of Victory.

level of specificity he provides in the accompanying texts; he even notes the proper yarn weight of the fringe. The brilliant color palettes he employed enliven the images, and their level of detail makes them seem more magnificent than Hope's simplified black-and-white illustrations (fig. 16). However, Hope's extant furniture creations demonstrate they were just as impressive in their use of colorful materials.[48]

The success of Smith's enterprise propelled him to publish another design book: *The Cabinet-Maker and Upholsterer's Guide* (London, 1826). Similar to Smith's 1808 *Collection*, this work includes 152 intricate engravings of decorative arts designs such as chairs, candelabras, drapery, and wardrobes, about half of which are hand colored (fig. 17). However, the *Guide* differs in its inclusion of lengthy prose rather than the perfunctory plate descriptions of the earlier book. Smith provides an erudite exploration of the core components of art making for his reader, including geometry, perspective, color, shadow, and ornament, before delving into interiors. These additions distinguish Smith's book from his predecessors and align it more with the treatises on painting and sculpture that had circulated in Europe for centuries. Nevertheless, he extols the legacy of Chippendale, Adam, Hamilton, Denon, and Hope in his introductory remarks as crucial to the formation of his contributions to the field.

In what was quickly becoming a saturated market, the impetus for James Barron (active 1805–1839) to produce another pattern book was likely financial. Barron, who advertised himself as a seller of Venetian blinds, a patent holder of roller blinds, and a brass founder, included price lists for his wares in his 1814 publication *Modern and Elegant Designs of Cabinet and Upholstery Furniture*.[49] Whether or not Barron himself executed the designs for his pattern book is unclear, but the sixty-eight plates, the majority hand colored, conveniently highlight his shop's wares. Ample attention is paid to draperies as well as furniture ornamented with brass, but scant textual descriptions accompany the illustrations (fig. 18). Barron's publication must have reached the hands of some of the best Philadelphia cabinetmakers, as several pieces of furniture made there closely conform to illustrations in this book. Furthermore, Barron's hardware impressed Bostonian craftsmen who frequently imported brass from the English designer.

The German-born publisher Rudolph Ackermann (1764–1834) also recognized the lucrative nature of design compilations and, like La Mésangère, produced serial publications. Trained initially as a carriage maker, he moved to London in 1787 and established a printing shop that came to specialize in color-plate books. Ackermann valued the arts and even financed a drawing school in his storefront from 1795 to 1805.[50] In 1809 he commenced a monthly magazine, much like La Mésangère's *Collection*, called *The Repository of Arts, Literature, Commerce, Manufactures, Fashions, and Politics* (London, 1809–28). In addition to current reviews of plays and politics, each month showcased a bespoke selection of furniture with descriptions about the upholstery and suggestions for use. There were even four fabric samples pasted into each monthly issue with notes regarding suitability (fig. 19). Judging from the number of American pieces of furniture that were inspired by Ackermann's designs, his magazines were widely circulated.[51]

Fig. 17. George Smith, "Bookcase for a Study," plate 140 in *The Cabinet-Maker and Upholsterer's Guide* (London, 1826), hand-colored engraving (Courtesy Winterthur Museum, Garden & Library)

Fig. 18. James Barron, Three Sofas, plate in *Modern and Elegant Designs of Cabinet and Upholstery Furniture* (London, 1814), hand-colored engraving (Courtesy Winterthur Museum, Garden & Library). The lion's-paw feet, fantastical dolphin-like creatures, and floral painted decoration included in these sofas appear in Classical furniture produced in the major American centers highlighted in this volume.

Fig. 19. Cover of Rudolph Ackermann, *The Repository of Arts, Literature, Commerce, Manufactures, Fashion, and Politics*, no. 3 (March 1809), engraving and textile samples; "Ladies Secretaire" and "Parlor Chair," plate 14 in Rudolph Ackermann, *The Repository of Arts, Literature, Commerce, Manufactures, Fashion, and Politics*, no. 3 (March 1809), hand-colored engraving (Courtesy Winterthur Museum, Garden & Library)

At the same time Smith issued his *Cabinet-Maker and Upholsterer's Guide*, the father and son duo Peter (1765–1844) and Michael Angelo (1794–1841) Nicholson produced *The Practical Cabinet-Maker, Upholsterer, and Complete Decorator* (London, 1826). Peter trained as an architect and mathematician and enjoyed an illustrious career as an educator, producing during his lifetime some twenty-seven treatises on subjects including geometry, railway masonry, staircases, and carpentry.[52] Michael was an accomplished draftsman and supplied illustrations for several of his father's projects.

The release of the Nicholsons' publication so close to Smith's was prescient, as the two books adhere in format. However, as Peter commented in the introduction, "It is a trite and oft-repeated observation that 'there is nothing new under the sun'; hence many imagine that every possible variety has already been covered . . . this however is far from the truth since though the number of forms may in some degree be said to be limited, their combinations are almost infinite."[53] Like Smith, the Nicholsons articulate the laws of geometry and perspective but far surpass their contemporary by devoting an impressive 135 pages to the subject. Following a glossary of technical terms, seventy-three plates present a range of styles and forms from tables to cornices to wine coolers (fig. 20). Hand-colored engravings are interspersed with simplistic black-and-white contour drawings or detailed black-and-white renderings with more refined shading. The choice of subject matter does not differ from Smith, but the Nicholsons include separate Gothic designs for almost every item of furniture rendered, demonstrating an aesthetic shift. In America, the Nicholsons' text as well as Peter's prior publications were well received, particularly in New York and Philadelphia.[54]

By 1829 another influential English publication appeared: *The Modern Style of Cabinet Work Exemplified* (London, 1829) by the prolific artist-designer Thomas King (c. 1790–1842). Little is known of King's career, but he published twenty-eight illustrated books between 1823 and 1848. His *Modern Style* enjoyed numerous editions up until 1862.[55] In the pithy

Fig. 20. Michael Angelo Nicholson, "Circular Table," plate in Peter Nicholson and Michael Angelo Nicholson, *The Practical Cabinet Maker, Upholsterer and Complete Decorator* (London, 1826), hand-colored engraving (Courtesy Winterthur Museum, Garden & Library). This piece exhibits a variety of surface ornamentation such as *vert antique* and gilding that American cabinetmakers, particularly those in New York and Philadelphia, embraced.

Fig. 21. Thomas King, "A Gothic Bookcase," plate in *The Modern Style of Cabinet Work Exemplified* (London, 1829), engraving (Courtesy Winterthur Museum, Garden & Library)

Fig. 22. John Hall, plate 27 in *The Cabinet Makers' Assistant* (Baltimore, 1840), lithograph (Courtesy Winterthur Museum, Garden & Library)

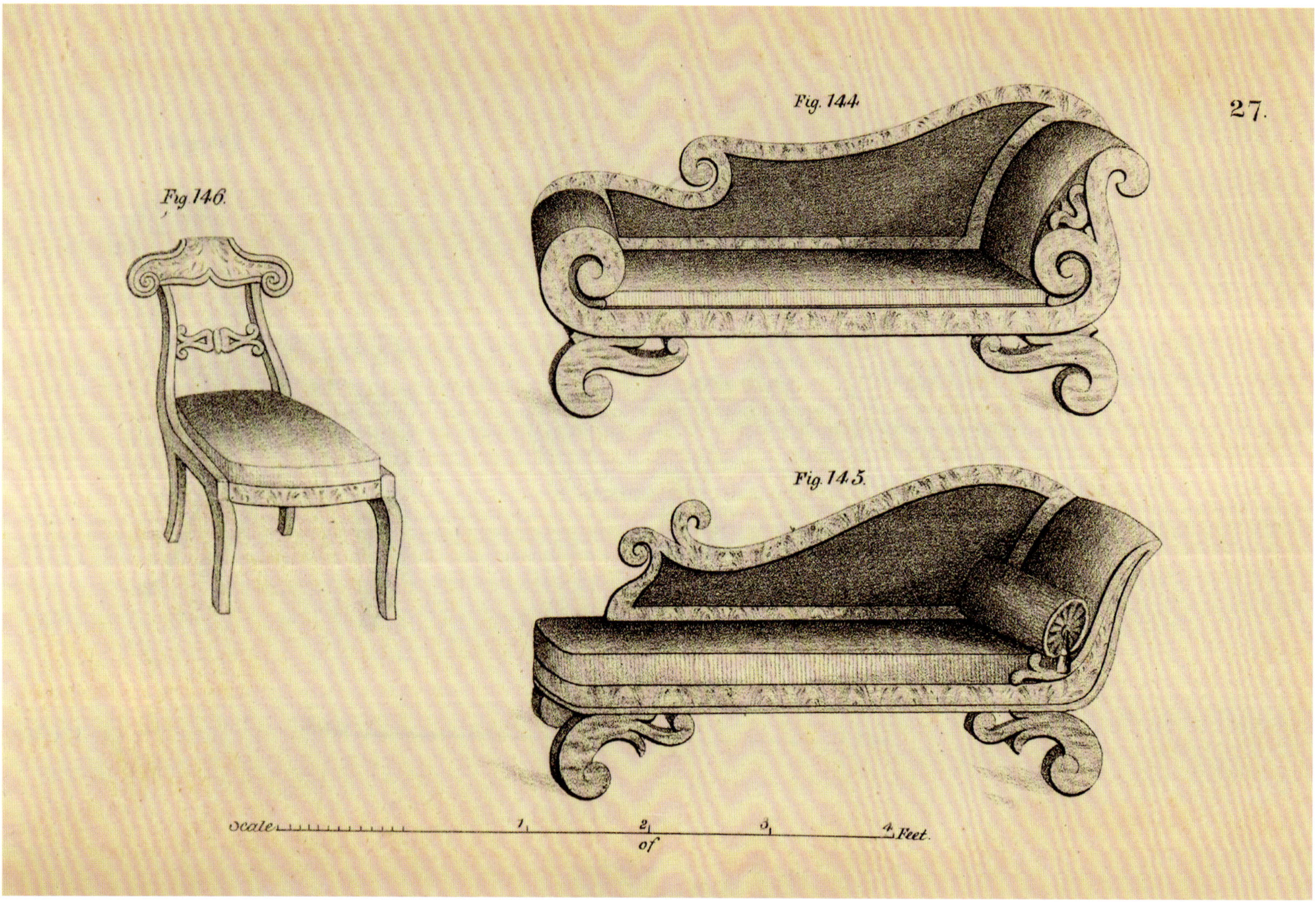

preface to this text, King muses on the evolution of what he calls the modern style, claiming that "as far as possible the English style is carefully blended with Parisian taste: and a chaste contour and simplicity of parts is attempted in all the objects, which, being in some degree confined in dimensions and form, present rather a difficulty in the adaption of Grecian, Roman, and Gothic Ornaments."[56] Although a few appear in color, the book of over seventy plates is predominantly composed of black-and-white contour drawings (fig. 21). Numerous American craftsmen drew upon King's designs and emulated his preference for veneer and inlay as well as bold scrolls, acanthus leaves, and rosette motifs. Conspicuously absent are animalia in any form such as lion's-paw feet, griffins, dolphins, or eagles that peppered earlier pattern books.[57]

The artisan John Hall (1804–c. 1855) looked to King when he created *The Cabinet Maker's Assistant* (Baltimore, 1840).[58] Exactly when Hall left England for America is unknown, but he was working in Baltimore as a draftsman by 1835. The beginning of Hall's preface includes a phrase derived from King but with two crucial changes. Hall wrote, "As far as possible, the style of the United States is blended with European taste," whereas King used the words "English" and "Parisian."[59] Hall touches on the essential point that although the United States was undoubtedly indebted to Europe the American Classical style was nevertheless distinct. Hall's forty-three black-and-white plates do not include overtly Classical motifs but demonstrate the shifting preference for more restrained forms with heavy proportions, less gilding, elliptical curves, and S-scrolls now known as the Grecian Plain style (fig. 22).

Regionalism in American Classical Furniture

The breadth and diversity of European pattern and design books available to American cabinetmakers of the Classical era was staggering. Furthermore, affluent Americans could travel to Italy, France, and Greece to see ancient monuments for themselves, along with the added benefit of observing the furniture that was actively being created in Britain and France. Some purchased examples, pattern books of their own, or even ancient works of art to bring stateside. The Classical influence permeated American taste.

Classical furniture from the major urban centers of America has much in common. After all, each location was inspired by many of the same published drawings of the art and architecture from the ancient world, and many of the same English and French pattern books. American cabinetmakers in this period were crafting similar furniture forms and embracing new interpretations in seating and table designs, as well as those for secretaries, beds, cellarettes, and others.

However, due to their economic, historical, and cultural makeups, the four urban centers of Boston, New York, Philadelphia, and Baltimore were resolutely distinct in the early nineteenth century which contributed to regional variations. Classicism is defined by conspicuously carved and ornamented surfaces, but Boston and Salem focused on the most chaste interpretation of the style. The city's long history and status as a somewhat-faded mercantile powerhouse likely led to a conservative approach focused on English Regency design, but by no means were Boston's cabinetmakers and carvers producing simple wares. Following a disastrous fire during the American Revolution, New York rose like a meteoric phoenix in the following decades to emerge as the country's largest and most prosperous city. Not surprisingly, the most exuberant and sculptural interpretations of American Classicism originated here, with deep ties to French sources. Philadelphia sustained its cultural and commercial importance following the Revolution and its subsequent ten-year stint as the national capital. The city also retained a vibrant furniture trade powered by craftsmen well versed in international trends or of European origin, who introduced some of the country's earliest Classical furniture as well as bold, volumetric forms that spoke to the moxie of consumers in Philadelphia and beyond. Baltimore was the youngest of these metropolitan locales, having charged to prominence during and after the Revolution. The newfound wealth powered a building boom and the cabinetmaking trade, which ranged from a local specialty in painted furniture to more formal and robust architectonic wares. In Washington, D.C., public officials desired to furnish the President's House and the Capitol in a befitting manner and so brought the new Classical style into official government spaces.

The rise and fall of the Classical cabinetmaking trade in each of these cities is inextricably linked to larger national and international trends. Shifting economic, political, and religious forces in Europe drove artisans to seek superior opportunities across the Atlantic in fits and spurts over the early nineteenth century. Wars and financial crises took their toll on the cabinetmaker's trade throughout the era. Thomas Jefferson's Embargo Act of 1807 and the War of 1812 were particularly disastrous for American commerce, as were the financial panics of 1819 and 1837. The geographic separation of Boston, New York, Philadelphia, and Baltimore from the cotton and sugar fields of the South did not isolate cabinetmakers from the impact of slavery. The wealth generated by Southern plantation owners and the Northern merchants, banks, and insurance firms that represented them is inextricably tied to the furniture trade, alongside many other aspects of the American economy. During periods of prosperity, the prodigious scale of furniture manufacturing in the four cities enabled those cabinetmakers overseeing large-scale operations to capitalize on the export market, shipping their goods down the coast to Southern U.S. ports and enjoying an increasingly transatlantic reach to the Caribbean and South America.

It is not always possible to ascribe an object to a particular place of origin with certainty. Over the course of building their holdings of Classical furniture, not to mention the research done in preparation for this catalogue, some furniture in the Schrimsher Collection was reattributed to another location: Boston to Salem, New York to Philadelphia, Philadelphia to Baltimore, and vice versa. Identifying the regional origin of American Classical furniture can be challenging, given the overlapping forms, motifs, use of materials, and types of ornament and construction. Yet when considering a particular piece of furniture, identifying a handful of attributes commonly used in a specific region will usually lead in the right direction.

Notes to the Reader

This catalogue is the first comprehensive assessment of the Classical furniture in the Schrimsher Collection. The contributing authors selected the objects that they felt best represented the style of the city centers discussed in this volume. To standardize the catalogue entries, the authors agreed to the following formatting guidelines. Dimensions are listed as height, width, and depth unless otherwise noted. If a piece is asymmetric, the dimensions given are at its greatest height, width, or depth. Provenance commences with the oldest owner first. The direct passage of an object from one owner, auction house, or dealer to the next is indicated with a semicolon. A break in the provenance is indicated by a period between the two parties. Research into these ownership gaps is still ongoing. The inclusion of the term "with" before a name indicates the object was in the possession of a dealer rather than a collector.

The materials listed for each object were identified by sight unless otherwise indicated. Certain pieces in the collection, for instance, have undergone microanalysis. Detailed findings from these tests and other conservation reports are available in the Schrimsher Foundation collection files. Primary materials appear first, followed by a semicolon to differentiate them from secondary ones; a further semicolon is followed by surface treatments and any other materials.

1. Samuel Henry Butcher, *Aristotle's Theory of Poetry and Fine Art* (New York: Macmillan, 1932), 97.
2. "Federal era" is the term used to describe the first few decades of the United States following the Revolution. Because the Neoclassical style was popular during the Federal era, the term "Federal" has been used in past as a synonym to refer to the proportionate, elegant, and Greek-inspired buildings constructed up to 1830. However, recent scholarship favors the use of *Neoclassical* and *Classical* to refer to the styles of decorative arts produced during the Federal Period. See Matthew Thurlow, "American Federal-Era Period Rooms," in *Heilbrunn Timeline of Art History*, November 2009 (New York: Metropolitan Museum of Art, 2000–), https://www.metmuseum.org/toah/hd/fede/hd_fede.htm.
3. Johann Joachim Winckelmann, *Reflections on the Painting and Sculpture of the Greeks*, trans. Henry Fusseli (A. Millar: London, 1765), 2.
4. Odile Nouvel-Kammerer, "Discourse on Ornament under the Empire," in *Symbols of Power: Napoleon and the Art of the Empire Style 1800–1815* (Paris: American Federation of the Arts and Musée des Arts Décoratifs, 2007), 28.
5. For more information on Winckelmann's influence, see Katherine Harloe, *Winckelmann and the Invention of Antiquity: Aesthetics and History in the Age of Altertumswissenschaft* (Oxford: Oxford University Press, 2013); Alex Potts, *Flesh and the Ideal: Winckelmann and the Origins of Art History* (New Haven: Yale University Press, 1994).
6. James Stuart and Nicholas Revett, *The Antiquities of Athens* (London, 1762), 1:i.

7. James Grout, "Stuart and Revett—And LeRoy," Encyclopedia Romana, last modified 2024, https://penelope.uchicago.edu/~grout/encyclopaedia_romana/greece/architecture/classicism.html.
8. Adriano Aymonino, "'The True Style of Antique Decoration': Agostino Brunias and the Birth of the Adam Style at Kedleston Hall and Syon House," in *Robert Adam and His Brothers: New Light on Britain's Leading Architectural Family*, ed. Colin Thom (Swindon: Historic England, 2019), 104.
9. Robert Adam, *The Ruins of the Palace of the Emperor Diocletian at Spalatro in Dalmatia* (London, 1764), 1.
10. "Robert Adam: Neoclassical Architect and Designer," Victoria and Albert Museum, accessed May 4, 2024, https://www.vam.ac.uk/articles/robert-adam-neoclassical-architect-and-designer.
11. Robert and James Adam, *The Works in Architecture of Robert and James Adam* (London: T. Becket, 1773), 1: 6.
12. Nicholas C. Vincent, "American Furniture, 1730–1790: Queen Anne and Chippendale Styles," in *Heilbrunn Timeline of Art History* (New York: Metropolitan Museum of Art, 2000–), December 2009, https://www.metmuseum.org/toah/hd/chip/hd_chip.htm; James Lomax, "Chippendale, Thomas snr (1718–1779)," British and Irish Furniture Makers Online, Furniture History Society, last updated February 15, 2024, https://bifmo.furniturehistorysociety.org/entry/chippendale-thomas-snr-1718-79. For more information on Chippendale's *Director* and its influence, see Morrison H. Heckscher, "Philadelphia Chippendale: The Influence of the 'Director' in America," *Furniture History* 21 (1985): 283–95.
13. Morrison H. Heckscher, "Chippendale's *Director*: A Manifesto of Furniture Design," *Metropolitan Museum of Art Bulletin* 75, no. 4 (Spring 2018): 41. For more information on who owned copies of the *Director* in America before 1800, see Morrison H. Heckscher, "English Furniture Pattern Books in Eighteenth-Century America," in *American Furniture 1994*, ed. Luke Beckerdite (Milwaukee: Chipstone Foundation, 1994), https://chipstone.org/article.php/48/American-Furniture-1994/?s=sheraton.
14. Two more editions of this book followed in 1789 and 1794. "Hepplewhite, George (1786)," British and Irish Furniture Makers Online, last modified 2019, https://bifmo.furniturehistorysociety.org/entry/hepplewhite-george-1786.
15. Heckscher, "English Furniture Pattern Books in Eighteenth-Century America."
16. The first edition included three parts, an appendix, and sixty-nine plates. The second edition is virtually the same as the first but has an Accompaniment with fourteen additional plates. The third edition was issued in 1802. Heckscher, "English Furniture Pattern Books in Eighteenth-Century America."
17. Ibid.
18. John Morley, *Regency Design, 1790–1840: Gardens, Buildings, Interiors, Furniture* (New York: H. N. Abrams, 1993), 231, 233, 239.
19. Hamilton sold a selection of objects to the British government for 8,400 pounds. Later he gifted other parts of his collection to the British Museum.
20. *Collection of Engravings from Ancient Vases of Greek Workmanship: Discovered in Sepulchers in the Kingdom of the Two Sicilies but Chiefly in the Neighbourhood of Naples during the Course of the Years MDCCLXXXIX and MDCCLXXXX Now in the Possession of Sir Wm. Hamilton, His Britannic Maiesty's Envoy Extry. and Plenipotentiary at the Court of Naples*, 4 vols. (Naples, 1791–95). Tamara Fultz, "A Passion for Antiquity: Sir William Hamilton and His Vase Collection," Metropolitan Museum of Art, October 17, 2018, https://www.metmuseum.org/articles/sir-william-hamilton.
21. Tristram Hunt, *The Radical Potter: The Life and Times of Josiah Wedgwood* (New York: Metropolitan Books, 2021), 110–12.
22. Alexandra Alevizatos Kirtley has confirmed that in 1772 The Library Company of Philadelphia acquired a copy of d'Hancarville's *Collection of Etruscan, Greek, and Roman Antiquities from the Cabinet of the Honble. Wm. Hamilton*. See James N. Green, "The First Colorplate Books Acquired by The Library Company, 1763–1772," *Living Color: Collecting Color Plate Books at the Library Company of Philadelphia*, Library Company of Philadelphia, 2007, https://www.librarycompany.org/color/index.htm.
23. See Susan Pearce and Frank Salmon, "Charles Heathcote Tatham in Italy, 1794–96: Letters, Drawings and Fragments, and Part of an Autobiography," *The Volume of the Walpole Society* 67 (2005): 1–2.
24. Charles Heathcote Tatham, *Etchings, Representing the Best Examples of Ancient Ornamental Architecture; Drawn from the Originals in Rome, and Other Parts of Italy . . .* (London, 1799), 7.
25. Alexandra Alevizatos Kirtley and Peggy A. Olley, *Classical Splendor: Painted Furniture for a Grand Philadelphia House* (Philadelphia: Philadelphia Museum of Art, 2016), 75.
26. Tatham, *Etchings*, 3.
27. Barry Bergdoll, "Introduction," in *The Complete Works of Percier and Fontaine* trans. Yolanda Stern Broad (Hudson: Princeton Architectural Press, 2018), 6.
28. This was another publication that George Bridport owned.
29. Charles Percier and Pierre-François-Léonard Fontaine, *Palais, maisons, et autres édifices modernes, dessinés à Rome* (Paris, 1798), 6–7.
30. Nina Burleigh, *Mirage: Napoleon's Scientists and the Unveiling of Egypt* (New York: Harper, 2007), xii.
31. It was during this expedition that the team of artists and scientists discovered the Rosetta Stone.
32. Past scholarship has also used the term "Empire" to describe Classical furniture produced in America. However, recent scholarship prefers *Classical* because American cabinetmakers were utilizing a variety of sources for inspiration, not simply French Empire.
33. Nouvel-Kammerer, "Discourse on Ornament under the Empire," 31–32.
34. "Denon, Jean-Dominique Vivant," Dictionary of Art Historians, accessed June 4, 2024, https://arthistorians.info/denonv/.
35. Denon's original drawings are now in the British Museum.
36. Napoleon also tasked Denon with overseeing monument and decorative art production in France. He further assisted Napoleon by managing the looted artworks confiscated during Napoleon's military exploits. "Denon, Jean-Dominique Vivant."
37. Françoise Tétart-Vittu, "Biographie de Pierre de La Mésangère (1761–1831)," Encyclopaedia Universalis, last modified February 10, 2009, https://www.universalis.fr/encyclopedie/pierre-de-la-mesangere/.
38. See the chapters on Boston and Baltimore in this volume.
39. In the introduction to *Household Furniture and Interior Decoration* (London: Longman, Hurst, Rees, and Orme, 1807), Thomas Hope recognized the talents of Charles Percier, stating that he was even able to "improve, through the freedom and the gracefulness of his touch, on the merit of the original drawings" (p. 14).
40. The house was demolished in 1851. "Thomas Hope and the Regency style," Victoria and Albert Museum, accessed June 4, 2024, https://www.vam.ac.uk/articles/thomas-hope-and-the-regency-style.
41. Ibid.
42. Hope, *Household Furniture and Interior Decoration*, 5.
43. Ibid., 6–7.
44 Ibid., 14.
45. New York cabinetmakers Charles-Honoré Lannuier and the shop of Deming & Bulkley often looked to Hope for inspiration.
46. George Smith, *A Collection of Designs for Household Furniture and Interior Decoration* (London: J. Taylor, 1808), xiii.
47. Compare Smith's plate 54 with Chippendale's plate 17 for the Gothic style, and Smith's plate 81 with Chippendale's plate 134 for Chinese.
48. See Hope's *Gilded-Wood Bench*, before 1807, Metropolitan Museum of Art, New York (2014.136), and *Pier Table*, c. 1800, Victoria and Albert Museum, London (W.19:1, 2-1976).
49. "Barron, James (1805–1839)," British and Irish Furniture Makers Online, Furniture History Society, last updated April 20, 2023, https://bifmo.furniturehistorysociety.org/entry/barron-james-1814. In 1816 Barron published another design book *Interior Decorations*, with contributions by John Stafford, an upholder, appraiser, and auctioneer of Bath. It is unclear why he financed this project. For more information on Barron's various business endeavors, see Simon Swynfen Jervis, "John Stafford of Bath and His Interior Decorations," *Furniture History* 45 (2009): 145.
50. John Ford, "Rudolph Ackermann," Oxford Art Online, last modified 2003, https://www.oxfordartonline.com/.
51. Tom Devonshire Jones, "Ackermann's 'Repository' 1809–28," *The British Art Journal* 11, no. 1 (2010): 69–74.
52. E. Keith Lloyd, "Mr. Peter Nicholson, the Practical Builder and Mathematician," *Mathematical Gazette* 66, no. 437 (October 1982): 203–7.
53. Peter Nicholson and Michael Angelo Nicholson, *The Practical Cabinet-Maker, Upholsterer, and Complete Decorator* (London: H. Fisher, Son & Co., 1826), vi.
54. Aspects of the Nicholson books were appropriated and reprinted by American authors as early as 1818. See Andor Gomme and Gavin Stamp, "An American Forerunner? Minard Lafever and Alexander Thomson," in *"Greek" Thomson*, ed. Gavin Stamp and Sam McKinstry (Edinburgh: Edinburgh University Press, 1994), 203.
55. In his publications, King described himself as a draftsman, publisher, and furniture pattern drawer. It seems likely that he trained as a cabinetmaker or upholsterer but King never explicitly said as such. Robin D. Jones, "King, Thomas (fl. 1829–c. 1840)," in *Encyclopedia of Interior Design*, vol. 1, ed. Joanna Banham (London: Routledge, 1997). See also Thomas Gordon Smith, *Thomas King Neo-Classical Furniture Designs: A Reprint of Thomas King's "Modern Style of Cabinet Work Exemplified," 1829* (New York: Dover Publications, 1995), iii-iv.
56. King, *The Modern Style of Cabinet Work Exemplified* (London, 1829).
57. Smith, *Thomas King Neo-Classical Furniture Designs: A Reprint of Thomas King's "Modern Style of Cabinet Work Exemplified," 1829*, vi.
58. Roger W. Moss, "Hall, John G. (1804–c. 1855)," Philadelphia Architects and Buildings, last modified 2024, https://www.philadelphiabuildings.org/pab/app/ar_display.cfm/24997.
59. John Hall, *The Cabinet Maker's Assistant* (Baltimore: John Murphy, 1840), 3.

A Revolution of Style and Taste in Boston and Salem

CLARK PEARCE

English Influence in Boston

THE ENGLISH REGENCY variant of Classicism influenced all the major American urban centers to some degree but was particularly strong in Boston and Salem, Massachusetts. Thomas Seymour (1771–1848) was one of Boston's preeminent tastemakers, advertising in 1809 that he made furniture "in an altogether new style," undoubtedly the Boston version of the English Regency.[1]

Boston cabinetmakers eagerly absorbed the elements of the early Classical style, but they filtered out most of the outlandish and avant-garde flourishes seen in English work to better suit their local market. That same aesthetic dictated broad, flat surfaces of well-polished mahogany or rosewood, often inlaid with brass stringing that accentuated the architecture of the object, and sinuous curves that were sparsely adorned with a single Classical motif. The elements of compositions were carefully balanced and symmetrical, according to classical principles. This phase of Boston cabinetmaking is perfectly represented by a rosewood card table in the Schrimsher Collection attributed to Thomas Seymour (cat. 1).

***Side Chair*, c. 1822–1825**
(detail of cat. 12)

The influence of English Regency designers is seen in Boston in two ways: local cabinetmakers exactly copied a design from a pattern book, or at least followed the spirit of the designer's intent; or selected certain elements from pattern books to make an original confection. In the latter case, American cabinetmakers used English and French design compilations as source books rather than strict how-to manuals. Even if no literal element was lifted from the designs, they were useful as inspiration, and as primers on classical principles of proportion and scale.

With a few modifications, a sofa signed by William Hancock (1794–c. 1849) (cat. 4) closely follows the pattern of a plate in Thomas Sheraton's *The Cabinet-maker and General Artist's Encyclopedia* (London, 1804–06). As is common in American work, Sheraton's pattern was simplified to appeal to Boston's more spartan tastes, and to keep the cost down. The lion heads on the cylindrical arms and the drapery swag across the front were eliminated. The principal modification to the Hancock sofa was the addition of a cylindrical crest rail that is supported on the ends by scrolled and acanthus carving. Sheraton's daring Regency design was published around 1805, but would not have been acceptable to most Bostonians at that time. In the mid-1820s, however, when the later Classical styles were in vogue there, it proved to be a popular pattern.

Although rare in Boston cabinetwork, several designs by Thomas King were lifted by Boston makers directly from his

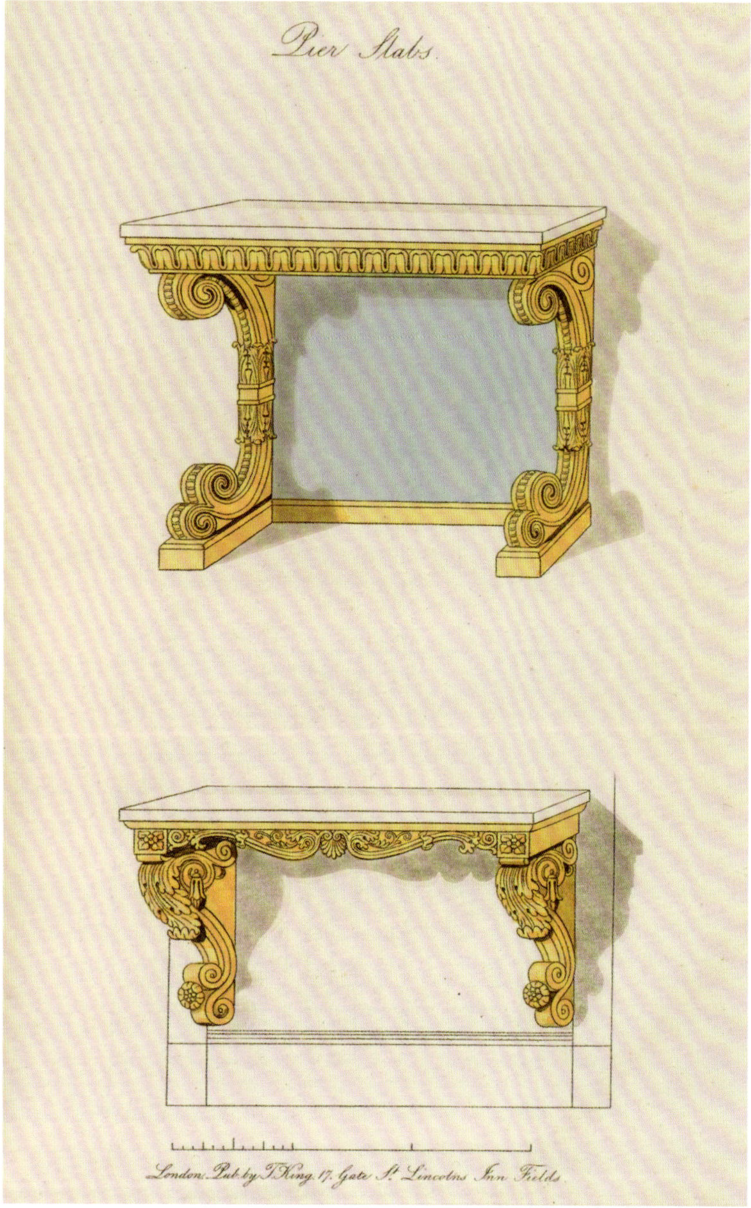

Fig. 1. "Pier Slabs," plate 22 in Thomas King, *The Modern Style of Cabinet Work Exemplified* (2nd ed, London, c. 1830), hand-colored engraving (Courtesy Winterthur Museum, Garden & Library)

Fig. 2. *Pier Table*, possibly attributed to Thomas Seymour, for Isaac Vose & Son or for George Archbald, carving by Thomas Wightman, 1823–1827, mahogany, chestnut; white pine, tulip poplar; marble, mirror glass, Colonial Society of Massachusetts (Courtesy Massachusetts Historical Society)

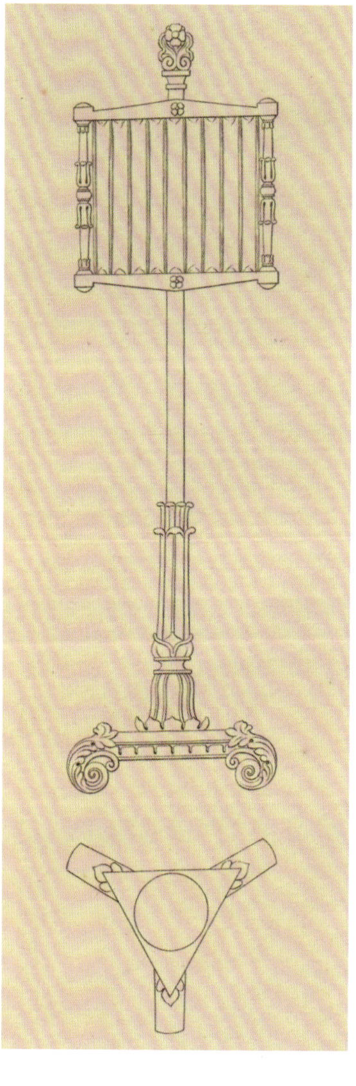

Fig. 3. Thomas King, "Screens," plate 26 (center image) in *The Modern Style of Cabinet Work Exemplified* (London, 1829), engraving (Courtesy Winterthur Museum, Garden & Library)

Fig. 4. ***Monopod Pier Table,*** **unknown maker, Boston or possibly Salem, c. 1825, mahogany, mahogany veneer; cherry, poplar; black and gold marble, mirror glass, Museum of Fine Arts, Houston, The Bayou Bend Collection, museum purchase funded by The Brown Foundation, B.98.13 (Courtesy Museum of Fine Arts, Houston)**

The Modern Style of Cabinet Work Exemplified (London, 1829). Plate 22 shows a later Classical "Pier Slab" with Greek double scroll ends and a frieze of carved Corinthian leaves (fig. 1).[2] This extraordinary design was copied line-for-line for a table, with its original Belgian black marble top, that is possibly attributed to Thomas Seymour, possibly for Isaac Vose & Son (Isaac Vose, 1767–1823) or George Archbald (1790–1870), with Thomas Wightman (1759–1827) supplying the carving (fig. 2).[3]

Another good example of a design pulled directly from King is an elegantly severe fire screen, with carved Corinthian and palm leaves, possibly made by Isaac Vose & Son or George Archbald (cat. 16). King's line drawing of the fire screen (fig. 3) is overly linear and stiff, which the Boston maker amply compensated for in his execution. Showcasing the skill of the carver, probably Thomas Wightman, the finished product is remarkably sculptural, abstracted, and idealized.

Many individual elements of George Smith's *A Collection of Designs for Household Furniture and Interior Decoration* (London, 1808) were selected for the work of Boston and Salem cabinet shops, such as the exaggerated winged paw feet that support a "chaise longue" in plate 65. Apparently, Smith was the first to introduce this ancient motif to the wider Anglo world. It was later used by many Boston, New York, and Philadelphia cabinetmakers, but Isaac Vose & Son, along with carver Thomas Wightman, perfected the motif on sofas.[4]

Smith's influence on Boston and Salem furniture was broad. Two commode tables in his *Collection of Designs* (plate 121), served as inspiration for a monopod table (fig. 4). Though these tables are rare in Boston and Salem furniture, this table is an extraordinary example of a mature Classical taste. It is also a good reminder of how talented urban New England cabinetmakers were at adapting—and often improving—imported designs.

"A Candelabra and Pedestal" in Smith's *Collection of Designs* (plate 139, right image) shows an elaborate columnar pedestal that incorporates an excellent rendering of the tall Greek Corinthian leaves that encircle the column just below the gadrooned "bowl" at the top. Although not picked up by Boston or Salem cabinetmakers until the mid-1820s, these repeating rows or circles of single-veined, reflexed leaves became the leitmotif of a simpler, more sculptural late Classical style in the region (see cats. 16 and 17).

Fig. 5. "Pedestals for Statues, Busts, etc.," plate 142 in George Smith, *A Collection of Designs for Household Furniture and Interior Decoration* (London, 1808), hand-colored engraving (Courtesy Clark Art Institute Library, Mary Ann Beinecke Decorative Art Collection). The pedestal at left with its tapered form and acanthus leaf design was appropriated by Boston cabinetmakers for table supports.

Plate 142 in Smith's 1808 edition shows "Pedestals for Statues, Busts, etc." (fig. 5). On the left is a heavy baluster-shaped pedestal that Boston cabinetmakers used, time and again, as single pedestals for card, dining, breakfast, and center tables. A card table in the Schrimsher Collection labeled by T. Hunt & Company (Timothy Hunt, d. 1874) employs just such a carved pedestal (cat. 9).[5] As expected, Hunt simplified Smith's design by stripping off the classical masks, intertwined vines, plinth, and paw feet to appeal to the local Boston audience.

At least one of Smith's designs was subtly adapted for a drop-leaf worktable that was probably made in a Salem cabinet shop (cat. 11). The design for this table appears as a "Backgammon Worktable" in Smith's *The Cabinet-Maker and Upholsterer's Guide* (London, 1826) (cat. 11, fig. 11.1]).[6] The form of the table in the Schrimsher Collection is essentially as Smith drew it, though the Massachusetts cabinetmaker eliminated the checkerboard and backgammon functions, and added carving to the ball feet, and an extra drawer above the bag for sewing necessities.

French Influence in Boston

Even though most Bostonians were devout anglophiles, French design was unexpectedly pervasive there. On the whole they revered English culture and governance and were horrified by the way the French Revolution devolved into chaos and tyranny. The esteemed General Gilbert du Motier, Marquis de Lafayette aside, Bostonians did not particularly welcome French *émigrés*, which helps to explain the paucity of French journeymen there.

Nevertheless, the early French Classical styles appealed immediately to those who were rich or prominent enough to be comfortable with more adventurous tastes. These consumers had the resources to travel to Europe and see firsthand the ancient world being brought into the modern one. By the 1820s, French furniture design had become more palatable, and fashionable imports were found in Boston (fig. 6).

Among a trove of eighty-five loose plates of furniture designs that descended from Boston cabinetmaker Henry Kellam Hancock (1788–1854), brother of William Hancock, no less than forty-seven are from Pierre de La Mésangère's *Collection de meubles et objets de goût* (Paris, 1799–1831), reinforcing the idea that Boston cabinetmakers and their clients were well versed in French furniture design. Also included in the cache are plates from the 1808 and 1826 editions of George Smith, James Barron's *Modern and Elegant Designs of Cabinet and Upholstery Furniture* (London, 1814), and Désiré Guilmard's periodical *Le Garde-meuble, ancien et moderne* (Paris, 1839–1935), along with a few anonymous hand-colored plates. All of these sheets are tattered and covered with pencil sketches of furniture with annotations and summations of bills, showing their heavy use in the workshop.

Fig. 6. Henry Sargent (1770–1845), *The Tea Party*, c. 1824, oil on canvas, Museum of Fine Arts, Boston, Gift of Mrs. Horatio Appleton Lamb in memory of Mr. and Mrs. Winthrop Sargent, 19.12 (Courtesy Museum of Fine Arts, Boston). Note that most of the furnishings in the painting depict imported French furniture, not Boston interpretations.

These plates are a rare survival but suggest their broader use in Boston and American cabinet shops than previously thought.[7]

Thus it should come as no surprise that La Mésangère's designs brought a cornucopia of inspiration and new furniture forms to Boston and other American cabinetmakers. Some French forms eclipsed English ones in Boston, like square pier tables, and what Bostonians called French secretaries (*secrétaires à abattant*). Many French designs were lifted wholesale and made in some numbers. Other forms that met with favor were French beds, bureaus with and without mirrors, dressing tables, and sideboards (lacking a central niche to store a cellarette). Bostonians apparently freely mixed French and English furniture throughout their houses, though at times they put the French-style pieces in the more public rooms, like front parlors and drawing rooms, and the English-inspired pieces in their dining rooms and bedrooms.[8] The explanation for this trend is unclear, but perhaps they felt that the French-style furniture was a bit too formal for their private spaces.

The Later Classical Style in Boston

While the English Regency style was very much alive in Boston, the later Classical style was gaining ground by 1815. This phase was characterized by designs that were more monumental in scale and chaste in ornament, with smoother, cleaner surfaces (see cat. 17). In many cases the decoration was the architecture, and vice versa. In 1816, trendsetter Thomas Seymour made a pair of card tables in an early version of the later Classical style for Peter Chardon Brooks (1767–1849), who made his fortune in marine insurance.[9] Seymour went on to develop and refine the form, which became an icon of later Classical furniture in the Boston vernacular (cat. 8). By 1818, Thomas Seymour, Isaac Vose, Joshua Coates (1774–1819), Thomas Emmons (c. 1781–1825), and George Archbald had each integrated the architecture of the ancients into modern furniture forms by merging the two (cat. 5), reaching the peaks of their respective abilities and careers in the 1810s and 1820s. The plates of La Mésangère were especially relevant and influential in this mature phase of Classical design in Boston. Although published almost a decade earlier, Thomas Hope's designs also found new relevance for Boston cabinetmakers and their clientele (see cat. 12, fig. 12.2).

One of the strongest expressions of the later Classical style in Boston was to be found at Tremont House, considered the first large-scale luxury hotel built in an American city. Designed by Isaiah Rogers in 1828, it opened its doors later the next year. In addition to a long list of firsts—running water, indoor toilets, hot baths, and a dining room dedicated to women only—Rogers meticulously incorporated ancient classical architecture into the design of the structure (fig. 7). He hired the best cabinetmakers in Boston to execute the interiors and as a result exposed them to a variety of Classical source material.

In the sixty-seven-page treatise *A Description of Tremont House with Architectural Illustrations*, the proprietors of the hotel specify the ancient structures that were recreated in the building's facade and interior spaces. The treatise includes thirty-one plates of floor plans, architectural line drawings, moldings, carvings, and diagrams of the hotel's mechanical innovations.[10]

The Doric portico entrance on Tremont Street for instance, was taken from James Stuart and Nicholas Revett's *The Antiquities of Athens* (London, v. 1 1762), titled simply "The front Elevation of the Doric Portico," chap. 1, plate 3. The honeysuckle blossoms on the underside of the cornice of the entablature are from the Parthenon.[11] Just inside the portico, the ceilings of the entrance hall and dining room are coffered and the rotunda above the stairs is paneled, all three taken from the Propylaea at Eleusis, at the Greek site of Attica.[12] The stained-glass skylight in the rotunda, made by the New England Glass Company, was modeled after fresco paintings from the Baths of Titus in Rome.[13] The columns and capitals in the Family Apartments were modeled after those on the Choragic Monument in Athens, again sourced from Stuart and Revett's *Antiquities*.[14]

This obscure yet precious publication documents the many Classical sources that Rogers used in the design of Tremont House. His careful rendering of ancient design and proportions in three dimensions gave Boston cabinetmakers and architects a considerable advantage in understanding and correctly incorporating Classicism into their work. The proprietors' list of all the craftsmen who contributed to the building of the hotel reads like a who's-who of the top Boston artisans of the day including cabinetmakers George Archbald, John Doggett (1780–1857), and Sherlock Spooner (1797–1881); upholsterers William Hancock and Thomas Hedges (1788–1832); carver Levi L. Cushing (active 1830s); and ornamental painter Edward H. Whitaker (active 1820s).[15] Craftsmen were exposed to new designs from pattern books and, more importantly, witnessed how their contemporaries reinterpreted classical material to suit current taste. It also codified the later Classical as a dignified style that would dominate design for decades to come.

Rich and Elegant, but Never Gaudy

Although the post-Revolution Boston economy was in the doldrums, the financial outlook and population began to surge beginning in 1790. Aside from the four years that the country was distracted by the War of 1812, and the panics of 1819 and 1837, this boom peaked in the 1830s and lasted into the 1850s. This newfound prosperity attracted entrepreneurs from inside and outside the city who made fortunes in national and international trade, marine insurance, water-powered manufacturing, and real estate, among other fields.[16] These newcomers contributed fresh expertise to the thriving metropolis. Many of

Fig 7. James Kidder (1793–1837), *View of Tremont House Boston,* c. 1834, engraving, Boston Pictorial Archive, Boston Public Library, 08_02_001490 (Courtesy Digital Commonwealth)

the men who made these fortunes were not members of the old Boston Brahmin class but found social acceptance in Boston's aristocratic society by emulating their ways and values, including a conservative aesthetic.[17] If anything, the willingness of the newly moneyed to embrace that dignified Brahmin taste gave it new life through the use of rich materials, refined craftsmanship, and restrained and elegant designs. Distinctly different from styles in New York, Philadelphia, and Baltimore, decorative carving and gilt brass ornaments were kept to a tasteful minimum—or eliminated completely.

Boston Craftsmanship

Alexis de Tocqueville wrote: "Craftsmen in aristocratic societies work for a strictly limited number of customers who are hard to please. Perfect workmanship gives the best hope for profit."[18] In Boston, craftsmanship was as important for buyers of expensive Classical furniture as the outward design, largely because the aristocratic and nouveau riche demanded it.

The interior finishing on the best Boston furniture is superb, with standards likely set by the notoriously fussy Thomas Seymour. He, in turn, had embraced the newly elevated standards of English and French work, most likely from a trickle of immigrant journeymen who brought with them fresh knowledge of these improvements. The top cabinet shop owners understood that these new construction standards could be used as a marketing tool to make their work stand out in a crowded and competitive field. Once established, these standards spread, in varying degrees, to other shops.

In the first half of the 1820s, it became customary for cabinet-grade or Honduras mahogany to be used in secondary areas like drawer bottoms, sides, and backs.[19] Additionally, any area made of a lighter secondary wood was given an orange-red mahoganizing wash—a standard English practice. This wash helped to divert the focus from these structural elements and give the object an evenly high level of finish. Although it added to the cost of the piece, cabinet-grade mahogany was also used for the substrates of the leaves on card and drop-leaf tables and for the cores of laminated plinths on similar table forms. These mahogany cores were then veneered on the visible tops of the leaves, and counter-veneered on the undersides to discourage cracks and warping that could form as the wood swelled and shrunk with the seasonal fluctuation of humidity. Consequently, one rarely sees Boston card tables with long shrinkage cracks in the tops.

French immigrant William Piquot (c. 1750–1829), who specialized in drawer making and other exacting casework, was a journeyman in Seymour's independent shop and for many years at the Vose shop. His cabinetwork is a study in perfection, meticulous and easily recognized, setting a high bar for others to emulate. Although none could match Piquot's skills, his work probably raised the quality of workmanship in other shops.[20] Occasionally, quarter-round moldings were placed on the joints between drawer bottoms and sides to keep small objects from falling into gaps, and to protect clothes from getting caught on rough edges. These subtle moldings, another English idea, also served to elevate the finish on the insides of drawers.[21]

The insistence on fine craftsmanship at the higher end of the market also extended to highly skilled and artistic specialists who worked—at considerable cost—for multiple shops. Thomas Wightman's distinctive and thoughtful carving was incorporated into the work of Seymour, Vose, Emmons, Archbald, William Fiske (1770–1844), Timothy Hunt, Cornelius Briggs (1787–1848), and surely others. Most of Wightman's carving depicted botanical forms of decoration from ancient Greece—acanthus leaves, anthemia, honeysuckle petals, flower sprays, leafy medallions, and Corinthian leaves. The latter are derived from carved motifs borrowed from Corinthian capitals and friezes and were executed in sharp, high relief and deeply undercut (cat. 16). His architectural ornaments also included Ionic capitals, reeding, and fluting.

Judging by the wide range of furniture forms and starkly different styles in Boston Classical work, there was considerable room for experimentation and creativity by Boston cabinetmakers. Compare the vast differences between the Emmons & Archbald pier table (cat. 5) and the pier table attributed to George Archbald (cat. 14). Even allowing for the decade between the two tables' production, their idiosyncrasies are striking. The absence of price books in Boston, like those published in London, New York, Philadelphia, and even Salem, may have something to do with this variety.[22] Price books were published to standardize prices that journeymen were to be paid for each aspect of their work, and for transmitting preferred designs that were codified for a given city. The absence of these books in Boston may have given cabinetmakers the creative freedom to express more of their own ideas. Concurrently, the lack of price books may have facilitated well-established cabinet shops to innovate and regulate their own construction methods, at times making it easier today to differentiate the unmarked or undocumented work of different shops based on labeled or documented work.

Fig. 8. Moses Swett (1804–1838), *View of William Hancock's Upholstery and Cabinet Ware-Rooms, 37–53 Cornhill Street*, published by Pendleton's Lithography, Boston, 1827–1828, lithograph, Boston Athenæum, Prints and Photographs Department, A B64B6 Sh.ha. (no. 1) (Courtesy Boston Athenæum)

A Selection of Boston Cabinetmakers

Given the prodigious research done by furniture conservator and scholar Robert D. Mussey Jr., much is known about the work of Thomas Seymour, Isaac Vose, Joshua Coates, and Thomas Wightman. The partnership of Thomas Emmons and George Archbald that began in 1813 remains less studied, but their extensive body of labeled work illuminates the scope and depth of their production. They dissolved their partnership in 1825, and a few years later Archbald bought Vose's old shop for himself. After the deaths of Vose, Coates, and Emmons, he went on to have a long career as Boston's best cabinetmaker until he retired to his farm in Hopkinton, Massachusetts, in 1844 following a devastating fire that destroyed his shop and other properties. Further motivation to retire was his displeasure "with the introduction of machinery into the trade."[23]

Although no labeled furniture from Archbald's shop is known, there is good evidence that he was working at the top of the market. In 1827, Samuel Atkins Eliot (1798–1862) and his wife, Mary, were building a new house at 31 Beacon Street, spending lavishly on the structure and the furnishings. They paid Archbald $2,263.50 for furniture in installments from 1826 to 1831 (none of it itemized, unfortunately).[24] An elaborate set of five bookcases that were made in 1830 for George Ticknor's (1791–1871) renowned library in Boston are likely by Archbald as well.[25]

After the death of hardware merchant Steven Salisbury (1746–1829), his widow, Elizabeth (1768–1851), redecorated the west end of their mansion in Worcester, Massachusetts. She turned to Archbald in 1831 for a new center table for the parlor, with her brother Edward Tuckerman (1775–1843) acting as her agent. He went to Archbald's shop to find a suitable marble-top center table, but was told by the proprietor that marble was "out of fashion" and that "Mahogany are only used now." Elizabeth purchased a mahogany-top center table from Archbald for $70, plus a sofa, a table, a set of twelve painted fancy chairs, two stools, and a low French bed. She also bought from William Hancock a patented spring-seat rocking chair that was covered in a "green medallion figured plush."[26] Another group of furniture made by Archbald was ordered by Henry Wadsworth Longfellow (1807–1882) and his wife Frances (1819–1861) in 1843, probably including two center tables, a bed, and a dressing bureau.[27] Beginning in 1828, Archbald was one of two Boston cabinetmakers (along with Sherlock Spooner) who were given plum contracts to make the non-upholstered furniture for Tremont House.

William Hancock labeled a fair number of pieces that he upholstered or retailed for other cabinetmakers. The image of his extensive warerooms demonstrates his importance as a major player in the Boston furniture trade (fig. 8), but our understanding of his operation is still somewhat thin. However, recent research has turned up another sign of his prominence: a substantial contract to supply upholstered seating furniture for Tremont House.[28]

William's brother, Henry Kellam Hancock, has been frustratingly elusive and apparently neither labeled nor inscribed any of his furniture. It is known that he ran a large shop on Orange Street in Ward 12 near the shops of Emmons & Archbald, and that he supplied frames for seating furniture and other cabinetwork for his brother's warerooms.[29]

The Classical work of Solomon Loud's (1787–1833) large shop on Newbury and Court Streets is completely unknown, although a few labeled Neoclassical card tables survive. The 1820 Boston census lists Loud as having eighteen employees, including eleven in manufacturing, making his shop one of the largest in the city. At his death in 1833 his estate was valued at $3,540.[30]

Much is known about chair maker Samuel Gragg (1772–1855), thanks to two troves of his personal and business records. Gragg's innovative "elastic" chairs, occasionally painted with peacock feathers by John Penniman (1782–1841), were an engineering marvel, but he had difficulty marketing them. Most of his other work consists of fancy-painted and "bamboo" chairs for the middle-class market. These chairs were his stock in trade and provided him with a decent living; the elastic chairs were not financially successful.[31]

The career of cabinetmaker Benjamin Bass Jr. (1775–1819) reveals the complexity of the furniture trade in the nineteenth century, and how complicated it was to make a living at it. An English Regency-style sideboard that Bass signed indicates his talent. Clearly a bespoke piece, it is almost a clone of sideboards that Thomas Seymour was making at the time, complete with carving by Thomas Wightman. At the time of Bass's death in 1819, an inventory of his business reveals that his shop made only a few pieces for the Boston elite. His main livelihood derived from a factory that made inexpensive tables, stands, and chairs. He further diversified his business by wholesaling cotton and selling imported mahogany and veneers to his competitors. One of his apprentices was James Barker (active 1814–1819), who became his business partner around 1814. A few years later they dissolved their partnership, and Barker set up his own shop with Seymour starting as foreman in 1817.[32] Two years later, when Barker's shop was experiencing financial difficulties, Seymour left the firm to join Isaac Vose & Son's shop as foreman, where he had a huge impact on Boston Classical furniture.

Timothy Hunt partnered with Simon H. Hunt (active 1819–c. 1830) from 1819 to 1827, in the business known as T. Hunt & Co. When the partnership dissolved, Simon opened a retail furniture warehouse.[33] Timothy continued in the cabinetmaking business until 1835. His work is known by at least five labeled pieces. Other than the card table in the Schrimsher Collection (cat. 9), his labeled work includes three somewhat middle-market French bureaus and a secretary.[34] As the furniture business in Boston became more mechanized and competitive in the 1830s, Hunt began to invest in real estate at a time when population and prosperity boomed. At his death in 1874 his estate was valued at $11,591, surely a higher amount than it would have been had he stayed in the furniture-making business.[35]

In addition to established cabinetmaking shops, it is important to take into account several other enterprises that employed and enriched many of Boston's talented cabinetmakers. For example, William Fiske, a prolific cabinetmaker who employed a large quantity of journeymen, produced a wide range of furniture for the middle market, but also produced clock cases. His labeled work demonstrates the breadth and scope of his output.[36] After his father and business partner died in 1797, Fiske moved his shop from Salem to Roxbury, where there was a thriving group of clock makers, including the Willard family, Stephen and Elnathan Taber, and William Cummins.[37]

According to Simon Willard's great-grandson and biographer, John Ware Willard, Fiske "made nearly all of his clock cases."[38] This may have been an exaggeration, as many other cabinetmakers are known to have made clock cases, including John Doggett, Thomas Seymour, Henry Willard, Charles Crehore, and William's brother Samuel Fiske. Fortunately, a tall case clock made by Aaron Willard (1757–1844) is accompanied by an original bill of sale for the case from William Fiske, dated May 21, 1806, which neatly documents his work for the Roxbury clock makers.[39] These Roxbury cases were luxury items and often as elaborate as the best furniture made in Boston (fig. 9). They probably supplied a steady stream of work and income for Fiske, making him one of the more prosperous cabinetmakers in Boston.

James Cogswell (1780–1862) was a well-respected journeyman in Boston. He worked in Thomas Seymour's shop from 1803 to 1806, and was a partner for the year of 1809, probably to help Seymour produce a large order of furniture

Fig. 9. ***Tall Clock*, works by Aaron Willard, case by William Fiske, with his invoice 1806 for making the case, mahogany veneer, white pine; brass, iron, lead, painted decoration, Sold at Christie's, New York, January 18, 2024, lot 499, Private collection (Courtesy Christie's Images)**

Fig. 10. ***Pianoforte*, John Osborne, 1822–1829, mahogany and rosewood veneers; brass, steel, silk, ivory, ebony, Old Sturbridge Village, Sturbridge, Massachusetts, 10-17-99 (Courtesy Gavin Ashworth)**

for Elizabeth Derby West's Danvers estate.[40] He partnered with Thomas Emmons in 1812, just prior to George Archbald's joining the firm in 1815.[41]

Perhaps about 1813, Lewis and Alpheus Babcock, along with Thomas Appleton, persuaded Cogswell to take charge of making the cases for their piano manufactory. He agreed, and brought with him an apprentice named John Osborne (1791/92–1835). Apparently the precocious Osborne learned so much about the making of piano works at the firm that he left to open his own piano manufactory in 1816. Although no record survives, Cogswell may have joined the Osborne shop (fig. 10) to make cases.[42]

By 1818 Boston pianos were made in the early Classical style, and their elaborate mahogany and rosewood cases were every bit as labor intensive and stylish as the work coming out of the Vose and Emmons & Archbald shops. It is not known how long Cogswell continued to make piano cases, but the piano business was booming in Boston. Cogswell is just one Boston cabinetmaker who is documented to have worked in the piano trade, but there had to have been a great many others who made cases for the numerous firms engaged in piano production well into the 1850s.

Boston Classical Furniture Forgotten and Rediscovered

By the early twentieth century, Bostonians had completely forgotten the excitement and gusto of the Classical style, along with the innovative and talented craftsmen who manufactured this distinguished furniture. By the 1950s the old families that had inherited Classical furniture referred to it disparagingly and relegated it to attics, summerhouses, or the offices of historical organizations. The old Boston aesthetic of genteel Classical design that emphasized rich materials and tasteful and minimal decoration was long dead. With the onslaught of the frilly elaboration of Rococo and Renaissance revivals and the Queen Anne style, how could that old Boston taste have possibly survived? The flood of derivative, cheap furniture in a watered-down Classical style had few, if any, aesthetic merits in the 1840s and 1850s and only accelerated the trend. It was not until the 1960s that a few prescient curators and collectors began to recognize Boston Classical furniture with the appreciation and wonder that it deserves.[43]

1. Robert D. Mussey Jr. and Clark Pearce, *Rather Elegant than Showy: The Classical Furniture of Isaac Vose* (Jaffrey, NH: Massachusetts Historical Society in association with David R. Godine, 2018), 9, 25n60; *Colombian Centinel* (Boston), September 27 and October 11, 1809.
2. Thomas King, *The Modern Style of Cabinet Work Exemplified* (London, 1829), pl. 22, "Pier Slab."
3. Mussey and Pearce, *Rather Elegant than Showy*, 197, figs. 214–15.
4. George Smith, *A Collection of Designs for Household Furniture and Interior Decoration, in the Most Approved and Elegant Taste* (London: J. Taylor, 1808), pl. 65. For other winged paw feet, see Mussey and Pearce, *Rather Elegant than Showy*, 104–6, 262, figs. 115–17, 326.
5. For other baluster pedestal tables, see Mussey and Pearce, *Rather Elegant than Showy*, 166, 228, figs. 188, 256.
6. George Smith, *The Cabinet-Maker and Upholsterer's Guide* (London: Jones & Co., 1826), pl. 8, "Backgammon Worktable."
7. This group of plates descended through Hancock's family. Though uncatalogued, they now reside at the Winterthur Library.
8. These observations are anecdotal, drawing upon paintings of Boston interiors, Auguste Edouart silhouettes, and hints from account and waste books.
9. Robert D. Mussey Jr. and Clark Pearce, "Classical Excellence in Boston: The Furniture of Isaac Vose, 1789–1825," in *Boston Furniture, 1700–1900*, ed. Brock Jobe and Gerald W. R. Ward (Boston: Colonial Society of Massachusetts, 2016), 259, fig. 9.
10. William Havard Eliot and Isaiah Rogers, *A Description of Tremont House with Architectural Illustrations* (Boston: Gray and Bowen, 1830). It is possible that the other proprieters of the hotel were involved in the publication: Thomas Handasyd Perkins, James Perkins, Andrew Eliot Belknap, William Havard Eliot, and Samuel Atkins Eliot.
11. Ibid., 5–7; James Stuart and Nicholas Revett, *The Antiquities of Athens* (London, 1762–96), 1:chap. 1, pls. I–IV. Rogers was faithful to the design, though he eliminated the pitched pediment from the original building. For his justification for using ditriglyphs in the entablature, Rogers quoted from Edmond Aiken, *An essay on the Doric order of architecture: containing a historical view of its rise and progress among the ancients* (London: T. Bensley, 1810), n.p. For an explanation of the dimensions of the intercolumniation that Rogers used, he quotes Peter Nicholson, *An Architectural Dictionary, Containing a Correct Nomenclature and Derivation of the Terms Employed by Architects, Builders, and Workmen . . .* (London: J. Barfield, 1812–19), 264–65.
12. Eliot and Rogers, *Description of Tremont House*, 8, pls. VIII, X, XIV. The coffered ceilings over the Tremont Street entrance and the main dining room were taken from The Society of the Dilettanti, *The Unedited Antiquities of Attica: Comprising the Architecture Remains of Eleusis, Rhamnus, Sunium, and Thoricus* (London: Longman, Hurst, Rees, Orme, Brown, and John Murray, 1817), n.p.
13. Eliot and Rogers, *Description of Tremont House*, 9, pls. VIII, IX. The skylight was executed by John L. Race for the New England Glass Company, but it is unclear where he sourced his Grotesque-style imagery. The fresco murals for the Baths of Titus were painted by Famulus in 81 CE; just prior to their demolition in the late eighteenth century they were documented by Nicholas Ponce, who published a book of engravings of the fresco designs in 1786. It is possible that this may have been Race's source. Nicholas Ponce, *Description des bains de Titus, ou collection des peintures trouvées dans les ruines des thermes de cet empereur* (Paris: L'Auteur and Barbou, 1786).
14. Also based on that source are the Ionic colonnades in the Reading Room and the General Drawing Room, which were taken from the Temple of Athena (Minerva) Polias, a Greek Ionian town in Priene, Turkey. Both structures are illustrated in Stuart and Revett, *The Antiquities of Athens*, 1:chap. 4, pl. III, and 2:chap 1, pls II–III, VII–VIII, X, respectively. Yet another colonnade in the vestibule of the hotel was copied from the Ionic Temple on the River Ilissus near Athens. This is also illustrated in Stuart and Revett, *The Antiquities of Athens*, 1:chap. 2, pls. I–VII. See also Ponce, *Description des Bains de Titus*, 26.
15. Eliot and Rogers, *Description of Tremont House*, 18n*, 19.
16. Edward L. Glaeser, "Reinventing Boston: 1630–2003," *Journal of Economic Geography* 5, no. 2 (April 2015): 119–153.
17. Page Talbott, "Classical Conservatism: Card Tables and English Regency Style in Boston, 1810–35," *Maine Antique Digest* (December 1989), 11c.
18. Talbott, "Classical Conservatism," 12c; Alexis de Tocqueville, *Democracy in America*, ed. J. P. Mayer, trans. George Lawrence (New York: Harper & Row, 1969), 466.
19. Honduras mahogany is a different species of mahogany that grows around Mexico's Bay of Campeche and Central America. It is not nearly as dense or beautiful as island mahogany. Because it looks a lot like island mahogany, it was used in secondary areas that would be seen occasionally but never used as a primary wood. It was less expensive than island mahogany, and therefore much used for drawer linings, card table wells, etc.
20. Mussey and Pearce, *Rather Elegant than Showy*, 242–44, figs. 286, 294–97.
21. Ibid., 244–45, fig. 293. Quarter-round moldings on the insides of drawers have not been seen on Philadelphia work, though there were plenty of English immigrant cabinetmakers there. They have not been seen on New York or Maryland work either.
22. *Articles of the Salem Cabinet-Maker Society, Associated June 26, 1801* (Salem: Joshua Cushing, 1801), Phillips Library, Peabody Essex Museum, NK2435.M3 S2 1801; Dean Thomas Lahikainen, "A Salem Cabinetmakers' Price Book," in *American Furniture 2001*, ed. Luke Beckerdite (Milwaukee: Chipstone Foundation, 2001), 152–219.
23. Mussey and Pearce, *Rather Elegant than Showy*, 196, 202n82.
24. Ibid., 158–59.
25. Ibid., 161. Some of these bookcases are now at Dartmouth College. Ticknor was also a founder and trustee of the Boston Public Library.
26. Mussey and Pearce, "Classical Excellence," 233–34. This is the same color and pattern plush found on the original show cover on the sofa in cat. 4.
27. Ibid., 124, 137n28.
28. *Description of Tremont House*, 18–19.
29. Page Talbott, "The Furniture Trade in Boston, 1810–1835: Check List," *The Magazine Antiques* 141, no. 5 (May 1992): 850, "Hancock, Henry K."
30. Ibid., 851, "Solomon Loud."
31. Michael S. Podmaniczky, "Samuel Gragg and the Elastic Chair," in *Boston Furniture, 1700–1900*, eds. Brock Jobe and Gerald W. R. Ward (Boston: Colonial Society of Massachusetts, 2016), 203–6.
32. Morrison H. Heckscher, "Benjamin Bass and Boston Sideboards: A Question of Attribution," in *Boston Furniture, 1700–1900*, eds. Brock Jobe and Gerald W. R. Ward (Boston: Colonial Society of Massachusetts, 2016), 240–43.
33. Hunt's partner Simon Hunt may have been a brother or cousin.
34. A second card table (private collection) can be firmly attributed to Hunt based on his typical construction. The carving can be attributed to Thomas Wightman, though executed in a very different style than the labeled card table. See cat. 9, note 2.
35. Talbott, "The Furniture Trade in Boston," 850, "Hunt, Timothy and Co."
36. Fiske's name is sometimes written as Fisk. Among the furniture forms that Fiske labeled, inscribed, or documented are four-column, pedestal, and lyre worktables, card tables, portable desks, dressing mirrors, drop-front desks, and a clock case.
37. Philip D. Zimmerman, "Early American Furniture Makers' Marks," in *American Furniture 2007*, ed. Luke Beckerdite (Milwaukee: Chipstone Foundation, 2007), 132–67.
38. John Ware Willard, *Simon Willard and His Clocks* (New York: Dover, 1968), 43, 117–18.
39. The Aaron Willard tall case clock with accompanying Fiske bill of sale sold at Christie's, New York, January 20, 2024, lot 499. The same clock was previously sold at Christie's, New York, January 26, 1985, lot 225.
40. Mussey and Pearce, *Rather Elegant than Showy*, 42, 47.
41. Talbott, "The Furniture Trade in Boston," 848, "Cogswell, James."
42. Darcy Kuronen, "Early Pianomaking in Boston, 1790–1830," in *Boston Furniture, 1700–1900*, eds. Brock Jobe and Gerald W. R. Ward (Boston: Colonial Society of Massachusetts, 2016), 318–22.
43. Mussey and Pearce, *Rather Elegant than Showy*, 1–4.

1

Card Table, c. 1815–1820

Attributed to Thomas Seymour (1771–1848); painted decoration attributed to John Ritto Penniman (1782–1841)
Boston
Rosewood, rosewood veneer; mahogany, white pine, white ash, ebonized wood; brass, painted decoration
29⅜ × 36 × 17⅝ in.

PROVENANCE: With George Subkoff Antiques, Inc., Westport, CT, by 1994; Purchased by Schrimshers, 1994.

As early as 1809, tastemaker Thomas Seymour was advertising in Boston newspapers that he was making furniture "in an altogether new style," almost certainly referring to the new "Grecian" style in the English Regency taste.[1] While this sleek and sophisticated rosewood card table is attributed to Thomas Seymour, it probably dates a little later than his early advertisements.[2] His design was skillfully filtered through the requirements of the Boston vernacular, with no outlandish flourishes, all the parts well integrated, and the use of rich materials in an understated way.

Here, the basic structure of the two hinged leaves resting on a shaped apron has not changed much from Neoclassical forms, but the straight legs in the four corners that previously would have supported the table have been eliminated. In their place, a central pedestal with four shorter, sinuous legs emanate from a thick plinth supporting the leaves and apron. References to the classical world abound in this re-imagination of an earlier Neoclassical card table, including the single columnar support, the plinth (like those upon which Greek temples were built), the lyre (which refers to the musical instrument of Apollo), and the brass lion's-paw feet found in Greek and Roman bronze furniture. Even the stamped brass rosettes on the scrolls of the lyre refer to those that were carved in the friezes of Greek temples.

Fig. 1.1. *Pier Table*, attributed to Thomas Seymour (1771–1848), painting by John Ritto Penniman (1782–1841), 1809, white pine, white ash; paint, brass, Nichols House Museum, Boston, 1961.11 (Courtesy Nichols House Museum and David Bohl)

Brazilian rosewood came into fashion during the English Regency style. An option for the most expensive furniture, the exotic import was usually reserved for best parlors or drawing rooms. Thomas Seymour had a great talent for composing the grain of wood veneers, seen here by his use of the same flitch of rosewood for both upper and lower leaf edges, set on an angle to catch the eye and to create dynamic drama. In true English Regency fashion, the beautiful wood is inlaid with subtle brass stringing to echo and accentuate the architectural form and contours of the table.

Imported gilt cast-brass mounts are another feature of this new style in Boston furniture. The ornament at the center of the apron depicts two crossed oak-leaf branches, tied together with a ribbon. It is a high-quality ornament with sharp casting, and is a pattern seen often at this time on similar card tables from Seymour's shop.

John Ritto Penniman was the best decorative painter in Boston, and probably added the delicate acanthus leaves on the arms of the lyre. Penniman's decorative painting appears on many pieces of Seymour's furniture, starting perhaps as early as 1804, just as the first manifestations of the English Regency style were taking hold in Boston.[3]

Another table made by Seymour and painted by Penniman in 1809 exemplifies the collaboration between the two craftsmen (fig. 1.1).[4] Decorative painting in other American cities, particularly Baltimore, was a mainstay during the Classical period, but was never as popular in Boston. The painted furniture that was made there was more formal and conservative in design, fitting with the prevailing Boston taste (see Appendix I).

1. Robert D. Mussey Jr. and Clark Pearce, *Rather Elegant than Showy: The Classical Furniture of Isaac Vose* (Jaffrey, NH: Massachusetts Historical Society in association with David R. Godine, 2018), 9, 25n60; *Colombian Sentinel* (Boston), September 27 and October 11, 1809.
2. A very similar card table from a private collection is attributed to Seymour and inscribed with the date 1818, making it an example made by Seymour in James Barker's shop. Photographs of the table and inscription are in the author's files.
3. Robert D. Mussey Jr. and Clark Pearce, "Classical Excellence in Boston: The Furniture of Isaac Vose, 1789–1825," in *Boston Furniture, 1700–1900*, ed., Brock Jobe and Gerald W. R. Ward (Boston: Colonial Society of Massachusetts, 2016), 259, 284n84; Robert D. Mussey Jr., *The Furniture Masterworks of John & Thomas Seymour* (Salem, MA: Peabody Essex Museum, 2003), 114–15, 314–17.
4. Robert Mussey and Christopher Shelton, "John Penniman and the Ornamental Painting Tradition in Federal-Era Boston," in *American Furniture 2010*, ed. Luke Beckerdite (Milwaukee: Chipstone Foundation, 2010), 2, fig. 1.

2

Basin Stand, c. 1815–1820

Attributed to Thomas Seymour (1771–1848)
Boston
Mahogany, mahogany veneer; Honduras mahogany, white pine; brass
29⅝ × 17¾ in. diameter

INSCRIPTION: In pencil on the back of two drawer fronts: "No 2."

PROVENANCE: Sale, Skinner's, Bolton, MA; Private Collection, by 1983; Sale, Christie's, New York, Jan. 22, 2016, lot 121; Dr. Larry McCallister (1935–2021), IN; Sale, Sotheby's, New York, Sept. 22, 2022, lot 179; With Clark Pearce, Essex, MA, 2022; Purchased by Schrimshers, 2022.

Unlike the card table (cat. 1), this charming little confection of a basin or wash stand is a wholly new and imaginative form that draws inspiration from the English Regency style. Simple geometric shapes—cylinders, circles, half circles, spheres—become important design elements. In the earlier Neoclassical style, wash stands were square, or triangular when intended to fit into a corner, but here the body of the stand is a completely round, freestanding form. The overhanging top, with turned, circular moldings around the opening for the wash bowl, repeat and accentuate the cylindrical form below. Extending the scheme, the shelf below is also outlined with a series of circular moldings.

The quest for design innovation sometimes overlooks the practical considerations of manufacture. There is no straightforward way to make this shape from solid wood, so the exterior must be veneered over a laminated cylinder, which took much skill and time to produce. Unlike many of his competitors, Thomas Seymour was a very skilled laminator, but this cylindrical form takes the process to a new level, undoubtedly making these tables expensive to produce.

There are many references to the ancient world seen here. In the eighteenth century Sir William Hamilton (1730–1803), as British ambassador to Naples, Italy, collected a Roman bronze folding tripod and bowl cast in a cylindrical form, retaining evidence that it had been buried in the lava of Mount Vesuvius. By 1774, he had donated it to the British Museum, where, among many others, Thomas Hope became aware of it.[1] This stand, like its Greek and Roman antecedents, has three legs, a bowl at the top, lion's-paw feet and lion heads (for drawer pulls instead of carrying handles). (For an example of an extant Greek tripod stand, see p. 288, fig. 1.) The Bostonian designer of the Schrimsher stand reinterpreted the ancient model, using "modern" furniture elements to stand in for the ancient ones.

Two elements on this table were plucked directly from Thomas Sheraton's *The Cabinet Dictionary*, and from George Smith's *A Collection of Designs for Household Furniture and Interior Decoration*. The turned legs on the stand have toes that bend outward, just as the front of "Bed Room Chairs" (fig. 2.1) do in Sheraton's book. The three stretchers that curve down from the pitcher shelf to capture the lower out-turned legs are seen in Smith's cartoonish "Dejuné Table" (fig. 2.2). Seymour would have likely had access to these two design books, and it is not inconceivable that he designed this basin stand himself. If so, it speaks to the creativity that existed in the best Boston furniture shops.

There may be as many as fifteen of these tables extant. None are labeled or documented and they are hard to attribute to any one maker. However, an example at the Peabody Essex Museum (PEM) in Salem, Massachusetts, offers a clue.[2] This is the sole example that employs the use of contrasting light-colored bird's-eye maple veneers for drawer fronts and leg stile blocks. This highly figured maple has been intentionally scorched with a hot instrument to heighten the contrast even further, a fussy, labor-intensive "extra" that only Seymour used. Several other features also point to his manufacture, such as the fine triple beads cut into the edge of the top, the use of plain spherical brass drawer pulls, and the cylindrical patinated and gilt brass collars at the tops of the turned legs. A recent discovery on the PEM table makes the attribution of this group to Thomas Seymour all but certain: two tiny pencil inscriptions on the backsides of two of the drawer fronts read "No 2," executed in his distinctive hand. The inscriptions probably indicate that he made at least two of these tables at one time, taking advantage of the economies of scale.

Fig. 2.1. Thomas Sheraton, "Bed Room Chairs," plate 30, in *The Cabinet Dictionary* (London, 1803), engraving (Courtesy Winterthur Museum, Garden & Library)

Fig. 2.2. George Smith, "Dejuné Table," plate 82 in *A Collection of Designs for Household Furniture and Interior Decoration* (London, 1808), hand-colored engraving (Courtesy Clark Art Institute Library, Mary Ann Beinecke Decorative Art Collection)

1. *Bowl*, 1st century BCE–1st century CE, bronze, The British Museum, 1774,0603.1.b.; Thomas Hope, *Household Furniture and Interior Decoration* (London: Longman, Hurst, Rees and Orme, 1807), 110–11, pl. XVII, fig. 5.

2. *Basin Stand*, Peabody Essex Museum, Salem, Massachusetts, 124.788, illustrated in Berry B. Tracy, Marilynn Johnson, Marvin D. Schwartz, and Suzanne Boorsch, *19th-Century America: Furniture and Other Decorative Arts* (New York: Metropolitan Museum of Art, 1970), cat. 13. The top of this table has been altered to eliminate the hole that the basin is meant to seat into.

3

Side Chair, c. 1820–1824

Attributed to Thomas Seymour (1771–1848) for Isaac Vose & Son; carving attributed to Thomas Wightman (1759–1827)
Boston
Mahogany; maple, tulip poplar; replacement upholstery
33¼ × 19¼ × 24¼ in.

PROVENANCE: Dr. Alan W. Feld, Las Vegas; Sale, Christie's, New York, Jan. 17, 2019, lot 1294; Purchased by Schrimshers, 2019.

In the years just before Isaac Vose Jr. closed his father's cabinet shop in January 1825, Thomas Seymour was at the top of his game producing Classical furniture. This klismos side chair beautifully demonstrates that status. Seymour started making this general pattern of chair perhaps around 1816, possibly copying an example imported from England. Textile manufacturing innovator Nathan Appleton owned a large set of chairs that probably date from this time, albeit a much simpler model.[1] After making countless variations in this overall pattern, Seymour's design had matured fully, with pitch-perfect proportions. Thomas Wightman's successfully integrated carving on the crest and middle stay rail completes the well-developed design. The flared horizontal fluting on the crest and middle rail is quite arresting, a pattern that so far has eluded precedent but most likely comes from a pattern book or an imported chair that came to Seymour's attention. There were at least two sets of chairs made with this lyre pattern, including a slightly different model owned by the Metropolitan Museum of Art.[2]

Well into the 1820s, Seymour continued to use the Regency-inspired small paw feet on chair legs, as well as delicate carved lyres on crest rails, at a time when the shop was also making later Classical chairs. There was a market for both in Boston.

None of the Classical chairs that we associate with Seymour are marked, labeled, or otherwise documented, and the question of attribution arises. Seymour is well known for his early Neoclassical chairmaking in his independent shop, and it stands to reason that he would have continued making chairs as foreman of James Barker's shop from 1817 to 1819 and Isaac Vose's shop from 1819 to 1824.[3]

One telltale feature of his Neoclassical chairs is the use of heavy maple or birch front and rear seat rails that are secured into the legs with neat double tenons. Another is the care he took to slightly bevel each sharp corner in all his joinery, seen and unseen alike. He also gave the rear faces of stiles a perfectly semicircular profile that is very unusual, if not unique, in American work.

Acting as a bridge between Seymour's Neoclassical and Classical seating work is an open-arm sofa in the English Regency style, probably dating to 1814–17, that is constructed like an armchair with an elongated seat.[4] It has all the features mentioned above, but with one additional quirky element: a tiny wedge-shaped shelf is cut into the inside surface of the leg adjacent to the maple rear seat rail.[5] This fussy joint, together with the earlier characteristics used by Seymour, allow numerous sets of Classical chairs to be attributed to him.

1. Robert D. Mussey Jr. and Clark Pearce, *Rather Elegant than Showy: The Classical Furniture of Isaac Vose* (Jaffrey, NH: Massachusetts Historical Society in association with David R. Godine, 2018), 123, fig. 135.
2. *Side Chairs*, Metropolitan Museum of Art, New York, 1971.180.29–30.
3. Robert D. Mussey Jr., *The Furniture Masterworks of John and Thomas Seymour* (Salem, MA: Peabody Essex Museum, 2003), 382–89.
4. Mussey and Pearce, *Rather Elegant than Showy*, 61, fig. 69; 264, fig. 328.
5. Ibid., 264, fig. 329.

4

Sofa, c. 1825–1828

William Hancock (active c. 1820–1849)
Boston
Mahogany, mahogany veneer; white ash, white pine, mahogany, birch or maple; brass, partial original under upholstery, replacement upholstery
34 × 89½ × 27 in.

INSCRIPTIONS: In pencil: "William Hancock"; stamped on brass castor cups: "BB&Co / Patent." (See Appendix II)

PROVENANCE: By descent in the Shea Family, Needham, MA; With Israel Sack Inc., New York, by 1988; Purchased by Schrimshers, 1988.

A sofa in Thomas Sheraton's *The Cabinet-Maker, Upholsterer, and General Artist's Encyclopaedia* illustrates an innovative but outlandish design for a sofa (fig. 4.1). The principal elements are the two enormous cylindrical arms that emphasize the geometric forms that are such an integral element in English Regency–style furniture. This plate was engraved in 1805, but it took nearly twenty years for Bostonians to warm up to the more adventuresome Classical designs of Sheraton's later work.

The sofa shown here is not labeled (a nearly identical sofa at the Metropolitan Museum of Art is), but William Hancock inscribed his name in pencil onto the sponge-decorated paper lining of the drawer side on the proper right arm.[1] William was the second of five brothers, all of whom became ambitious and entrepreneurial participants in the Boston and Philadelphia furniture trade. The oldest brother, Henry Kellam Hancock (1788–1854), trained in Boston as a chair maker and cabinetmaker. William trained as an upholsterer, and likely taught his younger brothers Belcher and John the trade. The youngest, James, became a clerk in the family businesses.[2]

After William's apprenticeship, he probably worked in Henry's shop as a journeyman upholsterer until 1825 when Henry moved to a shop on Washington Street and William opened his own business on Market Street (later Cornhill). The two men presumably continued to work together, Henry making seating-furniture frames for William to upholster, including his patented spring-seat rocking chairs. Of the five or six sofas of this pattern that are known, each is a slight variation on the last. They all have the cylindrical crest rail with pointed terminals, carved scrolls supporting the crests, and some version of Sheraton's carved stump feet.[3] Each bolster-like arm features a three-dimensional ring of molded mahogany encircling a pleated silk face that masks a hidden drawer.

A conclusion that Henry made these sofa frames in his chair and cabinet shop would be quite logical. However, there are four elements on this sofa that suggest another maker. First, the construction of the frame echoes Seymour's method of building sofas with hollow rectangular boxes at the ends of the frame, designed to secure the feet. Second, Seymour often used bed bolts with nuts that are sunken into the wood frames to attach the arms so that they can be easily removed for reupholstery. Third, the brass caster cups on the feet are stamped "BB&Co / Patent." This mark likely stands for "[James] Barron's Blinds & Company," a high-end manufacturer of furniture, curtain, and blind hardware in London and Birmingham.[4] Seymour and Vose apparently had a direct relationship with Barron, whose marked hardware is only seen on their documented or attributed work. Two other sofas from this group also have Barron's marked casters: the labeled sofa at the Metropolitan and another owned by Bernard & S. Dean Levy, Inc. The fourth element is the presence of carving done in the style of Thomas Wightman, Seymour's go-to carver, albeit at a lower level of quality. Since these sofa frames would have been wholesaled to Hancock, the carving may have been done by a journeyman or apprentice in Wightman's shop. All of this evidence opens the possibility that William Hancock also sourced sofa frames from the Vose & Son shop in the first half of the 1820s.

The under upholstery on the arms of this sofa is original and carries a shadow of the green stamped plush medallion show covers, the pattern of which was used to reproduce the modern red. Also original is the beautiful lead-filled cast-brass molding beneath the crest rail and around the front of the arms.

Fig. 4.1. "Sofa," detail of plate 2 in Thomas Sheraton, *The Cabinet-Maker, Upholsterer, and General Artist's Encyclopaedia* (London, 1805–6), hand-colored engraving, New York Public Library, The Miriam and Ira D. Wallach Division of Art, Prints and Photography: Art & Architecture Collection, ID: b13976291 (Courtesy New York Public Library Digital Collections)

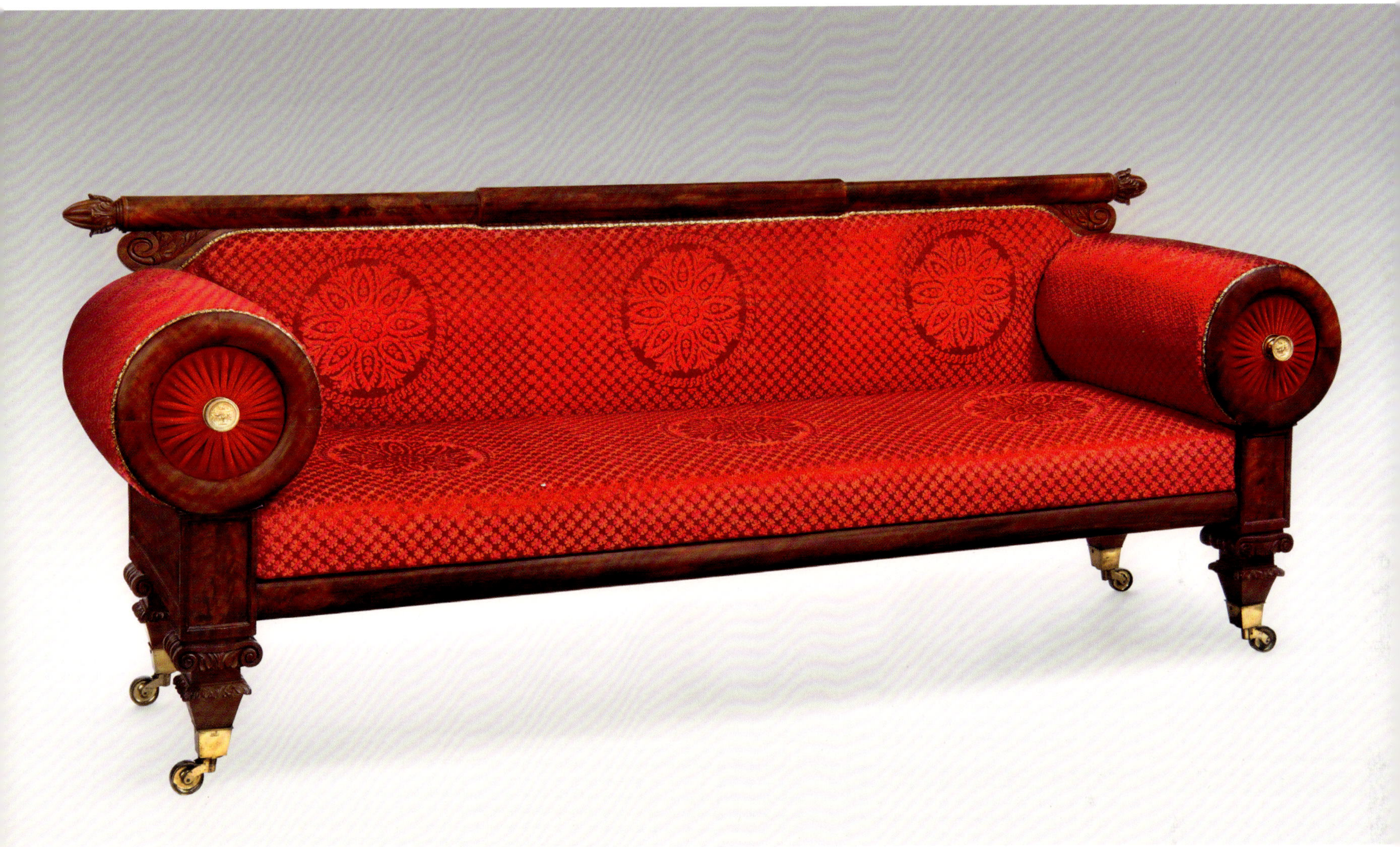

1. The similar sofa labeled by William Hancock is at the Metropolitan Museum of Art, New York, 48.164.1.
2. David H. Conradsen, "Ease and Economy: The Hancocks and the Development of Spring-Seat Upholstery in America" (MA thesis, University of Delaware, 1998), 4–8.
3. Thomas Sheraton, *The Cabinet Dictionary* (London, 1803), pl. 22.
4. James Barron, *Modern and Elegant Designs of Cabinet and Upholstery Furniture* (London, 1814). The advertisement for his hardware company is incorporated into this book.

5

Pier Table, c. 1813–1825

Emmons & Archbald: Thomas Emmons (c. 1781–1825) and George Archbald (1790–1870), in partnership 1813–1825
Boston
Mahogany, mahogany veneer; white pine, chestnut, ebonized wood; gray- and white-veined marble, mahoganizing wash, mirror glass, brass
33½ × 41 × 16¾ in.

INSCRIPTION: Stenciled on left rail: "EMMONS & ARCHBALD / No. 39 Orange Street / (BOSTON) / Cabinet, Chair & Upholstery / Manufactory." (See Appendix II)

LABEL: Paper label glued to the right interior corner: "G. Ticknor."

PROVENANCE: George Ticknor (1791–1871), Boston. Sale, Christie's, June 23, 1993, lot 203; Purchased by Schrimshers, 1993.

Hera, wife of Zeus, flies east through the clouds, her chariot drawn by a pair of stallions, in the form of a gilt brass ornament on the frieze of this French-style pier table (see Appendix I). The shop of Thomas Emmons and George Archbald, who began their partnership in 1813, specialized in these canted-corner pier tables, often making them in pairs. The mate would have likely featured a matching ornament of Zeus in his chariot, also drawn through the clouds by a pair of stallions, rushing west towards Hera.

Because their design is based on actual elements of ancient architecture, French-style square pier tables are among the most successful forms created in Boston in the later Classical style. The monumental scale of this table perfectly communicates the stability and longevity of ancient architecture. The deep curves cut into three sides of the plinth, the canted corners, and the compressed ball feet work to soften the severity of the purest antique taste for their largely Anglophile clientele. Surprisingly, comparatively few French-style pier tables are known to originate from the Vose shop, which may have retailed Emmons & Archbald pier tables. A beautiful rosewood pier table with the distinctive construction methods of Emmons & Archbald's work contains the stenciled label of Isaac Vose & Son beneath the slab.[1]

As expected on late Classical Boston pier tables, this example includes a knife-edge Grecian ovolo molding beneath the marble top, a feature indicative of this city's craft traditions. Boston cabinetmakers were also fond of flat fillet moldings of cross-banded mahogany on the aprons and pilasters to frame the crotch mahogany panels. The inner frame and glue blocks of the apron are chestnut. The substrate of the plinth is formed with a frame of four pine slabs. There is a resultant gap in the center of the underside of the plinth, shaped in a long rectangle that is two inches deep. This long gap is the most important characteristic for identifying Emmons & Archbald pier tables. Apparently no other cabinetmaker in Boston used this method.[2]

Adding to the monumental aspect of the table is the beautiful inch-thick charcoal-gray marble slab with white veining. Robert D. Mussey Jr.'s research identified the owner of a marble yard and manufactory in Boston in the 1820s. Scottish immigrant John Templeton advertised frequently in the Boston newspapers, listing the types of marble that he sold, offering evidence of the most popular marbles used by local cabinetmakers and their patrons. Not surprisingly, his best sellers appeared to be Italian white, Italian white-veined, and dove-colored, which is a soft gray with slight overtones of lavender.[3] All three are frequently seen on Emmons & Archbald tables, but the marble on this table does not seem to fit into any of Templeton's advertised categories. Chiseled on the underside, the coded shipping mark, a diamond shape with a dot at the center, was unique to the Emmons & Archbald shop, and was used by the European shipper to identify their marble slabs when they were unloaded in the port of Boston.[4]

A paper label on the inside frame of the apron is inscribed "G. Ticknor," indicating that the table was once owned by George Ticknor. He studied at Dartmouth College and became a professor at Harvard, eventually becoming the world's leading authority on the history of Spanish literature and a founder of the Boston Public Library. The Ticknors furnished their homes with stylish Classical furniture, patronizing both Emmons & Archbald and Isaac Vose & Son.[5]

---

1. Private collection. The inside rear rail is inscribed "Gardiner," possibly owned by a descendant of loyalist Dr. Silvester Gardiner (1708–1786). The Gardiner family (spelled with an *i*) was unrelated to the prominent Gardner family.
2. Robert D. Mussey Jr. and Clark Pearce, *Rather Elegant than Showy: The Classical Furniture of Isaac Vose* (Jaffrey, NH: Massachusetts Historical Society in association with David R. Godine, 2018), 249, fig. 306.
3. Ibid., 238–39.
4. The symbol on this and one other attributed table is a diamond shape with a dot at the center. A third attributed pier table is marked "HX." All three tables are in a private collection.
5. Mussey and Pearce, *Rather Elegant than Showy*, 159–67. One of his daughters donated a large group of her father's Classical furnishings to Hood Museum at Dartmouth College. At least three were probably made by Emmons & Archbald: a marble-top pier cabinet (F.965.90.8), a marble-top pier table (F.965.90.9), and a rosewood worktable (F.965.90.22).

6

French Secretary, c. 1820–1825

Emmons & Archbald: Thomas Emmons (c. 1781–1825) and George Archbald (1790–1870), in partnership 1813–1825
Boston
Mahogany, mahogany veneer; Honduras mahogany, birch, chestnut, tulip poplar, ebonized wood; mahoganizing wash, brass
58¼ × 36⅛ × 18⅜ in.

LABEL: Stenciled on the long drawer bottom in the interior, "EMMONS & ARCHBALD / No. 39 Orange Street / (BOSTON) / Cabinet, Chair & Upholstery / Manufactory." (See Appendix II)

PROVENANCE: Private Collection, MA; Given to Dr. Elmer Humphrey Copeland, Northampton, MA, as payment for treatment; By descent to his granddaughter Katherine Copeland Newhall, Bedford, MA; Sale, Kaminski Auctions, Beverly, MA, 2021; With Christopher Settle, Newton, MA, 2021; With Clark Pearce, Essex, MA, by 2021; Purchased by Schrimshers, 2021.

The French Secretary was an expensive yet relatively popular form in Boston. Almost none are inscribed, labeled, or documented in any way, making it difficult to assign them to any particular shop.[1] This example is one of only two known secretaries labeled by Emmons & Archbald and is nearly identical to the other at the Museum of Fine Arts, Boston (MFA).[2] One difference between the two is that the MFA example has three flat, veneered drawers behind the hinged doors in the lower half, where this secretary has an open space with one shelf.

The workmanship in these secretaries closely rivals those from the Vose shop, but they are distinguished on the basis of style and construction. The Emmons & Archbald examples are considerably taller than their Vose cousins. The interiors vary from secretary to secretary but are always drawn from the same pool of options. These include a double row of valanced cubby holes at the top, a tall center section with dividers for account books, and deep drawers at the bottom with flush-mounted brass plates and ring pulls that are hinged at the top and lay flush when not in use (to avoid contact with the drop leaf when closed). The thin dividers between compartments are neatly beaded on the facing edges, a feature not seen on Vose's secretaries.

The form was developed in France around the mid-eighteenth century as a more compact desk than the larger cylinder or slant-lid desks and often intended for use by women. When the Empire style took hold after the Revolution, they became more architectural, with plinths, friezes, and engaged columns, providing strong associations with classical themes. This French design was adopted almost wholesale in Boston and was known in newspaper advertisements and bills of sale as a French secretary.[3] Boston cabinetmaker Henry Kellam Hancock (1788–1854), owned an anonymous plate that shows a French secretary that looks like it could have inspired this example (fig. 6.1).[4]

The facades of Boston French secretaries, with their broad, flat, uninterrupted surfaces, provided great opportunities for cabinetmakers to create interesting compositions with large flitches of crotch mahogany veneers. In this case Emmons & Archbald selected four consecutive sheets of figured veneers in an arch pattern, reversing them first horizontally, then vertically, creating a dramatic image that is symmetrical on four sides. They continued this theme onto the frieze above, and even onto the vertical edge of the secretary's top, where they create an arcade of small, vertical plumes of crotch veneer. The upward-arching movement is broken only between the frieze and top board by a knife-edge Grecian ovolo molding.

The writing surface on this secretary is lined with tooled Morocco leather that may be original or an early replacement for baize fabric. The turnip-shaped feet are favorites in Emmons & Archbald's work. In this case, the front feet are ebonized, and the rear feet are polished mahogany. The MFA secretary has carved paw front feet with identical turnip-shaped back feet. Like the Emmons & Archbald pier table (cat. 5), the MFA secretary has a red wash applied to any surface that might be seen when moving or using it, adding to the uniformity of the finish throughout.

Fig. 6.1. Unknown artist, *French Secretary*, c. 1815, gouache on paper (Courtesy Winterthur Museum, Garden & Library)

1. Robert D. Mussey Jr. and Clark Pearce, *Rather Elegant than Showy: The Classical Furniture of Isaac Vose* (Jaffrey, NH: Massachusetts Historical Society in association with David R. Godine, 2018), 274. One other Boston cabinetmaker is known to have signed a French secretary. Joseph Laidain Jr., son of a French immigrant, was an apprentice or journeyman who may have trained or worked in the Vose & Son shop. His signed French secretary is in the collection of the Winterthur Museum, Garden & Library (1979.0026).
2. *French Secretary*, Museum of Fine Arts, Boston, 1985.335.
3. Though referred to in Boston as French secretaries, they were known in France as *secrétaires à abattant.*
4. Hancock owned at least forty-seven loose design plates by Pierre de La Mésangère, James Barron, George Smith, Désiré Guilmard, and some anonymous designers. These plates, along with a large collection of unused cabinet hardware, descended in Henry K. Hancock's family, and are now in the collection of Winterthur Library. The loose plates are tattered, annotated, and worn, evidence that they were used frequently in the day-to-day operations of his shop. Note the pencil sketch of a lyre above the French secretary in cat. 6, fig. 6.1. Hancock was one of the appraisers of Isaac Vose's estate, and it is not inconceivable that he bought the plates at one of several auctions of Vose's holdings in 1825.

7

Sideboard, c. 1820–1825

Attributed to Emmons & Archbald: Thomas Emmons (c. 1781–1825) and George Archbald (1790–1870), in partnership 1813–1825
Boston
Mahogany, mahogany veneer; chestnut, white pine, tulip poplar; brass
56 × 82½ × 27½ in.

PROVENANCE: Sale, Skinner Auctions, Feb. 27, 2000, lot 223; With Clark Pearce, Essex, MA, 2000; Private Collection, Boston, 2000; Sale, Brunk Auctions, Asheville, NC, Nov. 12, 2022, lot 683; Purchased by Schrimshers, 2022.

When a Boston Classical sideboard has a brass gallery, it almost always turns out to be a later addition, but that is not the case here. Instead, it is fastened to the top of the sideboard with hand-threaded bolts and large square nuts. The gallery is probably of English manufacture and features elements of Regency style, like lion heads biting lotus buds and clusters of grapes and leaves.

Emmons & Archbald made English-style sideboards, like this one with a center opening to store a cellarette, and French-style examples with four doors across the facade, with no niche for a cellarette. They offered two options for feet on their sideboards, paw feet or smooth *toupie* feet (French for "spinning top"). This one has both: paw feet with a fringe of carved leaves on the front feet, and gadrooned toupie feet in the rear. Titled "Stump Feet" in plate 23 of Thomas Sheraton's *The Cabinet Dictionary* (London, 1803), toupie feet were a shop favorite for case work of all kinds. In George Smith's *The Cabinet-Maker and Upholsterer's Guide* (London, 1826) he shows a *toupie* foot that is even closer to those used by Emmons & Archbald.[1] A shortcut that this shop took was the carving on the paw feet, which seems to follow the patterns of Thomas Wightman's simpler work but may have been rendered by one of his journeymen. Belying the influence of French design in Boston, the sideboards from this shop never employ brass knobs or handles, instead giving access only through keys left in the locks, or hand grips cut into the frames behind the overhanging drawers. Additionally, only about half of the known examples have brass capitals and bases on the engaged columns—an option to accommodate their client's wishes by emphasizing the rich materials and architecture in a clean and subtle way. The sideboards without cast-brass capitals and bases have simple carving or plain turning in those areas. This sideboard perfectly embodies the Boston preference for rich but understated furniture.

No doubt a bespoke example, this sideboard has options not seen on Emmons & Archbald's standard examples. Along with the brass gallery and the concave center section, extras include two baize-lined cutlery boxes atop the pedestals, and the elevation of the end cabinets themselves. The cutlery boxes are hinged on the outer sides and fitted with locks, with sides molded with what Smith calls the "Greek Scotia".[2] The complex concave curve was made from a section of a parabola, a mathematical formula used by the Egyptians and Greeks but not the Romans.

All of the labeled or attributed sideboards from this shop are built with the same formula of modular units, with two independent pedestals and a separate single assembly for the top and the three drawers. The top assembly is screwed to the tops of the pedestals; in models with a cellarette niche, a single framed mahogany panel is screwed to the backs of the pedestals. The backboards are assembled with three framed panels of tulip poplar, two vertical and a rectangular one in the center, all neatly made and screwed into rabbets. Consistent veneering patterns, solid (not paneled) sides, and the use of chestnut as a secondary wood reinforce an attribution to the Emmons & Archbald shop.

1. George Smith, *The Cabinet-Maker and Upholsterer's Guide* (London: Jones & Co., 1826), pl. LXXII, "Supporting Feet for Cabinets, Commodes & Footstools" (third row down, left image).
2. Ibid., pl. I.

8

Card Table, c. 1817–1820

Attributed to Thomas Seymour (1771–1848), for James Barker (active 1814–1819) or for Isaac Vose (1767–1823); carving attributed to Thomas Wightman (1759–1827)
Boston
Mahogany, mahogany veneer; mahogany, chestnut, white pine, tulip poplar; brass
30 × 36½ × 18 in.

PROVENANCE: Sale, Skinners Auction Gallery, Oct. 25, 1998, lot 463; With Gary Sullivan Antiques Inc., 1998; With Christopher Settle, Newton, MA, c. 1999; With Clark Pearce, Essex, MA, 2016; Purchased by Schrimshers, 2016.

In late 1816, Thomas Seymour, still working independently, introduced to Boston a new design for a pair of card tables when he fulfilled an order from Peter Chardon Brooks (1767–1849), explicitly identifying them as "Grecian" in his waste books.[1] The tops and aprons of Brooks's tables are similar to this example, but the pillars and bases are blocky and underdeveloped. By the time Seymour made the present table, he had perfected the form with sophistication and elegance. Subsequently, such tables became popular in Boston and were made in quantities by cabinetmakers of various skill levels. A labeled example at the Saint Louis Art Museum offers a roadmap for construction, workmanship, veneering, and carving that can be used to attribute unmarked or undocumented tables to Isaac Vose & Son.[2]

The design combines an Egyptian "pylon pedestal," Greek Ionic scrolls for the apron terminals and feet, and Greek torus and scotia moldings at the bottom of the pylon.[3] The workmanship is meticulous. The long, single flitch of crotch mahogany veneer on the top is impressive, with two more flitches from the same log applied to the playing surfaces of the two leaves. The four pieces of crotch veneer on the top of the plinth have grain that tapers, radiating outward and pointing to the ends of the plinth above the feet. The grain of the crotch veneers set inside the fillet moldings on the four sides of the pylon are carefully selected to conform to its taper. Such compositions were one of Seymour's great talents.

Thomas Wightman's carving plays a large role in the success of this table, with perfect spirals that taper gradually to an impossibly fine point in the Ionic scrolls on the apron and feet. A square collar of acanthus leaves at the base of the pylon is carved with deeply cut, naturalistic leaflets that seem to bend and sway in the breeze.

The sophisticated Greek scotia and elliptical ovolo moldings below the carving on the pedestal are complicated to execute because they are cut with the grain of the mahogany block running vertically rather than horizontally. The blades in the molding planes needed for this work had to be incredibly sharp and in the hands of a highly skilled cabinetmaker. The gentle undulation of the patterns and colors of the vertical grain creates a subtle beauty that straight-grain moldings can never achieve. Seymour used an English Regency-style molding on the top corners of the plinth, composed of a series of quarter-round disks that softened the severity of the form and added visual interest.

This table provides an excellent study of the classical principles of symmetry and balance. The visual weight of the plinth and its scrolled feet balances the longer but lighter apron assembly above. The single pedestal simplifies the design, eliminating the four legs of a Neoclassical model, and its taper suggests a sense of solidity.

---

1. Robert D. Mussey Jr. and Clark Pearce, "Classical Excellence in Boston: The Furniture of Isaac Vose, 1789–1825," in *Boston Furniture, 1700–1900*, eds. Brock Jobe and Gerald W. R. Ward (Boston: Colonial Society of Massachusetts, 2016), 259, fig. 9.
2. Robert D. Mussey Jr. and Clark Pearce, *Rather Elegant than Showy: The Classical Furniture of Isaac Vose* (Jaffrey, NH: Massachusetts Historical Society in association with David R. Godine, 2018), 2, fig. 3.
3. Though there is an element of accuracy in the use of the term "pylon" for these tapered pedestal shapes, a true Egyptian pylon refers to the two tapered monoliths that represent hills in an Egyptian temple that flank an architectural portal in the center, through which the sun rises and sets on certain days of the calendar year. The pylon shape that has been adapted here actually comes from the ends of the tapered monoliths that make up the three-part pylon.

9

Card Table, c. 1823–1825

T. Hunt & Co.: Timothy Hunt (d. 1874) and Simon H. Hunt (dates unknown), in partnership 1819–1827; carving attributed to Thomas Wightman (1759–1827)
Boston
Mahogany, mahogany veneer; mahogany, Honduras mahogany, birch, chestnut; brass
29⅛ × 36¹⁵⁄₁₆ × 17⅞ in.

LABEL: "T. Hunt & Co. / Cabinet & Chair / Manufacturers / No. 85 Newbury St. / Boston" (stenciled). (See Appendix II)

PROVENANCE: Sale, Bonhams Skinner, Marlborough, MA, Apr. 1, 2021, lot 1648; With Clark Pearce, Essex, MA, 2021; Purchased by Schrimshers, 2021.

Classical furniture scholar Page Talbott discussed Timothy Hunt's labeled work in a series of articles in *The Magazine Antiques* between May 1975 and May 1992.[1] Dealers, auctioneers, and collectors subsequently attributed much furniture to his shop. Almost all of those attributions have been wrong, built on the assumption that the carving on the pedestal, base, and legs—the most striking parts of the table—was likely executed by Hunt, or someone in his shop. In fact, the excellent carving was the work of specialist Thomas Wightman, who worked for many different cabinetmakers, including Seymour, Vose, Emmons & Archbald, William Fiske, Cornelius Briggs, Benjamin Bass Jr., and undoubtedly others.

The simple rectangular shape of the apron and swivel top with rounded front corners was standard for card tables in Boston in the later Classical style. It was the blank canvas upon which elaborately grained mahogany veneer was applied in book-matched patterns, and the edges of the two leaves almost always have applied, slightly rounded profiles of cross-banded ribbon-grain mahogany. The turned and carved baluster-shaped pedestal was much loved in Boston (see fig. 5, p. 40). The gadrooning that sits directly on the plinth, a vestige of English Regency–style silver and furniture, was also favored in the city.

Because no price books were published in Boston to regulate the methods of joinery and what journeymen should be paid for each process, the city's cabinetmakers had more freedom to establish their own particular methods of construction. Some long-lived shops standardized their preferences, allowing furniture scholars, curators, and collectors of Boston furniture to use these habitual, quirky idiosyncracies to formulate more accurate attributions.[2]

1. Page Talbott, "The Furniture Trade in Boston, 1810–1835: Check List," *The Magazine Antiques* 141, no. 5 (May 1992): 850, "Hunt, Timothy and Co."
2. Some of the characteristic construction features of Hunt's card tables are a swing rail that protrudes through the rear apron rail and is double wedged; a T-bar bolt that secures the top to the plinth through the pedestal, sunk into the medial rail and covered with wood to hide it; and a large decorative blacksmith-made wingnut securing the T-bar bolt, among a handful of other features. With knowledge of these methods, Hunt's work can be reliably separated from the products of the Seymour, Vose, and Emmons & Archbald shops.

10

Armchair, c. 1822–1824

Attributed to Thomas Seymour (1771–1848) for Isaac Vose (1767–1823); carving attributed to Thomas Wightman (1759–1827); upholstery attributed to Thomas Hedges (1788–1832) or Otis Packard (1804–1880)
Boston
Mahogany; birch; original under upholstery, replacement upholstery
33⅜ × 21⅞ × 24¼ in.

INSCRIPTIONS: In pencil, twice: "Walcott."

PROVENANCE: Probably Nathan Appleton (1779–1861) and Maria Theresa Gold Appleton, Boston; Greely Stevenson Curtis (1830–1987) and Harriot Appleton Curtis (1841–1923), Boston and Manchester, MA; Thence by descent at Sharksmouth, Manchester, MA. Possibly to a member of the Walcott family of Boston, by 2012. Sale, Louis J. Dianni Auction, Sunrise, FL, held at West Point, NY, Aug. 18–19, 2012, lot 142; With Christopher Settle, Newton, MA, Aug. 2012; With Clark Pearce, Essex, MA, Aug. 25, 2012; Purchased by Schrimshers, 2012.

About 1823, Thomas Seymour expanded his repertoire of chair styles beyond the English Regency model that he had employed since at least 1816 (cat. 3). Seymour's new style featured concave tablet crest rails that extend beyond the upper stiles, and a new vocabulary of stay-rail designs, akin to chairs seen on ancient Greek vases and bas-relief marble sculptures. Armchairs in the new style have supports cut in an S-shape with open scroll handholds at the top. These replaced the large, one-piece open scroll arms that wasted too much expensive mahogany.

The arms, arm supports, stiles, seat rails, and front legs are continuously carved with a single fat reed flanked by small single beads. Seymour's English Regency–style chairs usually have wide double-reed moldings, but in this later phase of his chairmaking, he preferred single reeds, perhaps to make a more muscular, less fussy but still finished look. On this chair, the rectangular tablet has a single rounded bead cut just inside the perimeter. The center of the crest is carved in the intaglio style, meaning that the carving is sunk below the surface, rather than above it (as in bas-relief). Intaglio carving derives from the exteriors of ancient Egyptian temples like those at Dendera, depicting deities and hieroglyphs (fig. 10.1). It was often used on English Classical furniture to invoke an association with the ancient themes that fascinated so many during the Classical movement.[1] Thomas Wightman was surely the author of this symmetrical grouping of husks and leaves and may have learned the technique from an English carver.

Fig. 10.1. *Roman Emperor Trajan as Pharaoh Making an Offering to the Gods*, carving from an exterior stone wall at the Temple of Hathor complex in Dendera, Egypt, c. 100–117 CE, limestone (Courtesy Alamy)

Thomas Hedges, an immigrant from London, was an upholsterer and limited partner in the Vose & Son firm, first joining the shop in 1818.[2] After Isaac Vose died in 1823, Hedges left the firm to start his own upholstery and decorating business. Because the assumed date range for this chair is c. 1822–24, Hedges is the probable manufacturer of the under-upholstery extant on this chair and its mates. In 1820 Hedges inscribed his work on a pair of chairs with similar intaglio husk carving, and on a sofa dated 1819.[3]

The seat's side and rear corners are sharp and at right angles with the seat top in the French manner, but the front edge shows a downward roll to the front seat rail. This design is found in Thomas King's *The Modern Style of Cabinet Making Exemplified* (London, 1829), among other pattern books, and became the standard pattern for high-end Boston Classical chair seat cushions.[4] If the chair was made after Vose's death in 1823, Vose's nephew, and Hedges's likely apprentice, Otis Packard, could have made the seat cushion.[5]

This chair was part of a large set of arm and side chairs that were used at Greely and Harriot Curtis's summer home, known as Sharksmouth, in Manchester, Massachusetts. Harriot probably inherited the chairs from her father, Nathan. Several 1880s photographs survive of the Curtis family sitting around a dining table in these chairs.[6]

1. Robert D. Mussey Jr. and Clark Pearce, *Rather Elegant than Showy: The Classical Furniture of Isaac Vose* (Jaffrey, NH: Massachusetts Historical Society in association with David R. Godine, 2018), 221–22, figs. 241–43.
2. Ibid., 273, "Appendix 2: Vose's Partners, Journeymen, Subcontractors and Apprentices: Thomas Hedges".
3. Ibid., 221, fig. 241. The chairs are reproduced in Page Talbott, "The Furniture Trade in Boston, 1810–1835: Check List," *The Magazine Antiques* 141, no. 5 (May 1992): 843, pl. III.
4. Thomas King and Thomas Gordon Smith, *Neo-Classical Furniture Designs: A Reprint of Thomas King's "Modern Style of Cabinet Making Exemplified," 1829* (New York: Dover, 1995), pl. 18 (bottom right image).
5. Mussey and Pearce, *Rather Elegant than Showy*, 146–47, fig. 162. Packard inscribed a sofa "Stuf'd [sic] by Otis Packard at / Isaac Voses [sic] Boston / August 24 / 1823 OP." Packard was in charge of upholstery at the Vose shop from 1823 until the shop was closed and auctioned off in 1825. It is unclear where he worked after that date.
6. The Harriot Appleton Curtis Photographic Collection, Historic New England.

11

Worktable, c. 1830

Unknown maker; carving possibly by Joseph True (1785–1873)
Salem
Mahogany, mahogany veneer; Honduras mahogany; brass
29 × 35½ × 20¼ in. (leaves extended); 29 × 20½ × 20¼ in. (leaves down)

PROVENANCE: With Eldred's Auction Gallery, East Dennis, MA, by 2013; With Christopher Settle, Newton, MA; With Clark Pearce, Essex, MA, by 2019; Purchased by Schrimshers, 2019.

The cabinetwork of Boston and Salem is often quite similar, with many Salem-made objects attributed to Boston. With its architectural, late Classical design, this worktable is a case in point. Once thought to be of Boston origin, it is one of a group of three tables that are from the same Salem shop. One of these is in a private collection and is well documented to Salem.[1] The cabinetmaker who made these tables remains unknown, but the carving specialist Joseph True may have rendered the carved elements on the leaf supports and ball feet. True executed a considerable amount of carving for the Salem cabinetmaking firm of Abraham Kimball (1798–1890) and Winthrop Sargent (active 1821–1843), who, in 1837, employed seventeen journeymen.[2] These worktables may have been made in Kimball & Sargent's shop.

The figured mahogany veneers on all the tables are superb, following the same pattern of layout. Single flitches of crotch veneer are glued to the center sections of the tops. The facades of the cases have grain patterns flashing in many different directions. The quatrefoil plinths are veneered with four flitches of crotch mahogany, book-matched in four directions, with the grain accentuating the corners that support the lively columns. The capitals on the columns are carved with a repeating Corinthian leaf pattern derived from Greek columns, a favorite motif frequently employed on Salem Classical furniture. The leaf supports on two of the three tables are carved with Ionic scrolls filled with banded lotus petals. Whether by True or someone else, the carver was certainly trained in the London style, which is characterized in part by little horseshoe-shaped gaps between alternating acanthus leaves. No Boston Classical carving looks quite like this work.

Meticulous attention has been paid to the construction details, even in places that would not be seen. For example, the underside of the plinth is counter-veneered with plain mahogany to discourage cracks in the edges from swelling and shrinkage. The upper drawer is fitted with an adjustable writing surface. Beneath that surface is a long, concealed drawer across the front designed for an inkbottle, sander, pens, and pen nibs, accessible only from the proper left side of the drawer. There, a flush-mounted and hinged brass ring pull provides access to this space. This is an innovative design that allocates additional scale to the writing surface.

George Smith's "Backgammon Work Table," plate 8 in his *The Cabinet-Maker and Upholsterer's Guide* (London, 1826), provided the model for this table, which was copied quite directly (fig. 11.1). Typical of American cabinetmakers' desire for a more practical product, the Salem shop modified the details of the original design to suit their customer's preferences.

Fig. 11.1. George Smith, "Backgammon Work Table," plate 8 in *The Cabinet-Maker and Upholsterer's Guide* (London, 1826), hand-colored engraving (Courtesy Alamy)

1. This other table is a somewhat simpler model, lacking the scroll carving on the leaf supports. It retains a paper label, inscribed in ink, underneath the hinged writing surface inside the top drawer: "This work table was a piece of the wedding furniture of Mary Osgood Deland, my mother. She was married Dec. 15, 1833 to John Hodges, my father. HHS." Both Mary Osgood Deland (1808–1903) and John Hodges (1802–1882) were born in Salem, and John was a third-generation ship captain out of Salem Harbor, and a longtime member of the Salem Marine and East India Marine Societies. "Mary Osgood (Deland) Hodges (1808–1903)," Wikitree, last modified January 5, 2023, https://www.wikitree.com/wiki/Deland-213. Photos of the Hodges table and its label are in the author's files.
2. Kathleen M. Catalano, "Abraham Kimball (1798–1890), Salem Cabinetmaker," *American Art Journal* 11, no. 2, (April 1979): 62–70.

12

Side Chair, c. 1822–1825

Attributed to Thomas Seymour (1771–1848) for Isaac Vose (1767–1823); carving attributed to Thomas Wightman (1759–1827)
Boston
Mahogany; birch; replacement upholstery
33¼ × 18¾ × 21 in.

PROVENANCE: Mrs. Donald (Gloria Curtis) Horn, Roslyn, New York, 1976. Peggy N. (d. 2000) and Roger G. Gerry (1916–1995), Roslyn, NY; Their sale, Christie's, New York, Oct. 7, 2004, lot 1562; Purchased by Schrimshers, 2004.

While overseeing the Vose shop as foreman, Thomas Seymour developed several new styles of chairs around 1822–23 to add to his later Classical repertoire. He probably based his model for this chair on an English example, like a c. 1810–20 pair with swagged drapery stay rails that were owned by the Quincy family.[1] By this time Seymour had adopted simpler joinery in the rear seat rail. The new design retained the familiar Greek klismos form but added curved tablet crest rails with raised panels of figured mahogany and carved, double-scroll ends. These crests were offered in two options: with ruffles of carved acanthus leaves, as seen here (fig. 12.1), or with carved palmettes.

Both models hewed much more closely to Greek chairs depicted on ancient vases, frescoes, and marble sculpture. They are also very close to Grecian chairs designed by Thomas Hope. Seymour may have been looking at Hope's *Household Furniture and Interior Decoration* (London, 1807), plate XXIV, no. 3, when he designed these chairs (fig. 12.2). Modifying Hope's design, he raised the height of the back to make room for the triple-fold drapery, reminiscent of Greek garments such as chitons or enkykla or Roman togas.[2] The carved half-honeysuckle blossoms placed in the lower corners of the swag create more strength.

The overall format of these chairs was also available in two options: the first was made in the scale and proportion of traditional upright dining chairs; the second was made with the same crest and drapery, but the stiles were extended further back in a long, deeply swept upward curve, more aligned with the proportions of Greek klismos examples and intended for parlor or drawing-room chairs. The front seat rails are carved with a series of reeds set at opposing angles, with an inverted V-shaped acanthus leaf at the center. This carving pattern was reserved for parlor chairs only. The dining chairs in this pattern always have some variety of horizontal reeding.

Chairs with the deeply swept backs were also constructed in a very different manner. The base of the chairs (the four legs and the four rails) were made in a separate unit, like a stool. The lower stiles of the backs were then tenoned into the tops of the side rails of the stool. Because Seymour knew that this was a potentially weak joint, he added long strips of mahogany to the top of the side rails, secured by two strong screws from the underside. The strips were cut on an angle to project over the top of the lower stile joints, holding them tightly in place. The tops of these strips were molded to conform to the stiles above, creating a continuous molded curve that extends all the way to the front seat rail, terminating in a scroll topped by a carved single-veined leaf.[3] Given the extra labor to manufacture the elaborate carving on the front seat rails, the extra mahogany needed to make the deeply swept backs, and the added strips on the side rails, these were surely expensive chairs. Judging by how many examples survive, however, they were popular with elite Bostonians.

1. Robert D. Mussey Jr. and Clark Pearce, *Rather Elegant than Showy: The Classical Furniture of Isaac Vose* (Jaffrey, NH: Massachusetts Historical Society in association with David R. Godine, 2018), 163, fig. 184; *Side Chairs*, Historic New England, Quincy House, Quincy, Massachusetts, 1972.54a.
2. On triple-fold drapery, see Christina Garton, "The Truth about Togas," *PieceWork*, March 13, 2020, https://pieceworkmagazine.com/the-truth-about-togas/.
3. Interestingly, this is not where this model of chair breaks over time; that indignity usually occurs at the joint of the tablet crests and the upper stiles, where two screws are the only things that hold them together.

Fig. 12.1. Detail of cat. 12 showing the crest with carved acanthus leaves

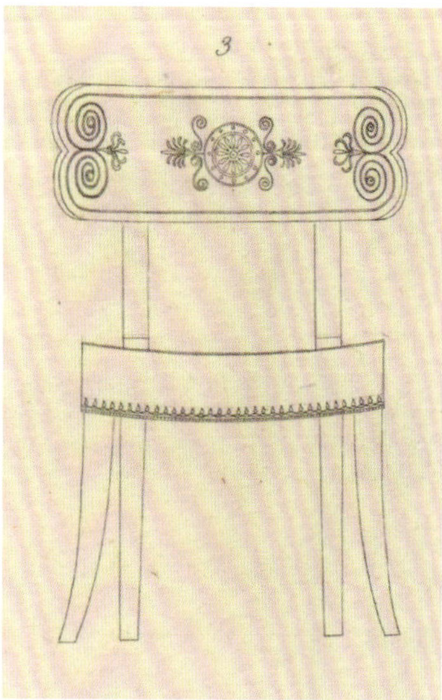

Fig. 12.2. Thomas Hope, detail of plate 24, no. 3, in *Household Furniture and Interior Decoration* (London, 1807), engraving (Courtesy Winterthur Museum, Garden & Library)

13

Pair of Side Chairs, c. 1830

Unknown maker; carving possibly by Joseph True (1785–1873)
Probably Salem
Mahogany, mahogany veneer; ash; replacement upholstery
32¼ × 17¾ × 19¾ in.

PROVENANCE: With Hirschl & Adler Galleries, New York. John W. Kluge, Morven, Charlottesville, VA. Sale, Christie's, New York, Dec. 16, 2005, lot 3; Purchased by Schrimshers, 2005.

The florid, leafy stay rails on this pair of side chairs are unusual and very close to those on another pair (fig. 13.1). That pair also has carving at the top of the legs that appears to be the work of the same Salem craftsman, perhaps Joseph True, who may have carved the ball feet on the Schrimsher drop-leaf worktable (cat. 11). The front seat rails on the other chairs have a series of carved leaf-and-dart, a Greek architectural motif often encountered in Salem Classical furniture but rarely in Boston work. Perhaps referencing Roman bronze furniture supports, the front legs on both pairs are turned and carved in a manner similar to those seen in Thomas King's *The Modern Style of Cabinet Work Exemplified* (London, 1829), plate 18.[1] King's pattern books were hugely influential in Salem.

Fig. 13.1. *Pair of Side Chairs*, unknown maker, probably Salem, c. 1830, mahogany, replacement upholstery, Private collection (Courtesy Charles Clark, Woodbury, CT)

Yet another pair of chairs that may also have been made in Salem have similarly turned legs with carving that closely relates to the ball feet on the drop-leaf worktable. They too have the repeating Greek leaf-and-dart carving on three sides of the seat rails. Their elaborately carved splats are of a different pattern but reminiscent of King's designs for chairs.[2]

Page Talbott's research suggests that the backs of the Schrimsher chairs relate to drapery-back models from Boston, like those seen from Isaac Vose's shop around 1823–25.[3] Though the carved stay rails on the chairs in this entry are more massive and ornate, they echo those of the Schrimshers' swag-back side chairs attributed to Vose (cat. 12). The tablet crest rails share similar raised panels of figured mahogany. The anthemions on the ends of the tablets on these examples, while larger and more florid, share commonalities with the more chaste design of the swag-back side chairs.

The patron of these chairs spent a considerable sum for the elaborate carving. There is more work to be done to confirm their place of origin.

1. Thomas King and Thomas Gordon Smith, *Neo-Classical Furniture Designs: A Reprint of Thomas King's "Modern Style of Cabinet Work Exemplified," 1829* (New York: Dover, 1995), pl. 18.
2. These chairs are illustrated in Stuart P. Feld, *Boston in the Age of Neo-Classicism, 1810–1840* (New York: Hirschl & Adler Galleries, 1999), 59, cat. 23.
3. Page Talbott, "Seating Furniture in Boston, 1810–1835," *The Magazine Antiques* 140, no. 5 (May 1991): 962, 967, pls. XVIII, XIX; Robert D. Mussey Jr. and Clark Pearce, *Rather Elegant than Showy: The Classical Furniture of Isaac Vose* (Jaffrey, NH: Massachusetts Historical Society in association with David R. Godine, 2018), 266–68, figs. 335–38.

14

Pier Table, c. 1835

Possibly George Archbald (1790–1870)
Boston
Mahogany, mahogany veneer; Honduras mahogany, tulip poplar, birch; Italian white-veined marble, mahoganizing wash, mirror glass
35¾ × 52 × 26 in.

PROVENANCE: With Vilnis Vitols, Strasburg, VA, before 2004; With Carswell Rush Berlin, Inc., New York by 2004; Purchased by Schrimshers, 2004.

Much like the Schrimsher card table (cat. 8), this pier table illustrates how American cabinetmakers arranged a pastiche of different architectural elements from ancient Egypt, Greece, and Rome and applied them to modern furniture forms. The prominent cavetto molding on the apron evokes the cornices on Egyptian temples; the front columns and rear pilasters are modeled after the pylons that form the facades of Egyptian temples.[1] Mixing their visual metaphor, however, they are topped by Ionic capitals (see Appendix I). The monumental scale of the table itself adds yet another element of Classicism to the mix.

The play of geometric shapes of the structure—the stepped squares beneath the pylons and pilasters, the rectangles that bridge those squares to form a trestle, the parabolic curves of the cavetto—adds to the sense of crisp order that underlies the table's composition. The deeply cut semicircle of acanthus and anthemion carving at the center of the plinth (fig. 14.1) is assembled from Greek architectural stone carving. This masterful flourish, when reflected against the large mirror plate, forms a full circle.

Fig. 14.1. Detail of cat. 14 showing carving at the center of the plinth

The design of this pier table is a tour de force. No English or European precedent is known, suggesting the innovation of a Boston cabinetmaker. The superb carving here was the work of an unknown carver who emerged following Thomas Wightman's death in 1827, perhaps an English craftsman who may have arrived in Boston about that time. But who was the cabinetmaker? Isaac Vose died in 1823, and Thomas Emmons died in 1825. That leaves George Archbald and Thomas Seymour still standing. Since Seymour continued to live in the neighborhood, it is not inconceivable that the two teamed up for a time after 1825, but there is nothing in the documentary record to corroborate that idea. The best indicator is the table's meticulous construction, possibly pointing to Seymour's having a hand in its manufacture—maybe even its design—while working for Archbald.[2] Seymour continued to make furniture after 1825, but whom he worked for is unknown. Either way, the odds are good that it was a product of Archbald's shop.

This table is one of a group of perhaps ten known similar pier tables.[3] Most have Egyptian black and gold marble, but this one has its original white slab with light gray veining. The top measures a hefty one inch thick, necessary to complement the effect of mass and solidity of the base. There is a good chance that the Archbald shop sourced this marble from Scottish immigrant John Templeton, who advertised his marble yard and manufactory frequently in the Boston newspapers.[4] The slab and looking-glass plate alone were costly, but the laborious and meticulous construction of the large cavetto apron frame and front pylons, the piles of mahogany veneers, and the elaborate carving, elevated this table and others like it into the upper reaches of expense.

1. For a discussion of pylons, see p. 62, cat. 8.
2. Though white ash was apparently not used in this pier table, it is employed in the two nearly identical card tables, cats. 15a and 15b. White ash was used almost exclusively by Thomas Seymour in Boston, and its presence may provide a hint about who may have made all three tables.
3. A pair of tables and another single table are currently held in Boston collections; another recently surfaced on eBay.
4. Judging by the order in which he enumerated the types of marble in his stock, white with gray veining was the second listed, indicating its popularity in Boston. Robert D. Mussey Jr. and Clark Pearce, *Rather Elegant than Showy: The Classical Furniture of Isaac Vose* (Jaffrey, NH: Massachusetts Historical Society in association with David R. Godine, 2018), 238–39; *Columbian Centinel* (Boston), February 18, 1824.

15a

Card Table, c. 1830

Unknown maker, possibly George Archbald (1790–1870)
Boston
Mahogany, mahogany veneer; Honduras mahogany, white ash, white pine, birch, tulip poplar; original green baize
29 × 36 × 18 in.

PROVENANCE: Private Collection, Beacon Hill, Boston, 2010 or before; By descent; Sale, Grogan & Company, Boston, Feb. 21, 2010, lot 239; With Bryan Riddle, Moore House Antiques, Charleston, SC; With Clark Pearce, Essex, MA, by 2011; Purchased by Schrimshers, 2011.

15b

Card Table, c. 1825–1830

Unknown maker, possibly George Archbald (1790–1870)
Boston
Mahogany, mahogany veneer; white ash, white pine, birch, tulip poplar
29 × 36 × 18 in.

PROVENANCE: With Peter Sawyer Antiques Exeter, NH, 1983 or before; Charles E. Buckley (1919–2011), St. Louis, MO, 1983; With Peter Sawyer Antiques, Exeter, NH, 2012; With Clark Pearce, Essex, MA, 2013; Purchased by Schrimshers, 2013.

The cabinetmaker that made the Schrimsher pier table (cat. 14), perhaps in the shop of George Archbald, also constructed at least two pairs of card tables that match it closely, probably made *en suite*.[1] Although not a true pair, the Schrimsher Collection has two similar card tables from this group with identical dimensions but minor inconsistencies in veneering and carving. Furthermore, one table (cat. 15a) has an original green baize playing surface, while the other (cat. 15b) has a mahogany one.

As noted in the previous entry, the carver for both the card tables and the pier table may have been an immigrant from London. That so little of this distinctive and masterful carving is seen in Boston or Salem suggests that he may have moved to New York or Philadelphia, where there was more demand for highly skilled carving. Like the pier table, the workmanship on these card tables is first rate.

The cabinetmaker adapted the pier table design to accommodate the card table form. Roman paw feet were used in place of the massive, squat melon feet on the pier table (see Appendix I). He added a shallow collar to the base of the single Egyptian pylon, carved with a Greek leaf-and-dart motif; the same pattern was added as a cap above the paw feet. To top off the classical themes, he added four carved Greek paterae, or rosettes, to the tops of the corners of the heavy plinth (fig. 15.1).

The rounded corners of the aprons feature single anthemions carved in relief with Ionic scrolls at the base. Many Greek ornaments were published in Peter and Michael Angelo Nicholson's pattern book *The Practical Cabinet-Maker, Upholsterer, and Complete Decorator* (London, 1826), which served as a compendium of Greek, Egyptian, and Roman architectural motifs.[2]

1. See footnote 2 in cat. 14.
2. Peter Nicholson and Michael Angelo Nicholson, *The Practical Cabinet-Maker, Upholsterer, and Complete Decorator* (London: H. Fisher, Son & Co., 1826), "Ornaments."

Fig. 15.1. Peter Nicholson and Michael Angelo Nicholson, "Greek Pateras," plate 30 in *The Practical Cabinet-Maker, Upholsterer, and Complete Decorator* (London, 1826), hand-colored engraving, New York Public Library, The Miriam and Ira D. Wallach Division of Art, Prints and Photography: Art & Architecture Collection, ID: b13982631 (Courtesy New York Public Library Digital Collections). Note the similarities between the paterae labeled fig. 4 and its carved counterparts on the plinths of cats. 15a and 15b.

15a

15b

16

Pole Screen, c. 1825

Possibly Thomas Seymour (1771–1848) for Isaac Vose (1767–1823), 1823–1824, or for George Archbald (1790–1870), 1825–1827; carving attributed to Thomas Wightman (1759–1827)
Boston
Mahogany, mahogany veneer; chestnut; replacement silk
H. 64¾ × 22½ × 18 in.

PROVENANCE: Sale, Northeast Auctions, Portsmouth, NH, Aug. 1, 1998; With Clark Pearce, Essex, MA, Aug. 3, 1998; Private Collection, Boston; Sale, Brunk Auctions, Asheville, NC, Nov. 12, 2022, lot 684; Purchased by Schrimshers, 2022.

During the last few years that the Vose firm was active, and perhaps up until Thomas Wightman's death in 1827, Thomas Seymour embraced a new style of severe late Classical furniture that relied heavily on Wightman's carving skills.[1] Defined by distinctive veined and reflexed leaf tips and long palm leaves often used on Corinthian capitals and friezes in ancient Greece, these motifs were documented by James Stuart at the Choragic Monument of Lysicrates, at the east end of the Acropolis in Athens. With partner Nicholas Revett, he published their drawings in *The Antiquities of Athens* (London, 1762, 1787, 1794, 1796).[2] As firsthand observers of ancient Greek architecture, their drawings were influential in the budding Classical movement.

English furniture designer George Smith returned to this motif in his *The Cabinet-Maker and Upholsterer's Guide* (London, 1826), plate 20, "Elements of Ornament Exemplified."[3] That same year Peter and Michael Angelo Nicholson published their pattern book, *The Practical Cabinet-Maker, Upholsterer, and Complete Decorator* (London, 1826), in which they show a "Tea Poy" and "Card Table" that incorporate Corinthian and palm leaves.[4] Shortly thereafter, Thomas King published the Corinthian-leaf design on the frieze of a remarkable "pier slab" with architectural double-scroll ends in his *The Modern Style of Cabinet Work Exemplified* (London, 1829), plate 1.[5]

The design for this fire screen is drawn directly from plate 6 of King's pattern book, (see p. 38, fig. 3).[6] Having an impeccable sense of late Classical design, Seymour, in collaboration with Wightman, simplified the trefoil plinth in order to highlight the exceptional carving above. The bell-shaped ring of inverted Corinthian leaves is also pulled from one of King's designs, at the base of the two pedestals on an "Occasional Table" in plate 48 in the same edition. The feet, the ring of reflexed leaves, the long, smooth palm leaves above, and the sequential tier of leaves on top were kept true to King's drawing, but Wightman gave the leafy elements a voluptuous, sculptural quality that is completely lacking in King's cartoonishly stiff images. Seymour and Wightman's work suggests a personal knowledge of classical forms and motifs gleaned from studying pattern books, perhaps owned by them or made available by one of their book-collecting patrons.

The leaf forms are deceptively simple. Wightman's steady hand is clearly seen in the perfectly inscribed lines that define the outside edges of the leaves, as well as in the sharp spined ribs that separate them.[7]

1. While this group of furniture that incorporates the carved Corinthian leaves is attributed to Thomas Seymour and Thomas Wightman of Boston, it is not inconceivable that these pieces were made in Salem, especially considering the dominance of Thomas King's designs in that city. His *The Modern Style of Cabinet Work Exemplified* (London, 1829) is full of designs that include carved Corinthian leaves.
2. James Stuart and Nicholas Revett, *The Antiquities of Athens* (London, 1762, 1787, 1794, 1796), 1:chap. 4, pl. III.
3. George Smith, *The Cabinet-Maker and Upholsterer's Guide* (London: Jones & Co., 1826), pl. XX, "Elements of Ornament Exemplified" (second row down, pair of leaves at left).
4. Peter Nicholson and Michael Angelo Nicholson, *The Practical Cabinet-Maker, Upholsterer, and Complete Decorator* (London: H. Fisher, Son & Co., 1826), "Tea Poy" and "Card Table."
5. Thomas King and Thomas Gordon Smith, *Neo-Classical Furniture Designs: A Reprint of Thomas King's "Modern Style of Cabinet Work Exemplified," 1829* (New York: Dover, 1995), iii, xvii–xviii. Thomas King published numerous design plates, pamphlets, and books between 1822 and 1840. Because he repeated many of his designs through the years, a plate from a later edition may have been in circulation a decade or more before. He may have published this design as early as 1822. There are no less than eighteen other designs in his 1829 compilation that employ Corinthian and palm-leaf motifs.
6. Ibid., pl. 6 (middle image).
7. The screen and finial are associated with the base of this fire screen. The finial is from an original Boston screen. The screen itself is a period one that is also very close to those that are pictured in King's *The Modern Style of Cabinet Work Exemplified* (London, 1829). To date, this Corinthian-leaf group consists of twelve examples in private collections and dealer stocks.

17

Center Table, c. 1830

Possibly George Archbald (1790–1870)
Boston
Mahogany, mahogany veneer; mahogany; brass
28½ × 50 in. (diameter)

INSCRIPTION: In pencil: "March 183_."

PROVENANCE: Sale, Aubert Auctions, Milton Hall, NH, July 15, 2016; With Christopher Settle, Newton, MA, July 15, 2016; With Clark Pearce, Essex, MA, by 2016; Purchased by Schrimshers, 2016.

The cabinetmaker that made this tilt-top center table perfectly captured the Boston aesthetic for rich materials, extravagant craftsmanship, and elegant yet restrained Classical design. Lacking any gilt brass ornaments, the highly figured crotch mahogany veneers, and the superb carving carry the day. This aesthetic is unlike the work from the other American cities. On the block beneath the top there is a pencil inscription, "183_": the last digit is obliterated by a small patch in the wood that was necessary when the pintle hinge for the top broke out.

Given the high quality of the design, carving, and veneering, George Archbald is possibly the table's author. Following the deaths of Isaac Vose, Thomas Emmons, and carver Thomas Wightman, Archbald's was the best cabinetmaking shop in Boston during the late 1820s and 1830s. George Ticknor (see cat. 5) probably commissioned him to build an extensive set of bookcases for his fabled book collection in 1829, and Archbald was selected to supply much of the furniture for Tremont House, the fashionable hotel that was designed the same year.[1]

Fig. 17.1. Jean-Nicolas-Louis Durand, "Détails Egyptiens tirés de Norden," plate 64 in *Recueil et parallèle des édifices en tout genre, anciens et modernes* (Brussels, 1800), engraving (Courtesy Heidelberg University Library). Note the leaf design on the column on the bottom row, third from the left.

The massive turned and carved pedestal, along with the paw feet, are the focal points of the table's composition. The unknown carver's work has similarities with the masterful carving on the plinth of the Schrimsher pier table (cat. 14). Both carvers seem to share a talent for classical motifs with smooth, elegant curves and lines, all deeply undercut for contrast. The ring of tall Corinthian leaves around the baluster section of this table is superbly executed, as is the collar of shorter inverted leaves that rest on the trefoil-shaped plinth. The baluster leaves have broad, smooth tops that resemble the lotus leaves on an Egyptian column that appears in line drawings by Jean-Nicolas-Louis Durand (1760–1834) in his *Recueil et parallèle des édifices en tout genre anciens et modernes* (Collection of All Types of Buildings Ancient and Modern; Paris, 1800) (fig. 17.1).[2] Apparently, the Corinthian people incorporated this Egyptian design into the architectural order that bears their name. The sculptural and archeologically correct carving belies the depth of knowledge that was necessary to create such work, not to mention the skill required to achieve the studied perfection seen here. With the demand for carving declining as the Grecian Plain style arrived in Boston, this carver, possibly an immigrant from London, may have moved south to New York or Philadelphia.

Although these large circular tilt-top tables are often called Loo tables in pattern books, Bostonians likely used them as breakfast or family dining tables. A similar table without carving on the pedestal is seen in the small dining room of the Greely Stevenson Curtis house at 28–30 Mount Vernon Street in an early photograph.[3] Mrs. Curtis's father, Nathan Appleton, also had a tilt-top breakfast table (perhaps the same one) in his dining room that was captured in another early photograph.[4] Whether used for games or less formal family meals, the top could be tilted up and wheeled on heavy, concealed casters to a corner or wall for storage.

1. Robert D. Mussey Jr. and Clark Pearce, *Rather Elegant than Showy: The Classical Furniture of Isaac Vose* (Jaffrey, NH: Massachusetts Historical Society in association with David R. Godine, 2018), 177, n. 85.
2. Jean-Nicolas-Louis Durand, *Recueil et parallèle des édifices en tout genre, anciens et modernes* (Brussels: JNL Durand, 1805), pl. 64.
3. Mussey and Pearce, *Rather Elegant than Showy*, 125, fig. 140.
4. Ibid., 107, fig. 119.

18

Wall Timepiece, c. 1827–1831

Works by Edmund Currier (1793–1853); carving attributed to Joseph True (1785–1873)
Salem
Mahogany, glass; Honduras mahogany; gold leaf, paint, iron, lead, brass
42 × 11 × 3⅝ in.

INSCRIPTIONS: Painted on lower reverse glass panel: "E. Currier / Salem"; inscribed on reverse dial and back of the pendulum bob: "Powell."

LABELS: Three printed Philadelphia clock repairer labels inside lower case, one inscribed "Moffett."

PROVENANCE: The Moffett family of Salem. The Powell family, Boston. Sale, Bonham's Skinner, Marlborough, MA, Oct. 20, 2021, lot 1165; With Clark Pearce, Essex, MA, Oct. 25, 2021; Purchased by Schrimshers, 2021.

The port city of Salem, famous during the Classical period for its international shipping—especially the China trade—made the town a magnet for merchants, ship captains, ship builders, and craftspeople from rural New England. Edmund Currier trained and set up shop in the small New Hampshire town of Hopkinton by 1815, but he decided to pull up stakes to ply his trade in the prosperous seacoast town in 1825.[1] Being an ambitious sort, he quickly joined the Salem Charitable Mechanic Association, which gave him access to many other prominent craftspeople and their networks.[2] Over the years, he became a trustee of the association, then vice president, and finally president from 1845 to 1847. He was eager to take part in the association's annual competitions for new inventions and machinery, winning several silver medals for his clock-making innovations. Given his interest in timepieces, he secured the role of maintaining and harmonizing Salem's public clocks. Currier trained at least seven apprentices whose identities are known. These efforts, and his apparently indefatigable personality, made him a well-respected man in Salem.[3] Remarkably, a daguerreotype of Currier is preserved at the Peabody Essex Museum in Salem.[4]

This gilt lyre wall timepiece is one of the most beautiful and elaborate expressions of the Classical form made in New England.[5] Not only is its ornamentation dazzling, it also combines several references to Greco-Roman mythology. The carved lyre evokes Apollo, the Greek god of music, poetry, and light, who is often depicted carrying the instrument. The large scallop shell at the base of the timepiece alludes to Aphrodite, goddess of beauty, love, fertility, and victory, who emerged from the sea, riding a shell to the shore.

The maker's name, "E. Currier / Salem," is painted on the lower reverse glass decorated tablet. Both painted panels are original; the upper one has an American shield at the center of the lyre. Classical clocks and timepieces were expensive in their day because movement making was labor intensive, and there were many specialists involved in their creation. The case was made by a local cabinetmaker, and then embellished by a carver and a gilder. Simultaneously, a specialist painted the reverse glass panels. Currier made the brass movement (or purchased it from a subcontractor) and installed the moving parts into the case.[6] A timepiece like this would have cost perhaps $45 to $60, a hefty sum in the 1830s. Gilt lyre wall timepieces by Edmund Currier are rare, with perhaps up to fifteen known examples.

The carving on the case is attributed to Joseph True, the preeminent carver in Salem after the death of Samuel McIntire in 1811. Born in Chichester, New Hampshire, True was another craftsman who migrated to Salem to take advantage of the greater opportunities there. Happily, some of True's account books survive for this period, revealing that he charged Edmund Currier on multiple occasions.[7] A nearly identical shell carving is on a chamber organ attributed to True.[8]

---

1. Paul J. Foley, *Willard's Patent Time Pieces: A History of the Weight-Driven Banjo Clock, 1800–1900* (Norwell, MA: Roxbury Village Publishing, 2002), 234.
2. Damon Di Mauro, "Edmund Currier Revisited," *Journal of the National Association of Watch & Clock Collectors, Inc.* 65/1, no. 461 (January–February 2023): 29. The Salem Charitable Mechanic Association was formed for the twin purposes of promoting the mechanic arts and practicing benevolence for its members.
3. Ibid., 29–38.
4. Peabody Essex Museum, Salem, 118669.
5. This type of clock is called a timepiece because it tells only time, lacking the ability to strike a bell to mark the hours or sound an alarm.
6. Robert C. Cheney, "Roxbury Eight-Day Movements and the English Connection, 1785–1825," *The Magazine Antiques* 157, no. 4 (April 2000): 613. Though he was a skilled clockmaker, it is known that Currier purchased some of his movements from Simon Johnson Jr. of Sanbornton, New Hampshire, in the 1830s and later.
7. The first entry in Joseph True's account book for carving for Edmund Currier was made in 1827; the last entry for Currier is in 1831, which is also the year that he went into partnership with his apprentice George B. Foster in a new business named Currier & Foster. Peabody Essex Museum, Phillips Library, Rowley, MA.
8. Peabody Essex Museum, Salem, 121452.A. The case of the chamber organ is attributed to Joseph True, George G. Hook, and William Hook, 1827.

E.CURRIER,
SALEM.

Perfectly Fitted, Burnished, and Bronzed: The Classical Furniture of New York

PETER M. KENNY

Some of the most vibrant, sculptural furniture ever produced in America sprung from the manufactories of New York following the War of 1812. This was an era of unparalleled economic growth and development that established the city as the chief commercial metropolis of the United States. The entrepreneurial master cabinetmakers who operated these workshops, as well as the myriad of journeymen and apprentices, upholsterers, carvers, gilders, and finishers they employed, have left behind a legacy of distinctive, richly ornamented Classical furniture that bespeaks the prosperity and cultural ambition of New York's social and economic elite, as well as that of patrons from the coastal South and beyond.

New York's advantageous situation as a deepwater port that remained ice-free year-round set it apart from other American cities along the Atlantic coast (fig. 1). This natural advantage as well as some key economic and transportation infrastructure developments in the aftermath of the War of 1812 catapulted New York ahead of Boston, Philadelphia, and Baltimore in terms of trade and commerce. With the signing of the Treaty of Ghent in December 1814, ending the War of 1812, the crippling British blockade of the eastern seaboard was lifted and the United States' commercial freedom was restored.

***Card Table*, 1815–1819**
(detail of cat. 35a)

The commercial opportunities presented at that moment spurred the farsighted decision by a group of New York merchants to establish a packet line between New York and Liverpool for the transportation of commodities, finished goods, and passengers to and from the United States and Great Britain on a predictable, regular schedule. The first packet line went into service in 1817, and within five years two more lines were established, with four monthly sailings to Liverpool, two to Le Havre, and one to London. By 1827, in addition to these foreign ports, regularly scheduled departures were sailing between New York and Greenock, Scotland; the British port of Gibraltar; multiple ports in Ireland; Havana, Cuba; Vera Cruz, Mexico; and Cartagena, Colombia. There also were lines between New York and the domestic ports of Baltimore, Richmond, Savannah, Charleston, Mobile, and New Orleans. According to *The Picture of New-York and Stranger's Guide* (1828), the "influence derived from the regular and rigidly observed periods of sailing to all the principal ports in this country and in Europe, now pervades every class and is productive of incalculable benefits to the trade and navigation of this port . . . producing an increased amount of business to all classes of society."[1]

The completion of the Erie Canal in 1825, an astonishing, publicly funded engineering feat, also led to a vast increase of trade in commodities, produce, and finished goods between New York's port and the interior part of the state, as well as

Fig. 1. William James Bennett (1787–1844), ***View of South Street, from Maiden Lane, New York City*****, c. 1827, watercolor on off-white wove paper, Metropolitan Museum of Art, New York, The Edward W. C. Arnold Collection of New York Prints Maps, and Pictures, Bequest of Edward W. C. Arnold, 1954, 54.90.130 (Courtesy Metropolitan Museum of Art / Art Resource, NY)**

states bordering the Great Lakes and the Ohio and Mississippi Rivers. After a visit to New York that same year, travel writer Anne Royall summed up the enviable results of all this investment in transportation infrastructure:

> I never saw more industry or more application to business of every description than in this city. . . No wonder New-York outstrips all her rivals! Her Clinton at her head, her Hudson and canals at her back, the Atlantic before her, covered with the wealth of nations, her citizens industrious, generous and enterprising, her whole system elevated and grand, she must succeed. Whilst others are debating the question of right and wrong New-York is acting.[2]

This was the bustling, competitive world of New York's master cabinetmakers, who strove not only for financial success but also for recognition as proud contributors to the city's commercial prosperity and as skilled, artistic practitioners of their craft. Collectively, their distinctive brand or style of furniture was known and appreciated throughout the United States, in certain port cities of the Caribbean basin, and as far afield as Rio de Janeiro and Buenos Aires. Individually, the name Duncan Phyfe (1770–1854) stood out above all others and was synonymous with the finest New York furniture in terms of design, materials, and workmanship. Working in lower Manhattan, Phyfe and his compatriots enjoyed the manifold advantages of the bustling port: a customer base bolstered by the rapidly accumulating wealth of the local mercantile elites and the Southern planters who came to the city in increasing numbers between 1815 and 1835 for business, entertainment, and shopping opportunities; a steady supply of the necessary materials of their trade, including island and coastal mahogany from the Caribbean, exotic rosewood from Brazil, white statuary and black-and-gold marble from Italy, and *ormolu* and lacquer-gilded brass ornamental hardware from France and England; and a regular influx of foreign craftsmen bringing with them design skills and French and British patterns that seasoned and transformed the New York Classical style.[3]

The official end of the War of 1812 and the lifting of the British blockade of New York Harbor brought great joy and renewed optimism to New York's merchants, tradesmen, and mechanics, including the cabinetmakers. The entire city celebrated with a grand illumination in February 1815, with master cabinetmaker Duncan Phyfe among the most enthusiastic participants in this glorious patriotic event.[4] According to a published account of the festivities, Phyfe strung a series of transparent lamps emblazoned with a portrait of George Washington and the names of U.S. naval heroes of the War of 1812 across Partition Street between his house and his shop and warehouse, and in his "centre store" he hung a "transparency with a figure resembling Justice and Liberty standing on a pedestal, the Eagle and Lion drinking out of a bowl [next to] emblems of commerce, and in the foreground, implements of war, destroyed and scattered around. . . . Mr. P[hyfe]'s elegant assortment of furniture was fancifully displayed in the window so as to produce on the whole a fine [effect]."[5]

Good economic times had returned and Phyfe hastened to capitalize on them with exceptional offerings in the latest antique or Grecian mode, known as the Classical style. So well-regarded and in such high demand was Phyfe's fashionable Classical furniture that one frustrated customer hoping to meet with him concerning an order she had placed months earlier lamented in a letter to a friend, "Mr. Phyfe is so much the United States rage, that it is with difficulty now, that one can procure an audience even of a few moments."[6] She had hoped for a meeting with Phyfe at his furniture-making and retailing establishment, which is depicted in a watercolor drawing at the Metropolitan Museum of Art (fig. 2). Here in Phyfe's "centre store" we see a salesman, maybe even Phyfe himself, with two elegantly attired female customers discussing perhaps the relative merits of two of his signature-style scroll-back chairs, one with an ogee-cross splat, the other with a more sculptural and costly carved lyre splat. The flowing, uninterrupted line of the seat rails into the scrolled rear stiles, and the incurvate, saber-shaped front and back legs on these chairs mark them as as modern interpretations of the ancient Greek klismos chair; the carved lyre splat symbolically alludes to the Greek god Apollo's instrument of cosmic harmony. Phyfe's klismos-type chairs, well established by this date, were in the vanguard New York Classical style. And although he was an essential figure in shifting the New York vernacular away from the lighter and more delicate Neoclassical designs of George Hepplewhite and Thomas Sheraton into this later, more sculptural and archaeologically accurate "antique" style phase, Phyfe was not alone.[7]

The Reception of the Antique in New York

Elizabeth Macaulay-Lewis and Matthew M. McGowan, editors of *Classical New York: Discovering Greece and Rome in Gotham,* make the observation that "neoclassical reinterpretations of Greek and Roman originals [ancient architectural ruins and archaeological fragments] . . . served as intermediaries between classical antiquity and the United States, where the reception of Greek and Roman art and architecture was rarely direct or based on firsthand contact with classical monuments, especially through the antebellum period (1790–1860)." They go on to suggest that when "considering the reception of classical antiquity in New York and across the United States, it is helpful to keep in mind a process of 'triangulation,' where books on classical art and architecture blend with Americans' experience of the neoclassical . . . imported from Europe" in the form of design and pattern books, casts, and other objects that resulted in what the authors refer to as a "'Neo-Antique' way of thinking, which was very much at home in America."[8]

Such a process occasionally resulted in the creative blending of established Neoclassical vernacular forms with more avant-garde published European designs. This synthesis is evident in the design of two closely related chests of drawers

Fig. 2. Unknown artist, *Shop and Warehouse of Duncan Phyfe, 168–172 Fulton Street, New York City*, 1817–20, watercolor, ink, and gouache on white laid paper, Metropolitan Museum of Art, New York, Rogers Fund, 1922, 22.18.1 (Courtesy Metropolitan Museum of Art / Art Resource, NY)

with doors, known in the New York trade as "French bureaus" (cats. 25a, 25b). These highly architectural case pieces have the heavier features of a French *commode antique,* including a facade flanked by wide pilasters, and a socle (or plinth) raised on carved lion's-paw feet painted *vert antique* in imitation of the color of excavated antique bronze (fig. 3). They maintain, however, in the drawer arrangement of the upper third of their cases a narrow frieze of two shallow drawers surmounting a deeper one, a characteristic feature of a distinctive type of Hepplewhite-inspired New York chest of drawers made from the late 1790s to about 1810. Thus, both continuity and change are embodied in this New York version of the French *commode antique,* and a "Neo-Antique" form made in a variety of iterations enters the mainstream of New York Classical design.

Other cabinetmakers engaged in this "Neo-Antique" way of thinking in even more creative ways, or else employed a "decorative architect" such as George Bridport (1783–1819) of London and later Philadelphia to do so on their behalf. They consulted published European works on Classical art and architecture to develop their more imaginative and sophisticated offerings, for example, the sculptural griffin card and pier tables that were something of a specialty of the Phyfe shop (cat. 20).[9] Charles Heathcote Tatham's *Etchings, Representing the Best Examples of Ancient Ornamental Architecture* (London, 1799) includes an evocative illustration of a fragment of an antique carved marble frieze in the Farnese Gardens in Rome depicting the partial body of a lion crouched amidst an arabesque of rolling acanthus leaves (fig. 4). The disposition and sculptural qualities of the creature's hind quarters and torso parallel those of the fantastical carved griffins employed by Phyfe (fig. 5). Although far from providing proof that Tatham's etching directly inspired Phyfe or his designer, this comparison nonetheless provides an intimation of the role that published images of antiquities may have played in creative design development.

Sadly, not a single inventory of a design library belonging to a New York cabinetmaker or other artisans in allied trades is known.[10] However, an 1808 inventory listing the contents of the library of New York architect-builder John McComb Jr., a nearly exact contemporary of Duncan Phyfe, includes such titles as "Antique Ornaments," "on Roman fragments," "Sheratons Cabinet Maker's Drawing-Book," and "Chippendales Designs," precisely the types of publications one might expect to find in the working library of a sophisticated New York furniture manufactory. McComb clearly had an interest in furniture, which may have led to his overseeing the designs for the tables and chairs made for the Common Council Chamber in the new City Hall in New York, completed in 1812.[11]

Published French furniture designs promulgating *le goût antique*, a style based on more archaeologically correct interpretations of the forms and ornaments of classical antiquity, were used in New York as early as 1803, when French immigrant cabinetmaker Charles-Honoré Lannuier (1779–1819) informed the public in his inaugural newspaper advertisement that he "makes all kinds of Furniture . . . in the newest and latest French fashion; and that he has brought for that purpose gilt and brass frames, borders of ornaments and handsome safe locks, as well as new patterns." Given the style of Lannuier's earliest documented work it is apparent that the "patterns" he refers to in this ad were almost certainly some of the early colored engravings from Pierre de La Mésangère's *Collection de meubles et objets de goût* (Paris, 1799–1831) (fig. 3). Another Frenchman in New York City, artist and naturalist Jacques-Gérard Milbert (1766–1840), wrote an account of his 1815 visit in which he was very specific about

Fig. 3. Pierre de La Mésangère, "Commode Antique," plate 49 in *Collection de meubles et objets de goût* (1802), colored engraving (Courtesy Winterthur Museum, Garden & Library). Note the *vert antique* treatment on the feet of the two tables and the *commode antique*.

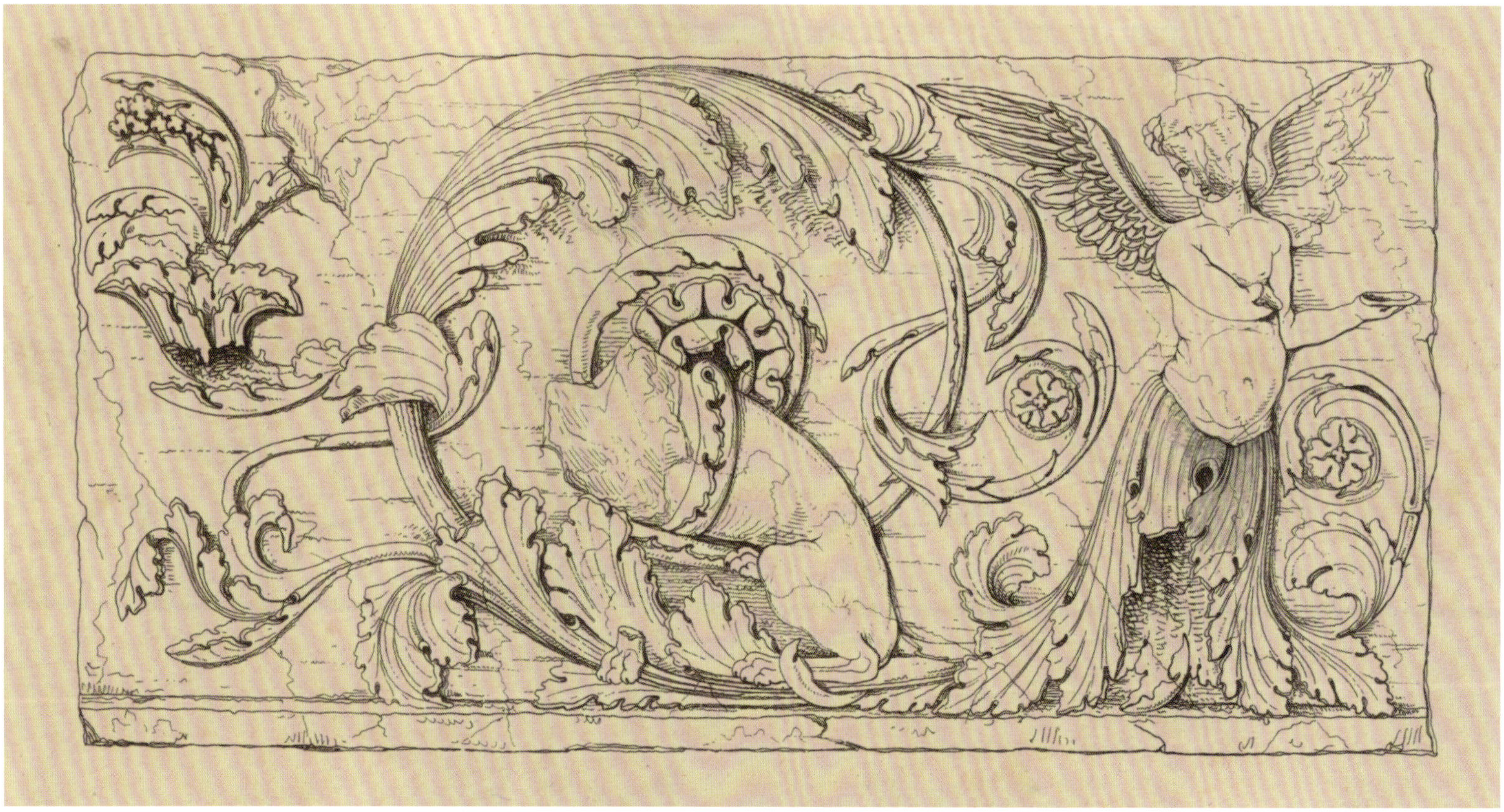

Fig. 4. Charles Heathcote Tatham, "Fragment of an Antique Frieze in the Orto Farnese at Rome," in *Etchings, Representing the Best Examples of Ancient Ornamental Architecture* (London, 1799), etching (Courtesy Winterthur Museum, Garden & Library)

Fig. 5. *Pier Table* (detail of griffin support), attributed to Duncan Phyfe, c. 1815–1820 (cat. 20)

the influence of French workmen and published French printed sources on New York vernacular furniture design during this period of stylistic change:

> Furnishings for the home . . . are either manufactured by the Americans or imported from France or England. Beds, tables, chairs, secretaries, etc. are made here, and they are superior in construction and solidity if not in taste and shape . . . However, to pay our country its due homage, I shall add that French workmen started this business in America and it is they who are developing it most successfully. They use the best models and books on furniture and interior decoration by Messieurs Percier and Fontaine.[12]

Milbert should largely be taken at his word. The essential forms and ornament that underpin New York Classical furniture have their roots in French Consular-, Empire-, and *Restauration*-period design. This is not to say that British design and pattern books or immigrant British craftsmen working in New York played no role in the development of the New York Classical style—they did, but their work, too, it can be argued, was heavily inflected by French furniture design. Phyfe's signature line of scroll-back klismos and curule chairs alluded to earlier were directly inspired by designs chronicled in the 1807 *London Chair-Makers' and Carvers' Book of Prices for Workmanship* and its 1808 *Supplement.*[13] And throughout this period in New York, furniture was either inspired by or copied directly from designs in British pattern books and fashion journals, such as those published by Thomas Hope, George Smith, Thomas King, and Rudolph Ackermann. A prime example of this is a Grecian couch or chaise longue attributed to Joseph Meeks & Sons (cat. 24) that is almost a line-for-line copy of plate 136 in George Smith's *The Cabinet-Maker and Upholsterer's Guide* (London, 1826).

In his introduction to *Household Furniture and Interior Decoration* (London, 1807), Thomas Hope is forthright in his admiration for French architect and designer Charles Percier, "who, having professionally devoted the first portion of his career to the study of the antique chef-d'oeuvres in Italy, now devotes the latter portion of his life to the superintendance of modern objects of elegance and decoration in France [including] . . . beautiful articles of furniture, of cabinet-work, and of plate."[14] Hope borrowed heavily from Percier and Pierre-François-Léonard Fontaine for his own designs for the furnishings of his Duchess Street house in London, which is the subject of his publication. Commentary describing a sofa or French bed in an 1822 issue of Rudolph Ackermann's *Repository of Arts, Literature, Commerce, Manufactures, Fashions, and Politics* (London, 1809–1828) also makes evident the profound sustained effect of French design on British furniture: "The taste for French furniture is carried to such an extent, that most elegantly furnished mansions, particularly the sleeping rooms, are fitted up in the French style; and we must confess, that, while the antique forms the basis of their decorative and ornamental furniture, it will deservedly continue in repute."[15] New York cabinetmakers, therefore, were exposed not only to the direct influence of French design but also to indirect French influence filtered through British design and pattern books, which undoubtedly had a formative effect on the look of New York Classical furniture.

Cabinetmakers of the City, the Masters, Well-Formed

The cabinetmakers of New York working between 1800 and 1840 were legion. Sadly, only a tiny percentage of them are known today for the roles they played in producing the thousands of pieces of surviving New York Classical furniture.[16] Many were highly skilled and, having attained the rank of journeyman, settled into careers in the shops of master cabinetmakers who served as their employers. Some journeymen became smaller masters of their own workshops and retail businesses. These were the ones British traveler Henry Bradshaw Fearon (c. 1770–1842) described in 1817:

> Cabinet-makers shops . . . are generally small concerns, apparently owned by the journeymen, commenced on their own account. These shops are perfectly open, and there is seldom any person in attendance. In the centre, a board is suspended with the notice, "Ring the bell." I have conversed with several proprietors: they state their business to have been at one time good, but there is now too much competition.[17]

Fig. 6. ***French Secretary*** **(detail of** ***ormolu*** **appliqué and capital, and die-stamped brass inlay), attributed to Duncan Phyfe, c. 1825 (cat. 29)**

Others accumulated or borrowed capital, or formed partnerships to increase investment and offset risk, and established larger manufactories and retail showrooms—the "cabinet warehouses" described in period newspaper advertisements and on cabinetmakers' trade labels (Appendix II). All of the New York cabinetmakers associated with the documented or attributed furniture in the Schrimsher Collection—Lannuier, Phyfe, Michael Allison (1773–1855), Thomas Constantine (1781–1854), the partnerships of Barzilia Deming (1781–1854) and Erastus Bulkley (1798–1872), and Joseph Meeks & Sons (Joseph, 1771–1868)—fall into this latter category. At the pinnacle of the trade in terms of their influence and the desirability of their offerings were Lannuier and Phyfe, whose artistic designs and superior workmanship captivated their early-nineteenth-century clients and modern collectors of Classical furniture alike.[18]

Lannuier was the essential figure at the forefront of the "French workmen" Milbert described as starting "this business in America [and] developing it most successfully." Lannuier unfortunately enjoyed only a relatively brief career in New York spanning sixteen years between his arrival from France in 1803 and his untimely death at the age of forty in 1819. Given Lannuier's early presence and influence in New York, it is hardly surprising that four new forms based directly on Consular- and Empire-period designs and specifically designated as "French" appear in the 1810 New York cabinetmakers' price book, as well as in a subsequent additional revised list of prices published prior to 1815. These include a French bureau (*commode antique*), French press (*armoire*), French sideboard (*desserte*), and French bedstead (*lit*), all of which are illustrated and discussed at length here (cats 25a, 34, 36a, 31). A fifth iconic French form that did not receive the appellation "French" appears in the pre-1815 additional revised list of prices, where it is rather prosaically referred to as a "square pier table" (*console*). Far from mundane, the finer examples of these highly architectural pier tables feature marble tops, marble or wood-veneered columns with *ormolu* caps and bases, *ormolu* appliqué at the center and front corners of their front aprons, a square plinth raised on lion's-paw feet, and looking-glass plates at the back. A sixth French form adopted in New York and produced in Lannuier's shop and then in substantial numbers by other makers throughout the 1820s and 1830s was the *gueridon* or center table (cat. 32). This form was not included in the New York price books of 1810 or 1817, and strangely did not appear in the 1834 edition despite the fact that it was an essential part of any stylish parlor throughout the era.[19]

Concomitant with the incorporation of these stylish new French forms into the New York vernacular was a breathtaking new vocabulary of applied, inlaid, and painted and gilded

Fig. 7. *Side Chair* (detail of back with freehand-gilded ornament in the crest rail), unknown maker, New York, c. 1825 (cat. 33)

Fig. 8. *Center Table* (detail of freehand-gilded apron ornament), attributed to Duncan Phyfe, c. 1825 (cat. 32)

carved ornament based on the antique. These included gilded, cast-brass appliqués for friezes, drawer fronts, table aprons, and plinths, and the crest rails on sofas and chairs; die-stamped inlaid brass in patterns reminiscent of the bands of repetitive geometric ornament on ancient Greek terracotta vases, and an array of carved leafage, lion's paws, and sculptural figures derived from ancient Greek and Roman mythology (fig. 6). Gilded cast-brass appliqués and column capitals and bases were either imported from France or England; the finest of these were exquisitely-chased and fire-gilded *ormolu* (see pp. 297–98). They could also be chemically treated and lacquered to produce a similar effect. Lannuier employed *ormolu* appliqués on some of his earliest documented furniture, and by 1815 to 1820 they were in fairly wide use and remained popular until about 1830.

Another type of ornament, freehand gilding, was considered a less expensive alternative to imported decorative metalwork (see p. 293). The earliest documented New York Classical furniture with freehand gilding dates to the early 1820s. Handsome effects were achieved with this technique on all the places where *ormolu* appliqués might have been used (fig. 7). And although its application can appear slapdash and amateurish on some lesser New York Classical furniture, a talented artistic gilder could achieve remarkable *trompe l'oeil* effects. A spectacular example of this finer variety can be seen on a center table of about 1825–30 at the Museum of the City of New York attributed to the Phyfe shop for Stephen C. Whitney (1776–1860) with a painted scagliola top encircled by dramatically shaded palmettes and scrolling acanthus that have the look of high-relief cast composition ornament.[20] A rosewood-grained and gilded center table (cat. 32), also attributed to Phyfe, has freehand-gilded apron ornaments every bit as exceptional as those on the Whitney example, with masterfully-rendered Baroque shells centering scrolling acanthus leaves (fig. 8). Other gilders had their own distinctive styles. Enough documented and firmly attributable Classical furniture is known from the shop of Deming & Bulkley to identify the hand of one of the gilders they employed. This unidentified artist's work appears on a monumental secretary bookcase in the Schrimsher Collection attributed to these partners (see cat. 23, fig. 23.1). Although finely rendered, the work is more linear and delicate than that of the artist who worked for Phyfe.

A third related decorative technique apparently used only in New York entailed the use of cut stencils, gold size or varnish, and metallic powders on an ebonized ground (see p. 293). The favored motifs were sprays of fruit and leafage. The combination of freehand gilding and stenciling on a single piece of furniture is not that uncommon; it was practiced in Philadelphia and Baltimore but never in Boston. On rare occasions, all three types of decoration can be found. The most spectacular piece of stenciled New York Classical furniture is a monumental ebonized and gilded secretary bookcase, circa 1830, in the collection of the Metropolitan of Art, thought possibly to be the work of cabinetmaker Robert Fisher (active 1824–1837).[21] An ebonized and gilded Grecian couch or chaise longue attributed to Joseph Meeks & Sons in the Schrimsher Collection employs this type of stenciled ornament in a more limited yet successful way in a series of lotus leaves along the length of its cavetto-shaped seat rails (cat. 24).

Three-dimensional sculptural carving, richly gilded and bronzed, is the true glory of New York Classical furniture. Dolphins, griffins, eagles, swans, and fantastical winged female figures (*chimères* as they are called in Percier and Fontaine's *Recueil de décorations intérieures*; Paris, 1801–1812) as well as hocked animal legs and lions' paws serve as pedestals and feet on a variety of tables, sofas, couches, and case furniture. Lannuier is widely credited as the first New York cabinetmaker to incorporate these sculptural elements into furniture. His documented and attributed tables with winged caryatids (cat. 35a) are acknowledged today as masterpieces of American furniture and are avidly sought after by museums and collectors. The first of these tables may have been produced in the Lannuier shop during the war years of 1812–15, and they remained a staple of his sophisticated furniture manufactory and warehouse, albeit an expensive one, until his death. An invoice from Lannuier dated June 19, 1817, lists a pair of caryatid card tables for $250 and a canted corner marble-topped pier table with gilded swans at the corners for $350.[22] Phyfe and possibly Michael Allison, another well-respected New York master cabinetmaker and lifetime competitor of Lannuier and Phyfe, tried their hands at these winged caryatid card tables (cat. 35b), but neither maker ever achieved the balance, beauty, and perfection of Lannuier's signature form.

Phyfe's response to Lannuier's winged caryatid tables were his card, center, and pier tables with griffin supports. About a dozen of these tables survive, including a pier table (cat. 20); none, however, have been attributed to a maker other than Phyfe. An engraved line drawing showing the outline of a griffin appears as plate 5 in *The New-York Book of Prices for Manufacturing Cabinet and Chair Work* (1817) (see cat. 30, fig. 30.1), among other known New York sculptural table standards. Lannuier's signature winged caryatids, swans, and dolphins are absent, which suggests Phyfe's outsized influence on the trade.[23]

Lannuier appears to have been a leading figure in the use of fantastical carved dolphins on New York Classical furniture. A suite of exceptional card tables and *encoignures* (corner tables) discovered in Cuba with highly animated dolphins having scaled, almost serpent-like bodies as front supports (fig. 9) may be the furniture recorded in Lannuier's 1819 estate inventory as "property abroad" consigned to a Captain Roy, who could have sold it on a stop at Trinidad de Cuba, a sugar-exporting port on the island's south shore.[24]

Deming & Bulkley also made these a shop specialty. By the early 1820s, these business partners were marketing in Charleston card tables manufactured in New York with exuberantly carved dolphin standards and feet, as well as some audacious and highly ornamented card tables with carved

Fig. 9. ***Card Table*** **(detail of dolphin support), attributed to Charles-Honoré Lannuier, c. 1815, mahogany, mahogany veneer; white pine, yellow poplar;** ***vert antique*****, gilded gesso, Chipstone Foundation, Milwaukee, Wisconsin, 2001.38 (Courtesy Chipstone Foundation). This is one of eight surviving tables Lannuier may have exported to Trinidad de Cuba.**

spread eagles for pedestals (cats. 22a, 22b). Dolphin feet appear on some of Phyfe's known card tables, but compared to those employed by Lannuier and Deming & Bulkley, these appear timid and small. Phyfe did successfully employ another type of painted and gilded carved dolphin, split down the length and applied to the faces of the scrolled arms mounted on the seat rails on some of his beautifully ornamented and proportioned Grecian sofas. For sheer flamboyance, however, few New York dolphin sofas compare to a group of closely related examples featuring entire scrolled ends from the floor up in the form of writhing, full-bodied dolphins covered in scales with gilded heads, fins, and tails (cat. 27). The designer and manufacturer of these sofas remain unidentified, but their work is the embodiment of the sculptural New York Classical style.

If Lannuier's brief but highly influential career was like a comet streaking across the night sky of Manhattan, Phyfe's was as fixed and steady as the North Star. His career in New York spanned half a century from the mid-1790s until 1847, over thirty of which he spent advancing and refining the Classical style. Compared to the work of other New York makers working in the mature, ornamented style of the 1820s, however, even Phyfe's most ornate painted and gilded furniture manages to convey a sense of timeless Classical repose. This controlled and somewhat conservative approach to design, even in such a highly ornamented style, was a talent and trademark that he maintained throughout his career.

In the wake of Lannuier, Phyfe continued to find inspiration in furniture designs of the period of the Bourbon Restoration in France (1814–1830). Around 1820 to 1825 Phyfe introduced a version of the French *secrétaire à abattant*, or fall-front desk, and a second elegant, compact French type of secretary bookcase called a *bonheur du jour* with a mirrored cabinet top surmounting a pier table base. The most elaborate examples are veneered in rosewood with *ormolu* appliqués and capitals and bases on the veneered columns and die-stamped brass inlay (cat. 29). Fine mahogany examples of these forms without the appliqués and inlays were also made for a lesser price.

Phyfe followed the French *Restauration* style in the increasing simplification of his furniture of the mid- to late 1820s. The key design elements were gleaming, extraordinarily beautiful mahogany veneers and veneered columns with *ormolu* capitals and bases. Additional new forms in this period include box sofas, cheval glasses, fire screens, and a variety of case furniture and table forms all utilizing veneered columns. Other makers followed suit as seen in a fine quality French bureau in this refined *Restauration* style from the workshop of a Phyfe acolyte (fig. 10).

With gilded cast-brass decorative hardware on the wane and virtually disappearing from use by the 1830s, brilliantly figured veneers and voluptuous curves became the focal points and essence of the final phase of New York Classical furniture design. Known today as the Grecian Plain style, furniture from this last phase features scroll-sawn console supports and deeply coved or ogee-shaped table aprons, cornices, drawer fronts and seat rails on sofas, and baluster-shaped or faceted center supports for pillar and claw-foot tables, all covered with

Fig. 10. ***French Bureau*****, manner of Duncan Phyfe, c. 1825, mahogany and mahogany veneer,** ***ormolu*** **mounts, brass, Schrimsher Collection**

gorgeous shaded and crotch mahogany veneers or occasionally Brazilian rosewood. Phyfe's is the most conservative yet the most beautiful of all New York Grecian Plain–style furniture and hews closely to published French designs by La Mésangère. Other more adventurous New York makers of the 1830s, the Meeks firm in particular, took wild flights of fancy with their energetically scrolled creations (cat. 39, fig. 39.1).

Ernest F. Hagen, an immigrant cabinetmaker who arrived in New York in 1844 from Hamburg, Germany, and served as Phyfe's first biographer, had no love for New York Classical furniture. In 1907, he published his now famous "Duncan Phyfe Memorandum," in which he states: "about 1820 although the workmanship was perfect [the furniture] gradually degenerated in style at first to the questionable 'American Empire' and after 1830 to the abominable heavy Nondescrip [sic] veneered style of the time the Cholera first appeared in New York."[25] Harsh words, no doubt. Luckily, Hagen was not the final arbiter in this matter, and considerable connoisseurship has been brought to bear on this furniture over the last few decades by scholars and collectors who came to appreciate and celebrate the finest examples of New York Classical furniture.

Are there some strange, heavy, overbearing clunkers out there? Yes, and new ones, it seems, regularly come to light. Strong opinions on 1830s New York Classical furniture still abound, including about Joseph Meeks & Sons' Gothic-Classical mash-up pier table (cat. 39), a fascinating piece of furniture from a firm that appears to have been attempting through its diverse and exuberant offerings to brand itself perhaps as the anti-Phyfe, as well as to engage with the emerging Gothic Revival, which along with the Rococo Revival would sweep away the Classical style in the 1840s and 1850s. It is reassuring to know that some things never seem to change in the city that never sleeps.

---

1. A.T. Goodrich, *The Picture of New-York and Stranger's Guide to the Commercial Metropolis of the United States* (New York, 1828), 278. The destinations of the packet ships given above is also on p. 278 of this source. For comprehensive surveys of the growth and development of the New York port and packet lines, see Robert Greenhalgh Albion, *The Rise of New York Port, 1815–1860* (New York: C. Scribner's Sons, 1939), and Albion, *Square-Riggers on Schedule* (Princeton: Princeton University Press, 1938).
2. Anne Royall, *Sketches of History, Life and Manners in the United States* (New Haven, 1826), 261. Here as well is a comprehensive list of the dates of the month ships sailed for the ports mentioned above. For more on Anne Royall, pioneering female journalist, see Cynthia Earman, "An Uncommon Scold: Treasure-Talk Describes Life of Anne Royall, *Library of Congress Information Bulletin* 59, no. 1 (January 2000), https://www.loc.gov/loc/lcib/0001/royall.html.
3. For documentation on furniture shipped from New York to ports in the United States, see Forsyth M. Alexander, "Cabinet Warehousing in Southern Atlantic Ports, 1783–1820," *Journal of Early Southern Decorative Arts* 15, no. 2 (November, 1989), 1–42. For New York furniture shipped to Rio de Janeiro, see Peter M. Kenny, "From Bedford to New York to Rio and Back: The Life and Times of Elisha Blossom, Jr., Artisan of the New Republic," in *American Furniture 2003*, ed. Luke Beckerdite (Milwaukee: Chipstone Foundation, 2003), 238–69.

4. Grand illuminations were city-wide celebrations at night when window displays and the exteriors of shops, public buildings, and homes would be simultaneously lit with candles, torches, and oil and gas lamps, often culminating in a fireworks display. A grand illumination occurred again in New York in 1825 for the Grand Canal Celebration, marking the completion of the Erie Canal.
5. *New-York Evening Post*, February 28, 1815, quoted in Peter M. Kenny, Michael K. Brown, Frances F. Bretter, and Matthew A. Thurlow, *Duncan Phyfe: Master Cabinetmaker in New York* (New York: Metropolitan Museum of Art, 2011), 36.
6. Sarah Elliott Huger, New York, to Harriet Pinckney Horry, Charleston, January 4, 1816, quoted in Kenny et al., *Duncan Phyfe*, 128.
7. Although "Classical" is the style term used in this catalogue to describe furniture made in this later phase of Neoclassicism, "antique" and "Grecian" were the preferred period terms. These three style terms are used interchangeably throughout this essay. According to Thomas Sheraton's *The Cabinet Dictionary* (London, 1803), the word *antique* is "generally applied to such painting and sculpture, or architecture, as were executed at the period, when these arts arrived to their utmost perfection among the Greek and Romans" (quoted in Kenny et al., *Duncan Phyfe*, 68). The word "Grecian" appears frequently in New York as a descriptor in period newspaper advertisements and in the New York cabinetmakers' price books of 1817 and 1834.
8. Elizabeth Macaulay-Lewis and Matthew M. McGowan, eds. "Classical New York," in *Classical New York: Discovering Greece and Rome in Gotham* (New York: Fordham University Press, 2018), 4–5.
9. George Bridport, a decorative painter who worked and trained in London, relocated to Philadelphia in 1807, where he worked with architect Benjamin Henry Latrobe on designs for sophisticated furniture and interior decoration in the antique taste in Philadelphia, Baltimore, and Washington, D.C. Still working out of Philadelphia, he advertised his services to New Yorkers as a "Decorative Architect and Furnisher" capable of rendering designs for furniture, mantels, etc., in New York's *Evening Post*, September 18, 1818.
10. For an example of an inventory of a design library belonging to a Boston cabinetmaker see Clark Pearce, "A Revolution of Style and Taste in Boston and Salem," in this volume, p. 40.
11. *1808 Catalogue of Books on Architecture Etc. Belonging to John McComb, Junr.*, Misc. Mss. McComb, Manuscript Department, New-York Historical Society. Design drawings of carved tablets and pilasters for the marble mantels in the new City Hall in New York survive at the New-York Historical Society, and it has been suggested that he may have had a hand in the overall design of the armchairs made by Honoré Lannuier for the Common Council Chamber in 1812. See Peter M. Kenny, Frances F. Bretter, and Ulrich Leben, *Honoré Lannuier Cabinetmaker from Paris: The Life and Work of a French Ébéniste in Federal New York* (New York: Metropolitan Museum of Art, 1998), 77, 139–41. The Academy of Arts in New York, formed by subscription in 1802, maintained a study collection of plaster copies of antique and modern Neoclassical sculpture, as well as a library consisting of books of "views, designs, and drawings, chiefly related to antique subjects," including "the celebrated engravings of *Piranesi* in 24 superb volumes, presented to the Academy by NAPOLEON BONAPARTE." Members of the academy were drawn from practicing artists, engravers, and architects. That "mechanics," a class of artisan that included cabinetmakers, ever gained access to such a collection and library, seems unlikely, though some who engaged with architects on projects certainly may have had the chance. In addition, Ithiel Town's extraordinarily complete architectural library was open and made available for study to other New York architects and likely to their elite patrons in "*The Architecture Room* of Ithiel Town and M. E. Thompson in the [Merchants] Exchange," which was designed by Thompson in 1825 and completed in 1827. Both the American academy and the Architectural Room of Ithiel Town and Martin Euclid Thompson are described in Goodrich, *The Picture of New-York and Stranger's Guide*, 369–71, 376.
12. Jacques-Gérard Milbert, *Picturesque Itinerary of the Hudson River and the Peripheral Parts of North America*, translated and annotated by Constance D. Sherman (Ridgewood, NJ: Gregg Press 1968), quoted in Kenny et al., *Honoré Lannuier*, 43n36; Charles Percier and Pierre-François-Léonard Fontaine, *Recueil de décorations intérieures* (Paris, 1812). The *Recueil de décorations intérieures* was issued as six loose, engraved plates in a series of twelve installments between 1801 and 1812, and were sold in bookstores, print shops or by subscription. In 1812 all of these plates were published in Paris in a single bound edition under the same title.
13. See Kenny et al., *Duncan Phyfe*, 69–71.
14. Thomas Hope, *Household Furniture and Interior Decoration* (London: Longman, Hurst, Rees, and Orme, 1807), 14.
15. Pauline Agius, *Ackermann's Regency Furniture & Interiors* (Ramsbury, Marlborough, Wiltshire: Crowood Press, 1984), 143. The reference to the plate showing "A Sofa, or French Bed" appeared in the November 1822 issue of *The Repository*.
16. The subheading in this section paraphrases a line from Walt Whitman's "Manahatta," an ode to the poet's beloved city first published in *Leaves of Grass*, vol. 3 (Boston, 1860–61). The actual line from the poem reads: "The mechanics of the city, the masters, well-form'd, beautiful-faced, looking you straight in the eye." In nineteenth-century New York a mechanic was any of a number of skilled artisans including cabinetmakers, carpenters, carvers and gilders, chairmakers, coopers, masons, printers, sailmakers, and ship joiners, to mention just some. There has been no precise count made of the total number of cabinetmakers working in New York between 1810 and 1840. Yearly counts have been made for the years from 1810 to 1819 when the total number of working cabinetmakers ranged from a low of 206 in 1814 to a high of 304 in 1819. For a tabulation of active cabinetmakers in New York, 1803–1819, by year, see Kenny et al., *Honoré Lannuier*, 45.
17. Henry Bradshaw Fearon, *Sketches of America: A Narrative of a Journey of Five Thousand Miles through the Eastern and Western States of America*, 2nd ed. (London: Longman, Hurst, Rees, Orme, and Brown, 1818), 24, quoted in Kenny et al., *Honoré Lannuier*, 45.
18. For the New York cabinetmaking trade between 1815 and 1840, see Michael K. Brown and Matthew A. Thurlow, "Life of a Master Cabinetmaker," in Kenny et al., *Duncan Phyfe*, 23–63; Peter M. Kenny, "Lannuier's Life and Work in New York, 1803–19," in Kenny et al., *Honoré Lannuier*, 31–101. The presence of other known French cabinetmakers working in New York, either in Lannuier's shop or on their own, is discussed here. Also insightful and well-documented is Catherine Hoover Voorsanger's discussion of the trade: "'Gorgeous Articles of Furniture': Cabinetmaking in the Empire City," in *Art and the Empire City: New York, 1825–1861*, ed. Catherine Hoover Voorsanger and John K. Howat (New York: Metropolitan Museum of Art; New Haven: Yale University Press, 2000), 287–325.
19. For the triumph of French forms in New York, see Kenny et al., *Honoré Lannuier*, 81–98. The twenty-seven-year gap between the issuance of the 1817 price book and one issued by New York's journeyman cabinetmakers in 1834 indicates the durability of the richly ornamented and carved Classical style in New York, which was only beginning to be supplanted by the Grecian Plain style. There is a chance that in the interim between 1817 and 1834 a revised supplement to the 1817 price book listing the center table as a standard form may have been issued. It is interesting to note, however, that in March 1835 New York journeymen cabinetmakers "met to air their complaints and express special concern that the price book used by their masters was more than a quarter century old," which seems to explain the gap. See Sean Wilentz, *Chants Democratic: New York City & the Rise of the American Working Class, 1788–1850* (Oxford: Oxford University Press, 1984), 232.
20. Kenny et al., *Duncan Phyfe*, 220–21.
21. Voorsanger, *Art and the Empire City*, 515, cat. 223.
22. Kenny et al., *Honoré Lannuier*, 232. To appreciate the relative value of Lannuier's caryatid card tables versus a more standard type, consider the fact that a pair of mahogany card tables with four turned columns, gilded and *vert antique* lion's-paw feet, and *ormolu* appliqués on their aprons identical to those on the Lannuier tables are listed on a receipted invoice from Duncan Phyfe to James L. Brinckerhoff in 1816 for $135. For an image of one of the Brinckerhoff card tables and the receipted invoice, see Kenny et al., *Duncan Phyfe*, 80, fig. 81, and 276, appendix 1.5, 276.
23. New York cabinetmakers' price books formed the basis of labor agreements between the master cabinetmakers and the journeymen who worked for them by setting piecework prices for specific furniture forms and popular additional options. During the period when the Classical style was popular in New York, three separate price books were published, dated 1810, 1817, and 1834. When new furniture forms emerged or alterations to existing ones became necessary due to changes in fashion in the dynamic period during and just after the War of 1812, lists of revised and additional prices were issued. Two such lists are known in New York, one undated but likely published between 1811 and 1815, and the other dated 1815. The new forms and stylistic and technical changes included in these lists eventually were incorporated into the 1817 price book, which the employers and journeymen cabinetmakers continued to use, despite often contentious negotiations over wages until a new and long overdue edition was published seventeen years later. For the best treatment of American cabinetmakers' price books and their use, see Charles F. Montgomery, *American Furniture: The Federal Period in the Henry Francis du Pont Winterthur Museum* (New York: Viking Press, 1966), 19–26.
24. The inventory of the estate of Charles-Honoré Lannuier is in the Joseph Downs Collection of Manuscripts and Printed Ephemera, Winterthur Library. It is reproduced in full in Kenny et al., *Honoré Lannuier*, 238–39, appendix 9.
25. Ernest F. Hagen, "Duncan Phyfe Memorandum," undated but internal evidence indicates a date of 1907, reproduced in Nancy V. McClelland, *Duncan Phyfe and the English Regency, 1795–1830* (New York: Dover Publications, 1939), 315–17.

19a

Card Table, c. 1805–1815

Possibly Duncan Phyfe (1770–1854)
New York
Mahogany, mahogany and possibly primavera (blonde mahogany) veneer; tulip poplar, mahogany, white pine; brass
29 × 36 × 17½ in. (closed)

PROVENANCE: By tradition originally descended in the Delapaline family of Westchester County, NY. With Ginsburg & Levy, Inc., New York, by 1968; William Nathaniel Banks Jr. (1924–2019), Newnan, GA, 1968; His sale, Brunk Auctions, Asheville, NC, Sept. 12, 2020, lot 140; With Bernard & S. Dean Levy, Inc., New York, 2020; Purchased by Schrimshers, 2021.

19b

Sofa Table, 1805–1815

Unknown maker
New York
Mahogany, mahogany and rosewood veneer; mahogany, tulip poplar, white pine; brass
29¾ × 36 × 28¾ in. (leaves down); 56⅝ in. wide with leaves up

INSCRIPTION: Museum loan number painted in red on the face of one drawer: "L.1885.1."

PROVENANCE: Richard Townley Haines Halsey (1865–1942), New York. With Joe Kindig Antiques, York, PA. With Bernard & S. Dean Levy, Inc., New York, by 2020; Purchased by Schrimshers, 2021.

These two New York pillar-and-claw tables with their urn-shaped and lyre supports, elegantly-attenuated saber-shaped legs, crisp reeding, and distinctive waterleaf carving (fig. 19.1) are the epitome of a style universally recognized simply as "Phyfe." Hundreds if not thousands of surviving New York dining, Pembroke, card, sofa, and work tables share this same design vocabulary, far more than ever could have been produced in the Phyfe shop between about 1805 and 1820. Given his outsized reputation it is hard to argue that Duncan Phyfe was not the progenitor of this New York vernacular style, but separating his work from that of his many contemporaries continues to remain a challenge.

Excellent proportions and a superior level of materials and workmanship are factors that tend to trigger attributions to Phyfe by dealers, collectors, and connoisseurs, and this card table (cat. 19a)

Fig. 19.1. Detail of cat. 19a showing fine waterleaf carving on tops of legs and urn-shaped support

is no exception, having been assigned a Phyfe authorship by the dealer who sold it to the Schrimshers and the previous collector who purchased it. The top and its conforming apron, whose softly swelling curves are segments of ellipses, was described in the period as treble-elliptic and is the rarest of those found on New York tables of this type. The incurvate saber-shaped legs and the elliptical curves of the top are indicators of its early Grecian styling. Curvilinear profiles of Grecian architectural moldings based on the ellipse (rather than the circle as in Roman architecture) were praised by Robert Adam, who was among the first British architects to incorporate Grecian moldings and other details in his designs. Of elliptical curves, he wrote: "We have always given preference to the latter [i.e. Grecian over Roman], and have even thought advisable to bend them still more in many cases, particularly in interior furnishings, where objects are near and ought to be softened to the eye."[1]

This table also has the so-called "trick leg" support system that allows the top to be flipped open for card playing but remains entirely hidden from view when the top is closed. The two side legs are the trick legs. Each pivots backwards 45 degrees by means of a mechanical system of iron cams and rods hidden under the top and within the hollow pillar. Time-consuming and difficult to make, treble-elliptic pillar-and-claw card tables such as these commanded just over double the starting price for a journeyman cabinetmaker to produce than four-legged New York card tables with an extra fly leg at the rear. Unfortunately, in a closed position, they are poorly balanced due the extra weight of the iron mechanism and a lack of necessary support at the rear. The solution to this problem arrived by the early 1810s, however, when New York cabinetmakers adopted the British method of making tops that pivoted 90 degrees on the upper frame, thus obviating the need for trick legs on pillar-and-claw bases, which instead began to sport a wide array of columnar, lyre, and other sculptural supports (cats. 22a and b, 28, 35a and b, and 37).[2]

Pillar-and-claw sofa tables with low cross stretchers, though relatively rare, were made throughout the period of the Classical style in New York.[3] Fitted with casters, they were intended to stand in front of a sofa to allow the drawers fitted in each side—one operational and the other with merely a false front—to remain accessible. Like modern-day coffee tables, sofa tables were multi-use, serving as writing surfaces, places for tea or light meals, and even a venue for games of chess or draughts with opponents seated across from each other. The intimate personal and social activities that occurred around sofa tables were repeated at the far more popular Pembroke or drop-leaf tea or breakfast table, a form, not surprisingly, that survives in far greater numbers. Increasingly after 1820, circular center tables with either wood or marble tops eclipsed the popularity of both sofa and Pembroke tables.

This sofa table (cat. 19b) has the distinction of once being the property of collector Richard Townley Haines Halsey, one of the early proponents of Phyfe's fame. It was included in *Furniture Masterpieces of Duncan Phyfe* by Charles Over Cornelius, an illustrated book that accompanied the pioneering 1922 exhibition *Furniture from the Workshop of Duncan Phyfe* at the Metropolitan Museum of Art, which Cornelius curated but was in all likelihood conceived by Halsey while serving as a trustee. The sofa table is one of two illustrated and discussed in the book; Cornelius described them as "superb examples of finished workmanship," pointing out expressly the "beautiful and delicate stretchers" and "brilliantly contrasting veneering" around the drawers and in the crossbanding of the tops.[4] There is also a drawing of the elegant lyre support on this sofa table in one of several fold-out plates in the book that depicted various parts of the furniture and was intended as a sort of field guide to the Phyfe style (fig. 19.2). One would be hard pressed to better explicate the virtues of this graceful, well-balanced example of the cabinetmaker's art.[5]

1. Robert Adam and James Adam, *The Works in Architecture of Robert and James Adam* (New York: Dover Publications, 2006), 6, quoted in Calder Loth, "Notes on Moldings, the Change from Roman to Greek," Institute of Classical Architecture and Art, February 10, 2015, https://www.classicist.org/articles/notes-on-moldings-the-change-from-roman-to-greek/.
2. For a discussion and illustration of the trick-leg mechanism in New York pillar-and-claw card tables, see Peter M. Kenny, Michael K. Brown, Frances F. Bretter, and Matthew A. Thurlow, *Duncan Phyfe: Master Cabinetmaker in New York* (New York: Metropolitan Museum of Art, 2011), 74, 76, fig. 76.
3. For insights on American sofa tables in the Classical style, see Philip D. Zimmerman, "The American Sofa Table," *The Magazine Antiques* 155, no. 5 (May 1999): 744–53.
4. Charles Over Cornelius, *Furniture Masterpieces of Duncan Phyfe* (New York: Metropolitan Museum of Art, 1922), 77, pls. XLII and XLIV.
5. Ibid., 50. See fold-out plate facing page 50 for a drawing of the lyre support.

Fig. 19.2. Detail of cat. 19b showing the reeded and waterleaf-carved lyre supports, delicate cross stretcher, and contrasting veneers on the leg blocks

20

Pier Table, c. 1815–1825

Attributed to Duncan Phyfe (1770–1854)
New York
Rosewood veneer, mahogany; white pine, tulip poplar; gilded gesso, *vert antique*, gilded brass, marble, mirror glass
36¾ × 43½ × 18 in.

PROVENANCE: Margaret (1765–1842) and Robert Smith (1757–1842), Baltimore, MD; By descent to his son Samuel W. Smith (1800–1870); By descent to his daughter, Ellen Donnell Smith Von Kapff; By descent to her daughter, Ellen Von Kapff Wilson (1856–1944); By descent to her daughter, Elinor Donnell Wilson Poultney (1883–1974); By descent probably to her daughter, Ann Poultney Taylor (1912–2012); By descent probably to her sister Elinor Poultney Wagner (dates unknown); Sale, Christie's, New York, Jan. 20, 2012, lot 304; Purchased by Schrimshers, 2012.

Winged griffins with fearsome beaks, bulging rib cages, and powerful hindquarters are Duncan Phyfe's most profound and dramatic statements of the antique. Fantastical creatures whose mythic role was the guarding of ancient treasure, griffins impart a strange and almost preternatural aspect to a group of tables only recently attributed to Phyfe; they may well have been his response to the winged caryatid tables of his rival, Charles-Honoré Lannuier (see cat. 35a).[1] A potent statement on its own, this pier table originally was part of a large suite of rosewood tables with painted and gilded figural supports, including card tables (most likely an original pair); a large circular table with a deep apron, drawers, and a cloth-lined top for writing; and a tea table.[2] The nine full-bodied mythical beasts, plus two figures of a variant design with identical gilded eagle's heads but slimmer, wingless bodies and scrolled tails, on these tables would make them a commanding presence in any drawing room or parlor (see p. 90, fig. 5).

According to family history, the original owners of these tables were Robert Smith and his wife, Margaret, of Baltimore. Smith served as secretary of the Navy from 1801 until the end of President Thomas Jefferson's administration. In 1809, he was appointed secretary of state by President James Madison, a post he held until 1811, when he resigned from government service. Recognized in Washington, D.C. society as people of wealth and style, Robert and Margaret Smith were regular participants in the city's steady rounds of splendid balls and dinner parties. Margaret Bayard Smith (1778–1844), chronicler of the early years of Washington society, recounts an invitation she received in 1803 to a particularly "elegant and select party" given by Mrs. Robert Smith in honor of fellow Baltimorean Elizabeth Patterson Bonaparte (1785–1879), wife of Jerome Bonaparte, the younger brother of the first consul and soon to be French emperor Napoleon.[3] Madame Patterson Bonaparte shocked the sensibilities of those attending by wearing a revealing dress in the latest Parisian style that, according to Bayard, left her "almost naked" and so revealed that "no one dar'd to look at her but by stealth."[4] Given their likely date of manufacture, the Smiths' suite of griffin tables were not part of the decor at this elegant but scandalous soirée. Instead, they were probably purchased after the family returned to Baltimore, where they lived at a couple of addresses before moving about 1822–23 into an imposing house on Monument Square in Mount Vernon, the city's most fashionable neighborhood. Here they doubtlessly continued to burnish their reputation for entertaining in high style. Four griffin tables, three from the original suite—the card table, the large circular table with the cloth-lined top, and a tea table—as well as a late nineteenth- or early twentieth-century copy of this pier table were placed on loan by descendants of Robert and Margaret Smith to the Maryland Historical Society (now the Maryland Center for History and Culture) in 1945, and eventually donated in 1981.[5]

1. For a discussion and illustrations of griffin tables and their attribution to Duncan Phyfe, see Peter M. Kenny, Michael K. Brown, Frances F. Bretter, and Matthew A. Thurlow, *Duncan Phyfe: Master Cabinetmaker in New York* (New York: Metropolitan Museum of Art, 2011), 82–85, pl. 16, 182–83, pl. 29, 204–5.
2. One card table, the large circular table, and the tea table from the suite, as well as a later reproduction of this pier table are at the Maryland Center for History and Culture, Baltimore, Maryland (1981.66.1-3).
3. Gaillard Hunt, ed., *The First Forty Years of Washington Society Portrayed by the Family Letters of Mrs. Samuel Harrison Smith (Margaret Bayard)* (New York, 1906), 46.
4. Ibid.
5. The card table, the circular table with the cloth writing surface, and the tea table are illustrated and discussed in Gregory R. Weidman. *Furniture in Maryland, 1740–1940: The Collection of the Maryland Historical Society* (Baltimore: Maryland Historical Society, 1984), 188–89. The author would like to acknowledge Gregory Weidman for her kind assistance with this entry on the history of the residences of Robert and Margaret Smith in Baltimore and the provenance of the suite of griffin tables, and for informing him about the reproduction pier table in the collection of the Maryland Center for History and Culture, Baltimore. Weidman also offered up the not unreasonable possibility that the suite of griffin tables may have been made for Robert and Margaret Smith's son Samuel W. Smith on the occasion of his marriage in 1823 to Ellen Donnell.

21a

Worktable, 1810–1820

Possibly by Duncan Phyfe (1770–1854)
New York
Mahogany, mahogany and satinwood veneer; mahogany, tulip poplar, white pine; brass
29 × 22 × 18 in.

PROVENANCE: With Israel Sack, Inc., New York; Gloria Peltz (b. 1935) and Richard (b. 1937) Manney, New York; Sale, Sotheby's, New York, Jun. 23–24, 1993, lot 455. With Israel Sack, Inc., New York; Westervelt Company, Tuscaloosa, AL; Sale, Christie's, New York, Jan. 17, 2019, lot 1277; Purchased by Schrimshers, 2019.

21b

Worktable, 1810–1820

Attributed to Duncan Phyfe (1770–1854)
New York
Mahogany, mahogany veneer, satinwood or other light-wood inlay; mahogany, tulip poplar, white pine; brass
31¼ × 22 × 15½ in.

INSCRIPTION: In period cursive script on underside of marble top: "No [conjoined] 1."

PROVENANCE: Private collection, Chicago, IL; Sale, Pook and Pook, Inc., Downington, PA, Oct. 1, 2021, lot 991; Purchased by Schrimshers, 2021.

Elegantly whimsical in their animated stance, one appearing on the verge of taking a step forward and the other with knees gracefully bent as in a ballerina's plié, these two ladies' worktables are an uncommon take on a fairly common form. Described in the 1817 *New-York Book of Prices for Manufacturing Cabinet and Chair Work* as a " Square Work Table" and a "Canted Corner Work Table," both share the same slender, cabriole-shaped legs with console scrolls at the top, a thin lower shelf, and hairy carved feet in the distinctive hooked shape of a dog's leg.[1] Cabriole-shaped legs of this type appear on a variety of Classical New York table forms, including work, card, side, and dressing tables, and apparently were popular enough for drawings of them to be included at the top of plate 4 in the 1817 price book (fig. 21.1). Listed as an optional extra in the price book for "A Square Work Table" is a "plain tapered case to stand between the legs" and "screwed to the shelf." Although both of these examples have open lower shelves, which may have held a tea caddy or a silk corbeille or basket of needlework, a very closely related worktable with canted corners and a nicely fitted, tapered mahogany case below is known.[2]

A notable difference between these two worktables, in addition to the shapes of their upper cases, is in their tops: one has a mahogany veneer, while the other has inset white marble. The latter was

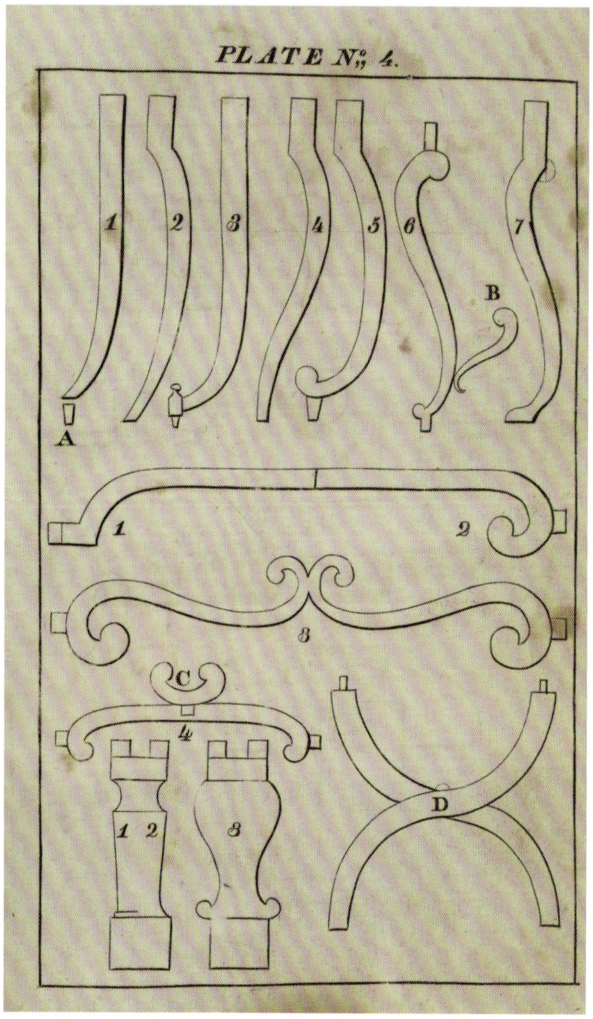

Fig. 21.1. Plate 4 in *The New-York Book of Prices for Manufacturing Cabinet and Chair Work* (New York, 1817), engraving, Metropolitan Museum of Art, New York, Harris Brisbane Dick Fund, 1939, 39.32.1 (Courtesy Metropolitan Museum of Art / Art Resource, NY). The legs on the square worktable, including the rectangular block at the top into which the aprons are mortise-and-tenoned is shown as number 7. The legs on the worktable with the canted corners have round tenons at the top, as shown in the leg marked number 6.

21a

particularly useful as it provided a safe, durable surface for mixing and serving alcoholic beverages or for blistering hot silver teapots. In 1815 Isaac W. Morrell (active 1811–1865), a warehouseman who sold imported New York furniture in Savannah, advertised "Lady's elegant work Tables with marble tops."[3] Having opened a furniture workshop and warehouse there about this time, Morrell later referred to himself in the *Georgian and Evening Advertiser* as "agent for D. Phyfe. New York."[4] A marble-topped worktable with canted corners at Winterthur Museum, Garden & Library labeled by Duncan Phyfe has a history of ownership in the Dearing family, who arrived in Athens, Georgia, from Charleston in the 1820s.[5] The canted-corner worktable in the Schrimsher Collection has an upper section so close in its proportions and in the disposition of its cross-banded and crotch mahogany veneers to the labeled example at Winterthur that assigning its authorship to Phyfe seems warranted. The attribution of the other worktable (cat. 21a) to Phyfe, though viable based on its related design and the overall quality of its materials and workmanship, remains less certain.

1. *The New-York Book of Prices for Manufacturing Cabinet and Chair Work* (New York: J. Seymour, 1817), 50–52, 53–55.
2. Ibid., pls. 4 and 6, unpaginated. For the closely related worktable with canted corners and tapered mahogany cases between the legs, see Leigh Keno and Leslie Keno with Joan Barzily Freund, *Hidden Treasures: Searching for Masterpieces of American Furniture* (New York: Warner Books, Inc., 2000) 176–77. A related worktable with a tapered mahogany case between console scrolls (replaced) that extend between the canted corners and a more compact plinth with incurvate, saber-shaped legs is in the collection of the Metropolitan Museum of Art (66.48.2). A virtual mate to this worktable is in the collection of the White House Historical Association.
3. *Republican and Savannah Evening Ledger*, May 2, 1815, 3, quoted in Peter M. Kenny, Michael K. Brown, Frances F. Bretter, and Matthew A. Thurlow, *Duncan Phyfe: Master Cabinetmaker in New York* (New York: Metropolitan Museum of Art, 2011), 174n2.
4. Quoted in Kenny et al., *Duncan Phyfe*, 40.
5. Ibid., 174–75, pl. 10.

21b

22a

Card Table, c. 1825

Attributed to Deming & Bulkley: Barzilia Deming (1781–1854) and Erastus Bulkley (1798–1872), in partnership 1818–1850
Mahogany, mahogany veneer, ash; tulip poplar, cherry or maple, white pine; paint, gilding, brass
30 × 37 × 18½ in.

PROVENANCE: Private Collection; Sale, Sotheby's, New York, Jan. 30, 1994, lot 1172; Purchased by Schrimshers, 1994.

22b

Card Table, c. 1825

Attributed to Deming & Bulkley: Barzilia Deming (1781–1854) and Erastus Bulkley (1798–1872), in partnership 1818–1850
New York
Mahogany veneer, white pine, ash; tulip poplar, cherry or maple, white pine; paint, gilding, brass
29¾ × 37¼ × 18⅝ in.

PROVENANCE: With F. J. Carey III by 1990; Purchased by Schrimshers, 1990.

Writing from New York in the late winter of 1816 concerning a custom order of furniture from Duncan Phyfe, Sarah Elliott Huger (c. 1775–1853) informed her Charleston cousin Harriott Pinckney Horry (1748–1830):

> Phyfe assured me that curled maple could not be worked in the shape I ordered but at an immense price; so high, that Mrs. L. he was sure could never be reconciled to give it for, what is generally so roughly used as Card Tables; Articles by the way that are now become obsolete in drawing rooms, which should only exhibit marble Tables on every pier, and a round centre one, corresponding in marble and finish with the side ornaments.[1]

Despite having her finger firmly on the pulse of the latest trends in furniture and interior decoration, Huger's advice from New York seems to have fallen upon deaf ears among socially elite Charlestonians, who kept up the local demand for card tables throughout the 1820s, especially those produced by the cabinetmaking partnership of Deming & Bulkley. With a manufacturing base in New York headed up by Barzilia Deming and a wareroom on Charleston's King Street operated by Erastus Bulkley, these partners developed an exclusive clientele and seemed to have enjoyed considerable success there for over twenty years.[2] Deming & Bulkley offered a complete line of high-quality and expensive cabinetwork, either ready-made or bespoke. Card tables, veneered with either rosewood or mahogany and invariably sold in pairs, were among their prime offerings. Approximately thirty are known today, the most numerous being those with sinuous, paired dolphins as front supports (figs. 22.1–3). Less common are the tables with painted and gilded spread eagles (cat. 22b) or tapered pylons with freehand-gilded lyres superimposed on the front. The vast majority of these tables have delightfully animated dolphin feet and many, unlike the present examples, are richly ornamented with freehand gilding on their aprons, tops and plinths in a style apparently unique to Deming & Bulkley (fig. 22.4).

One of the more intriguing aspects of these dolphin card tables is that almost never are the same combination of carved dolphin supports and feet found on different pairs of tables. Much like theme and variation in a piece of classical music, Deming & Bulkley would present the main melody with each new pair of dolphin card tables they made, then alter or change their design in some way. The Schrimsher Collection contains five Deming & Bulkley card tables, none of which is quite the same as the others (compare cat. 22a and figs. 22.1–3). In a society steeped in the art of entertaining and conspicuous display, Charlestonians may have demanded, or Deming & Bulkley shrewdly intuited, that the dolphin card tables on show in their drawing rooms should be just that much different than those of their social intimates and peers.[3]

Fig. 22.1. *Card Table*, attributed to Deming & Bulkley, c. 1825, mahogany, mahogany veneer; brass, Schrimsher Collection

Fig. 22.2. *Card Table*, attributed to Deming & Bulkley, c. 1825, mahogany, mahogany veneer; brass, Schrimsher Collection

Fig. 22.3. *Card Table*, attributed to Deming & Bulkley, c. 1825, rosewood; stencil gilding, *vert antique*, brass, Schrimsher Collection

22a

In 1820, Deming & Bulkley placed a notice in the Charleston *Gazette and Commercial Daily Advertiser* offering a "pair of card tables supported by a Spread Eagle," which they claimed to be "much superior" to any they previously offered and that "cannot be surpassed by any in the world."[4] The Schrimshers' spread-eagle card table (cat. 22b) and two other pairs provide an opportunity to see firsthand the subjects of this proud boast.[5]

Another New York shop, quite possibly that of Duncan Phyfe, made card tables with sculptural eagle supports. Two pairs are known with eagles carved of solid mahogany, canted corners, swivel tops, and standard New York reeded and carved saber-shaped legs.[6] These tables are finished in a clear varnish as opposed to Deming & Bulkley's rich polychrome surfaces. Although highly sculptural, they seem quite restrained by comparison. The dramatic composition and elaborate ornamentation of the Deming & Bulkley eagle card tables seems as Baroque in style as it does Classical. Furniture historian Richard H. Randall Jr. posited that eighteenth-century console tables with eagle supports in the manner of neo-Palladian British architects William Kent (1685–1748) and John Vardy (1718–1765) may have provided design inspiration for these later New York card tables rather than Charles Percier and Pierre-François-Léonard Fontaine's French Empire Napoleonic eagles with their allusion to Roman imperial taste.[7] Eighteenth-century British console tables, often made in pairs, feature large, facing giltwood eagles with spread wings perched atop rock outcroppings in much the same manner as those on Deming & Bulkley's card tables.[8] Miniaturized versions of these gilded spread eagles perched on rocky outcroppings appear in the pediments of British- and American-made looking glasses and girandoles into the 1830s and may be one of the ways earlier neo-Palladian Classical design was revived over time.

Fig. 22.4. Detail of cat. 22b showing gilded dolphin feet

1. Sarah Elliott Huger, New York, to Harriott Pinckney Horry, Charleston, March 5, 1816, Harriott Horry Ravenel Family Papers, 1694–1935 (1086.00), South Carolina Historical Society, Charleston, quoted in Peter M. Kenny, Michael K. Brown, Frances F. Bretter, and Matthew A. Thurlow, *Duncan Phyfe: Master Cabinetmaker in New York* (New York: Metropolitan Museum of Art, 2011), 128–29.
2. Information on Deming & Bulkley is based on the groundbreaking research undertaken on the partners and their cabinetmaking business by Maurie D. McInnis and Robert A. Leath for their article "Beautiful Specimens, Elegant Patterns: New York Furniture for the Charleston Market, 1810–1840," in *American Furniture 1996*, ed. Luke Beckerdite (Milwaukee: Chipstone Foundation, 1996), 137–74.
3. On the topic of the cultural sensibilities of Charlestonians and their love of display, see Maurie D. McInnis, *The Politics of Taste in Antebellum Charleston* (Chapel Hill: University of North Carolina Press, 2005), especially chap. 9, pp. 277–326. At odds in a sculptural sense with the fully three-dimensional carved dolphin feet are the front dolphin supports, whose backs are left flat and unadorned. Clearly evident on the backs are plugs used to fill holes left by the woodcarver's screw that held the roughed-out, S-shaped blanks firmly to the bench as the fronts were carved. When the card tables are against a wall, the viewer's perspective of the dolphin supports is good. Once the tables are brought out into the room, however, the flat backs of the dolphins are in plain view, an unfortunate lapse in the overall design, perhaps the result of a desire to speed production or to reduce the cost of the skilled labor that produced them.
4. McInnis, *The Politics of Taste in Antebellum Charleston*, 317n79.
5. A single example from one of the pairs is illustrated in McInnis and Leath, "Beautiful Specimens, Elegant Patterns," fig. 19, and in McInnis, *Politics of Taste*, pl. 14. One of the other pair is illustrated in J. L. Sibley Jennings, *Dolphin Tales: The Discovery of Related Southern Furniture of Exceptional Quality and Northern Mis-Attribution, or Move Over, Lannuier* (Washington D.C.: J. L. Sibley Jennings, 1990), 15, pl. 33. Jennings's publication is extremely useful for the number of card tables it illustrates and the provenance information it provides, but his attribution of these tables to unknown Charleston maker(s) has been thoroughly negated by McInnis and Leath in "Beautiful Specimens, Elegant Patterns."
6. One pair is split between the Museum of Fine Arts, Boston (58.19), and the Yale University Art Gallery (1930.2002); the other is in a private collection.
7. Richard H. Randall Jr., "Sources of the Empire Style," *The Magazine Antiques* 83, no. 4 (April 1963): 452–53.
8. For a British gilt eagle console table (c. 1740–50), with spread wings perched on a rock outcropping, see R. W. Symonds, "English Eagle and Dolphin Console Tables," *The Magazine Antiques* 18, no. 10 (October 1930): 304, fig. 1; 305, fig. 3.

22b

23

Secretary Bookcase, 1820–1830

Attributed to Deming & Bulkley: Barzilia Deming (1781–1854) and Erastus Bulkley (1798–1872), in partnership 1820–1850
New York
Rosewood, rosewood veneer, mahogany, painted and gilded ash in imitation of rosewood; mahogany, white pine, tulip poplar, ash; gilding, glass
95 × 48⅛ × 26¾ in.

PROVENANCE: With Anthony A. P. Stuempfig Antiques, Philadelphia, by 1990; Purchased by Schrimshers, 1990.

Imposing, architectural secretary bookcases in the Classical style are the latter-day equivalents of the eighteenth-century Baroque desks and bookcases made in Boston, New York, and Philadelphia: showpieces of the mercantile elite. Spectacular New York versions exist, including a gilded and ebonized example in the collection of the Metropolitan Museum of Art long attributed to Joseph Meeks & Sons (in partnership 1828–1835), and one of near equal brilliance in a private collection signed and dated 1829 by its maker, Robert Fisher (active 1824–1837).[1] This rosewood secretary bookcase, confidently attributed to the New York cabinetmaking partnership of Barzilia Deming and Erastus Bulkley, is only slightly less opulent and commands a place in the top tier of New York examples of this monumental form.

When purchased by the Schrimshers in 1990, this secretary bookcase, like so many other richly ornamented New York Classical pier tables and monumental case furniture like it at the time, was assigned an attribution to the aforementioned Meeks firm. Subsequent scholarship by Maurie D. McInnis and Robert A. Leath on Deming & Bulkley, who manufactured their furniture in New York but retailed it in Charleston in the 1820s and 1830s, has led to a reassessment of this earlier attribution. The freehand gilding on this secretary bookcase includes a stenciled border of grape vines around the perimeter of the lower cupboard doors and the fall front (fig. 23.1). In 1820, Deming & Bulkley, seeking to stimulate local interest in their New York–manufactured furniture, announced a raffle in the *Charleston City Gazette and Commercial Daily Advertiser* of "A most superb and complete set of Rose Wood Drawing Room FURNITURE," further adding that "The whole sett is made of real Rose Wood, with a Border in imitation of a Grape Vine, around every piece of it."[2] This grapevine border appears on the tops of several card tables dated around 1825 attributed to Deming & Bulkley and on

Fig. 23.1. Detail of cat. 23 showing the fall front with a freehand-gilded border of grapevines

Fig. 23.2. George Smith, "Book case Doors. Chinese. Egyptian. Gothic.," plate 106 in *A Collection of Designs for Household Furniture and Interior Decoration* (London, 1808), hand-colored engraving (Courtesy Clark Art Institute Library, Mary Ann Beinecke Decorative Art Collection)

the inner and outer faces of the boldly scrolled arms of an imitation rosewood-grained armchair, which was presented in 1821 by Erastus Bulkley to St. John's Lutheran Church in Charleston for the use of the minister on the altar.[3] In addition to the freehand-gilded grapevine borders on the fall front and cupboard doors, the ornament centering the cornice frieze is identical to one used on a card table attributed to Deming & Bulkley and a pair of card tables with painted and gilded spread-eagle supports.[4]

Also noteworthy are the glazed door panels with pointed arches and Gothic tracery, and the boldly carved front feet. The former are copied directly from plate 106 in George Smith's *A Collection of Designs for Household Furniture and Interior Decoration* (London, 1808), which illustrates bookcase doors in the Chinese, Egyptian, and Gothic styles (fig. 23.2). The lion's paws stand flexed with bulbous knees, with voluptuously carved acanthus leaves terminating in a sprightly upward flip at the base of the toes, and V-shaped reserves at the top with diamond-shaped facets like those seen on cut-glass tableware of the period. While decidedly different in form from the dolphin feet on Deming & Bulkley's better-known card tables, these lion's-paw feet, with their lush, undulating acanthus leaf carving, share a similar Baroque energy with their aquatic counterparts (see cat. 22, fig. 22.4).

1. Both of these New York secretary bookcases are discussed and illustrated in Catherine Hoover Vorrsanger, "Gorgeous Articles of Furniture: Cabinetmaking in the Empire City," in *Art and the Empire City, 1825–1861*, ed. Catherine Hoover Voorsanger and John C. Howat (New York: Metropolitan Museum of Art, 2000), 293–95; 293, fig. 239; 515, cat. 223.
2. *City Gazette and Commercial Daily Advertiser* (Charleston), April 11, 1820, and November 20, 1820.
3. Maurie D. McInnis and Robert A. Leath, "Beautiful Specimens, Elegant Patterns: New York Furniture for the Charleston Market, 1810–1840," in *American Furniture 1996*, ed. Luke Beckerdite (Milwaukee: Chipstone Foundation, 1996), fig. 30. As of 2024, the armchair was still at St. John's Lutheran Church in Charleston.
4. See ibid., fig. 30, for the rosewood-grained armchair and figs. 19 and 20 for one of the pair of eagle card tables with the identical freehand-gilded decoration on its front apron and freehand-gilded grapevines around the perimeter of its top. These card tables are on loan to the Charleston Museum. The exposed top at the front of the lower section of the Schrimsher secretary bookcase as well as its sides are also grained in imitation of rosewood.

24

Couch, 1829–1835

Attributed to Joseph Meeks & Sons: Joseph Meeks (1771–1868), John Meeks (1801–1875), Joseph W. Meeks (1805–1878), in partnership 1828–1835
New York
Rosewood-grained and ebonized mahogany, painted and gilded ash in imitation of rosewood; maple, tulip poplar; brass, replacement upholstery
35¼ × 85 × 24 in.

PROVENANCE: With R. T. Trump and Company, Philadelphia, by 1991; Private Collection; Sale, Sotheby's, New York, Jan. 1994, lot 1059. Sale, Christie's, New York, Oct. 8, 2004, lot 117; Purchased by Schrimshers, 2004.

Stylish and richly ornamented, this Grecian couch or *chaise longue* is a rare, literal copy of a published British furniture design executed by an American cabinetmaking shop (fig. 24.1). Moreover, its likely maker, the firm of Joseph Meeks & Sons, reprinted this design in barely altered form in an advertising broadside issued by the firm in 1833—unremarkable, perhaps, for a time when copyright protections were virtually non-existent, but extremely fortuitous when it comes to assigning authorship.[1] George Smith writes of his design, shown in plate 136 of his *The Cabinet-Maker and Upholsterer's Guide* (London, 1826): "This elegant chaise longue as to its design, may be considered wholly Grecian and is best adapted for the drawing room, or boudoir; in which case, the frame may be wholly of rosewood, and the seat and ends covered either with silk, Merino damask, or linen. If appropriated for the state apartment, the frame might then be finished entirely in gold."[2] State apartments aside, this relatively compact, rosewood-grained, bronzed, ebonized, and gilded couch was designed for rooms associated with women and their social pursuits, whether these be "withdrawing" after the evening meal to prepare tea and engage in conversation in the drawing room with other female guests while the men remained at the table drinking and discussing politics, or else socializing or engaging in private pursuits in their personal sitting room or boudoir, adjacent to their bedchamber. Other stylish and distinctive American examples of relatively compact size are known, including most notably a rosewood and brass-inlaid pair made for the Appleton family of Boston.[3] Smaller, gendered Grecian couches such as these speak to the taste and social pursuits of women in this period much in the same way as do elegant and multifarious worktables in the Classical style.

Fig. 24.1. George Smith, "Chaise Longue," plate 136 in *The Cabinet-Maker and Upholsterer's Guide* (London, 1826), engraving (Courtesy Winterthur Museum, Garden & Library)

A notable feature of Smith's "wholly Grecian" *chaise longue* design copied in the Meeks couch is the head of Silenus, the satyr-like Greek god of winemaking, and the tutor and jovial companion of Dionysus, jutting from the end of the sweeping top rail (figs. 24.1 and 24.2). Depicted with his characteristic bulbous nose and beard, Silenus often appears in Greek art as inebriated. Despite his debauched lifestyle, he was also considered intuitive, wise, and prophetic, Dionysian attributes that were, in the broadest sense, historically associated with women as opposed to the Apollonian qualities of order and rationality attributed to men.

---

1. Broadside for Joseph Meeks & Sons' Manufactory of Cabinet and Upholstery Articles, 43 & 45 Broad Street, New York, 1833, Metropolitan Museum of Art, New York, 43.15.8. The Meeks broadside is illustrated in Peter M. Kenny, Michael K. Brown, Frances F. Bretter, and Matthew A. Thurlow, *Duncan Phyfe: Master Cabinetmaker in New York* (New York: Metropolitan Museum of Art, 2011), 91.
2. George Smith, *The Cabinet-Maker and Upholsterer's Guide* (London: Jones & Co., 1826), 191.
3. One of the pair of smaller Appleton family Grecian couches is illustrated and described as one of a number of "ladies' Grecian couches" in Jonathan L. Fairbanks and Elizabeth Bidwell Bates, *American Furniture 1620 to the Present* (New York: Richard Marek Publishers 1981), 279.

Fig. 24.2. Detail of cat. 24 showing the bearded head of Silenus

25a

French Bureau, 1816–1820

Possibly Duncan Phyfe (1770–1854)
New York
Mahogany, mahogany and satinwood veneer; tulip poplar, white pine; brass
49 × 52 × 23 in.

25b

French Bureau with Secretary Drawer, 1816–1820

Possibly Duncan Phyfe (1770–1854)
New York
Mahogany, mahogany and satinwood veneer; tulip poplar, white pine; brass
49 × 51 × 23 in.

PROVENANCE (25a and 25b): William Christopher Rhinelander (1790–1878), New York; By descent to his daughter, Mary Rhinelander Stewart (1821–1893); By descent to her son, William Rhinelander Stewart (1852–1929); By descent to his son, William Rhinelander Stewart Jr. (1888–1945); By descent to his wife, Janet Newbold Stewart (d. 1986); Donated by Janet Newbold Stewart to the National Museum of Art, Smithsonian Institution, in 1969 and deaccessioned in 1986; With Margaret B. Caldwell, dealer, 1986; Gloria Peltz (b. 1935) and Richard (b. 1937) Manney, New York; Sale, Christie's, New York, Jan. 21, 2000, lot 195; Purchased by Schrimshers, 2000.

These beautifully matched French bureaus, one with a fitted secretary drawer with satinwood veneers, have an unbroken history of descent in the Rhinelander family until 1969 when they were donated to the Smithsonian Institution. According to family tradition, they were made on the occasion of William Christopher Rhinelander's 1816 marriage to Mary Rogers, daughter of wealthy New York landowner John Rogers. It is unusual to have two pieces of case furniture from one commission so exactly matched as to almost be a pair. This intentional alignment suggests that they may well have been his and hers wedding gifts or else purchased together by the young couple when setting up their household. The heavy, foursquare quality and strong architectural presence of these French bureaus are characteristic of French Consulat and Empire commodes in *le goût antique*, a style one would presume both Mr. and Mrs. Rhinelander

Fig. 25.1. Detail of cat. 25b

25a

favored. Style often triumphs over practicality, however—a situation just as likely to occur in New York as Paris, where it was reported in 1805 in the *Journal des dames et des modes*: "We so admired the forms of Antique furniture, originally destined to adorn immense spaces that we hurried to imitate them and to place them in small rooms for the use of small women who, for the sake of fashion, bruised their delicate limbs on angular forms, and are scarcely able to move an arm-chair."[1]

William C. Rhinelander was the namesake of William Rhinelander (1753–1825) of New York, a shipbuilder, merchant, and importer and processor of sugar. After the Revolution he acquired the confiscated sugar refinery and warehouse of loyalist Henry Cuyler, a New York landmark built in 1763, and renamed it the Rhinelander Sugar House. Rhinelander in turn invested the profits from his business ventures in New York real estate, a surefire way to pass on the kind of generational wealth that allowed his son to acquire beautiful home furnishings and live a comfortable life among his financial and social equals in New York. Sugar and cotton played an enormous role in the commercial success of New York, and local cabinetmakers were the beneficiaries of the wealth generated by trade in these commodities, of which the human cost is incalculable.[2]

These French bureaus include traits that relate to documented Phyfe case furniture: the flattened Grecian ovolo moldings with unusually sharp arrises along their leading edge (fig. 25.1); the proportions of the flat filets above and below the recessed, veneered section of the plinth; and the style of carving on the lion's-paw feet, with draped acanthus leaves, parted by a central vein, that terminate in a spoon-like shape above a pair of projecting, bulbous toes.[3]

1. Quoted in Ulrich Leben, *Molitor, Ébéniste from the Ancien Régime to the Bourbon Restoration* (London: P. Wilson, 1992), 116–17.
2. "The Rhinelander Family: An Old Colonial Fortune," *The New York Times*, June 23, 1878, 2.
3. For more on these particular features on documented and attributed Phyfe furniture, see the entry on the French pedestal-end sideboard and sarcophagus cellarette (cats. 36a and b) in this volume.

25b

26

Pair of Side Chairs, 1810–1820

Attributed to Duncan Phyfe (1770–1854)
New York
Mahogany; ash, tulip poplar; replacement upholstery
32¾ × 17¾ × 16½ in.

INSCRIPTIONS: Chiseled on rear seat rails: "V" on one chair and "XII" on the other; chiseled on slip seat of "XII" chair: "I"; painted museum loan numbers: "L2378.27" on "V" and "L2378.28" on "XII" chair.

PROVENANCE: Family of Governor William Livingston (1723–1790), NJ. Richard Townley Haines Halsey (1865–1942), New York; Philip Haas Hammerslough Jr. (1894–1978), Hartford, CT. With Jerome Blum, Lisbon, CT. With John Walton, Jewett City, CT; Robert M. Rosenberg (b. 1938), Weston, MA; With Clark Pearce, Essex, MA, by 2011; Purchased by Schrimshers, 2011.

Masterfully composed and exquisitely wrought, these klismos side chairs represent the acme of perfection in Phyfe's early Grecian style based largely on English Regency precedents. Their essential design almost certainly comes from the 1808 *Supplement to the London Chair-Makers' and Carvers' Book of Prices for Workmanship,* in which two plates illustrate the distinctive inward-curved or saber-shaped front and rear legs pointing in opposite directions, and the sweeping line of the inward-curved rear stiles, both characteristic features of the ancient Greek klismos. Phyfe's interpretation of this Regency form, of which these are two superlative examples, shows a firmness of line, proportional balance, and a pleasing economy of mass that makes them appear at once both elegant and robust. The carved "lyre bannisters," as they are described in the 1817 New York cabinetmakers' price book, are finely assembled sculptures consisting of two S-shaped yokes with waterleaf carving joined together with a tiny dowel at their base, a molded tailpiece, and a cross piece with ebony tightening keys, strung with ebony strings.[1] They are fussily constructed and fragile, yes, but perfectly framed and silhouetted symbols of Apollo's instrument of cosmic harmony.

These two chairs originally were part of a large set of as many as twenty-four that were among some of the objects sought after by early Phyfe connoisseurs. In 1909, they were lent by then owner Richard Townley Haines Halsey to the seminal Hudson-Fulton exhibition at the Metropolitan Museum of Art, where they were displayed in a special section dedicated to Phyfe's work drawn solely from Halsey's sizeable collection.[2] At a later date, ten additional chairs from the set were recovered from Mrs. Robert Gardner, a Livingston family descendant, and three more were gathered from different places and acquired by the noted Phyfe collector Louis Guerineau Myers (1874–1932).[3]

There were multiple options available to a patron ordering a set of klismos side chairs from Phyfe or other New York makers. In addition to lyre backs, a variety of other optional patterns are shown in plate 6 of *The New-York Book of Prices for Manufacturing Cabinet and Chair Work* (1817), including harp and ogee cross bannisters and a simple stay rail with a center ellipse flanked by carved Prince of Wales feathers. Saber-shaped front legs could be ornamented with a diminishing bead molding down the fronts, or carved in the shape of dog or lion's-paw feet with or without a hairy shank above. The narrow rectangular reserve above the hairy shanks might be ordered with carved waterleaves, or as was more common and seen on these chairs, a panel of fancy veneer. Phyfe, in particular, favored the use of a horizontal striped or fiddle-back pattern in this location as well as, on occasion, a veneered crest rail, though these more often have a crotch figure as on the Schrimsher chairs. The two known documented sets of klismos chairs made in the Phyfe shop in 1816 have the combination of veneered crest rails and carved saber legs.[4]

1. *The New-York Book of Prices for Manufacturing Cabinet and Chair Work* (New York, 1817), 107.
2. Three lyre-back side chairs from the collection of R. T. Haines Halsey, including the two Schrimsher chairs, are described, and one is illustrated, in Wilhelm Reinhold Valentiner, Henry Watson Kent, and Florence Nightingale Levy, *The Hudson-Fulton Celebration. Catalogue of an exhibition held in the Metropolitan Museum of Art commemorative of the tercentenary of the discovery of the Hudson River by Henry Hudson in the year 1609, and the centenary of the first use of steam in the navigation of said river by Robert Fulton in the year 1807 . . . New York, September to November, MCMIX* (New York: Metropolitan Museum of Art, 1909), 76, cat. 219, illustration facing p. 74.
3. Nancy V. McClelland, *Duncan Phyfe and the English Regency, 1795–1830* (New York: Dover Publications, 1939), 279–80. Sets of chairs were often sold in multiples of twelve. Two of these thirteen chairs, then in the collection of Mr. and Mrs. Andrew Varick Stout, are illustrated in *Duncan Phyfe and the English Regency*, where it is mentioned that one chair from the set is marked "XXIII," hence the belief that there originally were twenty-four chairs in the set. The partial set of thirteen chairs assembled by Louis Guerineau Myers is now in the collections of the American Wing at the Metropolitan Museum of Art, New York (65.188.2–.14).
4. Peter M. Kenny, Michael K. Brown, Frances F. Bretter, and Matthew A. Thurlow, *Duncan Phyfe: Master Cabinetmaker in New York* (New York: Metropolitan Museum of Art, 2011), 184–90, pls. 17 and 20.

27

Sofa, about 1820

Unknown maker
New York
Mahogany, mahogany veneer, painted and gilded ash; tulip poplar, white pine, mahogany; *vert antique*, gilding, replacement upholstery
37 × 98 × 25 in.

PROVENANCE: Mr. and Mrs. Edward Stone. Private Collection. Private Collection, Long Island, NY. With Hirschl & Adler Galleries, New York; The Westervelt Company, Tuscaloosa, AL; Sale, Christie's, New York, Sept. 25, 2013, lot 109; Purchased by Schrimshers, 2013.

Grecian sofas with integral, full-length dolphins of mahogany or painted and gilded ash forming their scrolled ends are iconic and have come to epitomize the sculptural dynamism of New York Classical furniture. Over a dozen of these sofas are known, with some design variations among them: yoked or scrolled crest rails as opposed to cylindrical ones, dolphin tails that flare outward instead of scrolling inward, and dolphin heads with a mouthful of vicious pointed teeth like the frightening *ketos* sea monster of the Perseus and Andromeda myth, as opposed to the more common snub-nosed variety seen here. All of these sofas relate closely enough in form and construction, however, for them to have been the specialty of a single shop. Despite the fact that these dolphin sofas have been known and published for more than sixty years now, furniture historians have yet to venture even an educated opinion as to their authorship. Charles-Honoré Lannuier and the cabinetmaking firm of Barzilia Deming and Erastus Bulkley are both documented as utilizing full-length, sculptural dolphins in their work, but one would never mistake them for the snub-nosed and heavily toothed variety used on these sofas. There are a number of Grecian sofas and couches with smaller gilded and bronzed dolphins mounted to the face of their fulcrum-like ends, some of which can confidently be attributed to the Phyfe shop. Again, however, these dolphins with their prominent duckbill-like snouts are nothing like the writhing sea creatures on the more dramatic examples. In 1818, a large consignment of furniture by cabinetmaker J. L. Everitt of New York was advertised for sale at the Charleston Auction Establishment, including "elegantly gilt" pier tables with marble tops, card tables "on new constructions," and "Grecian and Plain Dolphin Sofas."[1] Unfortunately, none of the sofas with these writhing, full-length dolphins have recovery histories in Charleston families.

On four of the dolphin sofas, including the Schrimsher example, inward-facing carved eagles flanking the crest rails rise phoenix-like up and out of the corners of the backs.[2] This design may have been inspired by Thomas Sheraton's *The Cabinet Dictionary* (London, 1803), plate 45, which depicts a drawing-room curule chair with similarly positioned eagles at the back (fig. 27.1). Another possible source may be plate 31 from the third edition of Thomas Chippendale's *The Gentleman and Cabinet-Maker's Director* (3rd ed., London, 1762), the original preparatory drawing for which is shown here (fig. 27.2). The influence of earlier eighteenth-century French and English sources on early-nineteenth-century New York Classical furniture has been suggested by Richard H. Randall Jr., who cites French architect Jacques-François Blondel's (1705–1774) engraving of a sphinx in his *De la distribution des maisons de plaisance* (Paris, 1737–38) as a direct source for a rosewood cellarette with gilded and bronzed crouched sphinxes supporting an ogee-shaped bottle case in the collection of the Yale University Art Gallery.[3]

Fig. 27.1. Thomas Sheraton, "Drawing Chairs," detail of plate 45 in *The Cabinet Dictionary* (London, 1803), engraving (Courtesy Winterthur Museum, Garden & Library)

Fig. 27.2. Thomas Chippendale, "Preparatory Drawing of a Sofa," 1760, published in reverse as plate 31 in *The Gentleman and Cabinet-Maker's Director* (3rd ed., London, 1762), pen and brown and black ink, brush and gray wash, Metropolitan Museum of Art, New York, Rogers Fund, 1920, 20.40.1(9) (Courtesy Metropolitan Museum of Art / Art Resource, NY)

1. *Charleston Courier*, December 28, 1818. The author thanks Maurie D. McInnis for this reference.
2. In addition to the present example, other dolphin sofas with flanking eagles are at the Chrysler Museum, Norfolk, Virginia, 71.407; Fort Hill, the home of John C. Calhoun, on the campus of Clemson University, Clemson, South Carolina; and a third, current location unknown, sold at Christie's, New York, January 20, 2017, lot 693.
3. Richard H. Randall Jr., "Sources of the Empire Style," *The Magazine Antiques* 83, no. 4 (April 1963): 452–53.

28

Pair of Card Tables, 1815–1825

Possibly by Michael Allison (1773–1855)
New York
Satinwood and mahogany veneer, ebony inlay, ebonized maple and mahogany; mahogany, white pine, maple; brass
29 × 36 × 17¾ in.

PROVENANCE: Estate of Elizabeth J. Shaw Benz, New York; Sale, Sotheby's, New York, Jun. 23–24, 1994, lot 461. With Leigh Keno Inc., New York, 1995. Westervelt Company, Tuscaloosa, AL; Sale, Christie's, New York, Sept. 5, 2013, lot 119; Purchased by Schrimshers, 2013.

Although a fairly common New York type of card table with a swivel top, canted corners, turned columnar supports, and a plinth with lion's-paw feet, these New York examples stand out among their peers for their brilliant interplay of russet-blonde satinwood veneers with ebony and light-wood inlays of Vitruvian scrolls, eight-pointed stars, and a Greek anthemion with flanking vines and tendrils. Inventiveness such as this is hardly unusual for the makers of American Classical furniture, who had at their disposal an immense store of antique ornaments to inspire novel interpretations of standard vernacular forms, transforming them into visually arresting objects such as this.

Fig. 28.1. *Chair*, unknown maker, after a design published by Thomas Hope (1769–1831), 1802–1810, mahogany, ebony, beech, and leather upholstery, Art Institute of Chicago, Robert Allen Purchase, Mary Waller Langhorne Memorial, and John and Neville Bryan Funds, 2009.127 (Courtesy The Art Institute of Chicago / Art Resource, NY)

Thomas Hope recommended the decorative use of brass-and-ebony or ebonized-wood inlays in furniture, stating, "These species of inlaying in metal, on a ground of ebony or dyed wood, seem peculiarly adapted to the nature of the mahogany furniture so much in use in this country, which they enliven, without preventing it, by any raised ornaments, from being constantly rubbed, and kept free from dust and dirt."[1] These comments referred specifically to illustrations of two Grecian side chairs he designed for his home at 10 Duchess Street in London (see p. 27). A chair after the Hope design, inlaid in ebony with an ancient Greek kithara, anthemia, stars, and a Greek key is in the collection of the Art Institute of Chicago (fig. 28.1).

Hope's elite method of ornamentation, a technique he notes was carried out to perfection in Paris, became more common in the hands of British manufacturers. In 1814, Venetian blind maker and brass founder James Barron (active 1805–1839) issued a catalogue of furniture ornaments and hardware available to cabinetmakers and upholsterers at his London and Birmingham locations. Included among his offerings were "highly polished" brass and wood ornaments "for inlaying in hard wood, either saw pierced or pressed."[2] Among these ornaments were a variety of stars with circular centers, including an eight-point star (fig. 28.2). Other specialist inlay makers, either by hand sawing or the use of a type of reciprocating scroll saw, made solid ebony inlays and Boulle work panels of ebony and light-wood for the use of cabinetmakers. The inlays on this card table are so precisely cut that it seems fairly certain it was the work of a specialist. The general dearth of Classical furniture from New York inlaid with ebony, or ebony and light-wood, suggests that it was not particularly popular there—even though polished brass-and-wood

Fig. 28.2. James Barron, "In Brass. In Hard Wood," in *Modern and Elegant Designs of Cabinet and Upholstery Furniture* (London, 1814), engraving (Courtesy Winterthur Museum, Garden & Library)

inlay surely was—and that this type of ornament, rather than being locally made, was imported on a limited basis or purchased abroad by a patron and supplied to the cabinetmaker responsible for this card table and its mate as part of a custom order. Although the identity of this New York cabinetmaker remains uncertain, this pair of card tables displays some design features that point to Michael Allison as a possible candidate: exceptionally heavy, high-knuckled feet with pronounced reserves carved around the claws, legs that terminate in a volute under the plinth, and tightly bunched compressed turnings under the uppermost balusters on the support columns. A similar design approach is apparent on a Pembroke table bearing an Allison trade label dated 1817 in the collection of the Metropolitan Museum of Art.[3]

1. Thomas Hope, *Household Furniture and Interior Decoration* (London: Longman, Hurst, Rees, and Orme, 1807), 35, pl. 24.
2. James Barron, *Modern and Elegant Designs of Cabinet and Upholstery Furniture* (London, 1814).
3. The Michael Allison Pembroke table in the collection of the Metropolitan Museum of Art (48.100) is illustrated in Peter M. Kenny, Michael K. Brown, Frances F. Bretter, and Matthew A. Thurlow, *Duncan Phyfe: Master Cabinetmaker in New York* (New York: Metropolitan Museum of Art, 2011), 80, fig. 82.

29

French Secretary, c. 1825

Attributed to Duncan Phyfe (1770–1854)
New York
Rosewood and tulipwood veneer, mahogany, mahogany with rosewood graining; mahogany, white pine; looking-glass plate, gilded brass, marble, leather
60 × 39 × 19¾ in.

INSCRIPTION: Stamped twice on edge of brass and steel lock: "PATENT."

PROVENANCE: With Hirschl & Adler Galleries, New York; Westervelt Company, Tuscaloosa, AL; Sale, Christie's, New York, Sept. 25, 2013, lot 144; Purchased by Schrimshers, 2013.

Elegant and compact with a gorgeous array of inlaid and applied gilded brass ornaments, this *secrétaire à abattant* or French secretary is among the purest of French forms made in New York. (In the 1834 *New-York Book for Manufacturing Cabinet and Chair-Work*, the form is called a French secretary.[1]) Richly ornamented rosewood examples such as this made before 1830 are relatively rare, with fewer than half a dozen known. All are attributed to Duncan Phyfe based on their precise workmanship, the use of die-stamped brass borders and line inlay, and the style of their carved feet: either lion's paws with acanthus leaves that spring upward from a crease at the base of the toes (as seen on a suite of rosewood furniture made by Phyfe for Robert Donaldson Jr. (1800–1872) of Fayetteville, North Carolina, and New York between 1822 and about 1826), or a round, ribbed, melon-shaped foot surmounted by an egg-and-dart collar. From the documented Donaldson furniture we are able to identify another trademark of Phyfe's richly ornamented Classical furniture: a wider than average brass line inlay on either side of the die-stamped brass inlay as seen on the fall front on the present example (see p. 92, fig. 6).[2]

Fig. 29.1. View of cat. 29 with the fall front open

Despite its strong architectural presence, this secretary stands a mere five feet tall. It presents best when the fall front is down, revealing its leather-lined writing surface and handsomely arranged interior enriched with *ormolu* appliqués and capitals and bases on the columns flanking a proscenium-like central opening (fig. 29.1). Placed at the back and sides of this opening are looking-glass plates that served the purpose of reflecting perhaps a fine silver and cut-glass inkstand, *objets d'art*, or a small sculpture meant to be appreciated in the round. All of the brass-inlaid rosewood secretaries have these mirrored openings on the inside. This type of interior—rather than one with pigeon holes for letters or receipts and tall, narrow slots for account books found on some New York examples—suggests a more culturally sophisticated use as collectors' cabinets, whose contents were stored and displayed for the private enjoyment of their owners or a small number of intimates in a library, lady's drawing room, or boudoir. Richly ornamented rosewood examples such as these clearly were a cut above average and were purchased at a premium cost.

Phyfe continued to make exquisite versions of this form in his most up-to-date Grecian Plain style, based on French *Restauration* furniture design. An extremely fine example in this style attributed to Duncan Phyfe, D. Phyfe & Sons, or D. Phyfe & Son (later iterations of the cabinetmaking firm) has the same type of mirrored proscenium in the interior as the examples from the 1820s and also shares their precise workmanship and superb proportions. Instead of *ormolu* and inlaid brass in exotic rosewood, however, it achieves the same jewel-like quality through the exclusive use of exquisitely figured crotch mahogany veneers, perfectly matched to the scale of its component parts.[3] With Phyfe, it seems, the richness of the materials used on the exteriors of these French secretaries telegraphed a purpose beyond a mere place to write and store correspondence and business records.

1. Peter M. Kenny, Michael K. Brown, Frances F. Bretter, and Matthew A. Thurlow, *Duncan Phyfe: Master Cabinetmaker in New York* (New York: Metropolitan Museum of Art, 2011), 214n3.
2. For the Donaldson suite, see ibid., 208–13.
3. Ibid., 231, pl. 45. *Secrétaire à abbattant*, 1835–47, Metropolitan Museum of Art, New York (1983.225).

30

Console or Side Table, 1810–1815

Charles-Honoré Lannuier (1779–1819)
New York
Rosewood veneer, mahogany, ash; white pine, mahogany, tulip poplar; *vert antique*, gilding, brass, marble
35¼ × 40½ × 21 in.

INSCRIPTIONS: Stamped twice: "H. Lannuier New York"; inscribed in period cursive script on the underside of the original marble top: "*Patterson* B. [. . .]" (See Appendix II)

LABEL: Printed paper label: "HONORÉ LANNIUER / CABINET MAKER, / (FROM PARIS), 'Keeps his Ware-house and Manufactory / AND CABINET WARE OF THE / NEWEST FASHION, / AT No. 60 BROAD STREET, / HONORÉ LANNUIER / EBENISTE / (DE PARIS) / LIENT SON MAGASIN / DE MEUBLES, LES PLUS / A-LA-MODE, / BROAD STREET No. 60 / NEW-YORK." (See Appendix II)

PROVENANCE: Private Collection; Sale, Sotheby's, New York, Jan. 8, 2021, lot 116; Purchased by Schrimshers, 2021.

Open, lightweight, and highly sculptural, this labeled console or side table by immigrant French *ébéniste* Charles-Honoré Lannuier at once also radiates the richness and monumentality of *le goût antique* as promulgated in the pages of Charles Percier and Pierre-François-Léonard Fontaine's *Recueil de décorations intérieures* (Paris, 1801–1812). The hocked lion's paws, identical to those used on multiple examples of Lannuier's winged-caryatid card tables, firmly ground a trestle base replete with carving, gilding, *vert antique*, and applied ornaments on nearly every available surface.[1] Even the white statuary-marble top was taken into consideration in the overall composition by making it thinner than usual so the minimally constructed base was able to withstand its weight. Lannuier, who was consistently challenged to adapt his intimate understanding of *le goût antique* to American taste, opted in this instance to transform a standard New York lyre as shown in plate 5 of the 1817 *New-York Book of Prices for Manufacturing Cabinet and Chair Work* (fig. 30.1) using *vert antique* with bronzed highlights, enveloping the serpentine arms at the base with lush, gilded acanthus carving, and centering cast composition masks in painted reserves above the bridge (fig. 30.2). A mahogany console or side table of nearly identical form in a private collection, but likely by Phyfe, more clearly reveals its function as a side or serving table with two drawers in the front apron and a low cross stretcher set back from the center for the service of food or other refreshments.

Unique in Lannuier's documented oeuvre, this table has undergone a careful program of conservation to successfully recover its original scheme of burnished oil gilding, painted *vert antique*, and ebonized surfaces, as well a significant amount of restoration of its applied composition ornaments and *ormolu* appliqués. Replacements were based on physical evidence and precedent provided by other documented examples of the cabinetmaker's furniture. For instance, the cast composition masks at the tops of the lyres are copies of one on the crown of the labeled Lannuier French bedstead at the Bartow-Pell Mansion in the Bronx, New York. The *ormolu* wreaths on the front corners, missing when the table was acquired, were chosen as replacements because of their use on several tables that bear the same printed bilingual label on this example, used by Lannuier between about 1805 and roughly 1812–15.[2] The *ormolu* appliqué at the center of the apron depicts winged caryatids flanking a central urn and is unique in Lannuier's known work. The finished casting is slightly coarser than usual, which may indicate that it was re-cast from another early nineteenth-century example, possibly even in Lannuier's shop, or at a later date. Affixed in the traditional manner, it is the only appliqué ever attached to the table in this location.[3]

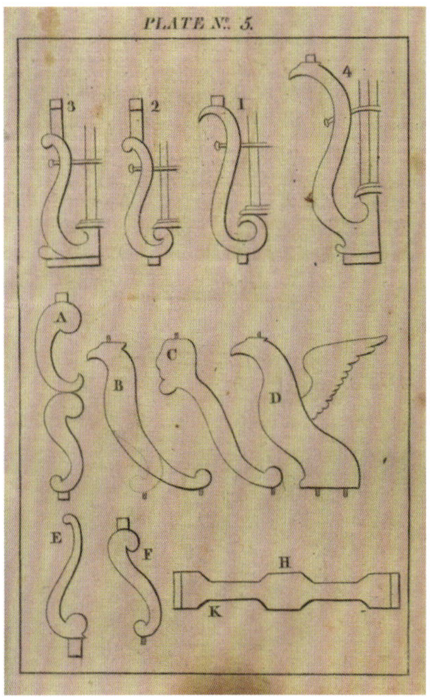

Fig. 30.1. Plate 5 in *The New-York Book of Prices for Manufacturing Cabinet and Chair Work* (New York, 1817), engraving, Metropolitan Museum of Art, Harris Brisbane Dick Fund, 1939 39.32.1 (Courtesy Metropolitan Museum of Art / Art Resource, NY). The large lyre at the top right (no. 4) represents the general outline used on the Lannuier console table.

Fig. 30.2. Detail of cat. 30 showing the richly ornamented lyre support

1. For winged-caryatid card tables by Lannuier with identical lion's-paw feet, see Peter M. Kenny, Frances F. Bretter, and Ulrich Leben, *Honoré Lannuier, Cabinetmaker from Paris: The Life and Work of a French Ébéniste in Federal New York* (New York: Metropolitan Museum of Art, 1998), cats. 66–67, 66–69, 80–82.
2. Honoré Lannuier, *French bedstead*, Bartow-Pell Mansion, Bronx, NY, 85.06.
3. A full conservation treatment report, including stratigraphy and scientific pigment analysis, is in the object file for this table at the Schrimsher Foundation.

31

French Bedstead, 1815–1820

Attributed to Duncan Phyfe (1770–1854)
New York
Mahogany, mahogany veneer; ash, white pine; *vert antique*, gilding, brass
49 × 55½ × 99 in.

PROVENANCE: Private collection, FL; Sale, Christie's, New York, Jan. 20, 2017, lot 695; Purchased by Schrimshers, 2017.

Mahogany bedsteads with turned and carved posts capped by gilded eagle heads were among the first pieces of furniture given the specific appellation "French" in the New York cabinetmakers' price books. A French bedstead appears for the first time in the 1810 *New-York Revised Prices for Manufacturing Cabinet and Chair Work.* In the new edition issued in 1817, two versions are listed: No.1 with straight front and rear posts as in the earlier model, and No. 2 with scrolled ogee ends, either plain scrolled or with carved eagle heads and a rectangular lower frame supported by winged lion's-paw feet, as on the present example.[1] What defined these bedsteads as French for New York cabinetmakers and their patrons is the fact that they were designed to be placed laterally against a wall with elaborate French-style bed curtains suspended from a canopy that was supported either by two upward-sweeping arms set into taller back posts, or else hung from a simple hook in the ceiling above the bed. With its ogee-scrolled ends front and back, which have the finer and more expensive feature of similarly shaped ogee end panels, one would suspect this French bedstead to have been dressed in the latter fashion.

Fig. 31.1. Detail of cat. 31 showing the *vert antique* and gilded treatment of the foot with ogee scrolls

Charles-Honoré Lannuier likely introduced these French bedsteads with carved and gilded eagle heads to New York. Two early examples by him are known: one is apparently a collaborative effort by Lannuier and his first cousin, Jean-Charles Cochois (1776–after 1808), a Parisian *ébéniste* who may have come to New York as early as 1804 and returned to France in the fall of 1808; the other is stamped four times by Lannuier and dates to about 1810 or possibly even a little earlier. Neither of these French bedsteads have the tall back posts that would have supported the upswept arms with a fixed canopy. Instead, like the present example, they may originally have been dressed with elaborate, fringed silk curtains suspended from a circular gilded, stamped brass crown or other upholsterer's device mounted to a hook in the ceiling. A rare invoice from upholsterer Peter Turcot (active c. 1807–1822) offers tantalizing hints of what one of these decorator's confections might have looked like. Dated June 22, 1816, and issued to dry goods merchant James L. Brinkerhoff (1791–1846) of New York, it lists charges of $16.00 for "Making 2 fancy Bed curtains"; $25.00 for "20 yds. fringe"; and an additional $25.00 for "a Large Eagle & Dart."[2]

A Phyfe attribution for this French bedstead is based on the design and execution of its gilded and bronzed lion's-paw feet (fig. 31.1), which are virtually identical to the feet on a Grecian sofa documented in a receipted invoice from Duncan Phyfe to this same Brinkerhoff, dated October 26, 1816.[3] In addition, the heads of the eagles on the tops of the ogee-scrolled ends share their distinctive smooth brows with those on the griffin tables also attributed to Phyfe (see cat. 20).

1. *The New-York Revised Prices for Manufacturing Cabinet and Chair Work* (New York: Southwick and Pelsue, 1810), 55, 96–97.
2. The Lannuier French bedsteads with carved eagles on their ends are illustrated and discussed in Peter M. Kenny, Frances F. Bretter, and Ulrich Leben, *Honoré Lannuier, Cabinetmaker from Paris: The Life and Work of a French Ébéniste in Federal New York* (New York: Metropolitan Museum of Art, 1998), 88, pl. 40, and 198, cat. 3; 48, pl. 14, and 199, cat. 4. The Peter Turcot invoice is illustrated on p. 121.
3. The Brinkerhoff Grecian receipted invoice is illustrated in Peter M. Kenny, Michael K. Brown, Frances F. Bretter, and Matthew A. Thurlow, *Duncan Phyfe: Master Cabinetmaker in New York* (New York: Metropolitan Museum of Art, 2011), 276, appendix I.5; the Grecian sofa and a detailed image of one of its lion's-paw feet are shown in plate 18 (p. 185), and figure 84 (p. 81).

32

Center Table, c. 1825

Attributed to Duncan Phyfe (1770–1854)
New York
Rosewood-grained curly maple and mahogany veneer, mahogany, white pine; white pine, tulip poplar, cherry; marble, *vert antique*, stenciled and freehand gilding
30 × 34 in. (diam.)

PROVENANCE: With Carswell Rush Berlin, Inc., New York by 2020; Purchased by Schrimshers, 2020.

Sumptuous and visually arresting, this marble-topped center table is a tour de force of faux-grained rosewood and stenciled and freehand-gilded decoration. It belongs to a small group of five rosewood center tables produced during the 1820s that can now be firmly attributed to the Phyfe workshop based on the discovery of a brass-inlaid example at Winterthur Museum, Garden & Library documented by an invoice from Phyfe dated August 21, 1822. Though slightly varied in design, all five tables share the same tripod pedestal base with a single column rising from a bud-like nest of gilded acanthus and lotus leaves, with a stepped lotus-leaf collar below. The gilded and *vert antique* lion's-paw feet with recessed brass casters are also highly distinctive and feature flared acanthus leaves that engage each spoke or leg of the plinth and lively foliate scrolls extending to the back as brackets (fig. 32.1).[1]

Fig. 32.1. Detail of cat. 32 showing the carved lion's-paw foot associated with the Phyfe shop, and the stenciled and freehand-gilded anthemion and lotus-leaf meander on the plinth

This center table is singular among its fellow Phyfe examples in its faux-grained finish rather than actual rosewood veneers. Even more unusual, this faux graining is applied on curly maple veneer, creating an iridescent effect that enhances the illusion that it is made of the most exquisite and exotic cuts of this costly imported Brazilian hardwood. Adding to the table's striking appearance is the stenciled and freehand-gilded decoration on the apron, column, and plinth, an expertly rendered combination of anthemia, lotus leaves, bellflowers, pinecone-tipped thyrsi, and scallop shells centering scrolled acanthus foliage (see p. 93, fig. 8), and separated by dies with eagle-headed kitharas on the apron.

The scallop shell is uncommon as an ornament in stenciled and freehand-gilded New York furniture. It can be seen as a carved ornament on Boston looking glasses and wall clock cases (see cat. 18). An ancient symbol associated with female deities, first of all Aphrodite, it was revived by Renaissance artists, most famously Sandro Botticelli in *Birth of Venus* (1485–86), and used extensively by architects and artisans into the Baroque period. Scallop shells like those on this center table remind us that Renaissance and Baroque prototypes may have provided as much inspiration as actual antique sources for furniture makers and the painters, carvers, and gilders they employed for decorative work.

1. The documented Phyfe center table is illustrated and discussed in Peter M. Kenny, Michael K. Brown, Frances F. Bretter, and Matthew A. Thurlow, *Duncan Phyfe: Master Cabinetmaker in New York* (New York: Metropolitan Museum of Art, 2011), 208, 210, pl. 32. The other Phyfe-attributed center tables include a magnificent example with a painted scagliola top in the collection of the Museum of the City of New York: see ibid., 220–21, pl. 40; one at Edgewater in Barrytown, New York, which has a replaced black-and-gold Egyptian marble top: see Richard Hampton Jenrette, *Adventures with Old Houses* (Charleston, SC: Wyrick & Co., 2000), 92, 93, 99; one at Vizcaya Museum and Gardens, Miami, Florida; and one with a brass-inlaid wooden top in the Platt-Cady Mansion, Fort Ticonderoga, New York. The author would like to thank Carswell Rush Berlin for bringing the center table at Vizcaya to my attention and Matthew A. Thurlow for the one at the Platt-Cady Mansion.

33

Pair of Side Chairs, c. 1825

Unknown maker
New York
Ebonized and bronzed hard maple; gilding, replacement chair caning
31⅝ × 18⅜ × 21¼ in.

INSCRIPTIONS: Stamped on the inside of the front seat rail: "VII" on one chair and "IX" on the other.

PROVENANCE: With Hirschl & Adler Galleries, New York, by 2021; Purchased by Schrimshers, 2021.

These sleek, sophisticated ebony and gold chairs are masterpieces of the New York chairmaker's, painter's, and gilder's art. Made in the mid-1820s, they are characteristic of the New York klismos chair form, which by this date tended to have cross splats, as on the present examples, as opposed to the lyres and crossed ogee banisters of the 1810s (cat. 26). Their overall proportions and the delicacy of the carved hairy dog's-paw feet relate closely to the earlier models; however, the broader crest rails and slightly heavier side seat rails with scrolled ends and prominent turned paterae signal a later date and a bolder interpretation of the antique style.

The ebonized, gilded, and bronzed surfaces of these chairs are in a remarkable state of preservation, having lost only a hint of their original luster. Shaded with india ink and a *sgraffito* technique that exposes the ebonized surface below, the freehand-gilded decoration is exceptionally well rendered, especially the beautifully proportioned and framed ornaments in the crest rails. The carved cross splats of gilded cornucopia, linked by bunches of bronzed grapes and surmounted by what looks at first glance like a flying, winged rosette, add a satisfying gravity and mass to the overall design.

Fig. 33.1. *Armchairs*, Duncan Phyfe (1770–1854), 1825–1827, birch, gilding, mahogany, Museum of the City of New York, 36.110.2A_B-1A_B (Courtesy Museum of the City of New York)

A noteworthy feature of these side chairs, two of an original set of twelve, is the gilded waterleaf carving at the tops of the rear stiles. This feature links them to three other exceptional New York sets of the 1820s, including a set of ten side and two armchairs of plain carved mahogany from the collection of the late Richard Hampton Jenrette (1929–2018) at Edgewater in Barrytown, New York; two ebonized and gilded armchairs now at the Museum of the City of New York (fig. 33.1) that were part of a larger set made for cotton speculator, ship owner, and investor Stephen C. Whitney (1776–1830); and a set of twelve ebonized and gilded side chairs at the Morris-Jumel Mansion in upper Manhattan.[1] The chairs from all three of these sets have the same incurvate scrolled backs with waterleaf carving at the top but vary in that they have upholstered backs, and, on two sets, powerful, Egyptianizing hocked front legs with large paw feet. The Whitney set may have been made at the same time as a spectacular center table that has been firmly attributed to Duncan Phyfe. Therefore, the scholar-dealer who sold these chairs to the Schrimshers has speculated that the set of Whitney armchairs were also issued from the cabinetmaker's shop, and, by extension, these chairs as well. Given their formal relationship to the Whitney set and their superb quality, such an attribution is certainly plausible but lacks grounding in documented examples of Phyfe's work in this style.[2] Even Phyfe's wealthiest clients typically patronized multiple New York shops when outfitting their houses, as was the case with wealthy New Yorkers Thomas Cornell Pearsall (1768–1820) and William Bayard Jr. (1761–1826) who purchased furniture from both Phyfe and Lannuier between 1807 and about 1815.[3]

1. Two side chairs from the same set as the Schrimsher side chairs are at the Los Angeles County Museum of Art (M.2006.51.28a–b), two are in the collection of Winterthur Museum, Garden & Library, Winterthur, Delaware, and the remaining six are in private collections. The accession numbers for the set of ten side chairs and two armchairs at Edgewater are 1982.006.01–12. The accession numbers for the Stephen C. Whitney ebonized and gilded armchairs at the Museum of the City of New York are 36.110.1–2a–b; three additional armchairs from this set are in private collections. The accession numbers of the set of twelve ebonized and gilded side chairs at the Morris-Jumel Mansion are 1990.1.1–12a–b.
2. For the pair of Schrimsher side chairs, see Hirschl & Adler Galleries catalogue information sheet (FAPG 21204D.001–002).
3. Peter M. Kenny, Frances F. Bretter, and Ulrich Leben, *Honoré Lannuier, Cabinetmaker from Paris: The Life and Work of a French Ébéniste in Federal New York* (New York: Metropolitan Museum of Art, 1998), 103–20.

34

French Press, c. 1820

Unknown maker
New York
Mahogany, mahogany veneer; tulip poplar, white pine; brass
83 × 63¼ × 25 in.

PROVENANCE: With Carswell Rush Berlin, Inc., New York, by 2021; Purchased by Schrimshers, 2021.

Tall French presses (*armoires* as they are called in France) with double- and single-panel doors were first listed as a standard form in the New York journeyman cabinetmakers' price book of 1810.[1] As one might expect, several signed or firmly attributable examples by Charles-Honoré Lannuier are known. Other documented French presses by Michael Allison and Duncan Phyfe exist, as do numerous others whose makers, like the present example, remain unidentified. The highly figured mahogany and mahogany veneers are of exceptional quality and were carefully selected by the maker. Of particular note are the cross-banded and book-matched crotch mahogany veneers in the upper and lower door panels (note the extra inlaid panels at the bottom of the upper ones), the flame-grained veneers at the sides, and the choice of solid fiddle-back mahogany for the door frames, precisely mitered at the upper and lower corners.

More practical but no less eye-catching for a furniture devotee are the four circular stamped brasses that cover bed bolts used to join the paneled sides to the central cupboard section (fig. 34.1), and the original use of iron and brass casters attached to the bottoms of the carved lion's paws and turned stump feet at the rear on such a massive case piece. These bed bolts were part of an unusual knock-down structural system that allowed the French press to be compactly crated for shipment and assembly upon reaching its destination, a distinct advantage for New York cabinetmakers involved in the export of furniture in the coastal trade or to Southern clients. Whether being transported in the hold of a ship, or else just conveniently rolled away from the wall for cleaning in a bedroom, this handsome and practical piece of case furniture embodies the French and German words for furniture or moveable objects, *meubles* and *möbel*.

The overall design and construction of this French press prioritizes this need to pack the component parts as flat and compactly as possible, much like a piece of military campaign furniture. Its structural system can be read in the front facade: vertical breaks are clearly visible near the front corners of the plinth and the cornice frieze, where separate center rails are joined with mortises and tenons to the brass-inlaid stiles and drawn tight with the bed bolts. The knock-down construction is different at the back, where loose, bridle, or slot mortises and tenons join the top and bottom center rails to the stiles and are fixed in place, when assembled, with screws (fig. 34.2). The flat top with a rounded nosing and a flattened Grecian ovolo molding below is separate and constructed like a shallow tray set upside down atop the frieze. There is a removable partition that divides the center of the case with cleats attached to either side to support original loose shelves, only two of which survive.

1. *The New-York Revised Prices for Manufacturing Cabinet and Chair Work* (New York: Southwick and Pelsue, 1810), 13.

Fig. 34.1. Detail of cat. 34 showing stamped brass bed bolt covers. These covers are replacements for the originals.

Fig. 34.2. Back view of cat. 34

35a

Pair of Card Tables, 1815–1819

Attributed to Charles-Honoré Lannuier (1779–1819)
New York
Rosewood and mahogany veneer; mahogany, white pine, tulip poplar, maple, cherry; gilded gesso and *vert antique*, gilded cast brass, die-stamped brass inlays
30¼ × 36⅛ × 17⅞ in.

PROVENANCE: Marchese Giuseppe Paternò, Castello di San Giuliano, Florence and Sicily. Sale, Sotheby's, New York, Apr. 29–May 1, 1981, lot 1068. Gloria Peltz (b. 1935) and Richard (b. 1937) Manney, New York; with Leigh Keno American Antiques, New York. Marilyn Teagan (1934–2015) and John Francis (1931–2022) Keane, Boston, MA; Sale, Bonhams Skinner, Marlborough, MA, Nov. 19, 2021, lot 54; Purchased by Schrimshers, 2021.

No other collection of American furniture, public or private, can boast winged-caryatid card tables, arguably among the finest and most sculptural pieces of American Classical furniture, by the two leading cabinetmakers of New York. For many years, the last owner of the card table attributed here to Duncan Phyfe (cat. 35b), William N. Banks Jr., as well as some furniture scholars, believed it to be the work of the acknowledged master of the form, Charles-Honoré Lannuier.[1] Only since the focused research and discoveries surrounding a major exhibition at the Metropolitan Museum of Art on Lannuier's life and work in New York and a subsequent one on

35b

Card Table, c. 1820

Attributed to Duncan Phyfe (1770–1854)
New York
Rosewood, satinwood and mahogany veneer; mahogany, white pine, tulip poplar, maple, cherry, ebonized mahogany; gilded gesso and *vert antique,* gilded cast brass, inlaid brass stringing, die-stamped brass inlay, replacement wool baize
29¼ × 35¾ × 18 in.

PROVENANCE: Ravenel Family, Charleston, SC; By descent to the Frost family, Charleston, SC; By descent to the Pringle family, Charleston, SC; By descent to Oliver Pringle Brown, Newnan, GA; Purchased by her cousin, William N. Banks Jr. (1924–2019), Newnan, GA, in 1968–69; Sale, Brunk Auctions, Asheville, NC, Sept. 12, 2020, lot 35; Purchased by Schrimshers, 2020.

Phyfe are we now able to distinguish the figural furniture produced in the workshops of these two talented masters.[2]

If imitation is the sincerest form of flattery, then Phyfe was surely an admirer of Lannuier's winged-caryatid card tables, a design Lannuier developed and perfected by about 1815 with the aid, perhaps, of a fresh influx of French workmen who helped to define his sophisticated furniture manufactory in the years following the end of the War of 1812.[3] For inspiration Lannuier may have mined the pages of Charles Percier and Pierre-François-Léonard Fontaine's *Recueil de décorations intérieures* and Pierre

Fig. 35.1. Detail of cat. 35a (attributed to Lannuier) showing winged caryatid

Fig. 35.2. Detail of cat. 35b (attributed to Phyfe) showing winged caryatid

de La Mésangère's *Collection de meubles et objets de goût,* where numerous examples of fantastical mythical creatures such as these were illustrated. Percier and Fontaine referred to winged caryatids as *chimères ailées* or winged chimeras: wondrous, dream-like, even bizarre creatures composed of incongruous parts—a human female head, bird-like wings, and vegetation in the form of acanthus and lotus leaves.[4]

Aside from the disparate lower sections on these Lannuier- and Phyfe-attributed card tables—dolphins versus hocked lion's-paw feet, and plinths with canted versus circular corners—they are remarkably similar in their overall design. Both employ exotic rosewood veneers, die-stamped brass inlays, applied *ormolu* appliqués centering their front aprons, and candelabrum-form gilded and *vert antique* rear supports. It is in the execution of their winged caryatids, however, that the two tables diverge: Lannuier's figure displays a cool, almost abstract quality in keeping with the precepts of Neoclassicism (fig. 35.1), while Phyfe's, with its tousled wing feathers and rather disagreeable countenance (fig. 35.2), seems to more fully embrace the bizarre suggested by Percier and Fontaine. The Phyfe winged figure also lacks the subtlety and finesse of Lannuier's interpretation. Note the small, nick-like cuts all over the wings intended to add definition and texture to the feathers (see p. 291). Those in the outermost tier below the wing tips are of particular note and appear *de minimis* and amateurish compared to the delicate, carefully modeled ones on the Lannuier figure, achieved through the careful re-cutting of the gesso layer underneath the gilding.[5] There is little question as to who was following whom in the manufacture of these tables. Twenty winged-caryatid card tables either labeled, stamped, or otherwise firmly attributed to Lannuier are known, including this rare pair with dolphin feet rather than lion's paws.[6] Only five can confidently be attributed to Phyfe.[7] The ratio of surviving caryatid card tables by Lannuier compared to Phyfe, who had a larger operation and worked through the late 1810s and 1820s when antique sculptural forms such as these were *de rigueur*, would seem to tell the story: this was Lannuier's autograph model, which Phyfe poached—conceivably, but far from certainly—in order to fill the void left by Lannuier's untimely death in 1819. Phyfe's true *métier*, on the other hand, was his bold antique-style griffins (see cat. 20), which Lannuier, as far as we know, neither imitated nor tried to adapt to his work.

Even though Lannuier employed his winged caryatids on other table forms, including marble-topped pier tables where they graced each of the front corners, and an extraordinary center table or *guéridon* with four such supports evenly spaced under the circular apron, Phyfe seemed less inclined to use them as table supports. Only two sofa tables most likely made in his shop have winged caryatids on each side of their center sections.[8]

1. For attributions of cat. 35b to Lannuier, see Jonathan L. Fairbanks and Elizabeth Biddle Bates, *American Furniture 1620 to the Present* (New York: Richard Marek Publishers, 1981), 266, and Maurie D. McInnis and Robert A. Leath, "Beautiful Specimens, Elegant Patterns: New York Furniture for the Charleston Market," in *American Furniture 1996*, ed. Luke Beckerdite (Milwaukee: Chipstone Foundation, 1996), fig. 10.
2. For our evolving understanding of Lannuier and Phyfe's figural tables, see Peter M. Kenny, Frances F. Bretter, and Ulrich Leben, *Honoré Lannuier, Cabinetmaker from Paris: The Life and Work of a French Ébéniste in Federal New York* (New York: Metropolitan Museum of Art, 1998), 91–97, and Peter M. Kenny, Michael K. Brown, Frances F. Bretter, and Matthew A. Thurlow, *Duncan Phyfe: Master Cabinetmaker in New York* (New York: Metropolitan Museum of Art, 2011), 84–85, 204–7.
3. In May 1816, the partnership of A. Frichot & Lannuier at No. 60 Broad Street was announced in the *New-York Gazette & General Advertiser*. A. Frichot is probably the Parisian *ébéniste* Pierre-Aurore Frichot (1785–1867). Another French *ébéniste* who worked in Lannuier's shop was John Gruez, who fashioned himself as "*EBENISTE DE PARIS*" and "*Successeur d' H. LANNUIER*" in his trade label published in *Longworth's Directory* in 1821. He also advertised in 1819, shortly after Lannuier's death, that he had "taken the establishment of the late Mr. Lannuier" and that he had "for several years superintended the interior part of Mr. Lannuier's business." Kenny et al., *Honoré Lannuier*, 42, 51–52.
4. Charles Percier and Pierre-François-Léonard Fontaine, *Recueil de décorations intérieures* (Paris, 1801–12), 33, plate XXXIX.
5. On the Lannuier caryatid a reddish-brown bole or clay was applied on the areas where the gold was brightly burnished: the top shoulder feathers, the volutes on the wing tips and the fillets that extend back from these to the inner wing feathers, and the filets and stars on the mid-band. The non-burnished areas on the Lannuier caryatid were either water or oil gilded directly on the gesso layer. Evidence discovered by Christine Thomson during the conservation of the Phyfe-attributed caryatid card table indicated that no bole was used originally on the winged figure and hence there were no brightly burnished gilded highlights to contrast with the matte oil gilded surface. The pair of Lannuier-attributed caryatid card tables underwent extensive restoration after they were purchased by Marilyn and John Keane (see provenance). This work was undertaken by R. Wayne Reynolds who used as his guide for re-gilding the winged figures on a pair of card tables attributed to Lannuier in the American Wing at the Metropolitan Museum of Art (1995.377.1–2) that survived in remarkable original condition and had been extensively analyzed for the gilding technique used on Lannuier caryatids such as these. A summary of these findings is given in Kenny et al., *Honoré Lannuier*, 188. The winged figure on the Phyfe-attributed caryatid card table has also undergone extensive restoration of its gilded surface. Conservation treatment reports for the Phyfe- and Lannuier-attributed card tables are in the collection files of the Schrimsher Foundation.
6. In addition to this pair of card tables (cat. 35a), the only other documented and attributed Lannuier furniture with dolphin feet include three pier tables, a center table, and a French bedstead. For images and a discussion of this furniture, see Kenny et al., *Honoré Lannuier*, cats. 5, 108, 109, 112, 115.
7. Nineteen of Lannuier's winged-caryatid card tables are illustrated and discussed in Kenny et al., *Honoré Lannuier*, cats. 66–84. For an image of the twentieth table, see Peter M. Kenny, "Opulence Abroad: Charles-Honoré Lannuier's Gilded Furniture in Trinidad de Cuba," in *American Furniture 2004*, ed. Luke Bekerdite (Milwaukee: Chipstone Foundation, 2004), fig. 10. The mate to this Phyfe-attributed caryatid card table is still in the possession of descendants of its original owner in Charleston, South Carolina. Another pair was sold at Christie's, New York, Sept. 25, 2013, lot 101. One of this pair is illustrated and discussed in Kenny et al., *Duncan Phyfe*, 85. A fifth example, once owned by Jacqueline Kennedy Onassis, is illustrated in Lorraine Waxman Pearce, "Lannuier in the President's House," *The Magazine Antiques* 81, no. 5 (May 1962): fig. 5. A related Phyfe-attributed card table with winged caryatids at the front corners and harps mounted on their backs is illustrated and discussed in Kenny et al., *Duncan Phyfe*, 206–7, pl. 31.
8. One sofa table is in the collection of the White House Historical Association; the other is at the Bayou Bend Collection and Gardens, Museum of Fine Arts, Houston (B.71.206).

36a

French Sideboard, 1815–1825

Attributed to Duncan Phyfe (1770–1854)
New York
Mahogany, mahogany veneer; white pine, tulip poplar; gilding, *vert antique*, brass
51½ × 76⅜ × 23¾ in.

LABEL: Printed paper label: "KNITTLE COLLECTION / Auctioned / Nov. 1962. 4."

36b

Cellarette, 1820–1825

Attributed to Duncan Phyfe (1770–1854)
New York
Mahogany, mahogany veneer; white pine, tulip poplar; gilding, *vert antique*, brass
24 × 24½ × 19¾ in.

LABEL: Printed paper label: "KNITTLE COLLECTION / Auctioned / Nov. 1962. 4."

PROVENANCE (36a and 36b): Rhea Mansfield (1883–1955) and Earl (1883–1962) Knittle, Ashland, OH; Their sale, Garth's Auctions, Delaware, OH, Nov. 1962. Sale, Sotheby's, New York, Sept. 27, 2012, lot 215; Dr. Larry McAllister (1925–2021), Muncie, IN; Sale, Sotheby's, New York, Sept. 22, 2022, lot 197; Purchased by Schrimshers, 2022.

Massive sideboards with open center sections and matching cellarettes containing the bottles of wine served at the table became essential pieces of furniture for the most fashionable American dining rooms in the period between 1815 and 1840. This monumental French sideboard and sarcophagus-shaped cellarette can both be confidently attributed to Duncan Phyfe. The sideboard is virtually identical in form, dimensions, veneer selection, and the style of its carved lion's-paw feet to one that once belonged to Phyfe. It varies only in its use of Roman Doric columns with *ormolu* capitals and bases instead of Ionic columns with carved and turned mahogany capitals and bases, and the front of its plinth is flat and veneered as opposed to the recessed veneered panel between two flat fillets on the Phyfe family example.[1] It seems unlikely they were originally made *en suite* due to the markedly different design of their lion's-paw and acanthus carved feet; on the sideboard they drape downward (fig. 36.1), whereas on the cellarette, gilded acanthus leaves spring upward from a crease behind the toes (fig. 36.2). Both styles of lion's-paw and acanthus feet are found on documented and attributed case furniture from the Phyfe shop, but the model with upward-springing acanthus appears to be the later of the two, coming into use about 1820 or slightly earlier.

The person for whom this furniture was originally made remains shrouded in the mists of time. The history of ownership in the early to mid-twentieth century, however, is quite interesting and suggests a way these functionally related but disparate pieces of furniture may have been brought together. Their earliest known owners were Earl and Rhea Mansfield Knittle, collectors and dealers of early American antiques who lived and worked in Ashland, Ohio, for most of their lives.[2] The Knittles moved to New York City for a brief period in 1909, the same year as the *Hudson-Fulton Celebration*, a ground-breaking display of American fine and decorative arts, was mounted at the Metropolitan Museum of Art.[3] Included in the exhibition was an entire section dedicated to the work of Duncan Phyfe. With their shared interest in American antiques and a family connection to Henry V. Weil, an antiques dealer in New York, it would not be surprising if it were here that the Knittles first encountered furniture by Phyfe and in his iconic style. They also most likely kept up with current scholarship on American decorative arts, including perhaps Thomas Hamilton Ormsbee's 1930 publication *Early American Furniture Makers: A Social and Biographical Study*, in which the matching Phyfe family sideboard and cellarette were illustrated for the first time.[4] Whether the Knittles, armed with this knowledge, embarked at some point on assembling an *en suite* Classical Phyfe sideboard and cellarette of their own, or else acquired them from another enterprising dealer with the same goal in mind, perhaps the aforementioned Weil, unfortunately remains an unanswerable question. A coat of modern green paint has been applied to the feet of both the sideboard and cellarette, which appears to cover earlier and possibly original layers of *vert antique* applied to the feet in order to imitate ancient excavated bronze. While intended to refresh worn and degraded surfaces, these matching layers of green paint on the feet also quite handily served the purpose of bringing these stylistic cognates into closer harmony still.

1. The Phyfe family sideboard and its *en suite* cellarette are illustrated and discussed in Peter M. Kenny, Michael K. Brown, Frances F. Bretter, and Matthew A. Thurlow, *Duncan Phyfe: Master Cabinetmaker in New York* (New York: Metropolitan Museum of Art, 2011), 195–97. The present example and the one originally owned by Duncan Phyfe and presumably made in his shop are hybrid examples of the French sideboard listed in *The New-York Book of Prices for Manufacturing Cabinet and Chair Work* (New York, 1817), 71–73, which had an enclosed cupboard section with two doors flanked by columns supported by a plinth and two additional lion's-paw feet below. Opening the center section allowed a handsome and useful storage space for the cellarette when not in use tableside.
2. Rhea Knittle was also an accomplished scholar who published her first article on Zanesville, OH, glass in *The Magazine Antiques* in 1924, the year the magazine was founded. In 1927, she authored *Early American Glass*, a comprehensive and authoritative book on the subject that remains in use today, and a decade later embarked on what was intended to be a fifteen-volume set of booklets she described as an "economic and social history and an historical survey of the industrial, decorative and fine arts in Ohio from 1767 to 1847." Rhea Knittle claimed that her love of American history and material culture was inspired by her family, in particular her mother, Elma Allee Mansfield, who in 1899 was divorced from her husband, Judge Cloyd Mansfield, and subsequently remarried well-known New York antiques dealer Henry V. Weil. Peggy Mershon, "Rhea Mansfield Knittle Made a Name in Antiques," *Mansfield News Journal*, September 5, 2015, https://www.mansfieldnewsjournal.com/story/news/history/2015/09/05/rhea-mansfield-knittle-made-name-antiques/71772860/.
3. Mershon, "Rhea Mansfield Knittle. . ."; *Hudson-Fulton Celebration*, Metropolitan Museum of Art, New York, September–November 1909.
4. Thomas Hamilton Ormsbee, *Early American Furniture Makers: A Social and Biographical Study* (New York: Archer House, 1930), pl. 33. The Phyfe sideboard and cellarette are also illustrated and discussed in Nancy McClelland, *Duncan Phyfe and the English Regency, 1795–1830* (New York: Dover Publications, 1939), 79–80, pl. 107, and Kenny et al., *Duncan Phyfe*, 195–97.

Fig. 36.1. Detail of foot on cat. 36a

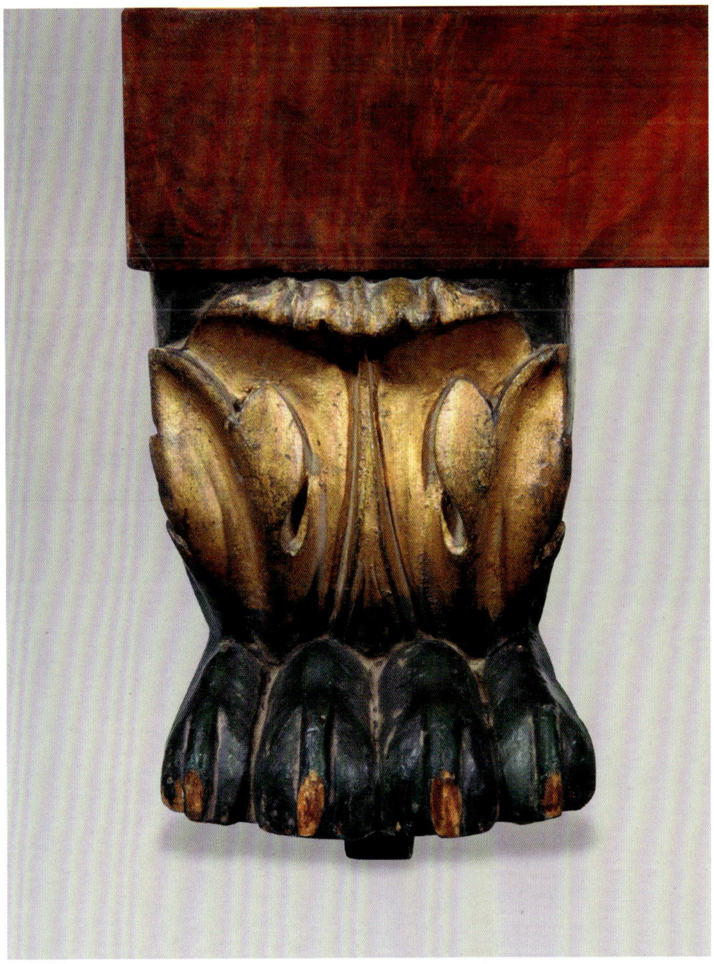

Fig. 36.2. Detail of foot on cat. 36b

37

Card Table, 1820

Duncan Phyfe (1770–1854)
New York
Rosewood and amboyna veneer, rosewood-grained maple, ebony; white pine, tulip poplar, maple; gilded gesso, gilded brass
29½ × 36 × 18 in.

LABEL: Paper label: "D. PHYFE'S / CABINET WAREHOUSE, / No. 170 Fulton-street, / NEW-YORK. / N.B. Curled Hair Matrasses, Chair, AND / Sofa Cushions. / AUGUST, 1820." (See Appendix II)

PROVENANCE: Private Collection; Sale, Sotheby's, New York, Jan. 28–30, 1988, lot 1820; With Israel Sack Inc., New York; Purchased by Schrimshers, 1988. Sale, Christie's, New York, Jan. 20–21, 2006, lot 867 (bought in).

Duncan Phyfe, with a few rare exceptions, did not label or sign his furniture. As New York's preeminent cabinetmaker, he may have believed that his fine, well-crafted work spoke for itself. A group consisting of five card tables with round corners, including the present example, a handsome pedimented writing table and bookcase, and a trestle-base worktable all with identical printed labels dated August 1820, however, is an anomalous exception to this general rule and begs the question of why Phyfe chose to mark this furniture at this particular moment in time.[1] It has been suggested that he may have labeled the pieces to promote them in export markets in response to the increased competition and the failed economy in the wake of the Panic of 1819. Whatever his reasons, the furniture in this group is quite distinctive and opens the door to other Phyfe attributions, especially for card tables with round corners, a design feature that became widely adopted by New York cabinetmakers during the 1820s and into the 1830s.

Fig. 37.1. Detail of cat. 37 showing the top of the card table rotated 90 degrees, revealing a printed Phyfe label on marbleized paper in the well, and wool broadcloth fitted to the top edge of the apron

Phyfe employed an imaginative technique to make the round corners on his card tables, designing them as separate structural elements formed by laminating a core of two kerf-sawn boards between two thinner ones, resulting in a multi-ply board that was bent round and dried in a caul that applied even pressure while the hide glue holding the laminates together dried. The round corner elements were then dovetailed on their ends to the front and side aprons and overlaid with plaques of rosewood or mahogany, depending on the wood of choice for the card table. Prepared in advance, these corner elements were essentially stock parts that speeded production and ensured that a different type of corner joint, such as a vertical miter, did not open and crack or read through thin veneers. Phyfe had used such laminated round corners earlier on his astragal-end tambour worktables, but we see an innovative leap forward in the use of standardized parts by 1820 on these round-cornered card tables.[2]

The almost skeletal framework of this card table belies its fine detail and the superior quality of its materials and workmanship. Rare honey-colored amboyna burl, a tropical hardwood from Southeast Asia, is combined with Brazilian rosewood and brass stringing in the veneered top, the Grecian ovolo molding at the top of the apron and the brass inlaid band at the bottom are of true ebony, while the crisply turned rosewood-grained uprights and cross stretcher also have passages ebonized to match. The *ormolu* appliqué centering the apron is of excellent quality and identical to one on a far more elaborate Phyfe-attributed card table.[3] When the hinged top is pivoted 90 degrees it glides on a worn but original band of green wool broadcloth (fig. 37.1) and when opened it reveals a playing surface lipped originally for a cloth of the same material. The feet at first glance may appear to be elaborate gilded, cast-brass casters but are of carved mahogany. This curious trick of the eye was enjoyed, perhaps, by the workmen in Phyfe's shop and the original purchaser of this compact showpiece at a southern port, such as Savannah, where Phyfe employed an agent to sell his wares and is known to have sent at least fourteen shipments of furniture between 1817 and 1823.[4]

1. For the four other labeled card tables, see Peter M. Kenny, Michael K. Brown, Frances F. Bretter, and Matthew A. Thurlow, *Duncan Phyfe: Master Cabinetmaker in New York* (New York: Metropolitan Museum of Art, 2011), 200–202, pls. 26 and 27, and appendix 2, 287.
2. For a discussion and an illustration of the laminate construction of the rounded corners on Phyfe card tables see Kenny et al., *Duncan Phyfe*, 85–87. For examples of Phyfe's astragal-end worktables, see ibid., 168–73, pls. 8–10.
3. This card table, with a gutsy gilded and bronzed fluted columnar support and heavy gilded lion's-paw feet highly similar to those on the center table in cat. 32 is illustrated and discussed in Stuart P. Feld and Wendell Garrett, *Neo-Classicism in America: Inspiration and Innovation, 1810–1840* (New York: Hirschl & Adler Galleries, 1991), 37.
4. Kenny et al., *Duncan Phyfe*, 39–40.

38

Pair of Side Chairs, 1815–1820

Unknown maker
New York
Rosewood-grained and gilded maple and cherry; brass, replacement upholstery
32 × 18 × 18 in.

PROVENANCE: Mr. and Mrs. John Rieger, New York. With Carswell Rush Berlin, Inc., New York, by 2009; Purchased by Schrimshers, 2015.

Light, colorful, painted, and gilded chairs with rush or cane seats, products of the rush-seat or fancy chairmaker's art, were made in countless numbers in New York and in the other cabinetmaking centers along the eastern seaboard of the of the United States from the 1790s through the 1830s. Also made within this time frame, but far less common, were more substantially constructed painted and decorated chairs with caned or upholstered seats. Outstanding examples of these in the Schrimsher Collection include a Philadelphia klismos side chair signed by its decorative painter, John Philip Fondé (cat. 42), and a Baltimore example attributed to the Finlay shop (cat. 63) that arguably are the finest American Classical chairs known. Even though New York chairs of this type were never as bold in form, they were nonetheless a welcome and brilliant addition to a high-toned parlor or drawing room. The New York shops that produced these chairs stayed carefully within the bounds of the standard scroll-back klismos form (cat. 26). They are constructed of maple and cherry and either rosewood-grained, like the Schrimsher example and its mate, one of which is shown here, or bronzed or ebonized with gilded carved elements, with freehand-gilded decoration trailing down the rear stiles and front legs, and on their crest and front seat rails (as in cat. 33). An invoice from Duncan Phyfe for a suite of rosewood-veneered furniture made for Robert Donaldson Jr. of Fayetteville, North Carolina, in 1822 includes "14 Ornamental Chairs," which offers a particularly apt period term to describe these chairs.[1]

These two chairs, part of an original set of at least six and possibly more, are unique among New York ornamental chairs.[2] Their relief-carved crests and ogee bannisters echo those of their mahogany counterparts, but their paneled, elliptical-bowed front seat rails and fluted and gilded front legs, features of French chairs in the late Louis XVI style, make them distinctive among their peers. The gilded saw-tooth pattern that encircles the tops of the legs, again isolated to these chairs, is a typical Neoclassical ornament seen in inlaid linear form in the light and dark wood banding on earlier Neoclassical furniture, and later in die-stamped brass and wood borders typical of New York Classical card and pier tables. The ogee bannisters that form the splat are of a type rarely seen on New York klismos chairs, a design that nonetheless appears in plate 6 of the 1817 *New-York Book of Prices for Manufacturing Cabinet and Chair Work*. Also uncommon are the relief-carved and gilded crossed torches in the crest rails, their billowing flames rendered dramatically with almost a cartoonist's flair. The painted and gilded decoration on the chairs remains intact, although an original gilded composition ornament is missing at the center of the front rails. The tight seat upholstery attached with bright brass tacks to the tops of the seat rails, like other aspects of these chairs, is out of the ordinary but borne out by the physical evidence.

1. Peter M. Kenny, Michael K. Brown, Frances F. Bretter, and Matthew A. Thurlow, *Duncan Phyfe: Master Cabinetmaker in New York* (New York: Metropolitan Museum of Art, 2011), appendix 1.7, 278.
2. One chair from this set is in the collection of the Metropolitan Museum of Art (2009.356a, bb). Another is in a private Virginia collection. The remaining two were with Carswell Rush Berlin, Inc., as of September 2023.

39

Pier Table, 1830–1835

Joseph Meeks & Sons: Joseph Meeks (1771–1868), John Meeks (1801–1875), Joseph W. Meeks (1805–1878), in partnership 1828–1835
New York
Mahogany, mahogany veneer; white pine, tulip poplar; marble, mirror glass
36½ × 43 × 19¾ in.

LABEL: Badly deteriorated fragment of a paper label, which in its original form reads: "MEEKS & SONS' MANUFACTORY / CABINET-FURNITURE / Nos 43 & 45 Broad Street / NEW-YORK." (See Appendix II)

PROVENANCE: Lee B. Anderson (1918–2010), New York; Sale, Doyle Auctions, Kensington, MD, Sept. 19, 2012, lot 1428; Dr. Larry McAllister (1935–2021), Muncie, IN; Sale, Sotheby's, New York, Sept. 22, 2022, lot 197; Purchased by Schrimshers, 2022.

In July 1868, an obituary in the *New York Herald* reported the death of "Mr. Joseph Meeks of this city . . . at the ripe age of 97 years" who "nearly eighty years ago began the wholesale and retail furniture trade in Broad Street, and for many years supplied the markets, from Boston to New Orleans, with the most expensive, elegant, and durable cabinet-work made in America."[1] Like his contemporary Duncan Phyfe, Joseph Meeks grew rich investing the profits from his furniture-making business in New York real estate on Broad Street and its vicinity. Even though Joseph worked in the New York cabinetmaking trade from the 1790s, strangely not a single piece of furniture is documented to the Meeks shop until he went into partnership with his sons John and Joseph W. in 1828, when the firm began to label its work. Earlier in the 1820s, Joseph W. was sent by his father to New Orleans to manage a satellite furniture warehouse that later was operated by another brother, Theodore (1812–1904). These three sons, and eventually a grandson, continued to operate the family cabinetmaking business after the elder Meeks's retirement about 1835 and then until his death in 1868, when they dissolved the firm in order to turn their attention to managing their vast real estate holdings.[2]

This pier table was probably made in the early 1830s, just a couple of years after Joseph Meeks & Sons first began to operate out of a new five-story brick furniture manufactory with an elegant showroom at 43 and 45 Broad Street. Here and at their Chartres Street branch in New Orleans, Joseph Meeks & Sons offered a wide array of furniture illustrated along with a price list in a now famous advertising broadside published in 1833.[3] Seventeen of the forty-four items depicted on the broadside were taken directly from designs in George Smith's *The Cabinet-Maker and Upholsterer's Guide* (London, 1826). The vast majority of the original Meeks designs on the broadside are in the new and final phase of the Classical mode in New York, often referred to as the Grecian Plain style, which eschewed the earlier painted and gilded sculptural elements, brass inlays, *ormolu* appliqués, and stenciled and freehand-gilded ornaments, and relied instead on clean, curvaceous lines and artfully deployed rosewood or mahogany veneers. This pier table is a Gothicized version of the Grecian Plain style.[4] Its dramatic black-and-gold Egyptian marble top and undulant apron are identical to those on another labeled Joseph Meeks & Sons table featuring the shop's highly distinctive, exuberant console scroll supports (fig. 39.1). Superbly crafted with the finest thick mahogany veneers, these two pier tables reveal the adventurous, imaginative mindset of a firm intent on forging its own identity in the crowded landscape of New York furniture making. Sadly, only seven years after it was established, Joseph Meeks & Sons' capacious new workshops and furniture showroom on Broad Street were destroyed in the Great Fire of 1835, a catastrophic event that more than likely precipitated the elder Meeks's retirement from the firm as well the relocation of the business to a more fashionable and conspicuous address at 14 Vesey Street. The new shop was just steps off Broadway and around the corner from the recently opened Astor House, New York's first luxury hotel, designed by Isaiah Rogers (1800–1869), the same architect responsible for Boston's magnificent Tremont House (see pp. 41–42).

Fig. 39.1. *Pier Table*, Joseph Meeks & Sons, 1830–35, mahogany and mahogany veneer; pine, ash; marble, mirror glass, Metropolitan Museum of Art, Gift of Emil and Dolores Pascarelli in Honor of Catherine Hoover Voorsanger, 2001, 2001.640a,b (Courtesy Metropolitan Museum of Art /Art Resource, NY)

1. *The New York Herald Tribune*, July 24, 1868.
2. For a complete history of the Meeks family of cabinetmakers, see Jodi A. Pollack, "Three Generations of Meeks Craftsmen, 1797–1869: A History of Their Business and Furniture" (Master's thesis, Parsons School of Design, New York, 1998).
3. The Joseph Meeks & Sons broadside is illustrated in Peter M. Kenny, Michael K. Brown, Frances F. Bretter, and Matthew A. Thurlow, *Duncan Phyfe: Master Cabinetmaker in New York* (New York: Metropolitan Museum of Art, 2011), 91. It can also be seen in the Metropolitan Museum of Art's online collections catalogue (43.15.18).
4. The Meekses clearly were familiar with George Smith's furniture designs. There are a limited number of pieces in the Gothic style in the *The Cabinet-Maker and Upholsterer's Guide* (London, 1826), but they are more numerous in Smith's earlier *A Collection of Designs for Household Furniture and Interior Decoration* (London, 1808), which includes in plate 85 an illustration of a rectangular Gothic sofa table with a fixed top, square legs with tracery, and lancet arches on the aprons.

Fashionable Patterns / Splendid Assortments: Classical Philadelphia Furniture

ALEXANDRA ALEVIZATOS KIRTLEY

Described as having "the most fashionable patterns" and being designed with "splendid assortments" of decorations, furniture made in Philadelphia from the 1790s through the 1840s reflects the aspirations of the patrons, the influence of design publications and imported wares, and the skills of artisans both newly emigrated and from a local tradition that was more than one hundred years old. Philadelphia furniture makers created dynamic works of art during this seminal fifty-year period, with Neoclassical delicacy becoming bold Classical designs. They established the city as the capital of cabinetmaking, a position they would eventually cede to New York City. As Philadelphia's prosperous, upwardly mobile merchants enjoyed tremendous economic successes in the new republic of the United States, the city's artisans fulfilled commissions for elaborate furniture to adorn grand interiors. In an 1809 letter to Philadelphia merchant George Harrison, who with his wife Sophia commissioned magnificent furnishings, including a lyre-back klismos chair (cat. 41), the British-born architect and designer Benjamin Henry Latrobe (1764–1820) identified a tension, between humility and excess: "we are jammed, between our republican principles, [and] our aristocratic wishes."[1]

Card Table, **1825–1830**
(detail of cat. 46b–c)

When William Penn (1644–1718) arrived in 1681 to lay claim to the lands of the Lenape people that surrounded the Schuylkill and Delaware Rivers (known as the Lenapehoking), Dutch and Swedish colonists had inhabited the region for several decades. The wealth of natural resources and the hope for prosperous trade inspired the colony's name, Pennsylvania—quite literally, Penn's Woods. The felling of trees throughout the six counties (Bucks, Philadelphia, Chester, New Castle, Kent, and Sussex, and the shores of West Jersey) began immediately, and joiners were among the earliest colonial artisans to practice their trade.[2] Families such as the Claypooles created dynasties of joiners, and others like the Kinsey/FitzRandolph and Stapleford families relocated from Massachusetts to Pennsylvania because of the region's potential. Local walnut, maple, and cherry as well as imported Caribbean mahogany were used as the primary woods, with tulip poplar, oak, Atlantic white cedar, white and yellow pine, and ash as the common secondary woods.[3]

By the 1710s, furniture made in Philadelphia began to take on a distinctive style. Many artisans were connected by their shared Quaker faith, but the colony boasted a range of cultures. Non-Quaker and Quaker artisans and patrons alike had sophisticated tastes in line with their aspirations to achieve prosperity through trade with ports throughout the Atlantic world, especially in the Caribbean where scores of Philadelphia Quakers owned large plantations, belying their intolerance of

Fig. 1. ***Double Chest*, Thomas Gross Jr. (1775–1839), 1805–1810, mahogany; tulip poplar, yellow pine; brass, Philadelphia Museum of Art, Gift of Mrs. Leslie Legum, 1983, 1983-167-1a,b (Courtesy Philadelphia Museum of Art). The son of a carpenter, Gross was a free Black artisan who maintained a shop in Philadelphia from about 1805 through the 1830s.**

enslavement. Most early Philadelphia cabinetmakers hailed from England, with a handful of Scottish and Irish makers and a significant community of Europeans, predominantly German, Dutch, and French.[4] While long overlooked, Africans (both enslaved and free) worked as skilled artisans in all aspects of furniture making (fig. 1).[5] Carvers worked for joiners on interior architectural elements and on furniture, and by the 1740s they arrived from London in droves, adding energetic Rococo curves to interiors and furniture that already had its own vernacular reflecting a hybrid of influences. Along with imported furniture, books of architectural design were instructional primers for joiners and carvers, providing proportion and profiles. Booksellers advertised design treatises, and those books are consistently listed in probate inventories of artisans and patrons.[6] Joiners—who began to adopt the title of cabinetmaker by the 1760s—created shop patterns for furniture that formed and transmitted local designs; the value accorded to those patterns in probate inventories suggests their significance in perpetuating local preferences for rail profiles, carved and cut-through chair banisters, and fretwork.[7]

The Philadelphia cabinetmaking community was complex and active enough by 1772 that the master cabinetmakers united to produce the world's first known printed price book, *Prices of Cabinet and Chair Work*. The pocket-sized, thirty-six-page text established retail prices for furniture in mahogany and walnut and set fees paid to journeymen for their piecework.[8] Though a lagging indicator of style, the price book's listings and descriptions provide salient details about furniture commonly made in 1772, revealing forms unique to North America (such as the high chest) as well as aspects of work not included in the price list: glazing, upholstery, painting, and carving beyond basic shells on knees and rails. Surviving works indicate that although the furniture design books by British artisans Thomas Chippendale (1718–1779), William Ince (1737–1804) and John Mayhew (1736–1811), and Robert Manwaring (active 1760–c. 1770) were in Philadelphia, architectural treatises prevailed as foundational texts. During the Grand Federal Procession of July 8, 1788, which celebrated Pennsylvania's ratification of the U.S. Constitution, cabinet-makers Jonathan Gostelowe (1745–1795) and Jedediah Snowden (1724–1797) led the parade of cabinet- and chair makers carrying their artisan tools (scales and dividers) and Andrea Palladio's *Four Books of Architecture* (1570).[9]

As the new United States emerged in the 1780s and the former colonists wrangled to establish themselves as a sovereign nation, the Residence Act of 1790 established Philadelphia as the country's capital for a ten-year period while the federal city was being built north of the Potomac River on lands ceded by the state of Maryland. This was a watershed moment for Philadelphia. In keeping with William Penn's aspirations and the Enlightenment period's embrace of the ancient—or classical—Egyptian, Greek, and Roman world, Philadelphia was determined to become the Athens of America.[10] The city was replete with large public buildings, such as the State House (1753, now called Independence Hall), Christ Church (1755), and Carpenter's Hall (1773),

Fig. 2. *Cylinder Desk and Bookcase*, unknown maker, c. 1800–1805, mahogany with mahogany, satinwood, and maple veneers; light and dark wood string inlay, white pine, tulip poplar; brass, glass, ivory, replacement fabric, Philadelphia Museum of Art, Purchased with the Fiske Kimball Fund and the John T. Morris Fund, 2004, 2004-81-1 (Courtesy Philadelphia Museum of Art). Wood grain, veneer, and inlay enliven the otherwise planar surfaces.

and intellectual organizations, such as the Library Company (1731), the American Philosophical Society (1743), and artist Charles Willson Peale's portrait gallery (1782) and natural history museum (1786). Philadelphians Samuel Powel and John Morgan—both prominent Quaker scions—had gone on a Grand Tour of Europe in the 1760s and brought home the fervor for the Classical style that was spreading among the artistic circles of Europe.[11] Pierre-François Hugues, Baron d'Hancarville's 1766 illustrated catalogue of the encyclopedic collection of ancient vases acquired by the British ambassador to the Kingdom of the Two Sicilies, Sir William Hamilton (1730–1803), was available to read at the Library Company of Philadelphia in 1772. Among other influences, it provided the city's elite with the complete artistic lexicon of the ancient Greeks and Etruscans who lived on the Italian peninsula. In sum, Philadelphians embraced what German art historian Johann Winckelmann (1717–1768) had stated in 1755: "There is but one way for the moderns to become great, and perhaps unequalled . . . by imitating the ancients."[12]

Considering its history, institutions, and position as the capital of the United States from 1790 to 1800, its prosperous and ambitious merchant class, and its range of skilled artisans from broad backgrounds, Philadelphia was poised to take the lead artistically for America in the same way Athens had inspired the ancient world. Bold Classical designs of architecture and furniture demonstrated the taste of patrons as well as their knowledge of and enthusiasm for classical art.[13]

Furniture made in Philadelphia in the late 1780s and early 1790s adopted the slighter profiles, flatter surfaces, and geometric decorative patterning (fig. 2) popularized by cabinetmakers like Thomas Shearer in *The Cabinet-Makers' London Book of Prices* (1788), George Hepplewhite in *The Cabinet-Maker and Upholsterer's Guide* (London, 1788) and Thomas Sheraton in *The Cabinet-Maker and Upholsterer's Drawing-Book* (London, 1793).[14] Furniture profiles became slighter and more linear, and carving became less effusive yielding to decorative inlay, marquetry, contrasting veneers, and painted ornament in geometric patterns or floral arabesques. The emergence of these more delicate Neoclassical designs took cues from the profiles of classical art, with the backs of chairs shaped like a vase or a lyre and blond satinwood used for geometric inlay patterns, including the ubiquitous budding husks, which were later referred to as bellflowers. Artisans and patrons became more dependent on published folios that illustrated the new fashions with instructions about how to decorate, upholster, and use the increasingly specialized furnishings.

Philadelphia Neoclassical furniture is less exuberant than that of other cities (especially nearby Baltimore, where the Neoclassical style flourished best), possibly because the embrace was tempered by the formality brought to the capital city by the cadre of international consulates, ambassadors, prosperous merchants, and entrepreneurial artisans. Furthermore, in the wake of the French support of the Continental Army and an influx of French *émigrés* in the 1790s (including the Duc d'Orléans, the future king of France, and his brothers, the Duc de Montpensier and the Duc de

Fig. 3. *Chair*, unknown maker, c. 1795–1800, mahogany, ash; replacement upholstery, Philadelphia Museum of Art, The Henry P. McIlhenny Collection in memory of Frances P. McIlhenny, 1986, 1986-26-55 (Courtesy Philadelphia Museum of Art)

Fig. 4. *Stool*, c. 1840, white pine, painted and gilt decoration, Philadelphia Museum of Art, Gift of Mary Calwell, 1991, 1991-82-1

Pier Table, unknown maker, c. 1790–1800, tulip poplar, white pine; plaster composition ornament, painted and gilt decoration, marble, Philadelphia Museum of Art, Gift of Mr. and Mrs. Richard J. Hamilton II, 2017, 2017-110-1

Armchairs (from a set of 12), unknown maker, c. 1790–1800, ash, tulip poplar; plaster composition ornament, painted and gilded decoration, replacement upholstery, Philadelphia Museum of Art, Bequest of Fiske and Marie Kimball, 1955, 1955-86-2,3 (Courtesy Philadelphia Museum of Art). This set of seating (12 armchairs and 1 settee) was made to accommodate its original upholstery—an elaborate Beauvais tapestry woven with a Neoclassical lozenge and medallion design.

Beaujolais), Philadelphians were Francophiles, favoring the French-inspired round, turned legs with carved and reeded decoration over straight, tapered legs with inlaid ornament (fig. 3). The furniture and furnishings that arrived with foreign emissaries can account for the fact that, to date, Philadelphia is the only North American city where artisans made sets of armchairs (and usually a matching settee and pier table) with carved and white and gilt decoration made to accommodate sets of imported tapestries (fig. 4).[15] These large sets of formal parlor or drawing room furniture were *de rigueur* in the finest city and country houses of Europe, Britain, and Ireland. Like bow-shaped rooms and levées, Philadelphians who were solidly grounded in their republican government embraced aristocratic protocols and *accoutrements* for their drawing rooms and dance assemblies.[16] Upholsterer George Bertault (1771–1831) arrived in Philadelphia from Paris by 1792 and was the mastermind behind these commissions: he imported French tapestry coverings and commissioned seat armatures to suit them. Numerous artisans rose to that occasion, including Adam Hains (1768–1846), a Philadelphia-born cabinet- and chair maker of German ancestry.[17]

Among the most prominent cabinet- and chair makers in Philadelphia in the beginning of this period was John Aitken (c. 1760/65–1839), who was born and trained in Dalkeith, Scotland, arrived by 1785, and by 1790 advertised himself as the sole proprietor of a shop at Chestnut and Second Streets with furniture "of various patterns, some of which are entirely new, never before seen in this city, and finished with an elegance of stile [sic]."[18] Aitken was adept at producing sophisticated furniture in the Neoclassical style and rose to prominence quickly.[19] He stood out among his fellow artisans, including Philadelphia-born or -trained artisans like Jonathan Gostelowe (1745–1795), Daniel Trotter (1747–1800), Ephraim Haines (1775–1837), George Claypoole Sr. (1706–1793), George Claypoole Jr. (1733–1793), William Rigby (d. 1796), and Henry Connelly (1769–1826). As President George Washington and his wife Martha were preparing to return to civilian life, they commissioned Aitken to make "a desk for Miss Custis [Martha's daughter] & a screen for Mrs. Washington"; a tambour secretary for President Washington's office; and two sideboards and two dozen chairs for the new room they were designing for their Virginia mansion, Mount Vernon.[20]

Henry Connelly, a native of Carlisle in central Pennsylvania, first advertised a cabinet- and chair-making shop on lower Chestnut Street near Aitken in 1802. Connelly's documented furniture is elegant, if not conservative, but distinguished and often infused with French aesthetics. He received significant patronage and employed a bevy of journeymen who signed and dated their furniture—presumably to mark their piecework for payment.[21] When Ephraim Haines declined cabinetmaking and devoted himself to dealing in lumber, Connelly received the exclusive patronage of the French-born merchant Stephen Girard (1750–1831) (see cat. 44).

Other makers of the Neoclassical style, such as Richard Alexander (1780–1823) and Thomas Whitecar (1784–1822, pronounced *Whit-a-ker*), made a strong impact but have enjoyed less recognition, possibly because their careers were cut short. Whitecar was trained in England and brought a late Regency style to Philadelphia through a modified version of the klismos chair that became central to Classical furniture design (fig. 5a–b). Two chairs—one attributed and one documented to Whitecar—follow the pattern in plate 77 of French Neoclassical designer Pierre de La Mésangère's 1802 edition of *Collection de meubles et objets de goût* (Paris, 1799–1831). La Mésangère's elegantly drawn and colored designs were consumed by patrons and artisans of all types, and they significantly impacted what was made and how it was used. Most Philadelphia artisans were like Whitecar, branding their own style by combining aspects of La Mésangère's chic designs with the accessible ones of the Englishman George Smith in his *A Collection of Designs for Household Furniture and Interior Decoration* (London, 1808).

The more-than-forty-year career of the Irish-born Philadelphia cabinet and chairmaker Joseph B. Barry (1757–1838) spans the Neoclassical and Classical periods (fig. 6). Deft and adaptable, Barry maintained a consistently prominent reputation among patrons and fellow makers. He was likely born in Dublin but claimed to have been trained in London and advanced himself in Philadelphia by partnering with well-heeled furniture makers (the Scotsman Alexander Calder in 1794 and Lewis G. Affleck, son of Scotsman Thomas Affleck, in 1795) and then Irish-born lumber (mainly mahogany) merchants Cavanagh and Hearn from 1795 to 1798. Barry listed himself as an independent entity starting in 1798.[22] While more volumetric

Fig. 5a. ***Klismos Chair with Double Sphinx,*** **attributed to Thomas Whitecar, c. 1806–1810, mahogany, ash; upholstery removed, Philadelphia Museum of Art, Purchased with the Halberstadt Fund for American Decorative Arts 2022, 2022-24-1 (Courtesy Jason Wierzbicki, Philadelphia Museum of Art Division of Conservation)**

Fig. 5b. ***Chair,*** **Thomas Whitecar, 1809, mahogany, ash, pine, oak; replacement upholstery, Philadelphia Museum of Art, Bequest of Lydia Thompson Morris, 1932, 1932-45-100d (Courtesy Philadelphia Museum of Art)**

furniture based on archaeological models is the eponymous "Barry style," he began in the 1790s with subtle or Neoclassical references to classical art. Between 1779 and 1801, Thomas Jefferson sought him out to make furniture in the styles that Jefferson had admired in France and imported through Philadelphia before sending them on to Monticello.[23] Barry's ability to innovate, seek the most current fashions, and promote his furniture in far-afield markets established him not only as Philadelphia's headliner but also as consistently relevant in an increasingly competitive market.

The ambitious Barry ventured to Savannah, Georgia, in 1798 with a cargo of "well finished" mahogany furniture for sale, established an outpost in Baltimore from 1803 to 1804, and traveled to London and Paris to make purchases and find inspiration in 1811 and 1819.[24] In 1826, he traveled to Valparaiso, Chile, to connect with agents there to sell his wares.[25] In 1811, he announced that he had acquired the City Hotel, a profitable business that served as the depot for the transportation line between Philadelphia and Baltimore, thereby connecting him to markets for his cabinet wares.

Barry's booming shop had a constant demand for journeymen: as early as December 3, 1810, he advertised for two weeks in the *New York Mercantile* for four journeyman cabinetmakers who wished for steady employment in Philadelphia. Similarly, the cabinetmakers Aitken, Joseph Beale (1774–1841), John Jamison (active 1818–1833), Charles B. McElwee (active 1805–1818), and Lawrence Sink (active 1800–1823) shared a two-week advertising spot in early 1814 in the *New-York Gazette*, requesting that journeymen apply to each of them and promising liberal wages and steady work.

Benjamin Henry Latrobe arrived in Philadelphia in 1799 and quickly observed the potential for the city's patrons and artisans to create an ideal city—where, as he would say in 1811, "the days of Greece may be revived in the woods of America and Philadelphia become the Athens of the Western World."[26] Latrobe's impact on architecture in the United States is conventionally acknowledged, but less well known is his design of a residence in Philadelphia and the furniture and furnishings for their double drawing room for merchant William Waln (1775–1826) and Mary Wilcocks Waln (1780–1841) that shifted the visual language of Classical furniture design in America.[27] Construction on the house at the southwest corner of Seventh and Chestnut Streets was nearing completion in August 1808, when Mrs. Waln rallied Latrobe, her husband, and her friend Madame Louise-Alexandrine Eugénie Hulot Moreau (1781–1821, wife of Napoleon Bonaparte's exiled general Jean-Victor-Marie Moreau) to travel to New York. There, they met the French-trained *ébéniste* Charles-Honoré Lannuier (1779–1819) and his cousin Jean-Charles Cochois (1776–after 1808), who had solicited consultations for patrons seeking furniture designs in the French taste.

Fig. 6. Unknown artist, ***Silhouette of Cabinetmaker Joseph Barry***, 1830s, cut paper with metallic paint on wove paper, Philadelphia Museum of Art, Purchased with funds contributed by Forbes and Sara Maner, 2020, 2020-18-1 (Courtesy Philadelphia Museum of Art)

Upon his return to Philadelphia, Latrobe—a British expatriate who unabashedly promoted French taste—set about designing the drawing room furniture in a decidedly French Classical style. Latrobe worked closely with Aitken to execute the furniture (a sideboard, about twenty chairs, two card tables, a sofa, and two window seats) in this new-found aesthetic (fig. 7).[28] The sleek profiles of the klismos seating and the form of the sideboard as a French *console dessert* would not have been familiar to Aitken or others in Philadelphia, where still in 1807 Girard had ordered a set of ebony furniture in the conservative French designs of the 1790s (see fig. 3). After the triumph of the Walns' lavish commission, President James Madison and his wife Dolley commissioned Latrobe to design similar drawing room furniture at the President's House, and the klismos profile became the standard in Philadelphia—and indeed throughout the United States.[29]

The impact of Latrobe's designs extended far beyond the furniture Aitken made for the Walns: the work of the English decorative artist and architect George Bridport (1783–1819) and upholsterer John Rea (1774–1871) underscored the impact that surface ornament and upholstery had on Classical furniture in Philadelphia (fig. 8). Trained as a theatrical set designer, Bridport drew inspiration from his extensive library; specifically for the Waln commission, he relied on his personal copies of Charles Heathcote Tatham's *Etchings, Representing the Best Examples of Ancient Ornamental Architecture; Drawn from the Originals in Rome* (London, 1799); Charles Percier and Pierre-François-Léonard Fontaine's *Recueil de décorations intérieures* (Paris, 1801–1812); Nicholas Ponce's *Collection des tableaux et arabesques antiques* (Paris, 1805); and Thomas Hope's *Household Furniture and Interior Decoration*

Fig. 7. *Suite of Furniture*, designed by Benjamin Henry Latrobe, made by John Aitken, decorated by George Bridport, upholstered by John Rea, 1808, Philadelphia Museum of Art (Courtesy Philadelphia Museum of Art)

Klismos Chairs:
Tulip poplar, oak; caning, gilded and painted decoration, replacement upholstery, Gift of Marie Josephine Rozet and Rebecca Mandeville Rozet Hunt, 1935, 1935-13-9–10
Maple, oak; caning, gilded and painted decoration, replacement upholstery, Purchased with the gift (by exchange) of Mrs. Alex Simpson, Jr., and A. Carson Simpson, and with funds contributed by Mr. and Mrs. Robert L. Raley and various donors, 1986, 1986-126-4–7
Tulip poplar, oak; caning, gesso, gilded and painted decoration, replacement upholstery, Gift of Mrs. Swan McLean Grant, 1991-84-1

Card Table, mahogany, tulip poplar, white pine; brass, gilded and painted decoration, iron, cotton velvet, Purchased with the gift (by exchange) of Mrs. Alex Simpson, Jr., and A. Carson Simpson, and with funds contributed by Mr. and Mrs. Robert L. Raley and various donors, 1986-126-1

Sideboard, tulip poplar, a conifer (probably pine); gilded and painted decoration, metal rosettes, replacement mirror, cotton, Purchased with the gift (by exchange) of Mrs. Alex Simpson, Jr., and A. Carson Simpson, and with funds contributed by Mr. and Mrs. Robert L. Raley and various donors, 1986-126-3

Sofa, tulip poplar, maple; gilded and painted decoration, replacement caning, iron, brass, replacement upholstery, Purchased with the gift (by exchange) of Mrs. Alex Simpson, Jr., and A. Carson Simpson, and with funds contributed by Mr. and Mrs. Robert L. Raley, and various donors, 1986-126-2

Fig. 7a. Crest rail detail of *Klismos Chair*, 1986-126-5, above, second from right

Fig. 8. ***Pair of Chairs*****, unknown maker for John Hare Powel, 1815–1825, mahogany, mahogany veneer, white pine, ash; rosewood, ebony, cut brass inlay, replacement upholstery, Philadelphia Museum of Art, Purchased with the Thomas Skelton Harrison Fund, 1974, 1974-143-1,2 (Courtesy Philadelphia Museum of Art)**

(London, 1807).[30] Even after the extravagant commission was completed in 1808, the Walns continued to update their interiors, hiring Bridport in 1811 to design a sideboard made by George G. Wright (1780–1853) in Barry's shop and (like his neighbors George and Sophia Harrison) ordering furniture from Lannuier of New York City sometime after 1815.[31] The furniture Latrobe designed for the Walns and their post-1815 purchases deeply impacted taste and design in Philadelphia, from sparkling events that occurred at their house to, following the Panic of 1819, the demise of their fortune: on November 7, 1821, "a scene of gaiety" occurred outside their Chestnut Street house when "the splendid furniture of a ruined gentleman, was exhibited for sale, and to-morrow will be distributed under the auctioneers [sic] hammer to the four corners of the city."[32]

December 1814 saw the signing of the Treaty of Ghent that ended the United States' war with Britain the following February and the defeat of Napoleon at the Battle of Waterloo in June 1815. These geopolitical events coincided with another shift in aesthetic taste toward volume and more direct copying of classical motifs, which made for a watershed moment in Philadelphia furniture design. By this time, the taste for furniture was marked by a new boldness, with more volumetric profiles and a richness in the amount and variety of surface decoration and upholstery. Many of the old guard like Aitken chose not to adapt and declined business when they foresaw the dramatic change in furniture fashions, shop practices, warehousing, tools, and techniques.[33] Connelly, whose limited work in this period can be seen in a swivel-top card table in the Schrimsher Collection (cat. 44), retired in 1824.

This stylistic shift coincided with an economic headwind: the plunging real-estate market set the city in a decline and artisans began to leave, seeking work in the newly burgeoning population centers of Pittsburgh, Cincinnati, Louisville, Nashville, and New Orleans, as well as Washington, D.C., where work was plentiful due to the rebuilding of the federal city that the British had set ablaze on August 24, 1814. All of this opened opportunities for a new wave of *émigrés* to reshape the landscape with the new taste for furniture that wholly imitated ancient forms and decoration in a style referred to in the period as both Classical and Grecian. Gone were the subtle references to vases, arabesques, and architectural orders; in their place were volumetric, sculptural works that mimicked ancient furniture as seen in wall and vase paintings and marble reliefs. Furniture design continued to take its cue from architecture, and with houses built on grander scales, featuring improved technology for heating and lighting, larger rooms, and higher ceilings, the scale of furniture increased, carving became bolder, decorative techniques were layered and combined on one single piece, and upholstery was overstuffed and puffy with the advent of the spring seating in the mid-1820s. Anthony Gabriel Quervelle (1789–1856) and Michel Bouvier (1792–1874) from France; Thomas Cook (1789–1868) and Richard Parkin (1787–1861) from England; Robert West (1778–1870) from Ireland; and a slew of German and Danish artisans advanced the taste for the Classical style, while the stalwart Joseph Barry adapted yet again to meet the challenge.

It is unknown with whom or where Bouvier trained, but he arrived in Philadelphia as a master of the French designs of Percier and Fontaine. Bouvier enjoyed a long and successful career and received commissions from fellow Frenchmen Joseph Bonaparte (1768–1844), the deposed king of Naples, Sicily, and Spain, and merchant Stephen Girard. Working

Fig. 9. *Card Table*, Michel Bouvier (1792–1874), 1830, maple, mahogany, ebonized white pine, rosewood inlay; white pine, tulip poplar, yellow birch, chestnut, Private Collection (Courtesy Laszlo Bodo)

from a shop located among his fellow cabinetmakers, he advertised "a large assortment of Fashionable Furniture . . . Sideboards, Bureaus, Sofas, Card Tables, Secretaries, Book Cases, Chairs, Dining Tables," but only a small number of pieces can be documented to him (fig. 9).[34] Bouvier relied on restrained profiles, finely worked surfaces, and elegant decoration—all on the finest of woods, which he also sold from his shop in an attached lumber yard where at one time he advertised "about 300,000 feet of veneers, of different qualities." Bouvier also employed a man who made smalls, such as intricate mechanical parts and boxes for sewing tables.[35] Only a few doors down Second Street worked Quervelle, who may have trained with the former shop of his relative Jean-Claude Quervelle (1731–1778), an *ébéniste du garde-meuble de la Couronne* at Versailles. Quervelle created a hybrid style distinguished by compartmentalized compositions and lobed, convex demilune facades with complex arrangements of figured veneers (see cat. 49a–b). While these distinctive patterns are synonymous with Quervelle, they also reflect the impact of German-trained journeymen in Philadelphia.[36] Quervelle applied elegantly engraved labels for certain commissions and stamped elements of furniture that he exported and that could be assembled in a port, such as card table pillars.[37] Quervelle's furniture profoundly impacted Classical Philadelphia: convex stars and radial fans; animated supports such as carved dolphins for card table tops, marble

Fig. 10. *French Bedstead*, attributed to Anthony Gabriel Quervelle, 1825–1835, mahogany, mahogany veneer; yellow poplar; brass, Philadelphia Museum of Art, Purchased with The Herbert & Nanette Rothschild Memorial Fund in memory of Judith Rothschild, 1997, 1997-152-1a–d (Courtesy Philadelphia Museum of Art). Both Quervelle and Michel Bouvier received the patronage of Joseph Bonaparte, the exiled king of Naples and Sicily. Bonaparte lived in Philadelphia and at Point Breeze, his New Jersey estate overlooking the Delaware River, for which this French bedstead was made.

Fig. 11 Attributed to Anthony Gabriel Quervelle, *Furniture Sketch*, c. 1820–1835, graphite and pen and ink on wove paper, Philadelphia Museum of Art, Purchased with funds contributed by an anonymous donor, Mr. and Mrs. W. B. Dixon Stroud, John A. Nyheim, Dr. and Mrs. Robert E. Booth, Jr., and Anne R. and John F. Haley, Jr., 1995, 1995-12-4a,b v1 (Courtesy Philadelphia Museum of Art). The collection is comprised of fourteen sheets of sketches.

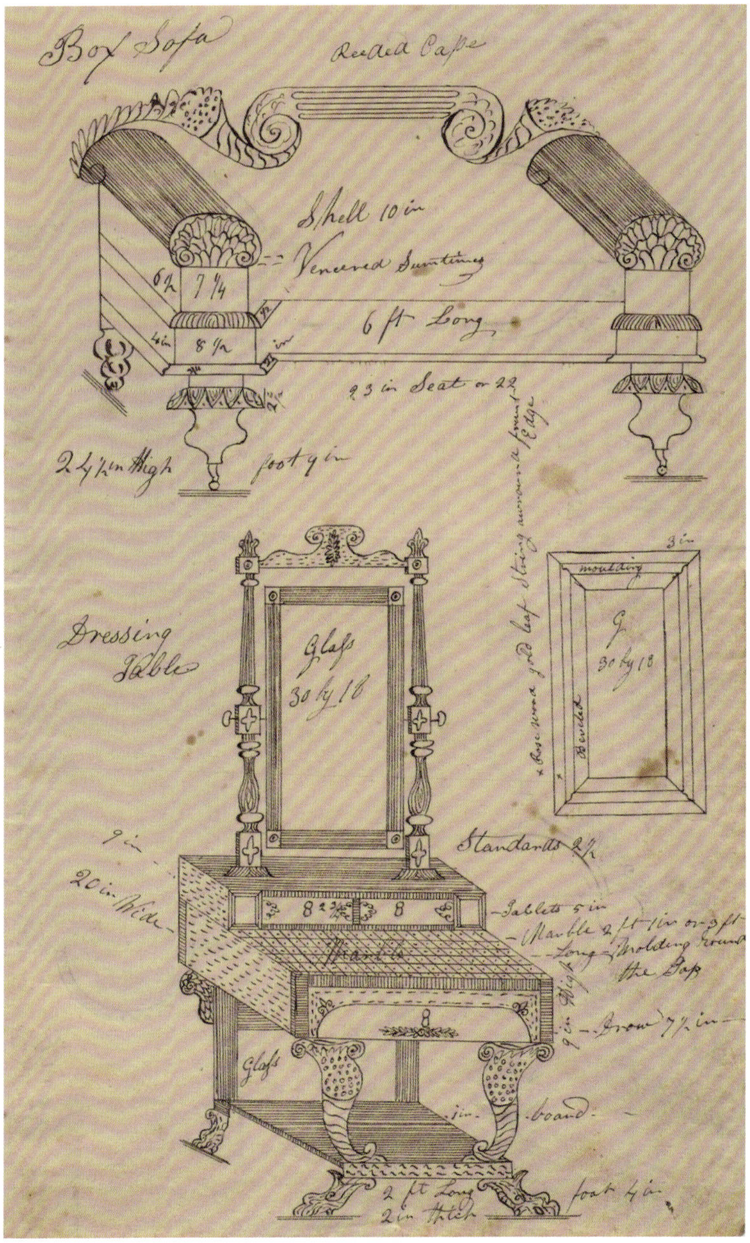

tops on pier tables, and sewing tables; and compressed volutes to suggest weight, such as on the feet of a French bedstead (fig. 10) made for Joseph Bonaparte. Many in Philadelphia copied his designs, and patrons across the country identified Philadelphia Classical taste through his unique brand—and sought it out (fig. 11). Combined with Barry's entrepreneurial forays into Southern markets, the dynamism of Quervelle's designs created a demand for Philadelphia furniture in the South, most notably in Virginia (including western Virginia), as well as in Savannah, Mobile, New Orleans, and points northward along the Mississippi River in Louisiana, Mississippi, Tennessee, Kentucky, and Ohio.

Barry, Bouvier, Quervelle, and other Philadelphia artisans regularly imported British and European furniture and elements such as *ormolu* mounts to ornament and incorporate furniture, and the impact of these imports on local manufacturers cannot be underestimated.[38] Bouvier advertised "Splendid Italian Marble Furniture . . . received directly from Italy, 1 Splendid real Mosaic Center Table, white marble pillar and base; 1 Statuary Centre Table."[39] Quervelle made at least two scroll-ended console tables to support painted slate tops and two center tables with elaborately inlaid marble tops.[40] Barry advertised in 1824 "2 Rich Sideboards, Buhl work and richly carved," a reference that has long associated him with the lavish set of furniture inlaid with brass marquetry (or Boulle work) made for the Gratz family of Philadelphia.[41]

These imports encouraged Philadelphia makers to step outside their bounds, adopt styles from around the world, and make extravagant sculptural works of art. For example, a pair of imported nearly six-foot-high candelabras owned in Philadelphia in the 1820s inspired a Philadelphia maker to make related ones.[42]

Arriving in Philadelphia between 1817 and 1819, British-born and -trained cabinetmakers Thomas Cook (1789–1868) and Richard Parkin (1787–1861) have only recently been recognized for their profound impact on Philadelphia furniture.[43] They operated a large shop at 56 Walnut Street, between Second and Third Streets, in the heart of the cabinetmaking district. Their furniture is marked by an academic severity, with designs directly referencing the archaeological models illustrated by Hope and the more accessible conceptions of George Smith; their later furniture gives a strong nod to the "Grecian" or Plain styles inspired by Peter and Michael Angelo Nicholson's *The Practical Cabinet-Maker, Upholsterer, and Complete Decorator* (London, 1826), George Smith's second book of designs, *The Cabinet-Maker and Upholsterer's Guide* (London, 1826), and Thomas King's *The Modern Style of Cabinet Work Exemplified* (London, 1829) (fig. 12). Furniture by Cook & Parkin is marked by a calm reservedness when compared with the energy of a Quervelle design. Features such as "distinctive demilune panels, large flat bosses with ovolo-molded edges, bosses with prominent convex centers surrounded by ovolo molding, and a variety of individualistic carved and gilded details predominate."[44]

The strength of Cook & Parkin's design sensibility and business savvy positioned them as leading makers of Philadelphia furniture in the Classical style. They competed with well-established stalwarts like Barry, and the more measured patterns of their Biedermeier-like designs of this period offered a counterpoint to Quervelle's more dramatic designs of the 1820s. Perhaps influenced by Cook & Parkin's success, Quervelle eventually adopted plainer profiles in the 1830s, as seen on his furniture for the Turnbull family at the Louisiana plantation Rosedown.[45] When Cook and Parkin began to work in separate spaces in 1829, it is unclear whether it was a strategic move that capitalized business for both. The partnership formally dissolved in 1833, but Parkin continued to make furniture at Barry's former shop location at 134 South Second Street, which Parkin had reimagined and named—in a nod to the London sculptor and designer George Bullock—Egyptian Hall.[46]

Fig. 12. *Library Table*, attributed to Cook & Parkin, c. 1827, rosewood, satinwood, Philadelphia Museum of Art, Gift of the Estate of Robert A. Goldstein in memory of Beatrice G. and Morton Goldstein, 2019-35-1 (Courtesy Philadelphia Museum of Art). The acanthus scrolls have a dolphin-like profile.

Barry moved to 129 South Walnut Street in 1825, where he shared space with at least one other maker, Robert West. Both Barry and West sold furniture to former president Andrew Jackson for his plantation, The Hermitage, just outside of Nashville, Tennessee.[47] While a large sofa is in a lyre form, the majority of the furniture is in the more austere so-called Late Grecian or Grecian Plain style, with a return to relying on the figure of the wood—both mahogany and rosewood—for the surface ornament accented by gilt stencils to emphasize the sculptural profiles (fig. 13).

The bedchamber furniture that Isaac Jones (1794–1868) made in 1833 for wine and liquor merchant Elijah Vansyckel (1788–1855) and Sarah Belinda Smith Vansyckel (1799–1871) epitomizes this final phase of Philadelphia Classicism: large sculptural furniture cloaked in prodigious amounts of highly figured veneers, gilt stenciled outlines with carving reserved for finials and cornices, and mirrors and upholstery wherever possible. The nine-piece suite is made of solid mahogany

Fig. 13. ***Pier Table*****, unknown maker, c. 1833, rosewood, tulip poplar, yellow pine; marble, mirror glass, patinated brass, Purchased with the Miller-Worley Fund for Excellence in American Art, 2018, Philadelphia Museum of Art, 2018-131-1a,b (Courtesy Philadelphia Museum of Art). The mirror at the back doubles the size of the gilt stencil ornament.**

Fig. 14. ***Secretary Bookcase*****, Isaac Jones, 1833, rosewood veneer, mahogany, mahogany veneer, tulip poplar; brass, silvered glass, gilt decoration, Philadelphia Museum of Art, Gift of Miss Pauline Townsend Pease, 1979, 1979-108-6 (Courtesy Philadelphia Museum of Art)**

veneered in showy mahogany and rosewood. The secretary bookcase (fig. 14) boasts the full range of decoration: carved ornaments, gilded brass mounts, papier-mâché decorated handles, silvered-glass doors, veneers, and gilt stenciled decoration. This sophistication of Classical design made Philadelphia furniture of the 1830s wildly popular in the American South. For example, Richard Thompson Archer (1797–1867), a Virginia-born plantation owner, visited Philadelphia in 1836/37 to establish markets for the cotton cultivated on his land by enslaved Africans. While in the city, he commissioned a reed organ for his wife, Ann Barnes Archer (1818–1892), with a writing table, worktable, and dressing table secreted inside the lid (fig. 15). The references to classical art could not be more conspicuous: the instrument is supported by caryatids memorializing the women of Karyai (or Caryae) in the Peloponnese, as seen on the Siphnian Treasury at Delphi (525 BCE) and the so-called Porch of the Maidens on the Erechtheion on the Acropolis (421–406 BCE) of Athens. Elegant lyres form the centerpiece of the base.

More than any single publication, it was artisans—cabinetmakers, upholsterers, and their allied tradespeople—who sought, proposed, developed, and shaped the taste for fashionable furniture in Philadelphia. They catered to a sophisticated and worldly group of patrons, allowing them to access the height of fashion in their own city. Patrons throughout the growing United States ordered furniture from Philadelphia makers, placing Grecian-style furniture into similarly styled and spacious Classical houses. Success in the manufacture of fashionable furniture was a source of pride for Americans at the time, and beginning in 1824, artisans entered their wares into the annual competitions at Philadelphia's Franklin Institute, which was founded to encourage creativity and ingenuity in the arts, sciences, and manufactures (see cat. 49a–b).[48]

Fig. 15. *Reed Organ*, Emilius Nicolai Scherr (1794–1874), 1836–1837, mahogany, mahogany veneer, maple, maple veneer, white pine; painted and gilded plaster, ivory, ebony, mother-of-pearl, white metal, brass, silvered glass, leather, wool baize, cut silk velvet, Philadelphia Museum of Art, Purchased with the Thomas Skelton Harrison Fund and with the gifts (by exchange) of the Titus C. Geesey Collection, Linda M. Girard Barlow, Sarah McLean Williams in memory of Mrs. William L. McLean, Lydia Thompson Morris, Lewine Russell, the Elizabeth Wandell Smith Collection, and Rhoda and Ira Albom, 2010, 2010-195-1 (Courtesy Philadelphia Museum of Art)

By the late 1820s, New York City's mercantile exchanges had begun to recenter the economic pulse of the Northeast to that city, but Philadelphia worked to maintain its reputation as the country's centerpiece for artistic instruction and Classical idealism. Philadelphians—artists and patrons alike—of the 1790s and the first decades of the 1800s embraced the city's ambition to be the Athens of America; it was more an aspiration than an accomplishment and more a vision than a triumph. Philadelphia Classical furniture was fashioned in bold forms and decorated with exuberantly carved cornucopia, lions and lions' feet, dolphins, lyres, shells, and Bacchanal garlands. Radial fans and compass stars were lobed in two dimensions and surfaces were framed with intricate gilt stenciling. Ambitious artisans imported Boulle work, *ormolu* mounts, marble slabs and specimen tops, and painted stones, and the entrepreneurs organized their shops to maximize their output and export their wares to eager markets in the American South. By the 1830s, German and Danish artisans brought a sleek, Biedermeier taste to the city, making less curvaceous forms with highly polished surfaces on figured veneers. Philadelphia Classical furniture of this period demonstrates the success of the pursuit to make furniture that mirrored that of ancient Egypt, Greece, and Rome, an enthusiasm sparked by the revival of classical arts in the eighteenth century. Philadelphia's artisans—chair and cabinetmakers, upholsterers, carvers, decorative painters, mount makers, and architects—catered to the tastes of a prosperous elite and succeeded by creating sculptural works of art that functioned as furniture.

1. Latrobe to George Harrison, June 20, 1809, quoted in Alexandra Alevizatos Kirtley and Peggy A. Olley, *Classical Splendor: Painted Furniture for a Grand Philadelphia House* (Philadelphia: Philadelphia Museum of Art, 2016), 91.
2. New Castle, Kent, and Sussex counties separated from Pennsylvania on June 15, 1776, to form what became Delaware. For the early period, the so-called "lower three counties" provided important wealth and patronage for Philadelphia. For a chest representing the Dutch tradition in early Pennsylvania, see Alexandra Alevizatos Kirtley, *American Furniture, 1650–1840: Highlights from the Philadelphia Museum of Art* (Philadelphia: Philadelphia Museum of Art, 2020), cat. 217.
3. Mahogany is recorded in joiners' inventories in the 1690s, such as Robert Ware, no. 177, 1698; Hector Watts, no. 179, 1698; and Robert Browne, no. 224, 1699. See Philadelphia Wills and Inventories (Microfilm, Joseph Downs Collection of Manuscripts and Printed Ephemera, Winterthur Library).
4. To date, no Spanish artisans have been documented, but trade with the Spanish colonies was established early and was brisk through the nineteenth century. James Claypoole's 1687 inventory lists "Spanish tables." Some artisans who arrived from England were Huguenot—that is, Dutch, Belgian, and French Protestants who emigrated from their ancestral lands to Britain.
5. Despite late nineteenth- and twentieth-century histories, it is well documented that Quakers enslaved people, including the prominent cabinetmakers Benjamin Randolph (1721–1791) and Thomas Affleck (1740–1795) and the upholsterer Plunkett Fleeson (1712–1791).
6. Books that appear frequently were by Andrea Palladio, Edward Hoppus, James Gibbs, and Abraham Swan. For inventories, see Philadelphia Wills and Inventories (Microfilm, Joseph Downs Collection of Manuscripts and Printed Ephemera, Winterthur Library) for John Mifflin (1759), William Leech (1764),

Henry Rigby (1768), Edmond Wooley (1771), John Derry (1777), and George Measam (1781).

7. See Henry Clifton (1771), George Pickering (1784), Peter Morgan (1780), Thomas Bryan (1794), and William Savery (1787), Philadelphia Wills and Inventories.
8. See Alexandra Alevizatos Kirtley, *The 1772 Philadelphia Furniture Price Book: An Introduction and Guide* (Philadelphia: Philadelphia Museum of Art, 2005). London cabinetmakers did not print a price book until 1788. The only surviving copy is a promised gift to the Philadelphia Museum of Art. It measures 6¼ in. long by 3⅝ in. wide.
9. See *Pennsylvania Mercury* (Philadelphia), July 10, 1788, 3. Carver George Measam owned a copy of Robert Manwaring's *The Cabinet and Chair-Maker's Real Friend and Companion, or, the Whole System of Chair-Making Made Plain and Easy* (London: Henry Webley, 1765) in 1781 and Thomas Affleck owned a copy of "Shippendale's [sic] *Director*" when he died in 1795. See Kirtley, *American Furniture, 1650–1840*, cat. 92.
10. The phrase was coined by Titian Leeds in his poem "Memorial to William Penn" (1729); Directors of the Library Company to Thomas Penn, May 31, 1733, in *The Papers of Benjamin Franklin*, ed. Leonard W. Labaree (New Haven: Yale University Press, 1959), 1:320–21. See also Alexandra Alevizatos Kirtley, "Athens of America," *The Encyclopedia of Greater Philadelphia*, last modified 2024, https:// philadelphiaencyclopedia.org/themes/ athens-of-america/. The painter Gilbert Stuart (1755–1828) frequently recalled his years in Philadelphia during the 1790s as the time "when I resided in the Athens of America."
11. See *American Travelers to Italy in the Eighteenth Century: A Journal of Samuel Powel* (Rome, 1764), ed. Sarah Jackson (Florence: Studio per Edizione Scelte, 2001).
12. Johann Joachim Winckelmann, *Reflections on the Painting and Sculpture of the Greeks*, trans. Henry Fusseli (London, 1765), 2.
13. See Kirtley, "Athens of America."
14. It is unknown exactly when Shearer's designs in the 1788 London price book or Hepplewhite's *Guide* arrived in Philadelphia, but Sheraton's *Drawing-Book* was advertised in 1794, less than a year after its release in London. See advertisement by bookseller John Ambler in Dunlap and Claypoole's *American Daily Advertiser* (Philadelphia), November 4, 1794, 4.
15. The Beauvais factory was founded in 1666 in Beauvais, France. By the eighteenth century, it became known for making tapestries for furniture covers. Charissa Bremer-David, *French Tapestries & Textiles in the J. Paul Getty Museum* (Los Angeles: The J. Paul Getty Museum, 1997), 76.
16. See Alexandra Alevizatos Kirtley, "Contriving the Madisons' Drawing Room: Benjamin Henry Latrobe and the Furniture of John and Hugh Finlay," *The Magazine Antiques* 178, no. 12 (December 2009): 56–63; Kirtley and Olley, *Classical Splendor*, 42–43 Kirtley, *American Furniture, 1650–1840*, cats. 117–19.
17. Kathleen Catalano and Richard C. Nylander, "New Attributions to Adam Hains, Philadelphia Furniture Maker," *The Magazine Antiques* 117, no. 5 (May 1980): 1112–16.
18. *Federal Gazette* (Philadelphia), June 10, 1790. The most complete biography of Aitken is in Kirtley and Olley, *Classical Splendor*, 67–73.
19. Aiken and six other master cabinet- and chair makers (Henry Ingle, Jacob Wayne, Samuel Claphamson, John Alexander, John Douglass, and Jacob Schreiner) led the cabinetmakers out of a labor dispute with the journeyman cabinetmakers that lasted from 1794 to 1796. See Kirtley and Olley, *Classical Splendor*, 68. One of the journeymen leaders was William Cocks (d. 1799), who hailed from York, England, and partnered with Aitken in ventures to sell furniture in ports in the South, including Charleston, South Carolina. William Camp (1773–1822) apprenticed with Cocks and then in 1801 moved to Baltimore where he was the leading cabinetmaker.
20. See the tambour desk (MV W-158) and chair (MV M-4058) at Mount Vernon, Virginia. The splat design for the chairs follows plates 33 and 36 in Thomas Sheraton's *The Cabinet-Maker and Upholsterer's Drawing-Book* (1793), and the tambour secretary follows a Shearer design illustrated in the 1793 edition of the *London Book of Prices*. During the time that Aitken was making this furniture, Lewis Affleck, the son of the prominent Scottish-born joiner Thomas Affleck (1740–1795) was working in Aitken's shop. Aitken hired a ship and delivered the Washingtons' furniture to Mount Vernon, likely conducting other mercantile pursuits along the way.
21. See Kirtley, *American Furniture, 1650–1840*, cat. 127.
22. Cornelius William Stafford, *The Philadelphia Directory for 1798* (Philadelphia: William W. Woodward, 1798), 20.
23. "Joseph Barry," *Thomas Jefferson Encyclopedia*, Monticello, last modified 2024, https://www.monticello.org/ research-education/thomas-jefferson-encyclopedia/joseph-barry/.
24. Before his 1811 trip, Barry advertised "fashionable articles . . . the newest and most fashionable Cabinet Furniture, superbly finished in the rich Egyptian and Gothic style." *Aurora General Advertiser* (Philadelphia), January 25, 1810, 1.
25. *Columbian Museum and Savannah Advertiser*, October 5, 1798. In February 1803, Barry opened a shop at 130 Baltimore Street in Baltimore. The following month, he moved his business to Light Street but ceased his Baltimore venture early in 1804. There are patent similarities between the labels of Barry and William Camp, who trained in Philadelphia and certainly would have known Barry. They both employ choice furniture designs from Thomas Sheraton's *The Cabinet-Maker and Upholsterer's Drawing-Book* (London, 1791–1793). For Camp's label, see the frontispiece in *Baltimore Furniture: The Work of Baltimore and Annapolis Cabinetmakers, 1760–1810* (Baltimore: Baltimore Museum of Art, 1947). For Barry's label, see William MacPherson Hornor Jr., *The Blue Book of Philadelphia Furniture* (Philadelphia: By the author, 1935), plate 432; see also cat. 40.
26. "Anniversary Oration to the Society of Artists" (May 8, 1811), in *The Papers of Benjamin Henry Latrobe*, vol. 3, *Correspondence and Miscellaneous Papers*, ed. John C. Van Horne and Lee W. Formwalt (New Haven: Yale University Press for the Maryland Historical Society, 1984), 76.
27. For a complete history of the commission and the furniture that survives from it, see Kirtley and Olley, *Classical Splendor*.
28. Latrobe wrote to William Waln, "I have designed a side chair & I think it will be tolerably handsome. It will at all events be new. But the pattern chair was the ugliest thing ever. I have ordered another pattern. To make a chair requires as much taste as to design one. Aiken has the sideboard already in hand." Latrobe to Waln, August 25, 1808, in *The Papers of Benjamin Henry Latrobe: The Microtext Edition*, ed. Edward C. Carter II (Clifton, NJ: James T. White & Co., 1976), 39/B6, 66/A6.
29. See Kirtley, "Contriving the Madisons' Drawing Room."
30. See Kirtley and Olley, *Classical Splendor*, Appendix B, 156–58. When Bridport died in 1819, these and the other erudite volumes in his library were sold at vendue in Philadelphia, where they certainly would have continued to impact the visual landscape.
31. See ibid., 62–65, cat. 5.
32. Rebecca Gratz, November 7, 1821, quoted in Kirtley and Olley, *Classical Splendor*, 65.
33. Aitken's father-in-law, James McDowell, died on July 12, 1815, and soon Aitken advertised that he was leaving the cabinetmaking business to become a farmer in Chester County. On April 16, 1817, John and Jane Aitken sold properties on Sixth and Chestnut to Thomas Hall for $16,500; Philadelphia County Deed Book MR13, p. 278, Philadelphia City Archives. Four more houses situated on that corner were included in Aitken's 1839 will; Will 9879, written March 15, 1839, proven September 30, 1839, Chester County Archives, Pennsylvania.
34. *United States Gazette* (Philadelphia), June 8, 1830, 3.
35. *Philadelphia Inquirer*, October 26, 1833, 3. His first wife was Sarah Anne Pearson Bouvier (1805–1826), the daughter of the confectioner Eliza Goodfellow (1767–1851). Goodfellow, who wrote what is considered to be America's first modern cookbook, remained close with Bouvier and rented space in several cabinetmaking shops, including Barry's former shop at 134 South Second Street, from 1826 until at least 1834.
36. Charles L. Venable, "Germanic Craftsmen and Furniture Design in Philadelphia, 1820–1850," in *American Furniture 1998*, ed. Luke Beckerdite (Lebanon, NH: University Press of New England for the Chipstone Foundation, 1998).
37. See a card table pillar in the collection of the Philadelphia Museum of Art (2008-128-1).
38. For example, local manufacturers made patinated brass mounts as less expensive alternatives to *ormolu* mounts made of mercury-gilded bronze.
39. *Philadelphia Inquirer*, July 21, 1834, 4.
40. The console tables are at Andalusia Historic House, Gardens, and Arboretum, PA (no number) and the Saint Louis Art Museum (1:1971); the center tables are in the Kaufman Collection (no number) and the Baltimore Museum of Art (1990.73).
41. *Poulson's American Daily Advertiser* (Philadelphia), September 11, 1824. Kirtley, *American Furniture, 1650–1840*, cats. 191–95.
42. *Imported candelabra*, Philadelphia Museum of Art, 1913-49c,d; Philadelphia candelabra, Munson-Williams-Proctor Institute, 60.58; Anna Tobin d'Ambrosia, *Masterpieces of American Furniture from the Munson-Williams-Proctor Institute* (Utica, NY: Munson-Williams-Proctor Institute, 2001), cat. 15.
43. See Carswell Rush Berlin, "'A Shadow of a Magnitude': The Furniture of Thomas Cook and Richard Parkin," *American Furniture 2013*, ed. Luke Beckerdite (Milwaukee: Chipstone Foundation, 2013), 156–95.
44. Ibid., 188.
45. See Thomas Gordon Smith, "Quervelle Furniture at Rosedown, in Louisiana," *The Magazine Antiques* 159, no. 5 (May 2001): 770–79.
46. See *Philadelphia Inquirer*, March 12, 1834, 12.
47. See Carswell Rush Berlin, "Presidential Appointments: Andrew Jackson and Three Philadelphia Cabinetmakers," *The Magazine Antiques* 184, no. 2 (March–April 2017): 74–83.
48. Quervelle's secretary bookcase made *en suite* with the two worktables in the Schrimsher Collection won the silver medal, which was the highest honor, in 1827. See Kirtley, *American Furniture, 1650–1840*, cat. 188 (PMA 1960-159-1).

40

Wardrobe, c. 1810–1812

Joseph B. Barry & Son: Joseph Brown Barry (1757–1838) and Joseph Brown Barry Jr. (1788–1862), in partnership 1810–1820
Philadelphia
Mahogany, ebonized mahogany; tulip poplar, yellow pine, Atlantic white cedar; silvered brass
92¾ × 104¾ × 24 in.

LABEL: (engraved by James Akin with copies of Thomas Sheraton's *The Cabinet-Maker and Upholsterer's Drawing-Book* designs): "Pier / A Lady's Dressing Commode / Tables / Joseph B. Barry & Son / Cabinetmakers & Upholsterers [cut out] / N° 132 South Second Street / Philadelphia / Drawing / A Sideboard with Knife Cases / Room Chairs / Orders for the West Indies or els[ewhere Executed in the neatest manner and] / Attended to [with the Strictest punctuality. / Drawn by J. Akin]." (See Appendix II)

PROVENANCE: Elizabeth Willing Powel (1743–1830), Philadelphia, or her nephew and adopted son and heir, Colonel John Hare Powel (b. John Powel Hare, 1786–1856) and Julia de Veaux Powel (1798–1845); By purchase of General Robert Patterson (1792–1881) and Sarah Ann Engle Patterson (1792–1875), 1830s; To their son Robert Emmet Patterson (1830–1906) and Mary Louisa Houston Patterson (1828–1908); To their son Francis Engle Patterson II (1863–1942) and Elizabeth Bella Hoopes Patterson (1864–1936), Waverly Farm, 5008 Kennett Pike, Wilmington, DE; To their daughter Anna (Nancy) Hoopes Patterson Lindsay (1887–1960) and Joseph Horace Lindsay (1885–1932); To their son Francis Engle Patterson Lindsay (1910–1963) and Louise Robinson Lindsay (1912–1960); To their son William Patterson Lindsay (1937–2013) and Zona Hertzog Lindsay (b. 1936); With New Life Furniture Systems, Newport, DE, and Garrison Grey Kingsley (1947–2023), Mount Cuba, DE, Nov. 2019; With Clark Pearce, Essex, MA; Purchased by Schrimshers, 2020.

The quality of wood and the steadfast attention to detail in the execution of this extraordinary wardrobe exemplifies the work of Joseph Barry. Faced with the finest flitches of mahogany and lined with aromatic cedar, the wardrobe fulfills its function of safeguarding precious textiles while also being a fashionable work of art. The label, which Barry edited with a cut-out and pen additions, documents that it was made at an auspicious moment: during the two years that Barry's shop was located at 132 South Second Street and just as his son Joseph Jr. had joined the business. While Barry dominated cabinetmaking in Philadelphia from 1798 to 1838, fewer than twenty pieces are documented to his shop. Most are post-1815, making this early work all the more significant. The flat surfaces and oval- and square-paneled door designs of this wardrobe, along with a secretary bookcase that Barry sold to Robert MacKay (1772–1816) and Eliza McQueen MacKay (1778–1862) of Savannah, are emblematic of Barry's furniture in the Neoclassical style.[1]

The Barry shop spared no expense on this wardrobe commission. The design of a central two-door cabinet (with trays and drawers) flanked by single door wings (for hanging clothes) derives from Thomas Shearer's plate 3 in *The Cabinet-Makers' London Book of Prices* (London, 1788, 1793). It is rooted in architecture: the four sections measure about 26¼ inches each, with the center projecting like the facades of contemporary houses. The facade proportions—particularly the cornice, crossbanded waist molding, and base—likely matched the room for which it was made, forming a seamless visual presence and possibly even masking the wardrobe as a built-in. The consistently matched figure of the mahogany on the posts, rails, drawer and tray fronts, and solid ends means that Barry used a single mahogany log for the structural timber on this commission; only the highly prized dappled (or horseflesh) mahogany found in the large oval and small square panels may have come from another log. The drawer hardware is silvered.

Barry cut out the part of the label that said "From London" because his business now included his son who was not from London or trained in London; however, the immaculate construction of the wardrobe exposes Barry's—and perhaps his journeymen's—training in and habit of construction in the best British traditions: in the central section, the five trays that are set above two stacks of drawers all slide directly against the sides of the cabinets. The wood grain of the bottoms of the drawers runs side-to-side and the bottoms of the ledger trays have floating panels, all of which is the common London method. The joints are precisely executed and each drawer, ledger tray, and door fits exactly into the sides of their respective cabinet. To protect the textiles stored inside from the elements, having nearly air-tight spaces was highly desirable for a wardrobe: the snugness of the construction limited exposure to dust, smoke, and air, while the Atlantic white cedar of the drawer and tray bottoms off-gassed and repelled destructive webbing clothes moths.

Wing wardrobes were often the most expensive items found in urban cabinet price books of the early nineteenth century, and they were certainly more common then than their survival today would suggest.[2] This example most likely stayed in one family's house from the 1880s to 2019; the quality of the wood and the subtlety of the design made it an attraction, and its usefulness made it a mainstay.

1. The secretary bookcase bears a label with the address of 134 South Second Street, dating it to between 1806 and 1809. It was originally owned by Robert Mackay and is at the Andrew Low House Museum, Savannah, Georgia.
2. Wing wardrobes were also made in Baltimore for wealthy merchants, including one likely made for the Bosleys by the Philadelphia-trained Baltimore cabinetmaker William Camp (1773–1822). Camp and Barry knew one another and even had very similar labels. See Gregory R. Weidman, *Furniture in Maryland, 1740–1940: The Collection of the Maryland Historical Society* (Baltimore: Maryland Historical Society, 1984), cat. 198.

41

Side Chair, 1815–1818

Attributed to Joseph Brown Barry (1757–1838)
Philadelphia
Mahogany; ash, tulip poplar; brass, replacement upholstery
33 × 18¾ × 21 in.

PROVENANCE: George Harrison (1762–1845) and Sophia Francis Harrison (1769–1851), Philadelphia; To their nephew (whose affairs George managed) Joshua Francis Fisher (1807–1873) and Eliza Izard Middleton Fisher (1815–1819); To their daughter Maria Middleton Fisher Coxe (1847–1933) and Brinton Coxe (1833–1892); To their son Edmund James Drifton Coxe (1881–1934) and Elizabeth Kean Michaux Turner Coxe (1883–1959); To their son Daniel Michaux Coxe (1904–1970) and Dorothy Weld Coxe (1906–1986), Philadelphia. With Robert Townshend Trump (1933–2015), Flourtown, PA; Purchased by Schrimshers, 1990.

Distinguished by their inswept front and rear legs and stiles, klismos chairs were—and perhaps remain—the design most emblematic of ancient furniture. The evolution of the klismos chair in early national Philadelphia originated with the embrace of French design, which arrived through publications, furniture makers, upholsterers, carvers, painters, and patrons. British designs dominated but were themselves infused with French taste, as observed in the title of Thomas Chippendale's *The Gentleman and Cabinet-Maker's Director* (London, 1754), in which "modern taste" refers to the publication's French designs. Long misinterpreted as an easy chair, a *bergère à oreilles*, or French chair, made in Philadelphia demonstrates the ease and eagerness with which the city's patrons in the 1760s embraced French seating furniture in a way not found in other British North American centers.[1]

Fig. 41.1. James Barron, detail of plate 39 from *Modern and Elegant Designs of Cabinet and Upholstery Furniture* (London, 1814), hand-colored engraving (Courtesy Winterthur Museum, Garden & Library)

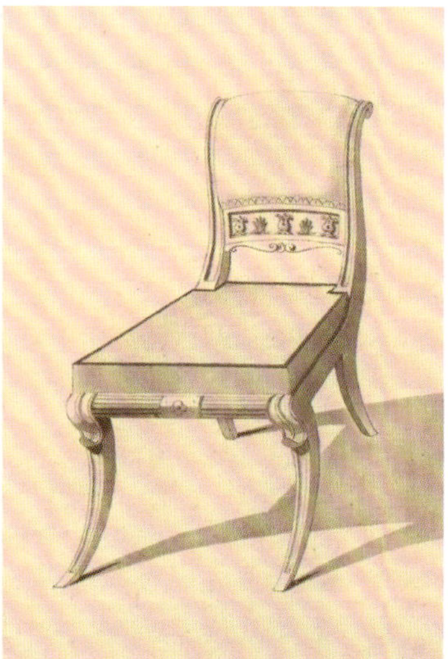

Fig. 41.2. James Barron, detail of plate 31 from *Modern and Elegant Designs of Cabinet and Upholstery Furniture* (London, 1814), engraving (Courtesy Winterthur Museum, Garden & Library)

It is within this tradition that Philadelphians' preferences for Neoclassical furniture of the 1790s tended towards British renditions of French furniture from the 1770s to the 1780s—that is, the furniture associated with the final years of the reign of Louis XVI and Marie Antoinette. These French-inspired attributes included turned front legs with conical feet and bound fasces as capitals, reeding, rounded seats, and intertwined urn banisters or fully upholstered backs (see p. 158). By around 1800, Americans were seeking direct cues, and likely the first klismos design copied in Philadelphia was plate 77 of the 1802 design by Napoleon Bonaparte's favored designer, Pierre de La Mésangère, in *Collection de meubles et objets de goût* (see p. 160, fig. 5a).[2]

This remarkably sophisticated klismos chair (one of a set) exemplifies the adaptation of ancient forms and motifs that was the genius of a cabinetmaker like Joseph Barry, who sought inspiration in Philadelphia and abroad. The crest rail is tenoned into the rear stiles, whose flat faces with inset panels match the design of the front legs. A lyre with brass rods mimicking strings forms the back of the chair and is set on an elegantly shaped and scrolled medial rail. The squared edges of the upholstered seat (a so-called French edge) are likely formed by the high, beveled edges of the slip seat frame. The swept front legs are capped by a scroll that provides a transition to the rounded, reeded fasces-like front rail. The design is an amalgam of two illustrations from James Barron's *Modern and Elegant Designs of Cabinet and Upholstery Furniture* (London, 1814): plate 39 for the back of the chair (fig. 41.1), and plate 31 for the seat, front rail, and legs (fig. 41.2).

The flat surface carving seen on the crest rail and acanthus-laden lyre is contrasted on the front rail by pronounced reeding and a deeply relieved rosette, which is similar to compositions Thomas Cook and Richard Parkin would later employ (see cat. 59). On the crest rail, a wreath of laurels is set above a cloaked, horizontal thyrsus, the often used—but more often misidentified—pinecone-tipped fennel stalk of Bacchus and his Maenads. Intended for architecture and sculpture, those motifs would have been readily available in illustrated texts such as Joseph Beunat's *Recueil des dessins d'ornements d'architecture* (Paris, 1813).[3] Related armchairs from the set at Winterthur Museum, Garden & Library feature teethy dolphins supporting squared arms that end in thyrsus handholds.[4]

George and Sophia Harrison commissioned the set of these chairs for their Philadelphia house on the southwest corner of Chestnut and Sixth Streets. Like their next-door neighbors, the Walns, they fervently embraced all aspects of French-inspired Classicism (architecture, furniture, and furnishings). Like the Walns, they even commissioned furniture from the Parisian-born *ébéniste* Charles-Honoré Lannuier of New York; these chairs would have been adjacent to Lannuier's furniture.[5]

George Harrison was a close confidante of the British-born Francophile architect Benjamin Henry Latrobe, who, with his

commission for the Walns' house, jump-started an enthusiasm for this flavor of Classicism. In 1809, a year after the Waln commission was complete, Latrobe lamented to Harrison about Americans and their discomfort with wanting refined goods: "we are jammed, between our republican principles, [and] our aristocratic wishes. They order these things better in France."[6]

---

1. Alexandra Alevizatos Kirtley, *American Furniture, 1650–1840: Highlights from the Philadelphia Museum of Art* (Philadelphia: Philadelphia Museum of Art, 2020), cat. 68. French-trained carvers such as Nicholas Bernard (1732–1789) and Martin Jugiez (1730–1815) were among the most sought-after in colonial Philadelphia, and more French artisans arrived after independence: carver Claudius LeGrand (d. 1801); paperers and upholsterers George Bertault (1771–1831) and Francis de l'Orme (dates unknown); numerous French painters, including Jean-Pierre Henri Elouis (1755–1840); and merchants/patrons Claudius Paul Raguet (1750–1793), Stephen Girard (1750–1831), and Louis Clapier (1765–1837).
2. See the chair attributed to Thomas Whitecar, 1806–10 (2019-112-1), and the armchair by an unknown maker, 1740–1750 (2022-24-1), at the Philadelphia Museum of Art.
3. For an excellent thyrsus, see *Bacchus* (no. XXXXIII), Borghese Gallery, Rome. A similar assortment of ornaments is found on a set of painted chairs made in Baltimore for Richard and Lydia Ragan of Hagerstown, Maryland; see Kirtley, *American Furniture, 1650–1840*, cat. 296.
4. Winterthur Museum, Garden & Library, Delaware, 2006.15.1 and 2006.15.2.
5. Brant Foundation, Greenwich, Connecticut; see Alexandra Alevizatos Kirtley and Peggy A. Olley, *Classical Splendor: Painted Furniture for a Grand Philadelphia House* (Philadelphia: Philadelphia Museum of Art, 2016), fig. 65.
6. Latrobe to Harrison, June 20, 1809. Ibid., 91.

42

Side Chairs (two from a set of ten), 1816

Unknown maker; painted by John Philip Fondé (1794–1831)
Ash, white pine, white oak; painted and gilded decoration, brass, replacement upholstery
31¾ × 18 × 21 in.

PROVENANCE: Major David Lenox (1753–1828) and Tacy Lukens Lenox (1783–1833), Philadelphia; To their niece and adopted daughter, Sarah Lukens Keene (1784–1866); Bequest to Episcopal Diocese of Pennsylvania; The diocese's sale, Samuel T. Freeman & Co., Philadelphia, Sept. 23–25, 1963, lot 332; Purchased by James Biddle (1929–2005) and Louisa Copeland (Biddle) Duemling (b. 1936); By gift to The Andalusia Foundation, 1980; Deaccessioned by order of the Trustees of The Andalusia Foundation to benefit acquisitions, 2018; With James M. Kilvington (dealer, b. 1950). With Clark Pearce, Essex, MA, 2019; Purchased by Schrimshers, 2019.

More than any other single work of art, the klismos chair typifies the shift from the references to ancient art that are found in Neoclassical furniture to the more archaeologically accurate designs that characterize furniture of the classical period. These chairs—two from a set of ten—encompass key attributes of a klismos chair: a tablet-shaped crest rail that extends far beyond the dramatically incurved stiles; a severely linear, trapezoid-shaped seat; incurved rear legs; and rounded front legs, which are variations on the standard Greek klismos that have four squared and curved legs. The front legs are painted with lotus-flower capitals, like the columns of the Egyptian temple at Luxor (another example of the mixing of motifs and styles in this period), and all of the surfaces are painted to mimic brass inlay and mounts.

When Major David Lenox and his wife Tacy Lukens Lenox commissioned the chairs in 1816 for their house on the banks of the Delaware River in Bristol, Pennsylvania, their final surface and upholstery treatment were undecided.[1] On another chair from the set, in the collection of the Philadelphia Museum of Art (PMA), the entire surface is grain-painted to mimic rosewood, and then covered with the current surface, which mimics maple graining. On the tablet backs of at least five of the chairs, a different decoration is suggested—painted scenes, designs, and even sketches for gilded brass mounts. Ultimately, the Lenoxes chose the maple graining and tablet backs covered in the seat fabric.

The maker of the set of these chairs has yet to be identified, but the complex sliding dovetail that joins the dramatically curved chair back to the seat suggests that the person was highly skilled at joinery and cabinetry. One strong candidate is the prolific chairmaker Joseph Burden (1771–1841), who received commissions from prominent patrons (including Benjamin Henry Latrobe) and won an award from the Franklin Institute in 1825 for an ingenious chair design; his ambitious brother Henry Roe Burden (1771–1819) is another candidate. Henry Burden left Philadelphia in the wake of the economic crisis of the post–War of 1812 and advertised in Washington, D.C., in November 1816. By January 5, 1818, the Philadelphia-born and -trained ornamental sign painter John Philip Fondé who painted these chairs had joined Henry Burden in D.C..[2]

On top of his lively rendition of maple graining, Fondé painted ornaments that simulate gilded brass strapwork and mounts. Shadows underneath give the ornaments dimensionality in a manner similar to coach and sign painting, the trade in which Fondé was trained. Single-hair brushstrokes of red vermillion add detail to the gilded decoration, and Fondé's inscription under the front rail of the PMA's chair is in the same paint used to make those details.[3] The overall composition of the painted decoration suggests a fictitious construction for the chair, belying the complex mortise-and-tenon and dovetail joints that are not located where the painted lines suggest they are.

The color of the wool moiré upholstery—replaced to match the original upholstery surviving on a chair from the set now at the Baltimore Museum of Art—was meant to complement the color of the maple graining. The texture of the wool contrasts with the sheen of the silk tufts, creating an interplay of matte and burnish similar to that of gilded surfaces.

1. The house was destroyed in 1963. The other chairs in the set are at the Andalusia Foundation (two chairs); Metropolitan Museum of Art, New York (1963.143); Winterthur Museum, Garden & Library (1964.26); Art Institute of Chicago (1970.436); Philadelphia Museum of Art (1977-299-1), Baltimore Museum of Art (2003.122); and Bayou Bend Collection and Gardens, Museum of Fine Arts, Houston (B.2007.2). For a full discussion, see Alexandra Alevizatos Kirtley, "The Painted Furniture of Philadelphia: A Reappraisal," *The Magazine Antiques* 169, no. 5 (May 2006): 142–43, and Kirtley, *American Furniture, 1650–1840: Highlights from the Philadelphia Museum of Art* (Philadelphia: Philadelphia Museum of Art, 2020), cat. 184.
2. Kirtley, "Painted Furniture of Philadelphia," 140–143, n.50.
3. Ibid., 140–143, n.37.

43a
Sofa Table, 1815–1820

Unknown maker
Philadelphia
Mahogany, mahogany veneer; tulip poplar, white pine, oak; brass, gilded brass
27½ × 36½ × 26 in. (with flaps down); 60¼ in. wide with flaps up

PROVENANCE: With Peter Hill, U.S. Antiques, Washington, D.C. by 1968; William Nathaniel Banks Jr. (1924–2019), Newnan, GA, 1968; His sale, Brunk Auctions, Asheville, NC, Sept. 12, 2020, lot 17; Purchased by Schrimshers, 2020.

43b
Worktable, 1815–1820

Unknown maker
Philadelphia
Mahogany, mahogany veneer; tulip poplar, white pine, oak; brass, gilded brass
31 × 23¼ × 15¼ in.

PROVENANCE: William Nathaniel Banks Jr. (1924–2019), Newnan, Georgia; His sale, Brunk Auctions, Asheville, NC, Sept. 12, 2020, lot 21; Purchased by Schrimshers, 2020.

While it is unknown whether these two tables share a provenance, their remarkable similarity combined with the rarity of their double crossed-lyre bases suggests that they were likely made in the same shop.

In ancient Greek mythology, the stringed instrument of the lyre was sacred to Apollo, the god associated with the arts, poetry, music, truth, and rational thought. Henry Wansey (c. 1752–1827), an Englishman who traveled to Philadelphia in 1794, noted at the house of William and Ann Willing Bingham "chairs . . . of the newest taste; the back in the form of a lyre, with festoons of crimson and yellow silk," which he surmised were purchased from the London firm of Seddon & Sons.[1] Originally heralded for its sweet, melodious tone, the lyre became more than just a symbol referencing classical art. By the 1810s, it represented beauty itself and was adopted as a central design element for tables, chair backs, settees, couches, and sofas. It frequently appeared in paintings and as painted decoration on wallpapers, walls, and furniture.

Distinguished by vertical strings (represented in brass) flanked by elongated S-scrolls, and topped with a crossbar and tuning knobs, the lyre was incorporated into the base of a lady's worktable in plate 26 of the appendix to Thomas Sheraton's *The Cabinet-Maker and Upholsterer's Drawing-Book* (London, 1793). Seen as a perfect complement to a lady's work in a parlor, the lyres in Sheraton's design are located between a central brace and support the two ends of a kidney-shaped vessel. On these tables the lyres have taken on the more conventional Philadelphia design of serving as the single-pedestal support. Lyre-based worktables constitute a well-known group made in Philadelphia and Baltimore, and while the turret-cornered design of the worktable box is familiar, the crossed-lyre base is highly distinctive on the worktable and, similarly, on the sofa table.[2]

The two lyres of the bases intersect at the center of the platform base, which is square shaped with canted corners and inswept sides. The base is supported by four projecting lion's-paw feet. The shape of the platform combined with the outward splay of the lion's-paw feet was a pairing commonly used on tables made in New York at this time, and their appearance on tables that were decidedly made in Philadelphia likely demonstrates the impact of journeymen from New York on Philadelphia furniture.[3] Struggling to meet demand, Philadelphia cabinetmakers Joseph Barry in 1810 and John Aitken, Joseph Beale, John Jamison, Charles B. McElwee, and Lawrence Sink in 1814 advertised in New York newspapers for journeymen to come to Philadelphia for steady work and good wages.[4]

The two-drawered worktable follows a much-used pattern, while the sofa table's design draws on the lyres used for card-table bases. Notably the crossed-lyre support presents an innovative twist and this sofa table is an early example of a type that became much more common in the 1820s and 1830s.[5] Sofa tables are not referenced in the 1811 *Journeymen Cabinet and Chairmakers' Pennsylvania Book of Prices*, which is a lagging indicator of taste, but the entry for "Pembroke table" describes the essential components of this table as well as a version with a shorter central section and longer flaps.[6]

1. Henry Wansey, *The Journal of an Excursion to the United States of North America in the Summer of 1794*, 2nd ed. (London, 1798), 123 (entry for June 8, 1794).
2. Henry Hawley, "Philadelphia Tables with Lyre Supports," *Bulletin of the Cleveland Museum of Art* 75, no. 1 (January 1988): 2–27.
3. See, for example, Peter M. Kenny, Frances F. Bretter, and Ulrich Leben, *Honoré Lannuier, Cabinetmaker from Paris: The Life and Work of a French Ébéniste in Federal New York* (New York: Metropolitan Museum of Art, 1998), figs. 89–90, pls. 70–71.
4. Joseph Barry, advertisement, *New York Mercantile*, December 3, 1810; John Aitken, Joseph Beale, John Jamison, Charles B. McElwee, and Lawrence Sink, advertisement, *New-York Gazette*, March 9, 1814.
5. See Alexandra Alevizatos Kirtley, *American Furniture, 1650–1840: Highlights from the Philadelphia Museum of Art* (Philadelphia: Philadelphia Museum of Art, 2020), cats. 176 and 177. For related card tables with matching bases, see Allison Boor, John William Boor, and Andrew Steven Harris, *Philadelphia Empire Furniture* (West Chester, PA: University Press of New England, 2006), fig. 63; Judith Hollander sale, Stair Galleries, April 2–3, 2016, no. 10.
6. *The Journeymen Cabinet and Chairmakers' Pennsylvania Book of Prices* (Philadelphia, 1811), 31. For another Pembroke/sofa table, see Kirtley, *American Furniture, 1650–1840*, cat. 179, fig. 55.

43a

43b

44

Card Table, 1815–1820

Possibly by Henry Connelly (1769–1826)
Philadelphia
Mahogany, mahogany and casuarina veneer; tulip poplar, yellow pine, oak; brass
28 × 38 × 18 in.

PROVENANCE: Sale, Neal Auction Company, New Orleans, LA, Nov. 21, 2015, lot 358; Purchased by Schrimshers, 2015.

The elegant curves of lyre support card tables made in Boston, New York, and Philadelphia, but only in the latter do dolphins form the lyre shape as on this card table (fig. 44.1). The menacing faces and scaly bodies of the dragon-looking dolphins are typical of ancient Roman depictions of the sea creatures. Related elements are found on numerous pieces of Philadelphia furniture of this period, forming the backs of chairs, the supports of tables (see cats. 47, 48, 50, and 51), and the feet of sofas and couches.[1] In contrast to the docile dolphins seen in ancient Greece, the Romans opted for a more threatening version, perhaps drawn from textiles they imported from Asia, where the dragon or sea serpent was apotropaic and embraced as beneficent and heralded luck. The liberal use of this dolphin form in Europe throughout the Renaissance, Baroque, and Classical periods may also have been influenced by trade with Asia; likewise, in Philadelphia, brisk trade with China and India could have encouraged the amalgamation of the ancient dolphin and the Asian dragon.[2]

The Schrimsher table has a D-shaped top that swivels clockwise to expand; the leaf, which opens with a hinge, is supported by the box below. The lyre base rests on a platform supported by four cabriole legs with acanthus carving at the top.[3] The front rail is decorated with mahogany and casuarina veneers. The latter is the light-wood crossbanding placed along the bottom edge of the rail.

The Schrimsher table relates to a pair made in Henry Connelly's shop in October 1817 for Stephen Girard, for the princely sum of $90, or about 30 percent more than a basic pair of lyre-based pillar-and-claw card tables.[4] The fan-shaped mahogany veneer work on the top and leaf of the Girard tables is considerably more elaborate than on this example, where the artisan used solid mahogany for the top and leaf. That feature combined with the different character on the dolphin carving demonstrates the range of work and the number of specialized artisans in Philadelphia's large cabinet shops.[5]

Fig. 44.1. Detail of cat. 44 showing dolphin lyre-shaped base

1. See Alexandra Alevizatos Kirtley, *American Furniture, 1650–1840: Highlights from the Philadelphia Museum of Art* (Philadelphia: Philadelphia Museum of Art, 2020), cats. 200 and 207.
2. Philadelphia's economy from 1784 onward was hugely bolstered by trade with Asia. See the exhibition catalogue Jean Gordon Lee and Philip Chadwick Foster Smith, *Philadelphians and the China Trade, 1784–1844* (Philadelphia: Philadelphia Museum of Art, 1984).
3. See Clark Pearce, Catherine Ebert, and Alexandra Alevizatos Kirtley, "From Apprentice to Master: The Life and Career of Philadelphia Cabinetmaker George C. Wright," in *American Furniture 2007*, ed. Luke Beckerdite (Milwaukee: Chipstone Foundation, 2007), 124–127; *Pair of Trick-Leg Card Tables*, maker unknown, c. 1810, Philadelphia Museum of Art (2021-95-1–2).
4. These tables are at Girard College. It was long thought that the Girard tables were a wedding gift for his niece. However, the tables descended in Girard's estate, and it is most likely that the shared date of the bill and the wedding were coincidental. See Robert D. Schwarz, *The Stephen Girard Collection: A Selective Catalog* (Philadelphia: Girard College, 1980), cat. 23.
5. Connelly ran a lucrative if unconventional cabinetmaking business. He primarily hired specialists and journeymen to make his designs as piece work, and the journeymen cabinetmakers all signed their work with their name and the date (see Kirtley, *American Furniture*, cat. 127). The 1820 Federal Census (accessed through ancestry.com), which was around the time this table was made and at the height of Connelly's success, shows that he had eight people working in his shop including a free Black boy. He retired to his wife's family's estate in Delaware in 1824.

45

Couch, c. 1823

Unknown maker
Philadelphia
Mahogany; white pine, tulip poplar; gilded brass, replacement upholstery
34½ × 90 × 24⅜ in.

LABEL: Formerly attached to the front rail, now attached to the underside of the seat: "This sofa came from the William Brown family / at Market and Chestnut Sts was in the / parlor. When the house was dismantled / Elizabeth Norris Brown took it to Fanny / Brown Coleman."

PROVENANCE: William Brown (1800–1842) and Deborah Norris Brown (1800–1864), Philadelphia; To their daughter Elizabeth Norris Brown (1824–1912); To her niece Fanny Brown Coleman (1861–1935), daughter of Deborah (Dollie) Norris Brown Coleman (1832–1904) and George Dawson Coleman (1825–1878), Lebanon, PA.[1] Sale, Briggs Auction House, Garnet Valley, PA, 2017; With Hirschl & Adler Galleries, New York; Purchased by Schrimshers, 2021.

This extraordinary couch represents the capacity of Philadelphia's furniture makers to use a design-book drawing as a starting point and add their own flair and local preferences to produce an elegant seat that beckons users to recline. The form developed out of Neoclassical designs for *bergère* chairs, "French Corner Chairs," and a "single headed Couch" in William Ince and John Mayhew, *The Universal System of Household Furniture* (London, 1762) and the "Chaise Longue" in Thomas Sheraton, *The Cabinet-Maker and Upholsterer's Drawing-Book* (London, 1793) and George Smith, *A Collection of Designs for Household Furniture and Interior Decoration* (London, 1808).[2] Each of these names—most especially couch, which derives from the French verb *coucher*, meaning "to lie down or sleep"—acknowledges the French source of this style of seating furniture. Popular from the seventeenth century onward, couches are defined as having no backs or partial backs and ends of different height, a design that encourages a single person to recline in them rather than being a seat for multiple sitters to share, as they might on settees, benches, and sofas.

Fig. 45.1. Detail of cat. 45 showing footrest with scallop-shell carving

In America, the curvaceous shape of the couch and the klismos feet have their roots in Philadelphia in Benjamin Henry Latrobe's 1808 elongated lyre design for what he referred incorrectly to as a sofa for the drawing rooms of William Waln and Mary Wilcocks Waln (see p. 162).[3] Made in the shop of John Aitken, it is painted and equally finished on all sides, meaning that it was intended to be circumambulated. On the Schrimsher couch, the tall end (or head) curves towards the seat to provide a comfortable support for the sitter's head, and an upholstered rest forms the foot. Only one face is ornamented, and this couch may have been one of a pair, with its mate's head and foot being on the opposite ends.[4]

The wooden base provided a lavish (and sturdy!) armature for the even more lavish expanse of upholstery; add to that the expense of the mahogany that is more elaborately carved than on any other surviving example. The base of the back arm support ends in a round medallion carved with a leafy dahlia-like flower, and the footrest is capped with an enormous and broadly lobed scallop shell on which a small gouge and chisel were used to create the lifelike details (fig. 45.1). The seat rails and the klismos feet are carved with sprays of acanthus. All in all, ornament envelopes the sitter.

This couch was likely made around the time that William and Deborah Norris Brown were married in 1823. While more daring designs were sometimes executed as less expensive painted furniture, this mahogany couch's grand size, lithe proportions, and elegant curves stand out from all other known seating furniture made in Philadelphia and suggest that the designer was well versed in earlier Neoclassical couches, such as those made in Baltimore and Salem, Massachusetts, in the 1810s.[5] A specialist would have undertaken the excessive carving, which relates slightly to that on a more substantial sofa made in the later 1820s.[6]

Deborah Norris Brown was painted in 1833 by the Philadelphia artist Thomas Sully (1783–1872). Sully sketched similar couches and seats of repose from the 1809 edition of Rudolph Ackermann's *Repository of Arts* (London, 1809–1828), presumably for practice in depicting his sitters reclining in them.[7]

1. While it has been suggested that the couch was returned to Elizabeth Norris Brown in 1912, this is not able to be documented and is highly unlikely since Mrs. Brown died in that same year. The couch does not appear in her inventory or will, which is accessible in Philadelphia City Hall, Room 180.
2. French forms infiltrated British design books, demonstrating how British—and by default American—patrons embraced French taste.
3. Shaped like an elongated lyre, the Walns' seat was neither a sofa (because it lacks a back support) nor a couch (because its ends are of equal height and tall), but rather it was a *récamier*, closely mimicking the double-ended and backless seat on which Madame Juliette Récamier (1777–1849) lies in the famous canvas by Jacques-Louis David (1748–1825) painted in Paris in 1800 now in the Musée du Louvre (INV 3708). See Alexandra Alevizatos Kirtley and Peggy A. Olley, *Classical Splendor: Painted Furniture for a Grand Philadelphia House* (Philadelphia: Philadelphia Museum of Art, 2016), cat. 2, fig. 124. Musée du Louvre (INV 3708; C 124).
4. See Alexandra Alevizatos Kirtley, *American Furniture, 1650–1840: Highlights from the Philadelphia Museum of Art* (Philadelphia: Philadelphia Museum of Art, 2020), cats. 198–99.
5. See Alexandra Alevizatos Kirtley, "A New Suspect: Baltimore Cabinetmaker Edward Priestley," in *American Furniture 2000*, ed. Luke Beckerdite (Milwaukee: Chipstone Foundation, 2000), 100–135, fig. 9; Charles F. Montgomery, *American Furniture: The Federal Period, in the Henry Francis du Pont Winterthur Museum* (New York: Viking, 1966), cat. 281.
6. See Allison Boor, John William Boor, and Andrew Steven Harris, *Philadelphia Empire Furniture* (West Chester, PA: University Press of New England, 2006), fig. 224.
7. See National Portrait Gallery, Catalog of American Portraits, Thomas Sully, *Mrs. William Brown*, 1833, oil on canvas, DLR02216; Kirtley and Olley, *Classical Splendor*, fig. 123. The portrait was sold at Skinner's in Boston in July 2013 and its current location is unknown.

46a

Card Table, c. 1830

Anthony Gabriel Quervelle (1789–1856)
Philadelphia
Mahogany, mahogany and walnut veneer; oak, tulip poplar, yellow pine, ebonized wood; wool baize, brass
30⅞ × 37⅛ × 18½ in.

LABELS: Printed on paper on the rear rail: "126 / ANTHONY G. QUERVELLE'S / CABINET AND SOFA MANUFACTORY, / SOUTH SECOND STREET A FEW DOORS BELOW DOCK / PHILADELPHIA"; retailer's label on underside (dates to before 1918, when Kyle's sold its stock and business to Strawbridge & Clothier): "J. Kyle's, 5342 Main St., Germantown, Philadelphia." (See Appendix II)

PROVENANCE: With J. Kyle's, Philadelphia, before 1918. Sale, Neal Auction Company, New Orleans, Sept. 10, 2011, no. 274; Purchased by Schrimshers, 2011.

46b–c

Card Tables, one of an assembled pair, 1825–1830

Attributed to Anthony Gabriel Quervelle (1789–1856)
Philadelphia
Mahogany, mahogany and rosewood veneer; tulip poplar, white pine; gilded decoration, brass
29 × 39 × 19½ in.

PROVENANCE (46b): Sale, Freeman's Auctions, Philadelphia, Apr. 22, 2007, lot 430; With Clark Pearce, Essex, MA; Private collection, Boston; Their sale, Brunk Auctions, Asheville, NC, Nov. 12, 2022, lot 695; Purchased by Schrimshers, 2022.

PROVENANCE (46c): Sale, Freeman's Auctions, Philadelphia, Nov. 19, 2006, lot 1431; With Clark Pearce, Essex, MA; Private collection, Boston; Their sale, Brunk Auctions, Asheville, NC, Nov. 12, 2022, lot 695; Purchased by Schrimshers, 2022.

Fig. 46.1. George Smith, "Work Table," plate 75 in *A Collection of Designs for Household Furniture and Interior Decoration* (London, 1808), hand-colored engraving (Courtesy Clark Art Institute Library, Mary Ann Beinecke Decorative Art Collection)

Born in France and trained in a shop around Paris, Anthony Quervelle brought a new angle on Classical furniture to Philadelphia, and the dynamic energy of his designs was embraced by patrons and impacted his fellow furniture makers. His shop on Second Street, just below Dock Street, was located in the premier furniture-making district. In comparison to the unique scrolled lions' paws on a pier table (cat. 54) and the scrolled dolphins on pier and worktables (cats. 47 and 49a–b), the pedestals on these card tables demonstrate how British designs—which were the predominant style despite significant French influence—inspired Quervelle. Each of the card tables has a swivel top with carved corners, a leaf veneered with burl woods in a fan-shaped, radial design, and a rectangular platform with incurved sides resting on exuberantly carved lion's-paw feet. Extravagant flame-grained veneers cover the primary surfaces of the tables, all arranged in a closely measured but creative way. The assembled pair of tables have gilt stenciling on their leaves that would have created a full circle when the two were pushed together to form a larger square table. Notably, the rear rail has a mahoganized surfaces, suggesting that the tables often stood—and were intended to stand—away from the wall.

The differences between the tables lie in their pedestals. The labeled table (cat. 46a) has a single column (laminated, turned, and veneered) on an enlarged square base. Decorative moldings are on the edges and a bold molding surrounds the squared base to provide an aesthetically pleasing transition from the vertical support to the horizontal platform. The other two tables (cats. 46b–c) have a massing of four J-shaped, squared supports with a gilded band of leaves just above where they turn outwards. Each support ends in tightly wound scrolls with turned bosses wrapped in gilded acanthus leaves.

The two designs are distinctive and noteworthy, and through them Quervelle has demonstrated his knowledge and use of British design books. For the J-shaped papyrus-sheathed supports, Quervelle adapted the Egyptian-inspired design from plate 75 in George Smith's *A Collection of Designs for Household Furniture and Interior Decoration* (London, 1808) (fig. 46.1); while Smith's 1808 *Collection* and *The Cabinet-Maker and Upholsterer's Guide* (London, 1826) were common sources for Philadelphia makers, Quervelle has shown his creativity in adapting the papyrus-shaft base of the worktable to this card table, reducing the scale, bundling four shafts together, and embellishing the terminal. A rendition of the papyrus shaft appears on an occasional table attributed to Quervelle that is the finest known example of that form (see cat. 53).[1] The central pedestal table is adapted from multiple plates for "Circular Loo Tables," "Card tables," and "Occasional Tables" in Thomas King's *The Modern Style of Cabinet Work Exemplified* (London, 1829).

Like his fellow artisans, Quervelle maintained a vigorous export business, which may explain why the single-pedestal table is labeled and the tables with more complex and fragile pedestals are not. Cabinetmakers were more likely to label wares intended for export than those they were selling locally. Additionally, it was easier to send the furniture to points overland or by sea in multiple pieces, and single-pedestal tables were often shipped in parts (in the case of cat. 46a, three: top and leaf, pedestal, and base).[2] The four-pronged pedestal tables would have required too much assembly to be shipped in parts, and they were much too vulnerable to ship assembled. On those tables, the slight differences in decoration and construction could be explained by the multiple artisans working in Quervelle's shop, which in 1840 boasted eight full-time journeymen—albeit a small shop compared to the factory-sized furniture shops that were beginning to appear in Philadelphia.[3]

1. Winterthur Museum, Garden & Library was recently given a tripod center table (2018.46.1) with papyrus shafts and related stencil work.
2. The Philadelphia Museum of Art has a round turned and carved pedestal (2008-128-1) bearing the same Quervelle label that was sent to New Orleans, where it was never assembled.
3. See the 1840 United States Federal Census, available online through Ancestry.com, https://www.ancestry.com/search/collections/8057/.

47

Pier Table, c. 1825

Attributed to Anthony Gabriel Quervelle (1789–1856)
Mahogany, mahogany and rosewood veneer; tulip poplar, pine; gilding, *vert antique*, marble, mirror glass
44 × 50 × 24 in.

PROVENANCE: John Shelby, MD (1785–1859) and Anna Maria Green Minnick Shelby (1793–1873), Nashville and Edgefield, TN; To their daughter Ann Minnick Shelby Barrow Kendrick (1813–1876) and (1) George Washington Barrow (1807–1866)[1] and (2) James Harvey Kendrick (1824–1886); To Kendrick's son James Harvey Kendrick Jr. (1848–1914) and Jane Lytle Foster Kendrick (1848–1911); To their daughter Susan Cheatham Kendrick Goode (1869–1906) and Captain Sidney Goode (1866–1899); To their son James Kendrick Goode (1889–1957); To Goode's second wife Mary Hord Wilson Goode (1900–1988), Mary Esther (Fort Walton Beach), FL; With Harold Paul Thames (1941–1996) and James Louden (dates unknown), Herron House Antiques, Montgomery, AL, before 1975; Judith Hollander (1941–2013) and Francis James Carey III (b. 1950), Penllyn, PA, by June 1975;[2] Offered for sale at the Philadelphia Antiques Show, April 1990; With Priddy, Beckerdite, and Flanigan, 1990; Purchased by Schrimshers, 1990.

With its noble presence and profuse yet neatly arranged decoration, this pier table represents the finest expression of Anthony Quervelle's dynamic version of Classical design. Quervelle employed a consistent pattern in his 1820s furniture: the unfurling of multiple curves throughout; the quality and arrangement of flame-grain veneers; the exciting use of fantastical animals and verdant leaves, flowers, and fruit in the carved decoration; the use of gilt stenciling to emphasize select areas; and the incorporation of color through upholstery or surface treatment. On his pier tables, Quervelle consistently used the shelf profile that is seen here and chose lions' legs for the front supports curved scrolls, or, as seen here, the Roman-style dolphin instead of straight columns.[3] While this majestic pier table is not labeled or signed, Quervelle's signature can be seen throughout the design.

The monumental pier table is part of a set of furniture ordered by the prominent Nashville physician John Shelby and his Philadelphia-born wife Anna Maria Green Minnick Shelby, which included the mate to this pier table (now at Winterthur Museum, Garden & Library), a couch (now at the Philadelphia Museum of Art, PMA), a center table (formerly owned by the artist Andy Warhol), and possibly a set of chairs (one of which is at the PMA).[4]

Among Quervelle's pier tables, this example and its mate stand out not only because of their dragon-like sea serpent front legs, but also the dynamic treatment of the S-shaped spray of acanthus leaves that are decorated in verdigris (restored) and tacked to the rear supports flanking the mirror (fig. 47.1). The shape of the acanthus supports mimics that of the front legs and lightens the profile of what is actually—at fifty inches wide—a substantially large table even for its form, suggesting the scale of the Shelbys's house. Flamboyantly carved cornucopia brackets at the top of each leg break the monotony of the front rail and connect to cornucopias on the other furniture in the set. The veneers on the central half-circle have been painstakingly laid out in the radial that was employed on only the finest furniture of the period; with the perimeter and the center highlighted by stencil decoration, the reflection in the mirror behind gives the illusion that it is a full circle.

Fig. 47.1. Detail of cat. 47 showing carved acanthus leaves

1. Their only child, John Shelby Barrow, died at the age of twenty-seven in 1855. He had two children, John Shelby Barrow II (1851–1908) and a daughter who died as a toddler. John II moved to the Northeast. The two pier tables, a center table, and the couch did not descend in his family, possibly because his mother lived for twenty-one years longer than he did.
2. It was acquired with the center table eventually purchased by Andy Warhol.
3. For a graphic showing this profile, see Robert C. Smith, "The Furniture of Anthony G. Quervelle, Part I: The Pier Tables," *The Magazine Antiques* 103, no. 5 (May 1973): 984.
4. Dr. Shelby attended medical school in Philadelphia where he met and married his wife. The furniture is connected by provenances that emanate from the Shelbys, who laid out an area east of Nashville that Dr. Shelby named Edgefield (now Shelby County). Dr. and Mrs. Shelby built two great Italianate houses for their two daughters: Boscobel (from the Italian meaning "beautiful woods") for Ann and Fatherland for Priscilla. Based on the provenances, their parents' furniture was divided between those two houses and then descended through their children and, in the case of this pier table, stepchildren. On March 22, 1916, both Shelby daughters' houses and an unknown quantity of household furnishings were consumed by a fire that ravaged the entire Edgefield section of Nashville. *Pier table*, Winterthur Museum, Garden & Library, 1975.0191. *Couch*, PMA, 1974-187-1; Alexandra Alevizatos Kirtley, *American Furniture, 1650–1840: Highlights from the Philadelphia Museum of Art* (Philadelphia: Philadelphia Museum of Art, 2020), cat. 200. *Center table*, Warhol's sale, Sotheby's, New York, April 30, 1988, lot 3231; PMA, 1992-61-1; Kirtley, *American Furniture, 1650–1840*, cat. 207. The Winterthur table was commissioned by the Shelbys and was then acquired by descendants of their neighbors and close friends, the Charlestonians-turned-Nashvillians Henry Middleton Rutledge (1775–1844) and Septima Sexta Middleton Rutledge (1783–1865) of Rutledge Hill, their Italianate house that still survives in East Nashville (Edgefield), Tennessee. Both houses are remembered in Nashville by streets and districts that bear their name. The current whereabouts of the center table are unknown to this author.

48

Side Chairs (three from a set of more than twenty), c. 1825

Attributed to Anthony Gabriel Quervelle (1789–1856)
Philadelphia
Mahogany, mahogany veneer; ash, birch; replacement upholstery
34½ × 19⅛ × 20¾ in.

PROVENANCE: James Monroe (1758–1831) and Elizabeth Kortright Monroe (1768–1830), Oak Hill, Loudoun County, VA; His sale, Jun. 3, 1831, from Oak Hill, VA; By tradition, purchased by a Pennsylvanian/brought to Pennsylvania. With J. Michael Flanigan, American Antiques, Baltimore, 2001; Purchased by Schrimshers, 2001.

James Monroe's political appointments abroad in the 1790s and early 1800s exposed him to the elegance and beauty of French art, and he and his wife Elizabeth became lifelong patrons of French furniture and furnishings. Elected as the fifth president of the United States in 1816, Monroe moved his family into the shell of a presidential house that retained significant scars from the British army's torching of it in September 1814. The Monroes urgently wanted Congress to repair and furnish the President's House, but the United States faced several financial crises during Monroe's presidency—chief among them the Panic of 1819. Despite these constraints, the Monroes were successful in acquiring fifty-three pieces of carved and gilded furniture for the central, bow-shaped drawing room (known today as the Blue Room) from Parisian *ébéniste* Pierre-Antoine Bellangé (1757–1827).

These three chairs from what was originally a set of more than twenty demonstrate the Monroes' interest in fashionable European designs.[1] The set was commissioned, most likely in preparation for their return to private life in Virginia.[2] Their close similarity to a sofa and chair at the Philadelphia Museum of Art and a set of furniture made for the Shelby family of Nashville, Tennessee, suggests that the Paris-trained Philadelphia cabinetmaker Anthony Gabriel Quervelle made them.[3] The root of the design is a klismos chair, which by the 1820s when this chair was made, had morphed with prevailing styles and adopted a softened, more relaxed profile. The legs and stiles are incurved in the typical style, while the arched crest rail departs from the severe, straight profile of a Grecian klismos (fig. 48.1). The crest rail shape and carving were inspired by contemporary British chairs, based on designs in plate 21 of Thomas King's *The Modern Style of Cabinet Work Exemplified* (London, 1829) and several in George Smith's *A Collection of Designs for Household Furniture and Interior Decoration* (London, 1826).

The quality of the carving creates visual depth and exudes energy. Fruit and flower-filled cornucopias frame C-scrolls placed in an upper and lower position on the medial brace. Evenly rendered acanthus-leaf sprays emanate from the front rail and extend to cover the rails and stiles. Most expressively, the front legs end in fabulous dolphins' heads, with the beaks precariously bearing all of the weight. Even C-scrolls behind the front leg are elegantly carved, leaving the flame figure of the mahogany veneer on the crest rail as the only uncarved primary surface. Executed in high-quality mahogany, the carving on these chairs complements the profile, creating a dynamic and unified design. A room or series of adjacent rooms filled with this set of chairs must have made a resplendent effect that satisfied the taste of a worldly couple such as the Monroes.

1. Other chairs from this set were published in Allison Boor, John William Boor, and Andrew Steven Harris, *Philadelphia Empire Furniture* (West Chester, PA: University Press of New England, 2006), fig. 194.
2. There is no evidence that the chairs were a public commission ordered with Congressionally appropriated funds for use in the President's House. The Schrimshers acquired six of the Monroe chairs. They donated one each to the Metropolitan Museum of Art, the White House, and the United States Department of State's Diplomatic Reception Rooms. Six others are at the Monroe house Highland (formerly Ash Lawn), near Charlottesville, Virginia, and two are at the James Monroe Museum and Memorial Library, Fredericksburg, Virginia.
3. See Alexandra Alevizatos Kirtley, *American Furniture, 1650–1840: Highlights from the Philadelphia Museum of Art* (Philadelphia: Philadelphia Museum of Art, 2020), cats. 200, 201, 207; see also cat. 47 in this volume.

Fig. 48.1. Detail of cat. 48 showing the arched crest rail and the cornucopias adorning the medial brace

49a–b

Pair of Worktables, 1827

Anthony Gabriel Quervelle (1789–1856)
Philadelphia
Mahogany, mahogany and rosewood veneer; tulip poplar, white pine; glass (49b replaced; two originals in drawer), brass
30¾ × 24 × 18 in.

LABEL: Pasted at the back of the top drawers: "A. G. QUERVELLE / United States / Fashionable / CABINET WAREHOUSE / NO 126 / South Second Street / Below Dock / PHILADELPHIA / Delmes Sculpt." (See Appendix II)

INSCRIPTION: On bottom of second drawer of 49b: "A L G / R G R / --90."[1]

PROVENANCE (49a): Robert Eglesfeld Griffith (1756–1833) and Maria Thong Patterson Griffith (1771–1854), Philadelphia; To their daughter Anne Catherine Griffith Coleman (1802–1886) and Edward Coleman (1792–1841) [no issue]; To their nephew Manuel Eyre Griffith (1837–1910) and Mary Ellen Robinson Griffith (1836–1912); To their daughter Mary Eyre Griffith Carter (1866–1929) and George Cuthbert Carter (1865–1947) of Oatlands, Leesburg, VA; To their son Robert Griffith Carter Sr. (1901–1981) and Charlotte Baldwin Insley Carter (1913–2003) of Virginia and Maryland; To their son Conrad Powell Carter (b. 1955) and Linda Lee Brittingham Carter (b. 1960), Laurel, DE; Advertised for sale, *Philadelphia Inquirer*, Aug. 20–27, 2004; With Timothy Campbell Naylor (b. 1963), Stevenson, MD, 2004; Purchased by Schrimshers, 2007.

PROVENANCE (49b): Robert Eglesfeld Griffith (1756–1833) and Maria Thong Patterson Griffith (1771–1854), Philadelphia; To their daughter Anne Catherine Griffith Coleman (1802–1886) and Edward Coleman (1792–1841) [no issue]; To their niece Annie Louisa Griffith (1833–1882); To her niece Anne Louise Griffith (1867–1957); To her niece Elizabeth Wilmer Griffith Page (1897–1994) and Edward Crozer Page (1891–1963). [Possibly to their grandson Francis James Carey III (b. 1950), Ambler, PA;] Barbara Marie di Giulio Boor (b. 1955) and John William Boor, MD (1947–2007); Their sale, Neal Auction Company, New Orleans, Nov. 21, 2015, lot 50; Purchased by Schrimshers, 2015.

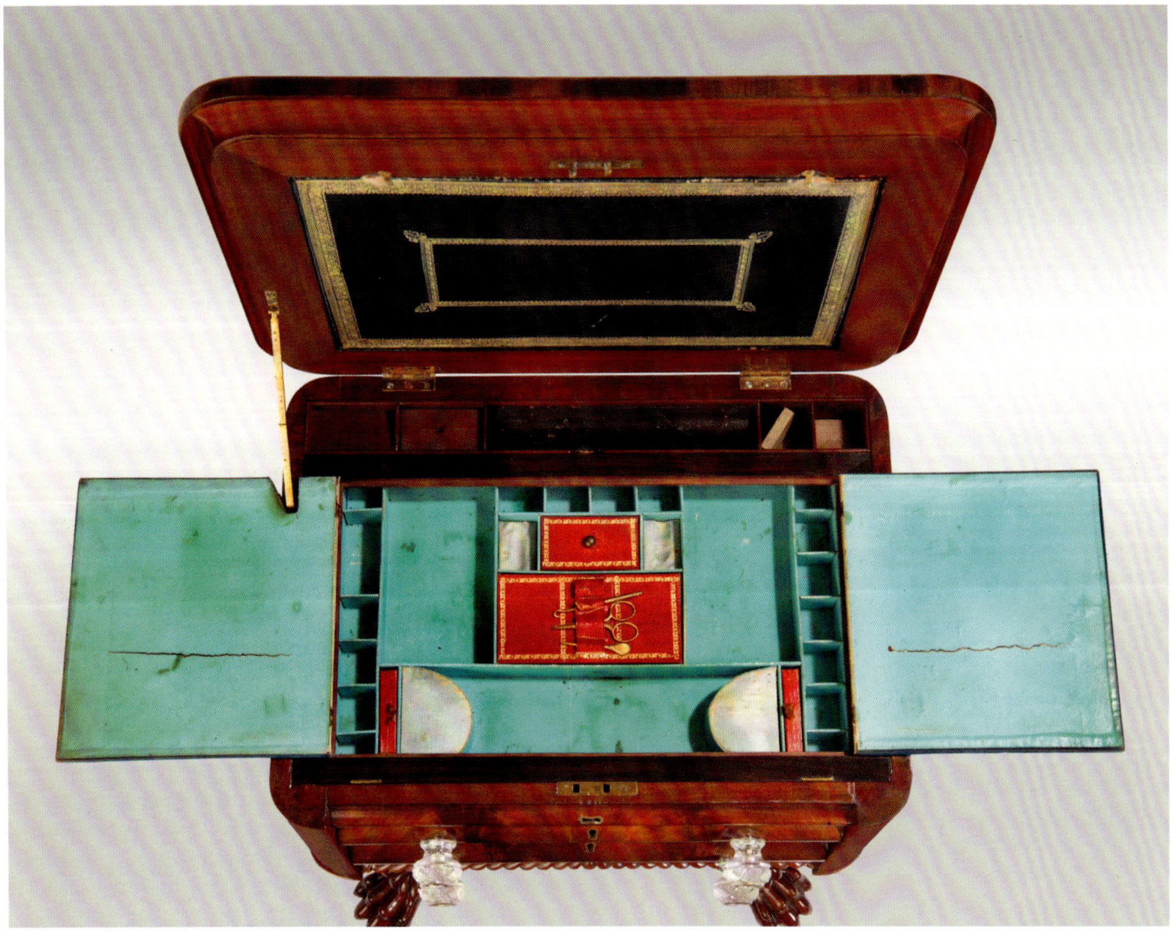

Fig 49.1. View of cat. 49a showing the interior writing surface

49a

49b

49c

Worktable, 1828–1830

Charles Haight White (1796–1876) and John Ferris White (1807–1852?), in partnership 1828–1840
Philadelphia
Mahogany, mahogany veneer; tulip poplar, white pine; brass
29 × 22 × 16 in.

LABEL: "Chas. H. & Jn. F. White / Upholstrey & Cabinet Furniture / WARE ROOMS / 107 & 109 Walnut St. / PHILAD[A]." (See Appendix II)

PROVENANCE: Barbara Marie di Giulio Boor (b. 1955) and John William Boor, MD (1947–2007); Their sale, Neal Auction, New Orleans, Nov. 20, 2010, lot 203; Private collection; Sale, Neal Auction, New Orleans, Feb. 3, 2023, lot 442; Purchased by Schrimshers, 2023.

From the genesis of their design in mid-eighteenth-century France, worktables were elegant stands made of fine materials. By the 1770s, French *ébénistes* added a compartmented lap desk–like box fitted with specialized *accoutrements* for writing and sewing onto a drawered base; this more complex table was easily moved around a room on castors. The preciousness of the materials and the excessive workmanship expended on them elevated the prominence of worktables, underscoring the significance of not only a woman's work but also the form as one necessary for women of means.

These three worktables are documented to their makers: two are an extraordinary pair made by the French *émigré* cabinetmaker Anthony Gabriel Quervelle; the other was made in the Philadelphia shop of the New Jersey–born White brothers, working in the style introduced by Quervelle.

The stunning pair by Quervelle are covered in the same dynamically flamed mahogany veneer on the front, sides, rear, and top, emphasizing their relationship as a single commission. The writing and sewing boxes are supported by four sinuously shaped S-scrolls, each ornamented with a turned boss at the top and carved acanthus leaves on the bottom. An extra scroll at the base of the supports gives them nearly the profile of a dolphin, which Quervelle used on other furniture (see cats. 47 and 50) and appears, not coincidentally, on the elaborate label appended to each of the tables.[2] The scrolls are set onto the familiar four-pronged platform with Quervelle's favored lion's-paw feet enhanced by effusive sprays of acanthus. The lid lifts and a tooled leather packet for notes is set on its underside; below is a velvet-covered writing surface and a bank of partitions for writing implements (fig. 49.1). All of the interior fittings are in navy blue with rosewood crossbanding. Using a discreetly located finger hole, the two-part writing surface opens to reveal a brilliant robin's egg blue papered sewing box; the red leather cushions and metal sewing implements are preserved on one of the tables, and the ghosts of where they once sat are visible on the other. The sides of the two drawers below are mahogany, a detail that suggests that they would have often been open while the table was in use as the epicenter of the room where women gathered to do their work.

The English-born Philadelphia merchant Robert Griffith and his wife, Maria, commissioned the pair of worktables as part of a multi-piece suite that included a monumental secretary bookcase now at the Philadelphia Museum of Art.[3] In 1827, the secretary bookcase was awarded a silver medal, the top prize, at the Franklin Institute's fourth annual juried competition for arts and manufactures for "excellence in the mechanical arts." In addition to the provenance and design elements that link these objects, the secretary bookcase's blue leather writing surface and its tooling matches that on the letter cases of the worktables.

The lidded, two-drawer case and the platform with lion's-paw feet of the White brothers' table are similar to the Quervelle pair, but they are supported by a single turned and carved pedestal. The White table is a dressing and sewing table, with a mirror set underneath the lid, rather than a writing surface. Altogether more restrained in its effusiveness, the White table retains an old surface that masks the mahogany, which has a less lively grain than the Quervelle pair made for the Griffiths.[4]

---

1. This likely refers to the children of Manuel Eyre Griffith (1837–1910) and Mary Ellen Robinson Griffith (1836–1912): Anne Louise Griffith (1867–1957), who would own the table, and her brother Robert Eglesfield Griffith (1868–1926). The date would then be "1890."
2. The choice of the finer label for the worktables is notable: while the secretary bookcase made for the Griffiths won the highest medal at the 1827 Franklin Institute competition, the labels on it are Quervelle's more rudimentary (less expensive) ones. See Alexandra Alevizatos Kirtley, *American Furniture, 1650–1840: Highlights from the Philadelphia Museum of Art* (Philadelphia: Philadelphia Museum of Art, 2020), cat. 188.
3. *Secretary bookcase*, Anthony Gabriel Quervelle, 1827, Philadelphia Museum of Art, 1960-159-1.
4. See Kirtley, *American Furniture, 1650–1840*, cat. 186. This worktable labeled by Charles White demonstrates that the Whites were capable of using highly grained veneers in creative ways when the patron asked (and paid) for it.

50

Pair of Card Tables, 1820–1825

Attributed to Anthony Gabriel Quervelle (1789–1856)
Philadelphia
Mahogany, mahogany and maple veneer; cherry; brass
29½ × 38 × 19 in. (closed)

PROVENANCE: Moses Levy (1756–1826) and Mary Pearce Levy (1762–1850), Philadelphia; To their daughter Martha Mary Ann Levy Milligan (1798–1889) and John Jones Milligan (1795–1875), Wilmington, DE; To their son George Baldwin Milligan (1825–1889) and Sarah Gough Carroll Milligan; To their daughter Elise Tiffany Milligan Bancroft (1860–1937) and Robert Hale Bancroft (1843–1918), MA; To their daughter Elizabeth Hope Bancroft Winsor (1895–1964) and Alexander Winsor (1894–1966); To Elise Hope Winsor Palmer (1919–2003) and Sanford Denison Palmer Jr. (1919–1990); With Carswell Rush Berlin (b. 1952), New York; Robert Ignatius Owens (1946–2022) and Elizabeth Harte Owens (b. 1950), MA; With Clark Pearce, Essex, MA, 2019; Purchased by Schrimshers, 2019.

Throughout the Neoclassical and Classical periods, the elegant lyre was coopted as a support for tables and a profile for the banisters of chair backs (see cats. 41 and 43a–b). In an inspired twist, the artisan who designed these tables—most likely the French *émigré* Anthony Quervelle— abandoned the more conventional lyre and incorporated scroll-shaped dolphins, downward-facing and dynamically looking out at the viewer. These are not the docile dolphins depicted in ancient Greek art, but rather the more menacing and scaley creatures designed by the ancient Romans; these features persisted through the Renaissance and Baroque periods and appeared in European design and ornament books from the late seventeenth through the early nineteenth century. For example, Thomas Chippendale incorporated them into designs for a candlestand (plate 145), a pedestal (plate 150), and a cistern (plate 151) in the third edition of *The Gentleman and Cabinet-Maker's Director* (London, 1762).[1] In classical mythology, dolphins were the attribute of Neptune, the god of the sea, and of Venus, the goddess of love; for Christians, they often represented the body of Christ.[2]

Benjamin Franklin (1706–1790), the Boston-born Philadelphia printer and intellectual, noted the distortion of the image of the dolphin when he was sailing from England to Philadelphia in 1726. Upon watching for, catching, and eating dolphins while at sea, Franklin recorded in his diary for September 2:

> Every one takes notice of that vulgar error of the painters, who always represent this fish monstrously crooked and deformed, when it is, in reality, as beautiful and well-shaped a fish as any that swims. I cannot think what could be the original of this chimera of theirs, (since there is not a creature in nature that in the least resembles their dolphin) unless it proceeded at first from a false imitation of a fish in the posture of leaping, which they have since improved into a crooked monster, with a head and eyes like a bull, a hog's snout, and a tail like a blown tulip.[3]

Franklin perfectly described the dolphin as carved on Philadelphia furniture of the early nineteenth century. Henry Connelly incorporated dolphins in his furniture designs of the 1810s (see cat. 44), and Quervelle often employed them as well: the incurved dolphin (or scrolls in the shape of incurved dolphins) on his tables, including on worktables (see cat. 49a–b).

The dolphins on these tables illustrate the most refined and expressive carving found on Philadelphia Classical furniture, and their innovative position gives the sense that the dolphins are moving the tabletops towards the viewer. The carving contrasts with the rectilinear tops that boast lively grained mahogany veneer outlined on the bottom edge by a burl maple crossbanding.

In typical Philadelphia fashion, the top and leaf are made with breadboard construction and veneered, and the remainder of the elements are mortise-and-tenoned, joined, or screwed. Although some carved elements on Philadelphia furniture of the Classical period are laminated, the dolphins and lions' paws on these tables are carved from the solid. This strategy would have made the dramatic curve of the dolphins less prone to breakage but also required an enormous amount of mahogany. The use of three round stub tenons to secure the leaf to the swivel top (instead of the usual two rectangular tenons) may speak to the larger size of the tables, which are thirty-eight inches square instead of the usual thirty-six inches.

The captivating design of these tables, with the imaginative incorporation of scrolled dolphins as supports, has not always been appreciated, especially to certain Colonial Revivalists: when describing one of these for his 1937 publication, Edgar G. Miller Jr. (1864–1940) wrote that it was a "monstrosity in the Empire style. . . . Two fierce-looking creatures of the ocean serve as legs and supports of the top . . . The time and skill spent on the carving on this card table were worthy of a better style."[4]

1. See Carswell Rush Berlin's entry in Allison Boor, John William Boor, and Andrew Steven Harris, *Philadelphia Empire Furniture* (West Chester, PA: University Press of New England, 2006), fig. 74.
2. The original owners of these tables were a Jewish man and an Episcopalian woman whose descendants acknowledged their Jewish roots but were well known as avowed Christians. It is not known what inspired their preference for the dolphins.
3. Benjamin Franklin, "Benjamin Franklin, Journal of a Voyage from England to Philadelphia 1726," American History from the Revolution to Reconstruction and Beyond, last modified 2012, http://www.let.rug.nl/usa/documents/1701-1750/benjamin-franklin-journal-of-a-voyage-from-england-to-philadelphia-1726.php.
4. Edgar G. Miller Jr., *American Antique Furniture: A Book for Amateurs, Vol. II* (Baltimore: Lord Baltimore Press, 1937), 803.

51

Armchair, c. 1825

Attributed to Joseph Brown Barry (1757–1838)
Philadelphia
Mahogany, mahogany veneer; cherry; replacement upholstery
37¾ × 24½ × 21 in.

PROVENANCE: John Rea (1774–1871) and Harriet Rea (c. 1785–1863), Philadelphia. With Hirschl & Adler, New York, 1994; Jack Warner (1917–2017) for The Westervelt Company, Tuscaloosa, AL (acc. no. 1994–0059); Their sale, Christie's, New York, Sept. 25, 2013, lot 121; Purchased by Schrimshers, 2013.

Philadelphia's embrace of French style began in the late Colonial period, and it increased after independence from Britain, buoyed by French *émigrés* who sought refuge and opportunity in a favorable climate for economic enterprise. Notables include the merchants Claudius Paul Raguet (active 1780–1793), Stephen Girard, and Louis Clapier (1765–1837); upholsterer George Bertault; wallpaper manufacturers Le Collay and Chardon; carver Claudius Legrand (d. 1801); cabinetmakers Anthony Gabriel Quervelle and Michel Bouvier; and political exiles Monsieur and Madame Moreau and Joseph Bonaparte. Even the British-born architect of numerous Philadelphia houses Benjamin Henry Latrobe promoted French design, encouraging his clients to look beyond "the slovenly and often filthy frippery of the French" to admire a French house for "the superiority of its design."[1] French influence is particularly discernable in Philadelphia seating design, beginning with a *bergère à oreilles* made in the 1760s and becoming especially notable with the Neoclassical and Classical styles preferred in Philadelphia, including the style of this high-backed armchair or *fauteuil à la reine*.[2]

In the 1780s, armchairs with framed and upholstered seats and backs had captivated Thomas Jefferson when he was an envoy in France; he returned to the United States with a set made around 1785 by the Parisian *menuisier* (joiner) Georges Jacob (1739–1814). The preference for these sets of armchairs, the uniformity of which can eliminate issues of precedence, was encouraged by upholsterer George Bertault who directed their manufacture by using specially imported French tapestries and fabric.[3] The throne-like *fauteuil* became a hallmark of French Classical design, a popular aesthetic that Napoleon used to promote his claim as inheritor of the Holy Roman Empire, and that also swept through Italy, Britain, and the United States. In the United States, sets of upholstered armchairs like this one were imported and made, based on published designs by Napoleon Bonaparte's architects Charles Percier and Pierre-François-Léonard Fontaine in *Recueil de décorations intérieures*. Pierre de La Mésangère also illustrated them in the serial publication *Collection de meubles et objets de goût*.[4] In Philadelphia, the residence of Napoleon's brother Joseph Bonaparte and Napoleon-supporting cabinetmakers Quervelle and Bouvier advanced the enthusiasm for this style.[5]

The particular design of this armchair has deliberate allusions to Roman republicanism, an imperial aesthetic popular in United States from the 1790s (consider Gilbert Stuart's portraits of George Washington as an orator) through the 1820s, when this example was made. The scrolls of the crest rail are a series of open volutes centering on a scallop shell, while the arms are supported by Roman-style dolphins, often employed on Philadelphia furniture of this period. The capitals of the squared front legs are carved with Greek- and Roman-style acanthus at the front and Egyptian-style papyrus on the sides.

It is not coincidental that this style had its zenith at the house of President James Monroe and Elizabeth Kortright Monroe. In this era (1816–24), furniture made by the Parisian *ébéniste* Pierre-Antoine Bellangé (1757–1827) was mixed with furniture made by local makers William Worthington (1775–1839) and William King Jr. (see cat. 83).[6] The design of this armchair would have been embraced by its original owner, the prominent Philadelphia-based upholsterer John Rea and his wife, Harriet, who were closely connected to presidential style: after Rea's success with the Waln commission in Philadelphia, Latrobe brought him to Washington, D.C., to execute the Madison commission and ongoing work at the Capitol. Following the burning of Washington, Rea returned at the behest of Thomas Claxton (d. 1821). Claxton served as the "doorkeeper of the US House of Representatives" for thirty-two years, beginning in his native Philadelphia in 1790 and moving to Washington with the government in 1800. Claxton's role went beyond simply being the official doorkeeper: Marie Kimball described him as "Jefferson's man-Friday in [the] task of furnishing" the executive mansion, a role he continued under James Madison and Monroe.[7] It was this role that put him in the position of hiring and collaborating with Rea.[8]

Several sets of Philadelphia-made *fauteuils* survive, including this one and a later set attributed to the British immigrant Richard Parkin (1787–1861). The Parkin armchair is made (extravagantly) entirely of rosewood with brass inlay on the front rail and lyre-arm supports. Joseph Barry and Rea were known to have collaborated, and the Rea armchair is closely related in its design and mortise-and-tenon construction to a set Barry made for Isaac and Dinah Minis of Savannah in 1827 and signed in the French manner with an *estampille*.[9]

1. Benjamin Henry Latrobe to William Waln, April 1, 1805, in *The Papers of Benjamin Henry Latrobe: The Microtext Edition*, ed. Edward C. Carter II (Clifton, NJ: James T. White & Co., 1976), 38/A6, 39/B6, 39/A6.
2. See Alexandra Alevizatos Kirtley, *American Furniture, 1650–1840: Highlights from the Philadelphia Museum of Art* (Philadelphia: Philadelphia Museum of Art, 2020), cats. 68, 115–19, 121, 122, 126, 128–31, 133, 159–67, and 189–90.
3. See ibid., 142–43, cats. 118 and 119.
4. A set of gilded *fauteuils* made in Rome has an early history in the United States and was given to the Philadelphia Museum of Art by Henry Livingston Lee (1872–1934) in 1931. They are currently on loan to the White House.
5. Anthony Quervelle and Michel Bouvier were both Napoleonists who emigrated to Philadelphia soon after Napoleon's final defeat at Waterloo—and possibly following Napoleon's older brother, Joseph Bonaparte, the former king of Naples and Sicily who moved to Philadelphia in September 1815. Joseph Bonaparte patronized Quervelle and Bouvier for furnishings for his Philadelphia house and his Delaware River estate, Point Breeze.
6. At the Capitol, seating was commissioned for the legislators from Thomas Constantine (1791–1849) of New York (see cats. 84 and 85).
7. Marie Kimball, "The Original Furnishings of the White House," *The Magazine Antiques* 16, no. 1 (January 1929): 36.
8. Rea was so fond of Claxton that he named his son Thomas Claxton Rea (1820–1846), perhaps also honoring Claxton's son Thomas (1794–1813), who died at the Battle of Lake Erie.
9. Kirtley, *American Furniture, 1650–1840*, cats. 189 and 190.

52a

Cellarette, 1825–1835

Unknown maker
Philadelphia
Mahogany, mahogany veneer; cherry, tulip poplar; brass
21⅝ × 24¹⁵⁄₁₆ × 13¼ in.

PROVENANCE: With J. Michael Flanigan, American Antiques, Baltimore, 2004; Purchased by Schrimshers, 2004.

52b

Cellarette, 1825–1830

Unknown maker
Philadelphia
Mahogany, mahogany veneer; tulip poplar, white pine; brass
29¼ × 23 × 18 in.

PROVENANCE: Anne Butler Carter Wickham (1797–1868) and William Fanning (W. F.) Wickham (1793–1880) Hickory Hill, Ashland, Hanover County, VA. Sale, Motley's Auctions and Realty, 2006; Private collection, on loan to the Wickham House at the Valentine Museum, Richmond; Sale, Sotheby's, New York, Jan. 22, 2011, lot 79; Purchased by Schrimshers, 2011.

With their design rooted in ancient sarcophagi, cellarettes that stored wine and liquor bottles offered an opportunity for artisans to create richly ornamented and sculptural works. Cellarettes were designed as an ensemble with sideboards or marble slab tables and were stored underneath them. Castors allowed them to be moved about the dining room, and wine and liquor were accessed from them. The genesis of this compact cellarette as an *accoutrement* of dining room furniture dates to at least the mid-eighteenth century, when Thomas Chippendale illustrated one as part of a sideboard ensemble with a frame for a marble slab (fig. 52.1). As early-nineteenth-century designers embraced ancient Egyptian, Greek, and Roman art and architecture, cellarettes became a visual trope with strong and direct references to the classical world.

South of Maryland, patrons favored bottle cases on stands, while in Maryland, Philadelphia, and New York City they preferred the more formal box on castors that was stored under the sideboard. The 1811 and 1828 Philadelphia cabinetmaker's book of prices include squared and oval cellarettes.

Both of these cellarettes are shaped—unapologetically—like sarcophagi. They have box-like bodies, raised pediments on the lids, and are set above the ground, one on two lion-shaped plinths that house the castors (cat. 52b) and one on four feet fitted with castors (cat. 52a). Like the cool surface of a marble tomb, the swirling grain of the mahogany provides the principal surface decoration, with carving limited to the lion supports underneath and the brackets and feet that flank it.

One cellarette is capped by a slightly domed lid (cat. 52a); the interior has nearly straight sides and a veneered panel front. Echoing the ancient architecture and marble sculpture on which the form is based, the case is supported by buttress-like scrolled acanthus carved feet and the sides are supported by console brackets—that is, tightly wound volutes covered with acanthus carving. The elaborate veneer and bold carving suggest that it was an extravagant commission; however, the interior surfaces are notably not veneered in mahogany, suggesting that its use was more about storage than service.

Conversely, the trapezoidal-shaped cellarette with the brass inlay (cat. 52b) and lion carved supports has an interior richly veneered in figured mahogany and partitions also made of mahogany. Plate 98 (fig. 52.2) of George Smith's *A Collection of Designs for Household Furniture and Interior Decoration* (London, 1808) illustrates the design for the cellarette with the lion plinths. The particularly sculptural modeling and character of the carving, suggest that the carver may also have worked in stone as well as made molds and patterns for metalworking and ceramics models.[1] The lion's pose is seen in ceramic, and the lion's countenance is familiar from prints and paintings, such as those by Edward Hicks (1780–1849) in his *Peaceable Kingdom* series.[2]

The recumbent lions appear on at least three known cellarettes of this same design, including one that was part of a large commission with a well-documented history of ownership by Simon and Mary Gratz of Philadelphia.[3] The Schrimsher example and another one in a private Southern collection conform to their original function as wine and liquor storage cases, while the Gratz piece was adapted into a wine cooler.[4] The elegance of this cellarette accords with its history of ownership by the Wickham family of Ashland, just outside of Richmond in Hanover County. The Wickhams were known for their sophisticated taste, and the restrained ornament on this cellarette would have complemented the Classical features and other furnishings of their house, which was completed in 1815.

Fig. 52.1. Thomas Chippendale and Matthias Darly (c. 1721–1780), "Frames for Marble Slabs," plate 176 in *The Gentleman and Cabinet-Maker's Director* (3rd ed., London, 1762), engraving (Courtesy Winterthur Museum, Garden & Library)

Fig. 52.2. George Smith, "Celeretts," plate 98 in *A Collection of Designs for Household Furniture and Interior Decoration* (London, 1808), hand-colored engraving (Courtesy Clark Art Institute Library, Mary Ann Beinecke Decorative Art Collection)

1. The best Philadelphia furniture and house carvers advertised that they carved in wood as well as stone, including, but not limited to, Martin Jugiez (c. 1730–1815), Nicholas Bernard (1732–1789), and James Reynolds (1736–1794). Carvers of the early nineteenth century followed suit, and carvings like these lions share features with individual busts, Persians, caryatids, and other sculptural elements that were often commissioned in stone and wood. See Alexandra Alevizatos Kirtley, "A New Suspect: Baltimore Cabinetmaker Edward Priestley," in *American Furniture 2000*, ed. Luke Beckerdite (Milwaukee: Chipstone Foundation, 2000), 100–135.
2. Hicks created over a hundred oil paintings in this series but only sixty-two canvases survive in public and private collections.
3. See Alexandra Alevizatos Kirtley, *American Furniture, 1650–1840: Highlights from the Philadelphia Museum of Art* (Philadelphia: Philadelphia Museum of Art, 2020), cat. 195.
4. Soon after the Gratz cellarette was made, the interior was fitted with a lead liner, a drainage spigot was drilled underneath, and the entire case was set on a full-sized plinth. What once was a cellarette for storing wine and liquor was transformed into a wine cooler.

53

Center Table, 1830–1835

Unknown maker
Philadelphia
Mahogany, mahogany veneer, maple veneer; tulip poplar, white pine; stencil gilding, brass
29½ × 41¼ × 41½ in.

PROVENANCE: Sale, Hindman Auctions, Cincinnati, OH, Mar. 10, 2022, lot 130; Purchased by Schrimshers, 2022.

More commonly referred to in the period as a circular table rather than a center table, a large, round-topped table like this one commanded the room in which it was set by creating a focal point whose design set the tone for the space. Great expense and effort were expended on ornamenting the tabletop. On this table (as opposed to those with marble tops), the top could be unlatched from the base and tilted up so that the triangular-shaped radial cuts of veneer, the dappled blond maple demilunes, and the gilded border could be viewed. This table is fitted with castors, so it could be moved around the room or placed out of the way with the top displayed vertically. Thus, the sculptural aspects of the three-legged support, pillar, and tabletop could be transformed into a more two-dimensional work of art.

The design for these large tables of the 1820s and 1830s is rooted in the much more modestly sized round-topped tea table of the mid-eighteenth century. Like this example, the precursor was supported by a pillar and three legs with claw feet (often also with castors), and the round top of the tea table also tilted up so that it could be admired and stored in a convenient location.[1]

This table is remarkably similar to an 1820s or 1830s drawing of a "Loo table" that is often ascribed to (but not documented to) the French *émigré* cabinetmaker Anthony Gabriel Quervelle (fig. 53.1). The feet, legs, pillar (including the two thin through-tenons), and top follow the drawing almost exactly, while the dimensions of this table are slightly larger. The radial placement of the veneers with the lighter-colored demilune ends is a decorative treatment often employed by Philadelphia artisans on circular tables as well as pairs of card tables, as illustrated in Quervelle's drawing (see also cat. 47). When two card tables were placed back-to-back, they produced the same effect as a single circular table.

Large circular tables like the Schrimsher example were used for dining, card playing, and supporting lighting fixtures at the center of a parlor, entryway, or library.[2] Prominently positioned in a room, they exemplified the sculptural potentials of furniture and became large-scale canvases for exhibition-like demonstrations of ornamentation—carving, veneer work, gilding, and painted decoration. The workmanship and range of decorative treatments—such as using gilding to emphasize the veneers and carving—found on the Schrimsher's Philadelphia table represent the finest expression of the form. Furthermore, the quality of the wood grain in the veneers underscores the fact that best artisans of this period could access the finest flitches of wood either by trading in lumber themselves, such as the lumber yard adjacent to Michel Bouvier's shop, or having privileged access to trusted lumber dealers.

1. Imported Chinese lacquer tables with narrative decoration inspired this design.
2. Curiously, they are absent from the 1811 and 1828 Philadelphia price books.

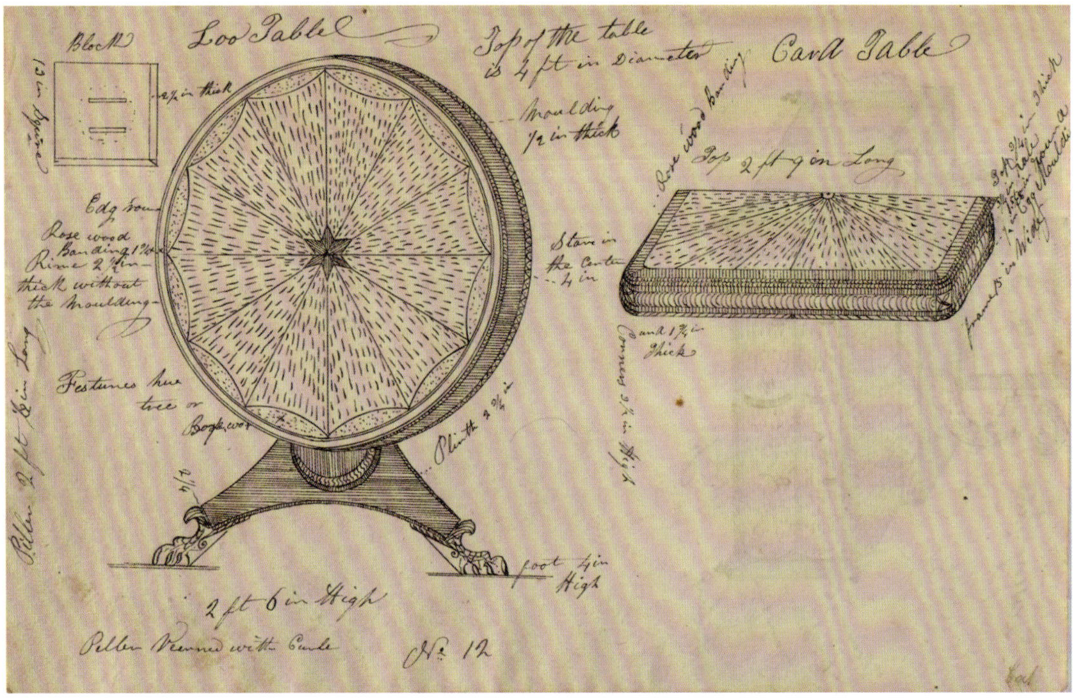

Fig. 53.1. Attributed to Anthony Gabriel Quervelle, *Furniture Sketch*, c. 1820–1835, graphite and pen and ink on wove paper, Philadelphia Museum of Art, Purchased with funds contributed by an anonymous donor, Mr. and Mrs. W. B. Dixon Stroud, John A. Nyheim, Dr. and Mrs. Robert E. Booth, Jr., and Anne R. and John F. Haley, Jr., 1995, 1995-12-2a,b (Courtesy Philadelphia Museum of Art)

54

Pier Table, 1829–1834

Attributed to Anthony Gabriel Quervelle (1789–1856)
Philadelphia
Mahogany; tulip poplar, white pine; gilding, marble, mirror glass, brass
38¼ × 45¾ × 25¼ in.

PROVENANCE: *Either* (1) Archibald Stuart (1795–1855) and Elizabeth Letcher Pannill Stuart (1801–1884), Patrick, Campbell, Smyth, and Washington Counties, VA, *or* their son William Alexander Stuart[1] (1826–1892) and Mary Taylor Carter Stuart (1831–1862), Campbell and Wythe Counties, VA; To their son Dale Carter Stuart (1858–1934) and Sally Preston White Stuart (1871–1931), Elk Garden, Russell County, VA; To their son Senator Harry Carter Stuart (1893–1963) and Marion Lee Cobbs Stuart (1897–1984), Elk Garden, Russell County, VA; To their daughter Marion "Lee" Stuart Cochran (1924–2017) and Justice George Moffett Cochran IV (1912–2011), Staunton, VA; Her sale, Jeffrey S. Evans & Associates, Harrisonburg, VA, July 3, 2021, lot 1278; Purchased by Schrimshers, 2021.

Or (2) Alexander Hugh Holmes Stuart (1807–1891) and Frances Cornelia Baldwin Stuart (1815–1885), Staunton, VA; To their daughter Margaret Briscoe Stuart Robertson (1855–1932) and Alexander Farish Robertson (1853–1938); To their daughter Susan Baldwin Robertson Cochran (1887–1975) and Peyton Cochran (1880–1969); To their son Justice George Moffett Cochran IV (1912–2011) and Marion "Lee" Stuart Cochran (1924–2017), Staunton, VA; Her sale, Jeffrey S. Evans & Associates, Harrisonburg, VA, July 3, 2021, lot 1278; Purchased by Schrimshers, 2021.

In 1829, French-born and -trained cabinetmaker Anthony Quervelle received a commission on behalf of President Andrew Jackson from the White House's interior furnisher, Louis Veron (1793–1853) of Philadelphia, for a set of furniture for the East Room. The commission included two marble-topped center tables and four pier tables with marble tops, silvered-glass (mirror) backings, and front supports in a rare combination of an eagle's head and lion's leg.[2] It was not the first time that Quervelle had received affirmation of the enthusiasm for his particular brand of combined French and British Classicism in Washington, D.C., but, with President Jackson proclaiming the White House to be "the people's house" and entertaining there regularly, it put Quervelle's bold designs on a prominent stage.[3]

The exuberant design of this pier table features the same bold elements found on the White House tables that reflect Quervelle's singular style of Classical expression (see also cat. 47). Here, below carved four-petaled flowers, the front legs are raised on faceted supports, requiring the curve of the lion's legs to be compact and exaggerated. The lion's paws—especially the claws—are tensed and well articulated, and the collars separating the facets from the compressed ball feet are carved. Gilt stenciled decorations in arrangements that complement the forms adorn the front legs, the central panel of the facet, and the frieze above the ball feet. The plinth set between the front legs is carved with an energetically scrolled garland of thickly veined acanthus leaves. At the center is a large three-leaf bouquet of acanthus, and recent conservation treatment by Christine Thomson revealed that the carved composition is accentuated by selected gilding to emphasize the design and increase the illusion of depth.[4] The reeded pilasters framing the mirror have gilt stencil designs at the bases. Most notably, the front and the rear supports are connected by a dramatic inwardly sweeping single rail. It creates an open, airy look, countering the bulky appearance of the lower shelf on similar marble-top pier tables. The mirror reflects back to the viewer this marvel of engineering an open space between the rail and the back.

Philadelphia's furniture makers supplied an eager clientele both locally and throughout the South with dynamically designed furniture, this one intended to fill the space of a window pier. Like sets of chairs, pier tables of this period are related to one another but are singular, never duplicative. While the arrangement of the front legs, the stenciling, and the gilded elements on this pier table relate it to others, the arced shape of the lower rear rail distinguishes this one.

1. William Alexander Stuart died of a sudden heart attack while he was in Philadelphia. The exact nature of his work there is still being researched, but it appears not to be related to the acquisition of this pier table.
2. The sixty-six-inch width of the White House pier table makes it more akin to a French *console dessert*. Their broad width is indicative of the oversized dimensions of the White House's East Room, which was and remains a stately reception room. It is notable that Veron—a French *émigré*—chose Quervelle while Philadelphia cabinetmaker Robert West (1778–1870) made furniture for Jackson's Tennessee house, The Hermitage, in the mid-1820s, and Joseph Barry (1757–1838) made furniture for the house after Jackson's presidency. "Presidential Appointments," *The Magazine Antiques*, March 21, 2017, http://www.themagazineantiques.com/article/presidential-appointments/.
3. Secretary of the Navy Samuel Lewis Southard (1787–1842) and his wife Rebecca Harrow Southard (1787–1863) commissioned furniture from Quervelle in 1827 for their Washington, D.C., residence.
4. The treatment report by Christine Thomson is on file at the Schrimsher Foundation.

55

French Secretary, 1820–1830

Unknown maker
Philadelphia
Mahogany, mahogany and maple veneer; tulip poplar, white pine; brass
63 × 30½ × 22¼ in. (with desk open: D. 35½ in.)

PROVENANCE: Sale, Christie's, New York, Jan. 26, 1995, lot 143; Purchased by Schrimshers, 1995.

Distinguished by a front panel that falls forward to form a writing surface that is set over a two-doored cabinet, secretaries epitomize Americans' embrace of French furniture design. The quiet elegance of these compact, neatly architectonic secretaries made them highly desirable, and Philadelphia examples were often topped by a rectangular pediment that boasted flitches of vibrant, blond maple veneer to accentuate the panels and pilasters. While many have gilded stencil decoration on their surfaces, this one is embellished with the more refined ornament of applied gilded mounts, which are most likely made of patinated brass.

Furniture artisans in Boston, New York, and Philadelphia relied on the same design sources for French secretaries. The pediment and three-part arrangement on this example represent the impact of German immigrants working in Philadelphia; at least six secretaries share this arrangement and date to the 1820s.[1] The design combines two published by Pierre de La Mésangère in *Collection de meubles et objets de goût*: the stacked exterior (pl. 563) and the arcaded interior (pl. 101). The surfeit of German artisans who arrived in Philadelphia beginning in the late 1810s influenced local designs by adding a pediment to the top and using maple veneers to form a geometric pattern on the facade that is emphasized on the interior.

Fig. 55.1. View of cat. 55 with fall front open

The whole is made of three separate units: the pediment, the secretary, and the two-doored cabinet, all of which sit on a framed-up base resting on carved lion's-paw feet at the front and turned feet at the rear. The front falls forward using scissor hinges (others have counter-weights) to reveal a dazzling tripartite elevation of drawers and pigeonholes separated by turned columns and centering on an open, arcaded niche (fig. 55.1). The drawers are faced with dappled maple veneer and divided by mahogany drawer blades, all of which underscore the geometric patterning favored by German artisans. Below, the doors mask four commodious drawers that, in familiar British fashion, run directly against the sides of the case. These attributes (the pediment, the geometric facade design, the exuberant interior) as well as certain construction nuances tie the group to an as-yet-unidentified shop. Given the combination of French, British, and German influences, this shop appears to have employed a group of artisans from disparate backgrounds who collaborated to make a distinctive design for a fashionable form.

This style of secretary is one of several French designs that infused Philadelphia furniture in the late eighteenth and early nineteenth centuries (see cats. 47, 56, and 60). In Philadelphia price books, newspapers, inventories, and invoices, *French* was used as an adjective to describe chairs, bedsteads, mirrors, and secretaries like this one. *Secretary*, meaning "one entrusted with confidential information," specifically refers to the front panel that, when unlocked, falls forward in order to access the desk space and interior drawers where, presumably, private papers and items were safeguarded. The central arcade allowed for the display of a cherished item, such as a statuette, a clock, or a portrait miniature. Notably—especially when compared to other urban centers—Philadelphians embraced this French-inspired design from the early eighteenth century onwards. For example, *escritoires* (sometimes called *scrutoires*) similar to one made by Edward Evans in 1707 show up commonly in probate inventories between 1704 and 1744. In the Neoclassical period, a related secretary was made about 1795–1805.[2]

1. This observation derives from the research of former Dallas Museum of Art curator Charles Venable; see Charles L. Venable, "Germanic Craftsmen and Furniture Design in Philadelphia, 1820–1850," in *American Furniture 1998*, ed. Luke Beckerdite (Milwaukee: Chipstone Foundation, 1998), 41–80.
2. See *Escritoire*, Edward Evans (1679–1754), 1707, Colonial Williamsburg, 1958-468; Alexandra Alevizatos Kirtley, *American Furniture, 1650–1840: Highlights from the Philadelphia Museum of Art* (Philadelphia: Philadelphia Museum of Art, 2020), cat. 122.

56

Cheval Glass, 1825–1830

Unknown maker
Philadelphia
Mahogany, mahogany veneer, maple; ash, maple; silvered glass, brass
69 × 41 × 27¼ in.

PROVENANCE: Sale, Skinner, Inc., Marlborough, MA, Aug. 19, 2021, lot 56; Purchased by Schrimshers, 2021.

Like the French bedstead, French secretary, French chair, and French wardrobe, the design of the cheval glass derives from French sources. *Cheval*—French for "horse"—refers to the sawhorse-like construction of the horizontal trestle that supports the two uprights. The uprights are turned and veneered and have a removable dowel that secures them to the base. Large screws set through the turned uprights and into the frame of the glass can be tightened or loosened so the user could adjust the angle of the reflection. This cheval glass lacks a support at the top of the uprights or above the glass, thus requiring the well-constructed and weighty base. The uprights are tapered to distribute the weight to the base, and two broad, solid mahogany scroll feet are secured (presumably with a sliding dovetail) into the base of the uprights, which is made of a substantial laminate of three mahogany boards. Castors allowed the cheval glass to be moved about a dressing chamber or bedchamber, where it would have had a sculptural yet elegant presence. Cheval glasses were placed in front of a window to capture light, but this example has the added convenience of brass candle arms to illuminate the user even in the dark. The reverse of framed silvered glasses were often upholstered, but the fine workmanship of the floating panel that supports this glass provided ample visual satisfaction.

French designs often reached patrons in Philadelphia through British sources as well as imported French furniture and French publications. In 1793 Thomas Sheraton published two designs for a "Horse Dressing Glass" in his *The Cabinet-Maker and Upholsterer's Drawing-Book*, appendix, pl. 17. Rudolph Ackermann declared in his serial *The Repository of Arts* for 1827 that "these moving glasses are now generally introduced in the sleeping-apartments and dressing-rooms of our nobility and persons of distinction."[1] In Philadelphia, they were more popular than the paucity of surviving examples suggests.[2] Philadelphia furniture price books for 1811 and 1828 delineated "Horse Fire Screens" and "Cheval Glasses," and newspapers of the time advertised cheval glasses for sale.[3] Samuel Kennedy (active 1800–1826) advertised in 1826 at his "Philadelphia Looking-Glass Factory" an "extensive variety of pattern, and of superior workmanship—Mantle, Pier, Toilet, Cheval, Pole, Mouth, Shaving, Travelling, &c. Looking Glasses," available in "Mahogany and fancy wood Frames; Brackets, and ornamental Carving and Gilding in general."[4]

The maker of this example engineered it well, abandoning an upper horizontal support to give it a more refined presence. The artisan seems to have known about Pierre de La Mésangère's *Collection de meubles et objets de goût*, primarily the "Glace à la Psyché" (plate 459), a large tilting mirror, and the "Ecran à Glace," or screen glass (plates 2, 17). Here, low-relief acanthus-leaf carving complements the shapes of the bud at the top of the uprights, reduces the mass of the lower cross support, and gently emphasizes the shape of the scrolled feet.

1. See Pauline Agius, *Ackermann's Regency Furniture & Interiors* (Ramsbury, Marlborough, Wiltshire: Crowood Press, 1984), 178.
2. The Philadelphia Museum of Art owns three: c. 1830, Classical style (2002-208-1), see also Alexandra Alevizatos Kirtley, *American Furniture, 1650–1840: Highlights from the Philadelphia Museum of Art* (Philadelphia: Philadelphia Museum of Art, 2020), cat. 202; c. 1840, Rococo Revival style (2023-96-1); and c. 1845, Gothic Revival style (1996-45-1).
3. See, among many, *Philadelphia Inquirer*, January 10, 1839, 3; *National Gazette* (Philadelphia), May 28, 1839, 3.
4. *National Gazette*, April 25, 1826, 3. The descriptions of Kennedy's looking-glass frames accord with designs that had appeared in publications by Charles Percier and Pierre-François-Léonard Fontaine (particularly their *Recueil de décorations intérieures*, Paris, 1801–1812) and Pierre de La Mésangère in France, and by Thomas Hope, George Smith, and Peter and Michael Angelo Nicholson in Britain, all of which influenced Philadelphia cabinetmakers.

57a

Side Chairs (set of four), 1834–1840

Attributed to Richard Parkin (1787–1861)
Philadelphia
Walnut, walnut veneer; tulip poplar; replacement upholstery
33¾ × 22 × 17¾ in.

PROVENANCE: John Jacob Snyder (1946–2013), Landisville, PA; His sale, Conestoga Auction Company, Manheim, PA, Sept. 13, 2014, lot 974; Purchased by Schrimshers, 2014.

57b

Side Chair, 1834–1840

Attributed to Richard Parkin (1787–1861)
Philadelphia
Rosewood; tulip poplar; replacement upholstery
33 × 17⅝ × 21⅛ in.

PROVENANCE: With J. Michael Flanigan, American Antiques, Baltimore; Purchased by Schrimshers, 2003.

Taking their cue from ancient art and architecture, early-nineteenth-century designers revived faithful imitations of ancient furniture known through archaeological excavations: sculpture, paintings on walls and pottery, and a very few remaining examples. Chief among those revivals is a chair known as a klismos. The Greek klismos is distinguished by having incurved front and rear legs and stiles; the Romans incurved the stiles more dramatically but straightened the front legs (see cat. 41). These chairs—four with wooden tablet backs (cat. 57a) and one with an upholstered back (cat. 57b)—represent the final expressions of the klismos form in nineteenth-century Philadelphia.

The French interpretation of the klismos chair design directly inspired Philadelphians. In 1802, Pierre de La Mésangère published a drawing of a woman seated in a modified klismos as plate 77 in his *Collection de meubles et objets de goût*; that design was followed almost exactly in at least two instances by Philadelphia artisans, including the English-trained Thomas Whitecar (1784–1822).[1] British-born architect Benjamin Henry Latrobe (1764–1820) designed his own version of a klismos in 1808 (see p. 162)—and possibly before. Like the collector Thomas Hope, who published his collection in *Household Furniture and Interior Decoration* (London, 1807), Latrobe closely followed the Greek archaeological models, with attenuated and tapering incurved legs and a long, horizontal tablet top that extended far beyond the stiles. Other British designers adopted the klismos, but modified and mollified it: George Smith in *A Collection of Designs for Household Furnishings* (London, 1808) made the curves less dramatic, added arms, and outwardly curved the back, while James Barron, in *Modern and Elegant Designs of Cabinet and Upholstery Furniture* (London, 1814), Thomas King, in *The Modern Style of Cabinet Work Exemplified* (London, 1829), and the sculptor George Bullock (1777–1818) set the tablet top within stiles between a medial brace and a carved crest rail. Some models feature upholstered backs and cabriole front legs. Front legs on these modified klismos chairs (called Trafalgar chairs in Britain) were incurved, straight, or turned, and sometimes even included Gothic decorative elements.

The design of the Schrimsher chairs was the innovation of Richard Parkin, the English-born and -trained cabinetmaker who in 1833 took over the renowned shop location of Joseph Barry at 134 South Second Street.[2] Parkin's take on the klismos chair became wildly popular and influential. Other makers adopted his design. He exported them to clients throughout Pennsylvania and in Virginia and Louisiana. His seating had individualized variations that suited patrons' needs and wherewithal as the architecture of their houses. This set of four (cat. 57a) is made of Pennsylvania walnut, while the single chair with the upholstered back (cat. 57b) is made of expensive and heavy rosewood.

Parkin added a facade to Barry's shop and renamed it Egyptian Hall, a concept likely inspired by (and modeled on) Bullock's Egyptian Hall at Piccadilly in London. Parkin's inventiveness made his shop a stunning success and profoundly impacted Philadelphia's Classical furniture design, perhaps most compellingly in the design of chairs like these in the late klismos style.

---

1. See Philadelphia Museum of Art, 2022-24-1; Alexandra Alevizatos Kirtley, *American Furniture, 1650–1840: Highlights from the Philadelphia Museum of Art* (Philadelphia: Philadelphia Museum of Art, 2020), fig. 48.
2. For detailed analysis and information on Parkin and his former partner Thomas Cook, see Carswell Rush Berlin, "'A Shadow of a Magnitude': The Furniture of Thomas Cook and Richard Parkin," in *American Furniture 2013*, ed. Luke Beckerdite (Milwaukee: Chipstone Foundation, 2013), 156–95.

57a

57b

58

Sofa, 1833–1837

David Fleetwood (1800–1855/60)
Philadelphia
Mahogany, mahogany and rosewood veneer; tulip poplar, white pine; brass, replacement upholstery
35 × 25½ × 82 in.

LABEL: Printed on paper, on top of rail, outback: "David Fleetwood / SUCCESSOR TO WM. B. FLING / Chair, Sofa & Cabinet, Upholstrey [sic] / WARE ROOMS / No. 95 / WALNUT STREET / PHILADELPHIA." (See Appendix II)

PROVENANCE: Sale, T. W. Conroy & Associates Auctions, Elbridge, NY, Jan. 26, 2002, lot 73; Purchased by Schrimshers, 2002.

Despite having immense talent as seen in the design and execution of this monumental sofa, Philadelphia cabinetmaker David Fleetwood is listed in the directories only briefly, from 1833 to 1837, and this is his only known work. Fleetwood was born in Delaware and married his first wife, Lydia Maria Ruth, a member of the prominent Stout family of Kent County, Delaware, in 1820 at the Second Presbyterian Church in Philadelphia.

Based on his label, which proudly proclaims that he is the successor to the eminent decorative painter and furniture maker William B. Fling (1737–1834), it is possible that Fleetwood trained with and was the foreman for the fancy and cabinet- and chairmaking shop of Fling and his son, Bennett (1797–1839). The address of 95 Walnut Street was the Flings' most recent location and placed the ambitious Fleetwood between Second and Third Streets, the heart of Philadelphia's furniture-making district—near luminaries like Joseph Barry, Robert West, Charles and John White, Anthony Quervelle, Michel Bouvier, Thomas Cook, and Richard Parkin, and, almost certainly, a bevy of turners, decorative painters, gilders, upholsterers, carvers, and others whose work supported fine cabinetmaking.

Despite his capacity to make elegant cabinet wares, Fleetwood tried his hand in politics and then advertised in May 1837 that he was selling his stock of "superior manufactured work": wardrobes, dressing bureaus with marble tops, a sideboard, center tables, sofas with spring seats, pier tables, and French and high-post bedsteads, rocking chairs, and pairs of bureaus (chests on chests) for bedchambers.[1] After a short stint in New Jersey, he and his second wife purchased eighty acres of farmland in Clinton County, Illinois, in November 1839 where they remained for the duration of their lives.[2]

The sofa described in Fleetwood's advertisement—with "elegant spring seat sofas"—aptly describes the design and structure of this example. Ornament is reserved only for areas that complement but do not overwhelm the profile. Instead of being scrolled, this sofa's crest rail is straight, supported by carved brackets at the ends. The arms are ovoid shaped and faced with elaborately carved scallop shells, which are surely the dominant feature of the design. The front rail has a carved twisted rope, or gadroon, on the lower edge, and the whole is supported by turned and carved bell-shaped feet. The surface decoration relies on the figure of the mahogany veneer and, just above the upholstered seat back, the subtle inclusion of a strip of rosewood veneer that is bracketed by two brass strips.

The upholstery would have been added by a specialist, and this sofa is an early example of spring seating. The coiled metal springs were set, tied, and stuffed inside the framed box that forms the seat; the box was suspended in the sofa and the seat was then toenailed to the front and rear rails with strips nailed below to secure it. The replacement upholstery recreates the lines, severe loft, and overall profile of the original treatment.

1. *Philadelphia Inquirer*, May 9–15, 12.
2. Fleetwood's first wife must have died but no records document the date or cause. He was remarried at the Presbyterian church in Lancaster, Pennsylvania, to Mary Ann Stehman (1812–1889) in 1834.

59

Pier Table, 1825–1829

Cook & Parkin: Thomas Cook (1789–1868) and Richard Parkin (1787–1861), in partnership 1819–29
Philadelphia
Mahogany, mahogany veneer; white pine, tulip poplar, maple; marble, mirror glass, gilded brass or bronze, stencil gilding
38 × 47¾ × 20 in.

LABEL: Stenciled underneath framing element underneath marble: "COOK & PARKIN / Keep mahogany and walnut / CABINETWARE / Mahogany ------- / At No. 56 Walnut St. / PHILADELPHIA." (See Appendix II)

PROVENANCE: Thomas Jefferson James (1776–1856) and Jane Bryne Claypoole James (1797–1864), Chillicothe, OH; To their daughter Elizabeth Claypoole James Dun (1821–1898) and John Graham Dun (1814–1895); To their daughter Miss Gertrude Dun (1850–1927), London, OH. Sale, New Orleans Auction, Jan. 26, 2002, lot 1014; Purchased by Schrimshers, 2002.

The stately elegance of this pier table both underscores the architectonic design on which it is based and exemplifies the work of one of Philadelphia's premier cabinetmaking partnerships working in the British idiom, that of Cook & Parkin. Trained in England, Thomas Cook and his wife arrived in Philadelphia in 1817, followed by Richard Parkin in 1819, and the two quickly formed a lucrative partnership. Carswell Rush Berlin has carefully identified and analyzed their work through the lens of their life experiences, demonstrating that Cook and Parkin stayed true to the design roots of Britain's late Regency while also creating innovative alternatives to the flamboyance of Anthony Gabriel Quervelle and the regalness of Michel Bouvier, their French *émigré* counterparts.

Designed to be placed against the wall (or pier) between two windows, pier tables were custom made to fit the space snugly, with the top also meeting the chair rail. Usually measuring 44 inches wide or less, the 47¾-inch width of the Schrimshers' example is notable. The inwardly curved molding beneath the top, which is known as a cavetto, is a bespoke departure from the more familiar Philadelphia version that is straight or ogee molded.

The columnar supports are possibly maple, turned on a lathe and then covered with an elegant and still perfectly stable mahogany veneer. The capitals and bases are punctuated by gilded and patinated brass (or bronze), likely imported. The front lion's-paw feet have a carved and gilded collar topped by metal mounts. Likewise, the gilt stenciled decorations on the apron and plinth are in a pattern that matches carving found on Philadelphia furniture of the period, including that made by Cook & Parkin.

Remarkably, the white marble top appears to be original. It is set on a robust dovetailed frame that provides sufficient stability. Similarly, the rails that form the mortise-and-tenon frame for the mirror are constructed of thick, solid boards. The wide mirror, which would have reflected light and color in a room, also appears to be original. The pier table may have been one of a pair or more, and the marble may also have matched a sideboard.[1]

Like so much stamped and labeled furniture, this table was marked by Cook & Parkin because it was shipped out of Philadelphia. The table was owned by a family of former Philadelphians who had moved to the booming trade town of Chillicothe, Ohio, around 1800. Ordering furniture from Philadelphia would not have been unusual for wealthy families, especially in a Midwestern town that was thriving in the era following the Panic of 1819.[2]

1. For advertisements of sets of pier tables and sideboards with marble tops, see the *Philadelphia Inquirer*, May 28, 1832, 3; March 9, 1836, 3; Joseph B. Barry & Co., advertisement April 29, 1836, 3; December 21, 1836, 3; January 25, 1837, 3; September 17, 1838, 3.
2. The British-born architect Benjamin Henry Latrobe, who had designed many buildings, interiors, and furniture in Philadelphia, provided the plans for Thomas and Eleanor Worthington's Adena, the most prominent residence in Chillicothe, in 1807.

60

Two Gondola Chairs, 1825–1830

Unknown maker
Philadelphia
Mahogany veneer, rosewood graining, ash; painted and stenciled gilding, replacement upholstery
31⅞ × 19¼ × 18 in.

INSCRIPTIONS: Chiseled on back rail of seat frame: "IIII"; chiseled on back rail of seat frame: "VII."

PROVENANCE: Herbert Archibald Fisher Jr. (1907–1977), Passaic County, NJ. With Garrison Grey Kingsley (1947–2023), Mount Cuba, DE, 2012; Purchased by Schrimshers, 2012.

Referred to as gondola chairs (or, in French, *chaise gondole*) because their straight sides and rounded ends resemble the ends of a gondola boat, the swank shape that was introduced in France around 1800, with the gentle chair's profile persisting through the 1830s.[1] The low, sloping backs and curved crest rails envelope the sitter, with the downward-slanting sides contributing to the sense of encirclement. The chic wooden framing is mahogany that is grain painted to mimic rosewood and decorated with gilded motifs in the prevailing Classical style. These two gondola chairs are from a set of at least eight, and their squared legs and gilded decoration relate them to furniture made in Philadelphia, where the form enjoyed a limited popularity. Gondola chairs made in New York mostly have open (not upholstered) backs with wooden splats.[2]

These chairs follow later patterns published by Pierre de La Mésangère in his serial *Collection de meubles et objets de goût* for a "Fauteuil en Gondole" (plate 494) (fig. 60.1) and a "Chaise de Salon" (plate 543) (fig. 60.2). George Smith referred to the design as a "Library Chair" in *A Collection of Designs for Household Furniture and Interior Decoration* (London, 1808), pls. 44–45. La Mésangère's one design shares the fully upholstered back of the Philadelphia chairs, though the incurved, klismos-like profile and the stance of the legs are more akin to his salon (or parlor) chairs. The gilded stencil decoration relates to the inlaid brass pattern found on klismos chairs that descended in the Powel family, and also to the gilded stenciling on a pier table and a secretary bookcase made by Isaac Jones for the Vansyckel family.[3]

With their strong French character, these chairs likely were part of a suite of furniture that may have included stools (La Mésangère's "Tabouret en X," plate 661), a couch ("Divan," plate 630, or "Canapé," plates 529, 626), and sideboards ("Console dessert," plates 570, 718).

1. While posh, truly bespoke furniture was not typically listed in Philadelphia price books of that period, advertisements in Philadelphia newspapers use the word *gondola* to describe these upholstered-back chairs. For example, see the advertisement of Moses Nathan, auctioneer, 84 S. Second Street (just above Walnut Street), "Rich Gondola Chairs, in plush," *Philadelphia Public Ledger*, October 30, 1848, 3.
2. Perhaps prompted by Mr. Fisher's loan of one of the Schrimsher chairs to the Newark Museum's 1963 exhibition *Classical America: 1815–1845*, Mrs. Van Horn Ely (Elizabeth Geist Ely, 1910–1986) donated two chairs each from this set to the Philadelphia Museum of Art (1965-84-1 and 1965-84-2), the Newark Museum of Art (also donated in 1965), and the Smithsonian Museum of Art (66.1039 and 66.1040). Mrs. Ely lived in Philadelphia and was a trustee of the Philadelphia Museum of Art. For a New York gondola chair, see the Metropolitan Museum of Art, 66.221.4. For the chairs in the PMA, see also Alexandra Alevizatos Kirtley, *American Furniture, 1650–1840: Highlights from the Philadelphia Museum of Art* (Philadelphia: Philadelphia Museum of Art, 2020), cats. 205–6.
3. See Kirtley, *American Furniture, 1650–1840*, cats. 180, 181, 204, and fig. 60.

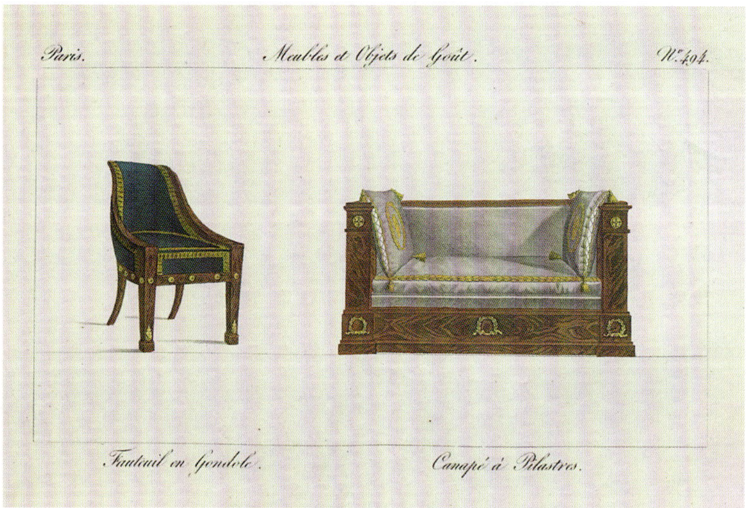

Fig. 60.1. Pierre de La Mésangère, "Fauteuil en Gondole", plate 494 (left image) in *Collection de meubles et objets de goût* (Paris, 1799–1831), hand-colored engraving (Courtesy Winterthur Museum, Garden & Library)

Fig. 60.2. Pierre de La Mésangère, "Chaise de Salon", plate 543 (left image) in *Collection de meubles et objets de goût* (Paris, 1799–1831), hand-colored engraving (Courtesy Winterthur Museum, Garden & Library)

61

Armoire, 1825–1830

Attributed to the shop of Anthony Gabriel Quervelle (1789–1856)
Philadelphia
Mahogany, mahogany veneer; tulip poplar, yellow pine; brass
95 × 84 × 30½ in.

PROVENANCE: By unknown descent. Purchased from an unidentified source in the 1980s by Martin J. Schoenberger, MD (1950–2019), and Stephanie Gilbert Schoenberger, MD (1952–2022), New Orleans, LA; Sale, Neal Auction Company, New Orleans, LA, Feb. 3, 2023, lot 407; Purchased by Schrimshers, 2023.

Columns, carved ornaments, and figured veneer cleverly animate the tripartite facade of this nearly eight-foot-high armoire. The monumental size suggests that it was designed for a large, high-ceilinged room whose architecture may have included related elements such as a columnar screen, pointed arches, and acanthus-leaf and volute carving. This distinctive repertoire of decoration relates this armoire to the documented work of Philadelphia's predominant French *émigré* cabinetmaker, Anthony Gabriel Quervelle.

An armoire is a cabinet in the French taste for storing clothing and bed linens that differs from an Irish- or British-inspired wardrobe, linen press, or clothes press or a Germanic *kleiderschrank*, all of which were much more commonly made and used in Philadelphia and southeastern Pennsylvania. Here, the double case doors of the armoire open at the center to reveal shelves for the storage of folded clothing and linens, punctuated by a central belt of two drawers; facing outward at each end of the case are full-height doors to shallow cabinets for hanging clothes. Though the 1828 book of prices for Philadelphia-area journeymen cabinet- and chairmakers describes "A French Wardrobe," it is a much more modest case piece that lacks the authentic French design seen here and in armoires made in Francophile communities, such as Louisiana.[1]

The panels of the central doors of this armoire are decorated with valances of carved acanthus leaves, and their central veins spiral to form volutes. At the center of the upper-panel valances are pinecones, here most likely a reference to the pinecone-tipped wand of fennel known as a thyrsus, an attribute of Bacchus that was widely recognized in the early nineteenth century as part of the repertoire of classical motifs. The thyrsus tip reappears on the plinth in between the columns in front of the armoire's end cabinets. The columns are cinched with a band of acanthus-leaf carving, complementing the doors. At the top, the armoire's cornice projects prominently but is otherwise plain, while the entire case is supported below by energetic dolphins in the familiar Roman model (fig. 61.1) (also seen on tables; see cats. 44 and 50). Their deeply contorted bodies emphasize the burden of supporting a large and heavy case.

While it is unknown who commissioned this armoire, the arrangement of its broad facade and its well-balanced carved composition make it the finest of its type to survive. It surely must have been part of an elaborately furnished house and was likely complemented by a suite of related Classical furniture.

1. *The Journeyman Cabinet and Chairmakers' Pennsylvania Book of Prices* (Philadelphia: Printed for the Society, 1811; repr. 1828), 80–81; Jack D. Holden, H. Parrot Bacot, and Cybèle Gontar, *Furnishing Louisiana: Creole and Acadian Furniture, 1735–1835* (New Orleans: Historic New Orleans Collection, 2009).

Fig. 61.1. Detail of cat. 61 showing dolphin foot

62

Secretary Bookcase, 1830–1835

Attributed to Henry Montgomery (active 1829–1840); carving attributed to Joseph Woodwell (1807–1899)
Pittsburgh, Pennsylvania
Mahogany, mahogany and maple veneer; pine, tulip poplar, Carpathian elm burl veneer; glass, brass
93 × 48 × 26 in.

INSCRIPTION: On lined paper attached to interior: "Lewis T Hamilton / Altoona / Blair County / Pa."

PROVENANCE: Lewis Peterson (Virginia 1791–1884) and Amelia Schriner Peterson (1794–before 1884), Philadelphia, and (by 1813) Pittsburgh; To their daughter Margaret Peterson Hamilton (1817–1910) and John Hamilton (1816–1903); To their son Lewis Theodore Hamilton (1859–1913) and Matilda McClure Greer Hamilton (later Caldwell, d. 1932), Jamestown, Dakota Territory (later North Dakota), and (after 1920) Altoona and Swarthmore, PA; To their daughter Theodora Hamilton Rutherford (1896–1952) and Thomas Rutherford (1894–1981), Swarthmore, PA. With Charles Clark, Woodbury, CT, 2023; Purchased by Schrimshers, 2023.

Fig. 62.1. Attributed to Anthony Gabriel Quervelle, *Furniture Sketch*, c. 1820–1835, graphite and pen and ink on wove paper, Philadelphia Museum of Art, Purchased with funds contributed by an anonymous donor, Mr. and Mrs. W. B. Dixon Stroud, John A. Nyheim, Dr. and Mrs. Robert E. Booth, Jr., and Anne R. and John F. Haley, Jr., 1995, 1995-12-4a,b (Courtesy Philadelphia Museum of Art)

In 1827, Philadelphia's French *émigré* cabinetmaker Anthony Gabriel Quervelle submitted a related secretary bookcase to the city's Franklin Institute for the exhibition and competition of "excellence in the mechanical arts."[1] That secretary bookcase, which was made *en suite* with a pair of worktables (cats. 49a and b) and is now in the collection of the Philadelphia Museum of Art (PMA), was awarded the highest honor—the silver medal. Conceived with the same overall composition, this secretary bookcase features the elegant fan on the secretary base and a bookcase above with attenuated glazing that are emblematic of the style that Quervelle created in Philadelphia that was eagerly embraced by Philadelphians. Other cabinetmakers—like brothers Henry and Benjamin (active 1820s) Montgomery, William Alexander (active 1837–1844), and Henry Bheares (sometimes Beares, 1800–1872)—brought these designs to Pittsburgh.

While the design of this secretary bookcase had its genesis in Philadelphia, nuanced features confidently point to its Pittsburgh manufacture. The convex and undulating rays that form a fan across the doors of the base of the secretary originated with Quervelle; however, the rounded square shape of this one differs from the demilune, or half circle, shape of those documented not only to Quervelle, but also to Philadelphia makers who adopted Quervelle's idiosyncratic design (fig. 62.1).[2] The pattern and execution of the two-dimensional carved acanthus and acorns in the corners relate to the documented work of Joseph Woodwell of Pittsburgh. On the secretary drawer are pulvinated diamonds: two horizontal ones on the fall-front drawer and two vertical ones framing it. Accentuated by figured veneer, the convex diamond design was one Quervelle employed on other furniture, including the PMA's award-winning secretary. Burl maple veneer on the interior drawer fronts adds light to the otherwise plain arrangement.

Perhaps even more than the secretary base, the execution of the bookcase closely mimics those made in Philadelphia. The cornice projects above a frieze covered with a carefully laid out pattern of mahogany veneers with a fiery figure. The design of the mullions is borrowed from variously published patterns, such as those at the back of the 1828 Philadelphia furniture price book, and similar ones are found on furniture made in both 1820s Philadelphia and Baltimore (see cat. 77). Notably, the columns flanking the glazing are integral to the doors (not separate like in Philadelphia), and the doors hinge from the sides—in the normal way.

Given the similarities to the drawing of the secretary bookcase, the design of this piece with more slender proportions can be ascribed to Henry Montgomery, the Philadelphia-trained cabinetmaker working in Quervelle's shop who signed his name as the journeyman who made the award-winning secretary and then relocated to Pittsburgh.[3] His brother Benjamin also likely trained as a cabinetmaker in Philadelphia and followed Henry to Pittsburgh; Benjamin is best known for signing a sideboard made in the Philadelphia style—an amalgamation of sketches of Classical sideboard designs.[4] This secretary bookcase, the Benjmain Montgomery sideboard, and a sideboard made by Alexander in nearby Sharpsburg have carved ornament that can be ascribed to Woodwell, who seemingly provided carving for Pittsburgh's finest cabinetmakers.[5]

A card tacked inside the case reveals its ownership by Lewis Theodore Hamilton, who was born in Altoona, Pennsylvania, attended Michigan Law School, and eventually settled in the Dakota Territory with his wife Matilda McClure Greer (later Caldwell). The Hamiltons were devout, multigenerational Presbyterians who moved from Philadelphia to Pittsburgh in 1813, and it is most likely that Lewis Hamilton inherited the bookcase from his family. Inspired by the Philadelphia form, this monumental and distinctively Pittsburgh-made secretary bookcase is as extraordinary as its Philadelphia model—and perhaps a unique example of a Pittsburgh secretary bookcase in the fully developed Classical style.

---

1. Quervelle himself referred to the form as a "Secretary & Bookcase"; see Alexandra Alevizatos Kirtley, *American Furniture, 1650–1840: Highlights from the Philadelphia Museum of Art* (Philadelphia: Philadelphia Museum of Art, 2020), 180.
2. Philadelphia Museum of Art, 1973-61-1. Quervelle's competitors in the Philadelphia cabinetmaking community pirated the distinctive fan design. A closely related secretary that is missing its bookcase top bears the stencil of Charles Haight White (1796–1876).
3. The inscription on the backboard—*H. Montgomery/ Sepr 27th 1827*—is the familiar format that Philadelphia journeymen used to mark their piecework for payment. See Kirtley, *American Furniture 1650–1840*, 2020, 154, 180.
4. Philadelphia Museum of Art, 1995-12-1 to -12.
5. See "How Do We Know a Pittsburgh Sideboard When We See One?" Oct. 22, 2009, https://urbanartantiques.com/2009/10/22/how-do-we-know-a-pittsburgh-sideboard-when-we-see-one. Alexander also stamped this pier table: sold at Pook & Pook, Inc., Downingtown, Pennsylvania, May 21, 2004, lot 358, current location unknown.

Baltimore Classical Furniture in the Schrimsher Collection

GREGORY R. WEIDMAN

In considering Baltimore Classical furniture, especially in light of the products of other major American cities of the time, it should be noted how Baltimore differs from those urban centers. In the 1810s and 1820s, Boston, New York, and Philadelphia were all long-established cities with rich cultural traditions and craft practices. Boston and its environs had experienced nearly two centuries of history, and New York and Philadelphia only a few decades less. Baltimore, however, had been little more than a village half a century earlier. Rather than experiencing many years of regular immigration, population growth, and physical expansion (the Revolutionary War years excepted), Baltimore virtually exploded onto the scene over a relatively brief period of time. Rather than having time-honored cultural preferences, craft traditions, and artisans' shops, both the makers and their clientele in Baltimore were, for the most part, recent arrivals.

By the 1810s, this burst of growth and activity led to the production of Classical furniture with an almost idiosyncratic style and aesthetic. Except for a small handful of forms and decorative elements closely related to similar pieces of Philadelphia manufacture, Baltimore for the most part went its own direction, with its own particular fashions, preferences, and taste.

***Sofa*, 1815–1830 (detail of cat. 65)**

Historical Background in Eighteenth-Century Baltimore

To describe Baltimore's mid-eighteenth-century beginnings as modest is certainly not an understatement. Although the town on the Patapsco River was founded and laid out in 1729, by 1752 it was still a small community. A description on a watercolor drawing of Baltimore, later turned into a well-known aquatint, notes only one hundred inhabitants, twenty-five dwellings, one church, two taverns, and a brewery, at a time when Philadelphia had about 15,000 inhabitants (fig. 1). The real growth began after the conclusion of the French and Indian War in 1763. Baltimore's geographic location—considerably farther west than Philadelphia, on the fall line near rich Pennsylvania farming hinterlands—and its deep harbor with easy access to the Chesapeake Bay, Atlantic Ocean, and Caribbean Sea began to drive growth. With the shift in Maryland's principal agriculture from tobacco to grain, enterprising young merchants from the British Isles and Pennsylvania established flour mills. Grain shipping to the West Indies and Europe and related industries such as shipbuilding began to thrive. The town's population was about 3,000 by 1770, around double that of Maryland's capital, Annapolis. The next year, a "friend to trade" complained in a Philadelphia newspaper that the town had "within a few years past carried off from

Fig. 1. After John Moale (1731–1798), *Baltimore Town in 1752*, lithograph, New York Public Library, The Miriam and Ira D. Wallach Division of Art, Prints and Photographs: Print Collection, EM3465 (Courtesy New York Public Library Digital Collections)

this city almost the whole trade of Frederick, York, Bedford & Cumberland Counties."[1]

During the Revolutionary War, with the other major port cities of Boston, New York, and Philadelphia blockaded, Baltimore was in an ideal position to profit—and profit it did. The town became a depot for food stuffs, iron, and military supplies for the Continental Army. Resourceful local merchants and courageous ships' captains came to monopolize the highly lucrative West Indian trade. When peace returned in 1783, a recent German immigrant opined, "Nothing was so favorable to the commerce of the place as the last war."[2]

Eager to join the action and seek their fortunes in post-Revolutionary Baltimore, immigrants from both Europe and other American cities and towns joined with members of the colonial land-owning gentry of Maryland in flocking to the city. Merchants, millers, manufacturers, land speculators, and wealthy planters arrived, including a substantial percentage of immigrants from the British Isles. The post-Revolutionary population exploded until the town became the third-most-populous city in the country by 1800.[3] Naturally, the physical city grew by leaps and bounds. Elegant town residences for the city's newly rich mercantile elite were built not far from the harbor near their places of business, and their country houses dotted the hills north and west of town. In 1796, French visitor François-Alexandre-Frédéric, duc de La Rochefoucauld-Liancourt (1747–1827) observed that there were "new houses building in every street" as the town spread outward. As one writer later described, Baltimore went from being "a group of cabins to a city changed" (fig. 2).[4]

Notably, among the recent arrivals who made their fortunes in the Federal era were newly rich entrepreneurs who became Baltimore's most powerful and influential citizens. Merchant princes such as Samuel (1752–1839) and Robert Smith (1757–1842), William Buchanan (1732–1804), William Patterson (1752–1835) and his sons, Robert Gilmor Sr. (1748–1822) and his sons, Solomon Etting (1764–1847), Jacob I. Cohen Jr. (1789–1869) and his brothers, Alexander Brown (1764–1834), William (1749–1824) and James (1776–1850) Wilson, Robert Oliver (1756–1834), and Isaac McKim (1775–1838) furnished their magnificent city residences and country houses with noteworthy examples of the distinctive work of Baltimore's furniture makers. However, it was not only newly wealthy immigrants who participated in this market. Members of Maryland's landed gentry including long-established families such as Carroll, Chase, Howard, Ridgely, and Rogers also became residents of the city and purchasers of the stylish objects made there.

Bonds among these disparate groups were formed not just through professions and sources of wealth but by religious affiliation as well. Many of Baltimore's most important

Fig. 2. Thomas H. Poppleton (1765–1837), Joseph Cone (1792–1831), and Charles Peter Harrison (1783–1854), *This Plan of the City of Baltimore*, 1822, hand-colored map, Library of Congress Geography and Map Division, 77691538 (Courtesy Library of Congress, Geography and Map Division)

and wealthiest merchants and civic leaders were Scots-Irish Presbyterians, but there were also prominent communities of Anglicans, Catholics, Quakers, and Lutherans. Also, although small (about fifteen extended families around 1800), the Jewish community in Baltimore was nonetheless important in the fields of banking and other mercantile interests and were very important as patrons of the cabinetmakers' arts. Religious affiliations sometimes influenced the selection of a certain craftsman (see cat. 75), even though patronage of leading makers such as William Camp (1773–1822) and Hugh Finlay (1780–1830) transcended all economic and religious communities.

After the turn of the nineteenth century, it was not always smooth sailing for Baltimore's largely shipping-based economy. European wars in the first decade harassed American vessels. Many Baltimore merchants responded by securing letters of marque, which were in effect licenses for privateering, a legal form of piracy. Using the small and speedy schooners known as Baltimore clippers, built in the city's Fell's Point neighborhood, a number of local merchants made considerable fortunes capturing enemy cargo in this risky enterprise. For example, veteran naval officer Joshua Barney's ship *Rossie* captured twenty vessels worth nearly $1.3 million during a four-month cruise in 1812.[5] The city was a leading center for privateering during the War of 1812, leading in September 1814 to the British attacking and seeking to capture the place they referred to as a "nest of pirates." Fortunately, the city's defenders at North Point, Hampstead Hill, and Fort McHenry successfully repulsed the British land and naval assault, leaving Baltimore mostly unscathed.

A brief period of prosperity and activity between 1815 and 1819 saw some of Baltimore's finest furniture commissions. As the city rebounded from wartime footing, prominent Quaker cabinetmaker John Needles (1786–1878) recalled that "when peace was made . . . my business so increased that I could not make furniture fast enough to sell."[6] This was all brought to a dramatic halt by the first major economic depression in the United States, the Panic of 1819. This event greatly affected all levels of society, including both craftsmen

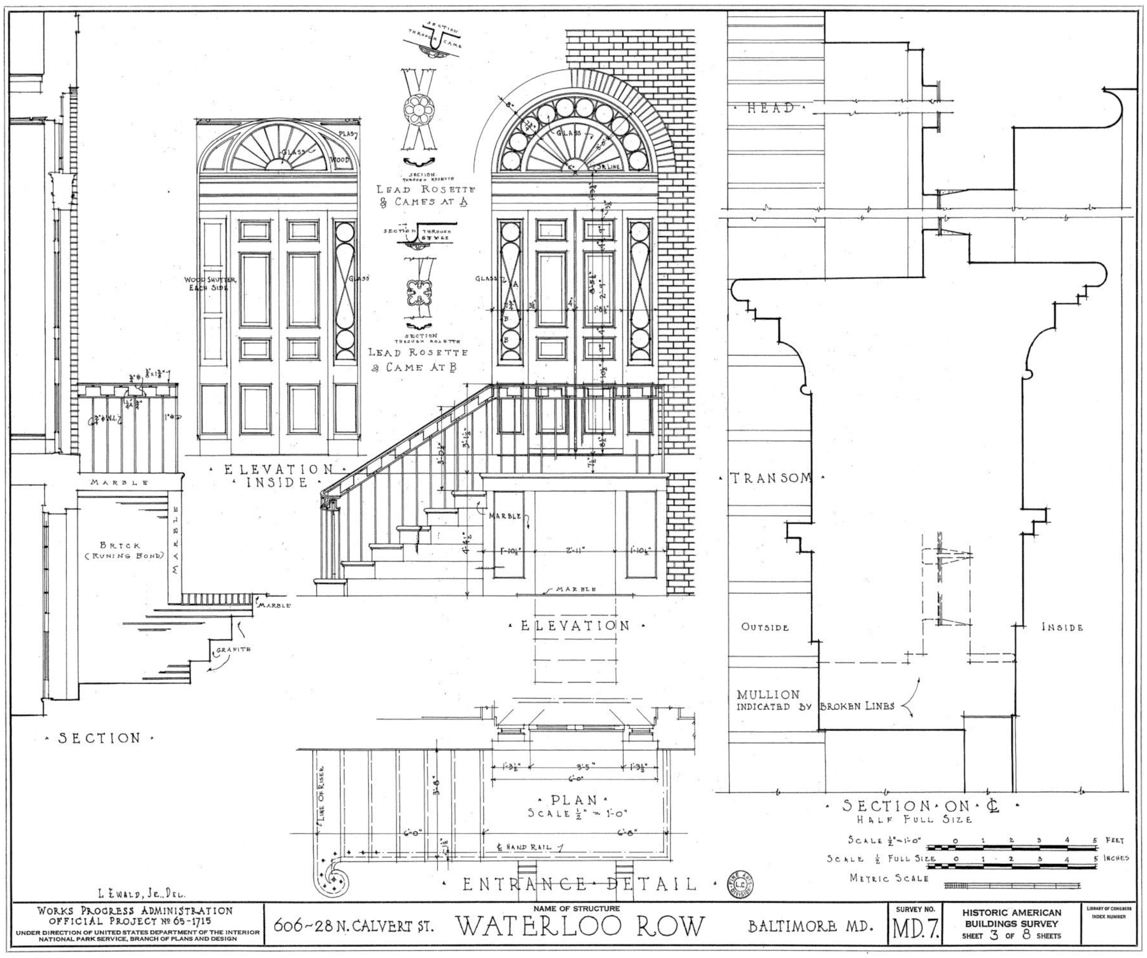

Fig. 3. Robert Mills (1781–1855), *Waterloo Row, 600 Block N. Calvert Street, Baltimore, Maryland,* 1816; Historic American Buildings Survey, HABS MD,4-BALT,16- (Courtesy Library of Congress). The plan shows the doorway to one of the elegant new townhouses built in Baltimore in the 1810s designed by noted American architect Robert Mills. The building was demolished in 1970.

and their clients. The economic climate of the 1820s saw a modest return to prosperity in the city, but the mood was definitely more subdued than the three previous decades had been. Not surprisingly, Baltimore cabinet furniture has a more conservative appearance at this time, with less of the showy surface ornamentation that defined the Neoclassical era.

Before the Panic, the first and second decades of the nineteenth century saw the construction of many magnificent townhouses, most three-bay but some of them large double-width, five-bay urban mansions (fig. 3).[7] There was a noticeable decline in the pace of the building of grand city houses, however, for a number of years in the early 1820s due to many lost fortunes and economic instability. In any case, virtually none of the impressive residences in the heart of the city on streets such as Water, Holliday, and Gay have survived. The moving of the most fashionable neighborhoods to new areas well north of the harbor, the rapid growth of the business and civic centers of the city in the second half of the nineteenth century, and subsequently the Great Baltimore Fire of 1904 virtually erased the physical evidence of Federal Baltimore in the center of the city. Gone are the grand houses once filled with stylish Classical furniture.

Cabinetmakers and Their Works in Federal-Era Baltimore

The cabinetmaking community in Baltimore in the early nineteenth century had evolved considerably from the immediate post-Revolutionary period. The leading cabinetmaker in the 1780s and early 1790s was London-trained immigrant Richard Lawson (1749–1803), who, with his American business partner John Bankson (1754–1814), executed some of the most sophisticated and highly ornamented furniture ever made in the new United States (fig. 4).[8] Notably, clients of Bankson & Lawson (in partnership 1785–1792) and their competitors were not just newly rich immigrants, they were also from old Maryland families, such as Charles Carnan Ridgely (1760–1829) of Hampton and Supreme Court Justice Samuel Chase (1741–1811). The latter moved from Annapolis to a new town house in Baltimore in 1788, where a chair in the collection of the Maryland Center for History and Culture can now be attributed to the Bankson & Lawson shop.[9] The impact of the Bankson & Lawson firm (along with other British-trained cabinetmakers such as William Singleton, active

Fig. 4. ***Sideboard,*** **attributed to John Bankson and Richard Lawson, Baltimore, c. 1790, mahogany, mahogany veneer, satinwood; yellow poplar, white oak, Diplomatic Reception Rooms, U.S. Department of State, Gift of Mr. and Mrs. Mitchell Taradash, RR-1967.0007 (Courtesy of the Diplomatic Reception Rooms, U.S. Department of State)**

1790–1803) on the local taste in Neoclassical furniture should not be underestimated. However, other than a handful of British immigrants, most of the other cabinetmakers working in the city by the 1790s were of Maryland origin.

Baltimore's early Neoclassical furniture is renowned for two salient characteristics: its close adherence to English design sources and its rich surface ornamentation. Although the first of these characteristics did not necessarily continue unabated into the later part of the period, the second certainly did, at least with regard to painted furniture. Regarding the strong relationship of Baltimore Neoclassical furniture to English sources, one scholar noted: "Nowhere in the young republic were the English prototypes adapted more faithfully or more ornately than in Baltimore."[10] Published design sources from which Baltimore cabinetmakers were inspired include George Hepplewhite's *The Cabinet-Maker and Upholsterer's Guide* (London, 1788), where pieces ranging from sophisticated "cabriole" sofas to the more basic "night tables" (commodes) were copied directly. Thomas Sheraton's *The Cabinet-Maker and Upholsterer's Drawing-Book* (London, 1791–93) inspired some of the most elegant and elaborate furniture made in the country (fig. 5).[11] Baltimore cabinetmakers also took inspiration from the distinctive designs of imported English pieces, such as oval and modified shield back chairs and sideboards not produced in other cities.

The true character of Baltimore Neoclassical cabinet furniture is most fully expressed in its elaborate inlaid ornament. The profusion of pictorial inlays and banding and veneers of exotic woods that embellish much of the city's furniture from 1785 to 1805 is especially noteworthy. Inlays range from a distinctive Baltimore bellflower to conch shells, eagles, blossoms, paterae, and numerous other designs, many probably made by specialist inlay makers. In addition to huge quantities of imported mahogany from the Caribbean and

Fig. 5. ***Dressing Table,*** **attributed to William Camp, c. 1800–1810, mahogany, satinwood, red cedar, tulip poplar; glass, Maryland Center for History and Culture, Gift of Eleanor S. Cohen, Eleanor S. Cohen Collection, 1938.7 (Courtesy Maryland Center for History and Culture)**

Central America, cabinetmakers used exotic imports such as satinwood, zebrawood, rosewood, and even casuarina from Australia.

By the first decade of the nineteenth century, the furniture that was filling the new residences of both the mercantile elite and landed gentry tended to be both vivid and colorful (fig. 5). In the late 1790s, a new taste was arising in the booming city, perhaps encouraged by Baltimoreans' continued reliance on British design books and their love for showy surfaces on furniture. Hepplewhite's *Guide* notes: "For chairs, a new and very elegant fashion has arisen within these few years, of finishing them with painted or japanned work," and Baltimore's consumers paid note.[12] At that time, those who had wanted the newly stylish sets of painted chairs and accompanying tables had to import them from England or New York. As the fad for painted furniture arrived in force by 1800, it was adopted to a great extent by those wishing to furnish their new homes in the latest taste. There to serve this growing market were a number of firms, but the leaders at the top end of the market were the brothers John (1777–1851) and Hugh Finlay, whose talent powered the growing popularity of "fancy" furniture.[13]

During this period, firms were established that would lead the cabinet furniture trade for the next two or three decades. Originally in partnership with Thomas Combs (dates unknown) (from 1799 until 1802), Baltimore County native Michael Jenkins (1778–1832) founded a family business that was to last (in one form or another) until 2009.[14] The wholesale lumber and undertaking were important sidelines to their cabinetmaking business. However, other than a fall-front secretary, dated 1806 and bearing Michael Jenkins's signature, no works documented by him are extant, although several by his sons and successors in business, including Anthony Hearn Jenkins (1814–1884) and Henry Worthington Jenkins (1814–1878), are known, and others have Jenkins family associations. Anthony signed two pieces (a card table and a writing table and bookcase), most likely when he was still working at his father's shop in the 1820s. These two examples and two other important Classical pieces with strong Jenkins family provenance help to fill this void for documented items dating before 1832.

New Jersey-born and Philadelphia-trained William Camp, the most prominent name of the era, was the acknowledged leader of Baltimore's cabinetmaking community for two decades. No other craftsman was even close to the number of acknowledgements in the press related to the quality of his shop's products. As noted in previous publications,[15] the size of his shop, as documented by the number of work benches for his journeymen (thirty-seven) and the amount of furniture listed in his estate inventory, were substantial.[16] Newspapers reported at least forty-six apprentices in his twenty-year career. The size of his ancillary business as a lumber merchant was also considerable, as documented in both newspaper advertisements and his probate inventory that included exotic woods from as far away as Australia.[17] Notably, he worked cooperatively with other prominent local craftsmen in this aspect of his business, including Edward Priestley, Michael Jenkins, and Walter Crook.

Edward Priestley (1778–1837) was one of Camp's principal competitors from the beginning. A native of Annapolis, he has the distinction of being the first to advertise the sale of Classical furniture in Baltimore: "Pillar and Claw" Pembroke tables in 1808.[18] Priestley could count the Lloyds, one of Maryland's richest and most prominent families, among his clientele. The attribution to Priestley's shop of the Lloyds' Wye House sideboard table with "mummy"-headed legs and other pieces made for another private family on Maryland's Eastern Shore is noteworthy. After his competitor Camp died, Priestley purchased both large quantities of lumber and thirty-one work benches at the estate sale.[19]

The last and youngest of the longtime leaders in cabinetmaking in Federal-era Baltimore was John Needles, a Quaker born and initially trained in Talbot County on Maryland's Eastern Shore. He began his long and successful career in Baltimore in 1808 as a journeyman in the shops of both Priestley and Camp. Needles's oeuvre is by far the best documented of any Baltimore cabinetmaker of the nineteenth century, thanks to his habit of labeling the products of his shop. Needles wanted to distinguish his meticulously constructed works from those of lesser craftsmen who sold their goods anonymously through commission merchants and street-corner auctions. In 1826, his warerooms at 54 Hanover Street were stocked with 160 pieces, an extensive array of goods that ranged from plain to elaborate.[20] He also had clients from Virginia to as far away as Louisiana, but lost money on a venture to export goods to South America.[21] Needles was always eager to introduce technological advancements such as steam power, which sometimes came at the price of fires in his shop.

The Classical cabinet furniture made in Baltimore is, for the most part, quite distinct from the products of the other major cities included in this volume. This is most clearly the case with furniture made in New York and Boston shops, which exhibits very little if any affiliation with Baltimore-made work. There is a closer connection with Philadelphia, but this is principally restricted to a few specific types of forms, features, and ornamentation. These include, most notably, the tables and sideboards embellished with carved "mummy" or "Persian" heads (cats. 72 and 73). There is also a group of similar lyre-based worktables (cat. 80). Some cabinet sideboards exhibit similarities, but most can be distinguished by the manner of carving (Baltimore's being generally less florid) or ornamentation of columns (Baltimore's distinctive bold reeding or column capitals).

The documented work of John Needles, however, can show a fairly close connection to Philadelphia design sources. He made a number of sideboards, center tables, and worktables that would be clearly attributed to Philadelphia were it not for the cabinetmaker's labels.[22] Given his close familial and religious connections to Philadelphia, this is not surprising. Also, as a canny businessman who exported furniture far and wide, he may well have simply wanted to widen his selection of designs to appeal to more clients.

Other than these few examples, Baltimore-made cabinet furniture of the 1810s and 1820s features a considerable

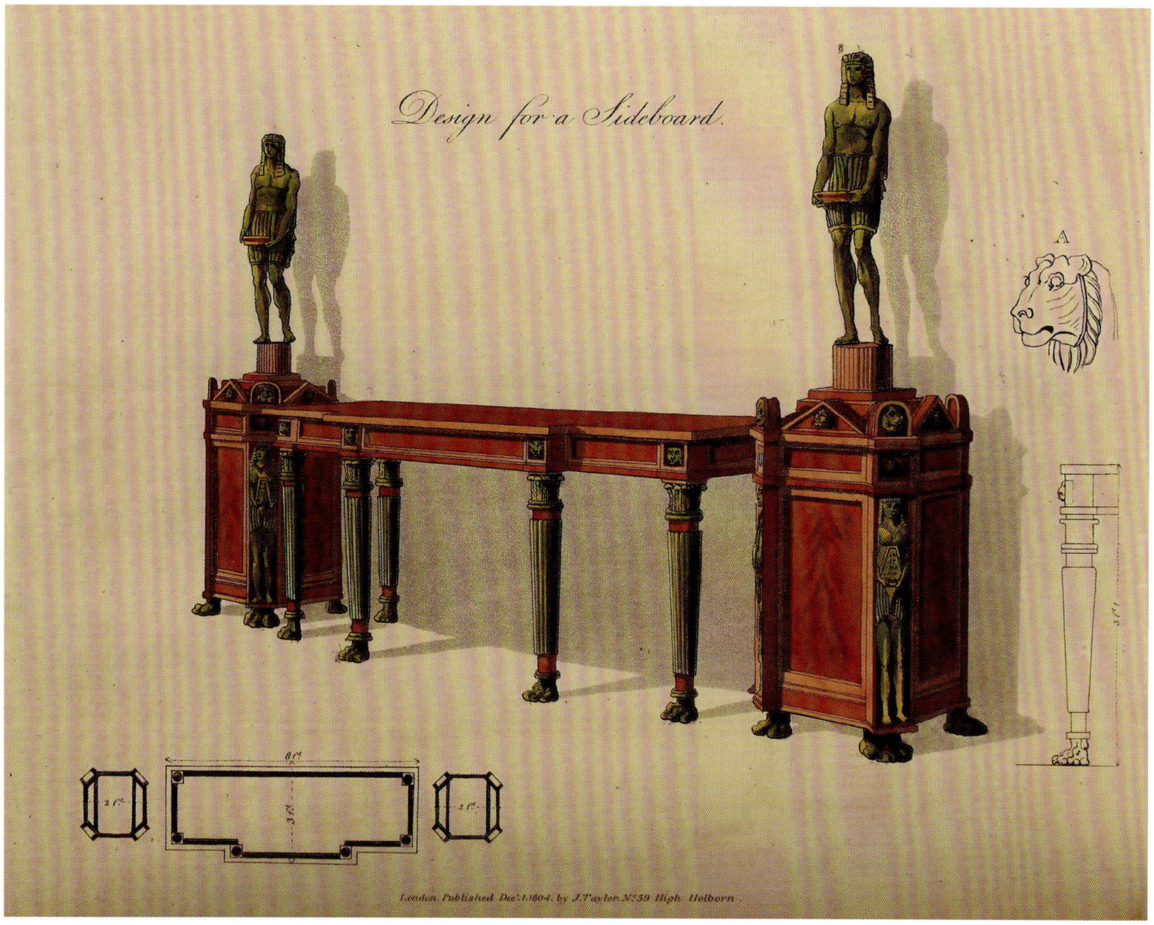

Fig. 6. George Smith, "Design for a Sideboard," plate in *A Collection of Designs for Household Furniture and Interior Decoration* (London, 1808), hand-colored engraving (Courtesy Clark Art Institute Library, Mary Ann Beinecke Decorative Art Collection). The Egyptian figures functioning as column supports recall the "mummy" or "Persian" heads found on Baltimore furniture. The reeding on the central columns also became a prominent characteristic of Baltimore Classical furniture.

number of decorative elements and forms that set the pieces apart from the work of other cities' craftsmen. Also, in a considerable contrast to earlier Neoclassical furniture made in Baltimore, makers' adherence to English design books and forms is less strongly seen. While there is some influence from publications such as George Smith's *A Collection of Designs for Household Furniture and Interior Decoration* (London, 1808) (fig. 6), perhaps inspiring case pieces such as sideboards and desks that combine both Grecian and Gothic designs, there is far less direct copying. Baltimore Classical cabinetwork in contrast to painted furniture tends to feature more conservative forms and ornamentation, perhaps as a result of the economic downturn following the Panic of 1819, especially in contrast to, for instance, the furniture of cabinetmakers such as Charles-Honoré Lannuier (1779–1819) and Barzilia Deming (1781–1854) and Erastus Bulkley (1798–1872) in New York or Joseph Brown Barry (1757–1838) and Anthony Gabriel Quervelle (1789–1856) in Philadelphia. The carved ornamentation of Baltimore Classical furniture in general is quite restrained and usually flatter than the voluptuous and florid carving seen on many Philadelphia pieces (see cats. 45, 47, and 48).

Baltimore Classical furniture can be idiosyncratic, such as in the use of bold, sometimes spiky reeding for columns, table pedestals, table and chair legs, square-back sofas, Grecian couches, and the like (cats. 75 and 78). Although Needles's work certainly has this feature, it is also seen on the documented and attributed work of several other Baltimore cabinetmakers, including Camp, Anthony Jenkins, Ralph Forrester (active 1814–1829), and others.[23]

Distinctive Baltimore case pieces include several noteworthy local Baltimore writing tables and desks with bookcase tops that have intricate and stylized Classical carving on the glazed doors (cats. 70 and 77), featuring elements such as anthemia, palmettes, and wreaths. Pilasters on the bookcase tops or lower cases usually have bold reeding topped by pointed water leaves. The cylinder lid for desks required a complex mechanism that only a few craftsmen had the ability to produce, including Camp, Needles, and possibly Priestley. These Baltimore craftsmen produced two different representations of the cylinder desk (cats. 73 and 76), a desk and bookcase form and the more unusual large cylinder desk embellished with carved "mummy"-headed therms on the corners of the case. Only one Philadelphia-made example of this form is known. These figures, derived from therms with Egyptian heads published in Smith's *Collection of Designs* can also be found on Baltimore cabinet sideboards. Both desks and sideboards

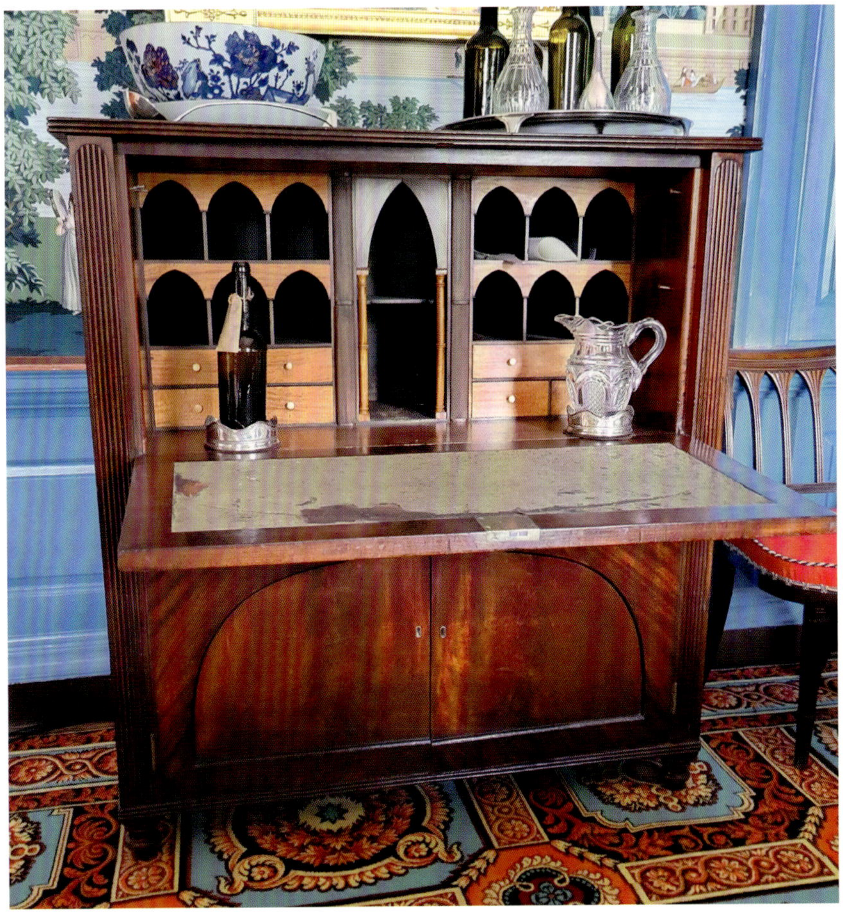

Fig. 7. *French Secretary*, attributed to William Camp, c. 1816, owned by Governor Charles Carnan Ridgely of Hampton, Baltimore County, mahogany, satinwood, tulip poplar, baize, brass (Courtesy Hampton National Historic Site, National Park Service). Though different in form from French secretaries produced in Boston, New York, and Philadelphia, the fall-front desk component of this secretary adheres to French examples.

also feature the synthesis of ancient classical elements such as carved motifs, columns, and paw feet with Gothic arched panels, also derived from Smith's design book. Rare forms in Baltimore cabinetwork are *secrétaires á abattant*, or French secretaries, including examples made by or attributed to Camp (fig. 7).[24]

There are a number of characteristic Baltimore table shapes. Unlike in other cities, a group of Baltimore pier tables have open legs with no mirrored backboard; those with marble tops were probably intended for use as small serving tables in dining rooms (cat. 75). Baltimore worktables come in a huge variety, one of the most unusual being the round "drum" table with drawers in the deep apron and supporting columns often featuring vase turnings with bold reeding. Both this type of table and larger round center tables often have radial veneers of flame mahogany. Although there are few card tables with acanthus-carved pedestals and knees and animal-paw feet, most have turned shafts (with or without bold reeding) and reeded saber legs (cat. 79). Sideboard tables had been very popular in Baltimore in 1790–1810, and that popularity continued into the era of the Classical style. Although local examples can have columnar legs (either boldly reeded or plain with Ionic capitals), a small but important group have "mummy" carved and reeded legs (including one of the finest examples of this particular form that was made in both Baltimore and Philadelphia, cat. 72).

In seating furniture, the two most ubiquitous forms—a side chair (cat. 78) and a square-back sofa with boldly reeded crest rails, arm supports, and legs—are actually late Neoclassical designs that continued to be made well into the late 1820s. The side chairs, which have reeded Gothic-arched splats, bell-shaped seats, and heavily reeded legs, have survived in considerable numbers. Although deriving some elements from New York and Philadelphia designs, they are interpreted in a purely Baltimore way. Notably, the klismos chair form in mahogany so frequently seen in other cities is not as common in Baltimore, partly due to the local passion for painted chairs. There are closely related Baltimore square-back sofas and Grecian couches with reeded elements that are also numerous. The Baltimore Classical Grecian couches have elegant lines but restrained ornamentation of reeded arms continuous with the seat rail and reeded saber legs. Some Grecian sofas with cornucopia-carved arms and leg brackets and lion's-paw feet were made in Baltimore, although the carving again tends to be flatter than that on Philadelphia examples.

In sharp contrast to table and case furniture, Baltimore Classical painted furniture, especially the work of leading

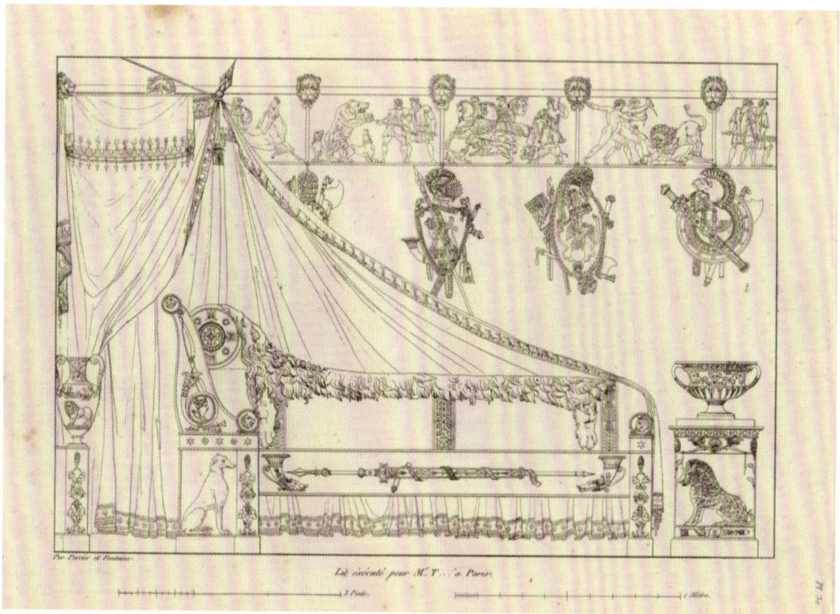

Fig. 8. Charles Percier and Pierre-François-Léonard Fontaine, "Lit éxecuté pour Mr. T ... à Paris," plate 33 in *Recueil de décorations intérieures* (1801–1812), engraving (Courtesy Winterthur Museum, Garden & Library)

manufacturer Hugh Finlay, shows considerable French influence, particularly in the decorative motifs on fancy furniture, many of which are derived from *Recueil de décorations intérieures* (Paris, 1801–12) by Charles Percier and Pierre-François-Léonard Fontaine (fig. 8). Classical painted furniture continues the Baltimore Neoclassical-era preference for highly ornamented pieces. This is most fully expressed in the "polychrome group" from the Finlay shop in the 1810s, painted in vivid colors such as chrome yellow, Pompeiian red, and bronze green with black accents (cat. 63). The later group of painted pieces features bold rosewood-grained grounds with red, brown, and black, heavily embellished with gilded ornament. The somewhat conservative style of most Baltimore Classical cabinet furniture is clearly eclipsed by the sophistication of the fancy work. In some Baltimore households one could find painted and cabinet furniture side-by-side in the same room: for example, painted klismos chairs in dining rooms alongside mahogany tables and sideboards.

The work of brothers John and Hugh Finlay dominated the top end of the market for painted furniture—"fancy" furniture as it was then called—both in the period 1800–1812 and then even more thoroughly in the later Classical period.[25] This followed the firm's notable commission to make furniture designed by Benjamin Henry Latrobe (1764–1820) for President James and his wife Dolley Madison in 1809, and Hugh Finlay's trip to London and Paris the following year. Following Hugh's return, the Finlays found their principal sources of inspiration in the works of designers such as Thomas Hope, George Smith, and especially Percier and Fontaine. Their incorporation of motifs from the latter is by far the most prevalent use of French designs in Baltimore Classical furniture. After 1816, when elder brother John left the painted-furniture business to open the Pavilion Baths, a recreational establishment, Hugh took the business to new heights, serving clients throughout Maryland and Virginia until his death in 1830. At its height before the Panic of 1819, the Finlay shop employed a total of sixty-eight men, women, and boys. Enough documented Finlay pieces dating from 1815 to 1822 survive to strongly attribute a sizeable group of closely related pieces. John resumed the business after his brother's death in 1830, but the Baltimore passion for painted furniture was waning. The last great suite of furniture documented from the Finlay shop, dated 1832, still survives intact and in situ in the Drawing Room of Hampton mansion at Hampton National Historic Site in Baltimore County.

In Baltimore Classical painted furniture, the most ubiquitous chair form features a distinctive klismos shape, having a raked back with tablet crest rail, short stiles, and turned front legs, inspired by ancient Roman, rather than Greek, designs. The Schrimsher Collection has one of the earliest and finest examples (cat. 63). Following the most stylish pieces made by the Finlays, chairs of this basic shape were made by literally dozens of Baltimore chairmakers in the post-1815 period and were exported and imitated far and wide. By this stage, most other types of important Classical painted furniture, such as sofas and tables, were almost exclusively the work of the Finlays.[26] Their dominance of the top end of the market after the War of 1812 does not necessarily include certain minor painted items, such as boxes and small stands, although these are clearly inspired by the Finlays' work and the ornament they used.

Baltimore's influence spread outward, partly through the work of emigrant cabinetmakers but primarily through exports of Baltimore furniture, which found clients in numerous locales beyond the city. This trade was already in motion immediately after the close of the Revolutionary War and continued to increase over time until it became truly big business for a number of craftsmen. The increasing widespread popularity of fancy chairs gave a boost to the business, since these lightweight items were easy to crate and ship, especially unassembled in pieces. Inexpensive Baltimore painted chairs reached locations as far away as South America and South Africa, but the stylish and costly painted parlor furniture of the Finlays was sent to their clients in western Maryland, the Eastern Shore, and southern Virginia. More expensive cabinet furniture from the shops of leading craftsmen such as Priestley, Jenkins, and Needles found buyers from western Pennsylvania to Louisiana.

Advances in scholarship on the careers of Baltimore's renowned furniture craftsmen have led to great strides in identifying works from several of the most important and prolific shops in the rapidly growing city. As additional labeled and documented examples by these firms become known, this understanding will continue to expand and be refined. Each city has its own distinct history and culture that is reflected in the works of those who lived and plied their trades there. As shown in the Baltimore examples well represented here, clear differences can be discerned that express the city's vibrant story.

In the last decade, scholarship on Baltimore and Maryland furniture has also expanded well beyond the traditional discovery and attribution of objects to shops to include different viewpoints and assessments.[27] With these new directions, the rich history of Baltimore furniture will gain important fresh perspectives.

1. Philadelphia "Friend to Trade," quoted in Jane Garrett, "Philadelphia and Baltimore, 1790–1840: A Study of Intra-Regional Unity," *Maryland Historical Magazine* 56, no. 1 (1960): 8; quoted in Gregory R. Weidman, *Furniture in Maryland, 1740–1940: The Collection of the Maryland Historical Society* (Baltimore: Maryland Historical Society, 1984), 70.
2. Raphael Semmes, *Baltimore as Seen by Visitors, 1783–1860* (Baltimore: Maryland Historical Society, 1953) 3, quoted in Weidman, *Furniture in Maryland, 1740–1940*, 70.
3. It became the second most populous a short time later, surpassing Philadelphia in 1830 until 1860.
4. Philip Freneau, "Maryland" (poem), quoted in Garrett, "Philadelphia and Baltimore, 1790–1840," 3.
5. "Privateer History," Pride of Baltimore II (website), last modified 2012, https://pride2.org/education/privateer-history/.
6. John Needles, "John Needles, An Autobiography," ed. Dr. Edward Needles Wright, *Journal of Quaker History* 58, no. 1 (Spring 1969): 16.
7. Among the leading architects active in Federal-era Baltimore were Benjamin Henry Latrobe, Maximilian Godefroy (1765–1848), Robert Mills (1781–1855), Robert Carey Long Sr. (1770–1833), and William F. Small (1798–1832).
8. For further information on Bankson & Lawson, see Sumpter Priddy III, J. Michael Flanigan, and Gregory R. Weidman, "The Genesis of Neoclassical Style in Baltimore Furniture," in *American Furniture 2000*, ed. Luke Beckerdite (Milwaukee: Chipstone Foundation, 2000), 59–99.
9. Weidman, *Furniture in Maryland, 1740–1940*, fig. 49.
10. Marilyn Johnson Bordes, *Baltimore Federal Furniture* (New York, Metropolitan Museum of Art, 1972), 13.
11. For a magnificent lady's cabinet dressing table attributed to William Camp, see, for example, Weidman, *Furniture in Maryland, 1740–1940*, fig. 148.
12. George Hepplewhite, *The Cabinet-Maker and Upholsterer's Guide* (London, 1788).
13. Firms like the Finlays and their competitors would not have considered their trade to be "cabinetmaking." They were chairmakers, fancy furniture manufacturers, ornamental painters, and gilders. Cabinetmaking in general required different skills to work wood and make cases, veneers, inlays, and finishes, though both trades may have used turning and upholstery at their manufactories.
14. The Jenkins family sold the firm in 1958, though the name was continued by the new owners for another fifty years.
15. Weidman, *Furniture in Maryland, 1740–1940*, 74; Gregory R. Weidman and Jennifer Goldsborough, *Classical Maryland, 1815–1845: Fine and Decorative Arts from the Golden Age* (Baltimore: Maryland Historical Society, 1993), 110ff.
16. Inventories, 1822, vol. 33, 571, Baltimore County Register of Wills, Maryland State Archives.
17. He offered 20,000 feet of San Domingo mahogany in the *Baltimore Evening Post*, December 1, 1806.
18. Alexandra Alevizatos Kirtley, "A New Suspect: Baltimore Cabinetmaker Edward Priestley," in *American Furniture 2000*, ed. Luke Beckerdite (Milwaukee: Chipstone Foundation, 2000), 100–151.
19. Ibid., 100.
20. Weidman and Goldsborough, *Classical Maryland*, 115–26.
21. Needles, "John Needles, An Autobiography," 15.
22. Weidman and Goldsborough, *Classical Maryland*, figs. 140, 142, 144.
23. Ibid., figs. 138, 153, 159.
24. Ibid., figs. 137, 165.
25. The Finlays' work has been featured in numerous publications, now dating back through five decades. See William Voss Elder III, *Baltimore Painted Furniture, 1800–1840* (Baltimore: Baltimore Museum of Art, 1972); Weidman, *Furniture in Maryland, 1740–1940*; William Voss Elder III and Jayne E. Stokes, *American Furniture, 1680–1880* (Baltimore: Baltimore Museum of Art, 1987); Weidman and Goldsborough, *Classical Maryland*; Lance Humphries, "Provenance, Patronage and Perception: The Morris Suite of Baltimore Painted Furniture," in *American Furniture 2003*, ed. Luke Beckerdite (Milwaukee: Chipstone Foundation, 2003); Alexandra Alevizatos Kirtley, "New Discoveries in Baltimore Painted Furniture," *Antiques and Fine Art Magazine*, Spring 2022, https://www.antiquesandfineart.com/articles/article.cfm?request=194; Alexandra Alevizatos Kirtley, "Benjamin Henry Latrobe and the Furniture of John and Hugh Finlay," *The Magazine Antiques*, December 9, 2009, https://www.themagazineantiques.com/article/benjamin-henry-latrobe-and-the-furniture-of-john-and-hugh-finlay/.
26. In their early work in the style, one set of Philadelphia-made furniture, the suite for Mr. and Mrs. William Waln was indeed somewhat influential; however, this was due more to the designer of the pieces, Benjamin Henry Latrobe, than to their geographic origin. Alexandra Alevizatos Kirtley and Peggy A. Olley, *Classical Splendor: Painted Furniture for a Grand Philadelphia House* (Philadelphia: Philadelphia Museum of Art, 2016). See also Elder and Stokes, *American Furniture*.
27. These recent studies include Michelle Fitzgerald's work on Quaker cabinetmaker John Needles's important activities as an abolitionist and Bethany McGlyn's scholarship on enslaved artisans who worked in early-nineteenth-century Annapolis. Michelle Fitzgerald, "The Furniture of John Needles," lecture for The Beltway and Beyond, Winterthur Museum, Garden & Library Virtual Conference, October 2020. Bethany McGlyn, "Who Built the City on the Severn?: Slavery, Material Culture, and Landscapes of Labor in Early Annapolis," (Master's thesis, University of Delaware, 2020). See also Tiffany Momon and Torren Gatson, Black Craftspeople Digital Archive, last modified 2024, https://blackcraftspeople.org/.

63

Side Chair, 1812–1830

Attributed to John Finlay (1777–1851) and Hugh Finlay (1780–1830), in partnership 1799–1816
Baltimore
Maple; cherry; painted decoration, stencil gilding, replacement caning
32⅝ × 19⅞ × 20½ in.

PROVENANCE: Possibly Arunah Shepherdson Abell (1806–1888) and Mary Fox Abell (1818–1859), Baltimore. Possibly by descent to their daughter Dorothy Margaret "Daisy" Abell Griffiss (1859–1929) and John Irving Griffiss (1856–1894). Margaret Mary Griffiss Fenwick (1890–1974) and Guy Bernard Fenwick (1881–1954), probably after c. 1915; By descent to their son Charles Cuthbert Fenwick (1924–2020) and Elizabeth White Fenwick; Sale, Sotheby's, New York, Jan. 24, 2022, lot 1504; Purchased by Schrimshers, 2022.

This chair is part of one of the most important and well-known sets of Baltimore painted furniture. Made when the Finlays were at their peak of sophistication and popularity, it reflects an international sensibility. The principal source for the ornamentation was Charles Percier and Pierre-François-Léonard Fontaine, *Recueil de décorations intérieures*.[1] The winged thunderbolts, fasces, crossed torches, and griffins with scrolled acanthus are taken from their published designs, which Hugh Finlay would have acquired during his visit to Paris in 1810.[2] The form derives from ancient Roman precedents, with turned front legs that stabilized the Greek klismos chair.

The color scheme is part of a distinctive polychrome group of Baltimore painted furniture that dates from about 1812 to the early 1820s. The key colors are Pompeiian red, dark bronze green, black, and, significantly, an intense yellow. This is chrome yellow (chromate of iron), first discovered on the farm of Isaac Tyson Jr. (1792–1861) in Bare Hills, seven miles north of Baltimore City, sometime shortly after 1808.[3] Art collector Robert Gilmor published this discovery in 1813 and the next year noted: "Perhaps in no part of the world has so much been discovered at one place. It furnishes the means of preparing a beautiful paint called chromic yellow, with which carriages and furniture are now painted in Baltimore."[4] Of note in this regard, the Finlays' coachmaking business had continued until at least mid-1813.

Fig. 63.1. Detail of cat. 63 showing griffins and *rinceaux* on the rail

There are two key documented objects that help to attribute the polychrome group to the Finlay shop. These are the set of side chairs made for dry-goods merchant Richard Ragan (1775–1850) of Hagerstown, Maryland, in 1815 and a suite executed for prominent Baltimore merchant James Wilson in 1819, both of which derive ornamentation from Percier and Fontaine.[5]

A Baltimore painted sofa made for the Bernard family of Rose Hill (later called Gay Mont) outside of Port Royal, Virginia,[6] may suggest an alternate provenance for the Schrimsher chair to that of the A. S. Abell family. The sofa is truly exceptional in several ways, not the least of which is having survived (though in damaged condition) a fire in 1956 that destroyed the center of the house. The sofa is visible in photos of the wide entrance hall at Rose Hill taken in 1941, 2008, and 2015. Its distinctive painted ornament, unquestionably from the Finlay shop, features a Percier and Fontaine–derived sword and spear motif on the front seat rail flanked by winged thunderbolts on the corners, the same as on a sofa owned by Alexander Brown, except the ground colors are reversed.[7] The seat rail of the Bernard sofa has a red ground and yellow corner blocks and saber legs with gilt curled tendrils on a red ground.[8]

Regarding the Schrimsher chair's provenance, it has long been recognized that Arunah Abell, who came to Baltimore in 1837 and founded the *Baltimore Sun* newspaper (the eventual source of his fortune) could not have been the original owner of the chairs. Even the mid-twentieth-century family provenance that claims the chairs were used at Woodbourne, one of Abell's several country houses, may not be accurate due to the descent of that house.[9] What is unquestionably true is that the chairs were owned by Margaret Mary Griffiss Fenwick (1890–1974) and her husband Guy Bernard Fenwick (1881–1954) at their estate in the Worthington Valley in Baltimore County, where they had moved shortly after their marriage in 1913.[10] Although it is possible that the chairs came to Mrs. Fenwick from her mother, Dorothy Margaret "Daisy" Abell Griffiss, the youngest of A. S. Abell's twelve children, there is a possibility that the set descended to her husband. Guy Bernard Fenwick was a great-grandson of John Hipkins Bernard (1792–1852) of Rose Hill, which he renamed Gay Mont after he married Jane Gay Robertson in 1816. The Bernards' daughter Gay Robertson Bernard (1817–1865) had moved to Baltimore in 1836 and married Charles B. Tiernan (sometimes recorded as Tieman, 1797–1886), a wealthy lawyer and son of Luke Tiernan (1757–1839), one of Federal Baltimore's merchant princes. The contents of Charles Tiernan's elegantly furnished Baltimore townhouse, recorded in his estate inventory, included a set of twelve chairs of fairly low value but placed in a principal parlor of the house along with expensive paintings and statuary.[11] The Tiernans' daughter Gay Bernard Tiernan (Mrs. Henry A Fenwick, 1842–1938) was Margaret Mary Griffiss Fenwick's mother-in-law. Perhaps she gave the set of painted chairs to help furnish the Worthington Valley house in the 1910s.

1. Charles Percier and Pierre-François-Léonard Fontaine, *Recueil de décorations intérieures* (Paris, 1801–1812).
2. As his brother John advertised in the *Baltimore American and Commercial Daily Advertiser* of December 19, 1810, Hugh Finlay forwarded to Baltimore "a number of Drawings from the first houses in Paris and London."
3. The yellow paint on this chair was analyzed by conservator Rian Deurenberg-Wilkinson of Fallon & Wilkinson. It was confirmed to be chrome yellow. See *Examination Report: Two Baltimore Painted Klismos Chairs, Attr. Finlay Brothers*, 6. The report is in the files of the Schrimsher Foundation.
4. This information was discovered and published by Lance Humphries in "Provenance, Patronage, and Perception: The Morris Suite of Baltimore Painted Furniture," in *American Furniture 2003*, ed. Luke Beckerdite (Milwaukee: Chipstone Foundation, 2003).
5. Gregory R. Weidman and Jennifer Goldsborough, *Classical Maryland, 1815–1845: Fine and Decorative Arts from the Golden Age* (Baltimore: Maryland Historical Society, 1993), figs. 111, 113. Among the polychrome group most closely related to the Abell chairs is the suite made for wealthy merchant/banker Alexander Brown (1764–1834), a card table in the Kaufman collection, a matching pier table in a private collection in Baltimore, and several other tables and pieces of seating furniture in private collections. For images of these pieces see Weidman and Goldsborough, figs. 114–19.
6. This sofa is mentioned, but not illustrated, in Tara Gleason Chicirda, "The Bowie Brothers of Port Royal, Virginia, and the Bernard Family Marble Chess Table," *MESDA Journal of Early Southern Decorative Arts* 38 (2017), note 19, https://www.mesdajournal.org/2018/the-bowie-brothers-of-port-royal-virginia-and-the-bernard-family-marble-chess-table/.
7. Weidman and Goldsborough, *Classical Maryland*, fig. 114.
8. The arm facing may also have a red ground, but these were fire-damaged and are now hard to distinguish. It is possible that the originally large set of chairs of which the Schrimshers' is one could have accompanied this extraordinary sofa.
9. Woodbourne was first acquired by Arunah Abell around 1857. After he bought Guilford, a larger country house, in 1872, the house passed to two of his sons, George W. Abell (1842–1894) and Edwin F. Abell (1840–1904). The latter's widow lived at Tivoli, another house on the expanded estate's property, until its sale in 1930. There is no known direct connection between the youngest Abell child Dorothy Abell Griffiss and the Woodbourne property. Information from the Passano-O'Neill file, Maryland Center for History and Culture.
10. Mrs. Fenwick sold nine of the chairs in 1964 or 1965 to Baltimore antiques dealer Norton Asner, who then sold the set to the Metropolitan Museum of Art. Five of the nine were deaccessioned by the Met in the early 1970s and are now in the collections of the Baltimore Museum of Art (65.167.2, 65.167.4), the Munson-Williams-Proctor Institute Museum in Utica, New York (65.167.3), the High Museum of Art in Atlanta, Georgia (65.167.7), and the Kaufman Americana Foundation (65.167.1). The Schrimshers' chair was one of a pair that remained in the Fenwick family until 2022.
11. Baltimore City Inventories, 1885–1886, RTB 129, 577, Maryland State Archives. The value of the chairs was $12.00 for the set of twelve, an appropriate value for seventy-year-old painted chairs.

64

Pair of Side Chairs, 1815–1830

Possibly by Hugh Finlay (1781–1830)
Baltimore
Tulip poplar, maple; painted decoration, stencil gilding, applied penwork, replacement caning
33 × 17½ × 16½ in.

PROVENANCE: By descent through the Hutchins family of My Lady's Manor, Baltimore County, MD; Probably originally owned by Col. William G. Hutchins (1800–1871), who married Sarah Anderson (d. 1830) in 1825; To James Alfred Hutchins (1826–1888) and Caroline Lowry Herring (1834–1920); To their son William Herbert Hutchins (1860–1905) and his wife Laura (d. 1937); To their daughter Garnet B. Hutchins (1891–1978); Sale, Milton J. Dance Auctioneers, Jun. 9, 1979, at the residence of Garnet Hutchins, Old York Road, Monkton, MD. With Colwill-McGehee Antiques, Baltimore, MD by 1994. Private Sale, Brunk Auctions, Asheville, NC; Purchased by Schrimshers, 2020.

There are several factors that suggest these chairs were made at Hugh Finlay's shop. The decoration of the crest rail with griffins and cornucopia flanking a central column is closely related to other Finlay chairs, including another Schrimsher side chair (cat. 63) and a set owned by merchant Alexander Brown.[1] The griffins' foliated scroll tails are also similar to those features on the Finlay-attributed tables owned by Alexander Brown. The ornament on the side seat rails appears on other Finlay-attributed sets.

However, the remainder of the chairs' gilded ornamentation—on the legs and stay and front seat rails—is quite broadly painted and does not have the crispness of the Finlay shop's characteristic work.[2] Also, the turning of the front legs is not typical of other Finlay chairs. This leaves open the possibility that the chairs were made at one of the numerous other fancy chairmaking shops in Baltimore after the War of 1812.[3] The Finlays' work was surely very well known among their competitors, and imitation is the sincerest form of flattery. By the time Classical painted chairs of this shape were made, the ground color used in the Finlay shop was almost exclusively chrome yellow (with red, dark green, and black ornament), rosewood grained, or black. Although it had been used on earlier Neoclassical fancy chairs, the vivid blue of these chairs does not seem to be a shade the Finlay shop typically used later. It is interesting to note that earlier Neoclassical painted chairs made in Baltimore could be found in a wider variety of colors than those made in the 1820s.

These chairs are from an original set of at least six and probably twelve. Another pair from the set is known to be at Colonial Williamsburg Foundation, another at the Baltimore Museum of Art, and final one in a Baltimore private collection.[4] The likely original owners were the Hutchins family of well-to-do farmers and shop owners who lived in far northern Baltimore County in the historic area known as My Lady's Manor.[5] At the 1979 auction where the family sold the chairs, they were described as a "Set of Decorated Adams Chairs."[6]

1. See, for example, William Voss Elder III, *Baltimore Painted Furniture, 1800–1840* (Baltimore: Baltimore Museum of Art, 1972), figs. 37, 338, 45; Gregory R. Weidman and Jennifer Goldsborough, *Classical Maryland, 1815–1845: Fine and Decorative Arts from the Golden Age* (Baltimore: Maryland Historical Society, 1993), figs. 111, 129.
2. Another possibility is that the chairs were made c. 1830, around the time of Hugh Finlay's death, when supervision of the quality of the shop's products was not as strong.
3. For a discussion of chairmaking firms in the post–War of 1812 period, see Gregory R. Weidman, *Furniture in Maryland, 1740–1940: The Collection of the Maryland Historical Society* (Baltimore: Maryland Historical Society, 1984), 87, 89.
4. Information courtesy of Stiles T. Colwill, Baltimore, Maryland. The chairs at Colonial Williamsburg are published in Ronald L. Hurst and Jonathan Prown, *Southern Furniture 1680–1830: The Colonial Williamsburg Collection* (Williamsburg, VA: Colonial Williamsburg Foundation, 1997), cats. 50, 178.
5. The son of the likely original owner also briefly ran a shop in Baltimore City in the post–Civil War era.
6. *Baltimore Sun*, June 5, 1979.

Fig. 64.1: Detail of cat. 64 showing crest and stay rails with painted decoration of griffins, cornucopia, and *rinceaux*

65

Sofa, 1815–1830

Attributed to Hugh Finlay (1781–1830)
Baltimore
Tulip poplar; painted decoration, stencil gilding, brass, replacement upholstery
36 × 95 × 24 in.

PROVENANCE: The James Wilson Family, Baltimore, *or* the Robert Smith Family, Baltimore. By descent to Mrs. James W. Wilson (née Ellen Von Kapff, 1856–1944) at 505 Park Avenue, Baltimore; To her grandson James Wilson Poultney (1908–1993). With G. K. S. Bush, Inc., c. 1990. Sale, Northeast Auctions, Mar. 21, 1999, lot 718, advertised as "Collection of the Wilson Family, Baltimore"; With J. Michael Flanigan, American Antiques, Baltimore, 1999; Purchased by Schrimshers, 1999.

In March 1819, southside Virginia plantation owner Humberston Skipwith (1791–1863) was billed by Hugh Finlay of Baltimore for furniture purchased at the time of his wedding to Sarah Nivison (1793–1822).[1] Among these, at the impressive cost of $140, was a sofa.[2] Referred to today as a Grecian couch, the sofa appears in a circa 1890 photo of the Drawing Room at Skipwith's Prestwould Plantation. The distinctive painted decoration on the rosewood-grained front seat rail and arm supports can clearly be seen and helps to attribute a number of nearly identical surviving pieces of Baltimore painted seating furniture to Finlay.[3] There are also at least two very similar sofas with reverse serpentine backs: one in a private collection in Maryland, which was originally owned by the family of the Rev. George Morrison of Long Green, in Baltimore County, and the Schrimshers' sofa.[4]

This group features identical painted and gilded decoration (fig. 65.1) that points to the Finlays' continued reliance on the Classical ornamentation in Charles Percier and Pierre-François-Léonard Fontaine's *Recueil de décorations intérieures* (Paris, 1801–12). In plate 29, titled "Fauteuil et Siege" (armchair and seat, fig. 65.2), the front seat rail of an armchair is decorated with a mount of similar design, featuring a central rosette flanked by elongated anthemions and stylized palmettes. The Schrimsher sofa's shape is an unusual variant on the form that was apparently made only in Baltimore: a Grecian sofa with a reverse serpentine back that is lower in the center. This form may have been inspired in part by Benjamin Henry Latrobe's designs for furniture for the Madison White House, which the Finlay firm had made, and for the William Waln family of Philadelphia, but both of those sofas were backless.[5]

The provenance of the Schrimsher's Baltimore sofa (and its relationship thereby to other major suites of furniture documented and attributed to Finlay) is significant, if somewhat convoluted. What is certain is that in the late 1920s, when the sofa was photographed for publication by Edgar G. Miller, it was in the residence of Mrs. James W. Wilson at 505 Park Avenue in Baltimore's historic Mount Vernon neighborhood.[6] After Mrs. Wilson's death, the house was sold, but the

Fig. 65.1. Detail of cat. 65 showing painted decoration on seat rail and leg

Fig. 65.2. Charles Percier and Pierre-François-Léonard Fontaine, "Fauteuil et Siege," detail of plate 29 in *Recueil de décorations intérieures* (Paris, 1801–12), engraving (Courtesy Winterthur Museum, Garden & Library)

sofa passed to her grandson James Wilson Poultney, who lived at the 505 Park townhouse from circa 1918 until the 1930s. The Wilson family were not the original owners of the house, however. The first owners were Mrs. James W. Wilson's maternal grandparents, Ellen Donnell and Samuel W. Smith (1800–1887), the only surviving son of U.S. Secretary of State Robert Smith (1757–1842), who moved into their new Park Avenue house in 1843. Photos of the interior of the house taken in the twentieth century show both pieces from Robert Smith's suite of New York furniture[7] and a center table from the Finlay shop later owned by James W. Poultney's mother, Mrs. William D. Poultney, née Ellinor Donnell Wilson (1883–1974).[8] The question, then, is was the sofa part of the famous large suite originally owned by James Wilson (1775–1851), or was it part of another very similar suite owned by Samuel W. Smith, who had married in 1823?[9] Both were major figures in the economic and social life of Baltimore and were great-great-grandfathers of Ellen Wilson.

---

1. Alicia Tucker, "Evenings at Home: Family Life in Southside Virginia, 1760–1836" (Master's thesis, College of William and Mary, Arts and Sciences, 1988), 99–100. According to Tucker, this and other furniture purchased that year were for Skipwith's new house in Norfolk. They would have been moved to Prestwould after his mother's death in 1826.
2. This is a high price for a painted rather than mahogany sofa. To compare, a mahogany square-back sofa made in 1817 by William Camp for Dr. Edmund Hilleary of Frederick cost $100.
3. These pieces include couches in the Museum of Fine Arts, Boston (1988.530), the Kaufman collection at the National Gallery of Art, Washington, D.C., and the Bayly parlor suite at Colonial Williamsburg (2003-1,1A; 2003-1,2; 2003-1,4A; 2003-1,4C). See Gregory R. Weidman and Jennifer Goldsborough, *Classical Maryland, 1815–1845: Fine and Decorative Arts from the Golden Age* (Baltimore: Maryland Historical Society, 1993), fig. 122; J. Michael Flanigan, *American Furniture from the Kaufman Collection* (Washington, D.C.: National Gallery of Art, 1986), fig. 59; Tara Gleason, "The Bayly Suite of Painted Furniture," *Antiques and Fine Art Magazine* (Spring 2003), fig. 3, https://www.antiquesandfineart.com/articles/article.cfm?request=385.
4. Weidman and Goldsborough, *Classical Maryland*, fig. 123.
5. Ibid., fig. 109; Alexandra Alevizatos Kirtley and Peggy A. Olley, *Classical Splendor: Painted Furniture for a Grand Philadelphia House* (Philadelphia: Philadelphia Museum of Art, 2016), fig. 117, cat. no. 2.
6. Also present were Finlay shop painted chairs; Edgar G. Miller Jr., *American Antique Furniture: A Book for Amateurs, Vols. 1–2* (Baltimore: Lord Baltimore Press, 1937), 1:fig. 339.
7. Gregory R. Weidman, *Furniture in Maryland, 1740–1940: The Collection of the Maryland Historical Society* (Baltimore: Maryland Historical Society, 1984), figs. 161–63. The Schrimshers' New York pier table (cat. 20), is also part of this suite.
8. William Voss Elder III, *Baltimore Painted Furniture, 1800–1840* (Baltimore: Baltimore Museum of Art, 1972), fig. 30.
9. See ibid., figs. 24–29.

66a

Pair of Card Tables, 1815–1830

Attributed to Hugh Finlay (1781–1830)
Baltimore
Tulip poplar; walnut, possibly maple; painted decoration, stencil gilding, brass
29 × 35½ × 17½ in.

PROVENANCE (66a): Elinor Merrell (1905–1993), New York, by 1993; Sale, William Doyle Galleries, New York, Dec. 1, 1993, lot 474. With Leigh Keno American Antiques, New York. The Westervelt Company, Tuscaloosa, AL; Sale, Christie's, New York, Sept. 25, 2013, lot 105; Purchased by Schrimshers, 2013.

66b–c

Assembled Pair of Card Tables, 1815–1830

Attributed to Hugh Finlay (1781–1830)
Baltimore
Tulip poplar; walnut, white pine, possibly maple; painted decoration, stencil gilding, applied penwork, brass
Each 28¾ × 36 × 17¾ in.

PROVENANCE (66b): Sale, Christie's, New York, Sept. 20, 2017, lot 186; Purchased by Schrimshers, 2017.

PROVENANCE (66c): Probably owned by James Clark of Baltimore (1840–1909) and his wife Elizabeth Booker (d. 1885) of Lynchburg, VA. By descent to their daughter Nannie P. Clark, Baltimore (Mrs. Robert Chester Smith, 1882–c. 1969); By descent to her son Robert Chester Smith Jr. (1912–1975), PhD, Professor of Art History, University of Pennsylvania; By descent to cousins of Robert Chester Smith Jr.; Sale, Sotheby's, New York, Oct. 11, 2001, lot 248; With J. Michael Flanigan, American Antiques, Baltimore, 2001; Purchased by Schrimshers, 2001.

66b

66c

These card tables exhibit the quintessential design and ornamentation of the best Baltimore painted furniture in the Classical style.[1] There are two phases of this style: the earlier phase, popular from about the time of the War of 1812 through the early 1820s, is a sophisticated taste featuring polychrome decoration emphasizing colors of yellow, red, and dark bronze green with black accents; the later phase, first introduced around 1817 and popular until the mid-1830s, features rosewood graining or black grounds with gilded ornamentation in imitation of the *ormolu* mounts on European examples, as seen here.

The first handsome pair of tables (cat. 66a) can be firmly attributed to the Finlay shop based on the ornamentation derived from Charles Percier and Pierre-François-Léonard Fontaine's *Recueil de décorations intérieures* (Paris, 1801–12) including the winged thunderbolt (fig. 66.1), crossed torches within a wreath, *rinceaux* with rosettes, and stylized palmette seen on the documented Wilson family pieces (cat. 65).[2] The X-base with S-scrolled brackets embellished with brass rosettes is found on a documented Prestwould card table, which is also rosewood grained.[3] In addition to the motifs on the apron, the barrel-and-ring turned pedestal with brass rosettes can be found on a similar pair of pier tables made by the Finlay shop for Governor Charles Carnan Ridgely of Hampton in Baltimore County in 1822.[4]

The attribution of the assembled pair of tables (cat. 66b–c) to the shop of Hugh Finlay is exceptionally strong. The tables are identical in all but one detail to the card tables made by Finlay in 1819 for Humberston Skipwith of Prestwould Plantation in Clarksville, Virginia.[5] The principal difference is in the center of the apron. The documented Prestwould table has a frieze of fruit and foliage in the center of the three-part apron rather than the stylized anthemion and cornucopia seen on the Schrimsher tables. Apart from this variance, the ornamentation and form of the tables are extraordinarily similar: both are rosewood grained (see p. 294, fig. 7), have a vase-turned central pedestal with gilt leafage at top over central gilded ring

Fig. 66.1. Detail of cat. 66a showing winged thunderbolt motif

turning, and both also have X-bases with scrolled brackets having gilded stylized palmettes and brass rosettes, ending on short turned legs on casters. In addition, the tops of both pairs of tables have a wide decorative banding of a central palmette and scrolled *rinceaux* of acanthus (fig. 66.2). The apron decoration on the Schrimsher tables, derived from the designs of Percier and Fontaine, is also related to those elements seen on the large suite of furniture made in 1832 by John Finlay for John Ridgely (1790–1867) of Hampton.[6]

A careful comparison of the painted decoration on the aprons reveals that the second pair (cat. 66b–c) reflects a somewhat more refined technique. Another particular enhancement of these tables is that the back of the aprons are painted and decorated to match the front. Card tables were meant to be brought out into a room when in use, so they needed to look elegant from any viewpoint. The tables would have been quite expensive when new, almost the equivalent of those rendered in mahogany. Hugh Finlay charged the aforementioned Skipwith $120 for the pair he purchased in 1819, the year the bottom fell out of the local economy in Baltimore.

1. Tom Armstrong, *An American Odyssey: The Warner Collection of American Fine and Decorative Arts* (New York: Monacelli Press, 2002), 174.
2. Charles Percier and Pierre-François-Léonard Fontaine, *Recueil de décorations intérieures* (Paris, 1812), see plates such as "Plafond de la Chambre à coucher de L'Empereur au Palais des Tuileries" and "Lit éxécuté pour M^{r}. T. à Paris"; William Voss Elder III, *Baltimore Painted Furniture, 1800–1840* (Baltimore: Baltimore Museum of Art, 1972), figs. 24–29.
3. Gregory R. Weidman and Jennifer Goldsborough, *Classical Maryland, 1815–1845: Fine and Decorative Arts from the Golden Age* (Baltimore: Maryland Historical Society, 1993), 98–99.
4. Ibid, fig. 128, see also figs. 125–6; tables from the Wilson family rosewood-grained suite; and the card table from the Bayly suite now owned by Colonial Williamsburg. See Tara Gleason, "The Bayly Suite of Painted Furniture," *Antiques and Fine Art Magazine* (Spring 2003), https://www.antiquesandfineart.com/articles/article.cfm?request=385.
5. Weidman and Goldsborough, *Classical Maryland*, figs. 120, 121. The top of the table can be seen in Alicia Tucker, "Evenings at Home: Family Life in Southside Virginia, 1760–1836" (Master's thesis, of William and Mary, Arts and Sciences, 1988), 96, fig. 12. Tucker's thesis is the first publication of this significant information; see also 99–100.
6. Ibid., figs. 129, 130. That suite can still be seen in the room for which it was originally made, the Drawing Room at Hampton mansion, Hampton National Historic Site, Towson, Maryland.

Fig. 66.2. Detail of cat. 66b showing palmette on top and striped rosewood graining

67

Pier Table, 1815–1830

Attributed to Hugh Finlay (1781–1830)
Baltimore
Probably tulip poplar; walnut; painted decoration, stencil gilding, brass
32⅜ × 47$^{15}/_{16}$ × 22½ in.

PROVENANCE: Sale, Christie's, New York, Oct. 8, 1998, lot 71; With J. Michael Flanigan, American Antiques, Baltimore, 1998; Purchased by Schrimshers, 1998.

As with the assembled pair of Baltimore painted card tables (cat. 66b–c), the attribution of this pier table to the shop of Hugh Finlay is very strong. The pier table closely relates to the card tables made by Finlay in 1819 for Humberston Skipwith of Prestwould Plantation in Clarksville, Virginia, with the exception of the ornamentation of the apron.[1] Differing from both the Prestwould and Schrimsher card tables, this pier table features wreaths and spears ending in stylized anthemions in a tripartite layout. The spear with anthemion motif is very similar to ornamentation seen on the seat rails of the Prestwould Grecian couch documented to Finlay, as well as a number of strongly attributed couches and sofas (see cat. 65).[2] Otherwise, this pier table and the Prestwould tables share many aspects of decoration and form, with rosewood graining, central pedestals, and cross bases with scrolled brackets, stylized palmettes, brass rosettes, and short turned legs on casters.

The most distinctive feature of this painted pier table is its faux marbleized top (fig. 67.1). Painted in varying shades of stone, tan, buff, white, and moss green, the original ornamentation of the top is not only a rare survival, but it was also an unusual choice for the period. The great majority of Baltimore Classical painted pier tables have marble tops, a much more practical choice, for their occasional use as serving tables. Even candelabra or vases could cause damage to a painted surface. Although the top of the Schrimshers' pier table has had a number of losses and stains, it has nevertheless survived in mostly original condition with no inpainting.

1. Gregory R. Weidman and Jennifer Goldsborough, *Classical Maryland, 1815–1845: Fine and Decorative Arts from the Golden Age* (Baltimore: Maryland Historical Society, 1993), figs. 120, 121.
2. Ibid., figs, 120, 122, 123; J. Michael Flanigan, *American Furniture from the Kaufman Collection* (Washington, D.C.: National Gallery of Art, 1986); Tara Gleason, "The Bayly Suite of Painted Furniture," *Antiques and Fine Art Magazine* (Spring 2003), https://www.antiquesandfineart.com/articles/article.cfm?request=385.

Fig. 67.1. View of cat. 67, showing faux-marbleized top

68

Fire Screen, 1820–1830

Attributed to Hugh Finlay (1781–1830)
Baltimore
Probably maple and tulip poplar; painted decoration, stencil gilding, brass, replacement upholstery
53½ × 15½ in.

PROVENANCE: Private Collection, Prince George's County, MD; Private Collection; Sale, Crocker Farm, Glencoe, MD, Sept. 15, 2012, lot 68; Purchased by Schrimshers, 2012.

The Finlay firm was known for making large and elegant suites of fancy furniture for the owners of fashionable Baltimore town houses. These suites are usually composed of sets of chairs, sofas, window seats, and card, center, and pier tables. However, there are other less common, often specialized forms that accompanied the standard parlor wares.[1] This fire screen, also called a pole screen or stand, is one such piece, an unusual form and rare survival, especially given its delicacy.

Although Antebellum-era pole screens are not uncommon, American examples with painted decoration are. Nevertheless, the form and ornamentation suggests this example is the work of Hugh Finlay's shop. The turning and painting of the shaft are very closely related to the rosewood-grained and gilded card tables (cat. 66b–c) and pier table (cat. 67) that are strongly attributed to Finlay on the basis of the documented Prestwould tables.[2] The rectangular screen is attached to the pole by metal rings and a screw clamp, enabling the sitter to adjust the height of the screen to protect their face from the heat of a nearby fire. The frame may have initially contained needlework by the young ladies of the household, which has not survived.

1. See, for example, William Voss Elder III, *Baltimore Painted Furniture, 1800–1840* (Baltimore: Baltimore Museum of Art, 1972), fig. 31. This is an extremely rare lamp stand with the same provenance as the Schrimsher painted sofa (cat. 65).
2. Gregory R. Weidman and Jennifer Goldsborough, *Classical Maryland, 1815–1845: Fine and Decorative Arts from the Golden Age* (Baltimore: Maryland Historical Society, 1993), figs. 120, 121.

69

Music Stand or *Étagère*, 1820–1835

Unknown maker
Baltimore
Tulip poplar, maple; painted decoration, gilding
53¾ × 18⅝ × 18¹⁵⁄₁₆ in.

PROVENANCE: Sale, Harris Auction Galleries, Baltimore, MD, Feb. 27, 2000, lot 105; Private collection, Baltimore, MD; With J. Michael Flanigan, American Antiques, Baltimore, by 2013; Purchased by Schrimshers, 2013.

Although this stand could simply be used as an *étagère* for the display of objects, music stands of this type have a series of open shelves meant for holding and storing sheet music in a parlor. They are thus a type of canterbury, although greatly differing in form from the traditional low, partitioned cart design described by Thomas Sheraton in his *The Cabinet Dictionary* (London, 1803).[1] This Baltimore example is more akin to tiered English stands of the Regency period, which sometimes also included a hinged top shelf that could be propped up on ratchets to view the music. Another Baltimore-made example in the collection of the Maryland Center for History and Culture was also clearly intended for use as a music shelf, having lyre-shaped partitions above the bottom drawer.[2] Alternatively, this stand could simply be used as an *étagère* for the display of objects.

Typically rendered from solid wood, American stands of this form with original painted decoration are rare. The design of the gilded ornamentation on a rosewood-grained ground is typical of Baltimore work. The front of the drawer is decorated with a central foliated rosette flanked by scrolled *rinceaux* (fig. 69.1), a motif frequently seen on pieces from Hugh Finlay's shop. Although the maker of this stand may have been influenced by Finlay, the gilded ornamentation is not as refined and expertly painted as generally seen on his documented and attributed work. The multiple ring turnings on the shelf supports and vase turned legs are seen on other Baltimore furniture.[3] With its simple turned elements and shelves, this stand could easily have been produced by one of the many makers of fancy chairs in Baltimore, including the long-running enterprises of Matthew McColm (active 1803–1849), John Hodgkinson (active 1822–1857), and Jacob Daley (active 1804–1847), to name a few of the most prominent.[4]

1. Gregory R. Weidman, *Furniture in Maryland, 1740–1940: The Collection of the Maryland Historical Society* (Baltimore: Maryland Historical Society, 1984), fig. 36. Thomas Sheraton, *The Cabinet Dictionary* (London, 1803), pl. 26.
2. Weidman, *Furniture in Maryland*, fig. 115.
3. See ibid., figs. 149, 152, 153.
4. For other craftsmen and related discussion, see ibid., 89.

Fig. 69.1. Detail of cat 69 showing painted drawer. The wear on the drawer indicates use but the central wreath and delicate *rinceaux* culminating in rosettes are visible.

70

Library Bookcase, 1820–1835

Possibly by Michael Jenkins (1778–1832) or his son
Anthony H. Jenkins (1814–1878)
Baltimore
Mahogany; pine, tulip poplar, Spanish cedar (Cedrela); glass, brass, replacement fabric
94 × 88 × 23½ in.

PROVENANCE: With Estate Antiques Inc., Charleston, SC, by 2003; Purchased by Schrimshers, 2003.

Although related in many ways to other known Baltimore desks and writing tables with bookcases, this large library bookcase is a tour de force and simply one of the finest extant pieces of case furniture in the Baltimore Classical style. At least one other example of similar scale is known, a related library secretary and bookcase in the Governor's Mansion in Austin, Texas, that has comparable mullions on the four glazed doors of the bookcase and richly carved corner spandrels below.[1] That impressive piece differs, however, in having a projecting (rather than recessed) center desk section over fan-paneled doors, and bow-fronted side sections in the lower case.

The possible attribution to the firm of Michael Jenkins is based on the similarity of individual elements to two pieces: a writing table and bookcase signed by his son Anthony H. Jenkins, and another Baltimore writing table and bookcase that descended in the family of Michael's brother William Jenkins (1767–1843).[2] The signed Jenkins writing table and bookcase is inscribed on the bottom board of the bookcase, as a journeyman might have done, rather than the master. Although possibly made after Michael's death in 1832, when Anthony took over the shop, it seems more likely that the younger Jenkins would have used his stenciled label on a piece made in his own shop, as he did on the labeled wardrobe in the Schrimshers' collection (cat. 71). The carving of the mullions (fig. 70.1) and the lobed feet on the wardrobe are very similar to those on the Schrimsher library bookcase. The similar piece with a Jenkins family provenance also has wreaths at the center of the glazed doors as seen here. Unfortunately, despite his long and successful career, only one piece signed by Michael has been recorded, a simple Neoclassical fall-front secretary dated 1806, a few years after the conclusion of his initial partnership with Thomas Combs (1799–1802).[3]

The drawer and case construction of the library bookcase are very refined and typical of Baltimore's best work but dissimilar from the shop practices associated with John Needles. Similarly, the carving on the doors and column capitals is different from that on the fall-front desk and bookcase (cat. 77) and the "mummy" cylinder desk (cat. 73), which suggests the number of expert craftsmen producing stylish wares in Baltimore. The most unusual features of the Schrimshers' library bookcase are the spandrels on either side of the arched opening at the center of the lower case (fig. 70.2). The Classical carving has a central pointed leaf flanked by pairs of curled tendrils and elongated oak leaves with acorns. The broad style of the carving is similar to Philadelphia cabinetwork, but the combination of motifs is distinctive.

1. The Friends of the Governor's Mansion purchased the piece from antiques dealer F. J. Carey III during a major restoration campaign at the mansion in the early 1980s.
2. Gregory R. Weidman and Jennifer Goldsborough, *Classical Maryland, 1815–1845: Fine and Decorative Arts from the Golden Age* (Baltimore: Maryland Historical Society, 1993), fig. 166. This and a similar writing table and bookcase were seen by the author in a private collection in north Baltimore in the 1980s.
3. Photographs seen by the author in the 1980s in regional research files, Museum of Early Southern Decorative Arts, Winston-Salem, North Carolina.

Fig. 70.1. Detail of cat. 70 showing mullion decoration

Fig. 70.2. Detail of cat. 70 showing spandrel carving of curled tendrils with oak leaves and acorns

71

Wardrobe, 1832–1837

Anthony H. Jenkins (1814–1884)
Baltimore
Mahogany, mahogany veneer; tulip poplar, pine; brass
80 × 52 × 25 in.

LABEL: Stenciled within a wreath on the inside of each door: "A H Jenkins / *Cabinet Maker* / No. 18 Light St / Balt." (See Appendix II)

PROVENANCE: With Hunt Valley Antiques, Cockeysville, MD. Sale, Alex Cooper Auctioneers, Towson, MD, Dec. 8, 2002, lot 894; Purchased by Schrimshers, 2002.

This labeled wardrobe documents one of Baltimore's most longstanding and important cabinetmaking firms. Anthony H. Jenkins led the second generation of a family that was in the cabinetmaking and undertaking business for over 150 years. The firm was founded by his father Michael Jenkins in 1799. Anthony was likely apprenticed to his father working there as a journeyman in the mid- to late 1820s, and he was prepared to assume running the family business immediately upon his father's death in 1832.[1] He advertised that the firm would continue "at the old stand No. 16 Light Steet, 2nd door south of the Methodist Meeting House."[2] In 1837 he brought into the firm his brother Henry Worthington Jenkins (1814–1878), who led the firm after Anthony's retirement in 1857.[3]

Although not the most elaborate or sophisticated piece of Baltimore furniture, the construction of the drawers confirms the Jenkins shop practice: the sides and bottoms are of poplar, with less refined dovetailing than work from the William Camp and John Needles groups; the curfing of the blocks on the bottoms is diagonal; and drawer stops and full dustboards are absent. All these individual elements help to distinguish the Jenkins shop's work in the later Classical period.

The label confirms the dating as mid-1830s, as would be expected from a late Classical piece with scrolled pilaster caps and feet. Typical of most pieces in this phase of the style, referred to as Grecian Plain, the aesthetic impact comes from the beautiful book-matched flame mahogany veneers on the paneled doors. The interior has a functional arrangement of four open drawer slides over three drawers of graduated sizes on the right. On the left are fragments of the hardware used for hanging clothes.

1. For another piece with this label, see the gondola-type chair at the Maryland Center for History and Culture: Gregory R. Weidman, *Furniture in Maryland, 1740–1940: The Collection of the Maryland Historical Society* (Baltimore: Maryland Historical Society, 1984), fig. 72.
2. *Baltimore American & Commercial Daily Advertiser*, September 25, 1832.
3. It was under Henry's name that the firm would be known until 2009, though the cabinetmaking services had been dropped in 1904 to concentrate on undertaking. The Jenkins family sold their interest in the business in the late 1950s. See Weidman, *Furniture in Maryland, 1740–1940*, 208.

72

Sideboard Table, 1820–1835

Possibly by Edward Priestley (1778–1837)
Baltimore
Mahogany, mahogany veneer; tulip poplar, white pine, yellow pine
48 × 72¼ × 24 in.

INSCRIPTION: Illegible chalk inscription in script on underside of bottom board.

LABEL: Shipping label: "Klipper, Webster & Co. / Wholesale and Retail Dealers in / FURNITURE / 6 S. Calvert Street, Baltimore, Md."; recipient's name in script: "Mr. Sarony / 37 Union Square / New York."

PROVENANCE: At the shop of Klipper, Webster & Co. (active 1869–c. 1891), Baltimore; Napoleon Sarony, 37 Union Square, New York, probably by 1884. Dr. Larry McCallister (1935–2021), IN; Sale, Sotheby's, New York, Jan. 26, 2013, lot 530. Private Collection; Sale, Sotheby's, New York, Jan. 18, 2018, lot 1195; Purchased by Schrimshers, 2018.

There are only a few furniture forms and decorative elements where Philadelphia and Baltimore work truly align, and pieces with carved "Persian" or "mummy" heads on tapered therms or reeded legs are notable among them. In Philadelphia, chests of drawers seem to be the most frequently made examples, along with a few desks and sideboard tables. In Baltimore, the most popular forms were cylinder desks (cat. 73), sideboards, and sideboard tables such as the one seen here. When comparing pieces from these two cities, it is often the details that help to distinguish them. This Baltimore sideboard table is characterized by the carved figures, the double-reeded molding of the top edge of the splashboard, the shape and heavy reeding of the legs, and the ovoid ring-turned feet. In contrast, a Philadelphia sideboard table at the Baltimore Museum of Art features distinctive mummy heads, carved oak leaves on trapezoidal therm legs, and vase-shaped acanthus-carved feet.[1]

Fig. 72.1. Detail of cat. 72 showing intricate carving of turbaned "mummy" head

Sideboard tables (formerly called hunt boards by collectors) were a popular form in Baltimore, especially in the earlier Neoclassical style, but not as common in the Classical idiom. Only a few with carved mummy figures have survived: a similar example formerly owned by Hirschl & Adler (current location unknown); one in the collection of Andalusia Historic House in Bensalem, Pennsylvania; and one in a private collection on Maryland's Eastern Shore.[2] The latter two have marble rather than mahogany tops, which required some difference in constuction and are thus difficult to compare. The drawers of the Schrimsher sideboard table feature refined dovetails, solid rather than curfed runners on the bottoms, mahogany sides and back, and tulip poplar bottoms. The bottom board of the top section is also tulip poplar, set within pine framing.

An attribution of the Schrimsher table to the shop of Edward Priestley is possible, if not confirmed, due to similarities to the documented marble-topped sideboard table in the Eastern Shore private collection in the panels over the legs, the reeding of the legs, and the shape of the feet.[3] The mummy heads, however, are quite distinctive from each other and were clearly carved by different craftsmen. Given that Priestley probably employed more than one carver, this does not completely rule out his shop. Priestley was also a lumber dealer, which provided him access to the richly figured "plum pudding" mahogany of the top. The mummy heads on the sideboard table also differ from those on the Schrimsher cylinder desk (cat. 73), as does the case construction.

The inscription on the bottom of the case unfortunately is indecipherable. The label on the backboard, however, clearly shows that the table was in Baltimore about fifty years after it was made. Furniture manufacturers and retailers Klipper, Webster & Co. shipped it to the studio of renowned professional photographer and artist Napoleon Sarony on Union Square in New York City. A newspaper account of the activities of the Tile Club of New York documents Sarony's visit to Baltimore in February 1884.[4]

1. William Voss Elder III and Jayne E. Stokes, *American Furniture, 1680–1880* (Baltimore: Baltimore Museum of Art, 1987), fig. 118.
2. Alexandra Alevizatos Kirtley, "A New Suspect: Baltimore Cabinetmaker Edward Priestley," in *American Furniture 2000*, ed. Luke Beckerdite (Milwaukee: Chipstone Foundation, 2000), fig. 22.
3. Ibid., fig. 1; Gregory R. Weidman and Jennifer Goldsborough, *Classical Maryland, 1815–1845: Fine and Decorative Arts from the Golden Age* (Baltimore: Maryland Historical Society, 1993), fig. 162.
4. *Baltimore Sun*, February 26, 1884. Klipper, Webster & Co.'s large establishment was located only about a block and a half from the hotel where Sarony was staying.

73

Cylinder Desk, 1820–1835

Unknown maker
Baltimore
Mahogany, mahogany veneer, satinwood; tulip poplar, Honduras mahogany, pine, marble, brass
51½ × 51 × 23 in.

INSCRIPTION: Signed in ink on underside of desk interior drawer along: "R H Gordon" and "Robert God" [with alphabet and doodles].

PROVENANCE: Possibly Josiah H. Gordon (1816–1887), Cumberland, MD; Possibly to his son Robert H. Gordon (1852–1910), Cumberland, MD. By descent in the Thomas family of Gaithersburg, MD, for three generations until c. 2000. With Peter Curran Antiques, Wilton, CT, by late 2000; With J. Michael Flanigan, American Antiques, Baltimore, by 2001; Purchased by Schrimshers, 2001.

Baltimore cabinet furniture in the Classical taste was inspired by a variety of elements from the ancient past, almost always filtered through English design sources. In the case of the unusual carved figures sometimes seen on stylish Baltimore case pieces and sideboard tables, one of the principal sources is George Smith's *A Collection of Designs for Household Furniture and Interior Decoration* (London, 1808). The heads of the figures on Baltimore pieces are generally called "mummies" or "Persians," but the carved, bearded figures with turbans and tassels seem to reflect Ottoman Turkish design of the period more so than ancient Egypt or Greece.[1] The form as seen on American furniture was present by the late 1810s, as the *New-York Book of Prices for Manufacturing Cabinet and Chair Work* of 1817 lists "tapered therms with mummy heads and feet."[2] This type of ornament was seldom if ever made in New York but was, however, made by both Philadelphia and Baltimore cabinetmakers.

Fig. 73.1. Detail of Cat. 73 showing reeded therm with a turbaned, bearded head and feet

These figures appear on both sideboards and cylinder desks made in Baltimore but not on chests of drawers and bureaus as frequently seen in Philadelphia. On Philadelphia examples, the figures are usually facing to the side, and the paneled therms typically have three narrow, rounded reeds, very different from the Baltimore type. On Baltimore case pieces, the bearded figures are virtually always combined with Gothic-arched panels on doors and other elements (fig. 73.1). This Grecian-Gothic combination is a hallmark of the local style whose elements are also derived from Smith's plates, though the English designer did not blend the two distinct styles in the same piece.

This cylinder desk is one of at least a half dozen known with "mummy" figures. Five are from Baltimore, and one is from Philadelphia.[3] These desks and related sideboards and sideboard tables have been variously attributed to leading Baltimore cabinetmakers including William Camp, John Needles, and Edward Priestley. No definitive attribution for the Schrimsher desk can be made, however. Based on close examination of ornamentation and construction, it is not from the same shop as the Camp-attributed cylinder desk at Maryland Center for History and Culture. Priestley's shop also cannot be confirmed on the basis of the documented Priestley sideboard table with mummy figures in a Maryland private collection. The carving of the figures on the two pieces is quite different and the Priestley piece has no drawer to compare construction techniques. Further, the drawer construction of the Schrimshers' desk is not related to John Needles's documented work.

The provenance of the Schrimshers' desk places it in Maryland for much of the twentieth century. A further possible factor in a longer Maryland history is the inscription on one of the small interior drawers over the writing surface. From the style of the inscription, Robert H. Gordon was clearly a child of perhaps six or seven years practicing his letters. A Robert H. Gordon of Cumberland, Maryland, the son of Josiah H. Gordon, a prominent lawyer and legislator, is one possible identification for the inscriber. Letters written by young Robert to his father in 1861 show some similarities in signature to the inscription on the Schrimshers' desk, although a definitive attribution is uncertain.[4]

1. For a thorough discussion of the design sources of the carved figures, see Alexandra Alevizatos Kirtley, "A New Suspect: Baltimore Cabinetmaker Edward Priestley," *American Furniture*, 2000, ed. Luke Beckerdite (Milwaukee: Chipstone Foundation, 2000), 100–151. See also Gregory R. Weidman and Jennifer Goldsborough, *Classical Maryland, 1815–1845: Fine and Decorative Arts from the Golden Age* (Baltimore: Maryland Historical Society, 1993), 131. Thomas Hope in his *Household Furniture and Interior Decoration* (London: Longman, Hurst, Rees, and Orme, 1807) also shows Bacchus figures with full beards.
2. *The New-York Book of Prices for Manufacturing Cabinet and Chair Work* (New York, 1817), 12.
3. Donald L. Fennimore and Robert T. Trump, "Joseph B. Barry, Philadelphia Cabinetmaker," *The Magazine Antiques* 135, no. 5 (May 1989): 1218, pl. VIII. The Schrimsher desk is identical to one sold at Sotheby's in Andy Warhol's sale. See Sale, Sotheby's, no. 6000, April 1988, lot 3171. The second one is in the collection of the Maryland Center for History and Culture (1982.58). For more information on this piece see Gregory R. Weidman, *Furniture in Maryland, 1740–1940: The Collection of the Maryland Historical Society* (Baltimore: Maryland Historical Society, 1984), fig. 100. Two others are in private collections. A final piece at the De Young Museum, Fine Arts Museums of San Francisco (1988.32.10), is identical in form to the Schrimsher desk but has reeded columns in place of carved figures.
4. The letters are in the Gordon Family Papers (Series 2 – Kate Gordon Correspondence, Box 2), Clements Library, University of Michigan. At the start of the Civil War in 1861, Josiah Gordon was imprisoned by the Union for his Confederate sympathies and activities. He received frequent correspondence from his wife and young son Robert. Several other Robert H. Gordons from Pennsylvania, New Jersey, Maryland, and Virginia were traced. None were the correct age or economic status to be children of original owners. A Robert H. Gordon (1827–1903), a banker from Norfolk, Virginia, could have made the inscription, but his father was unlikely to have been the original owner due to his economic status.

74

Pier Table, 1830–1840

John Needles (1786–1878)
Baltimore
Mahogany; marble, mirror glass
35½ × 40 × 21 in.

LABEL: Stenciled: "John Needles / Cabinet Maker / 54 Hanover St. / Balto" [within an oval wreath]. (See Appendix II)

PROVENANCE: Sale, Northeast Auctions, Portsmouth, NH, Oct. 27, 2006, lot 982; Purchased by Schrimshers, 2006.

The numerous labeled and documented works of longtime Baltimore Quaker cabinetmaker John Needles clearly show that the prolific craftsman produced furniture in a variety of styles.[1] His work ranges from very simple and plain (perhaps crafted mainly for his fellow Quakers and family) to highly elaborate and embellished, and there are a number of pieces whose Baltimore origin would be questioned were it not for his label. This pier table is one of those, which might otherwise be ascribed to Philadelphia. The carving of the feet and the column capitals is somewhat atypical of Baltimore work and other Needles furniture, and the overall form of the table with elliptical concave apron and mirrored back is similarly unusual.

The likely reason for Needles's diversity of styles and ornamentation is his acumen as a businessman, documented in both his autobiography and numerous advertisements in local newspapers.[2] Baltimoreans could distinguish the cabinetwork of different cities—newspaper advertisements of the time specified "sideboards of Boston, New York and Baltimore Style"[3]—so it was astute of Needles to offer a wide variety of tastes in his shop. Indeed, one advertisement from the mid-1820s lists over 160 pieces in his warerooms, significantly more than advertised by other cabinetmakers of the time.[4] Another of Needles's advertisements noted the availability of fashionable "Grecian," "Gothic," or "French" furniture.[5]

The stenciled label is on the underside of the framing supporting the top. This particular Needles label is usually found on pieces having design and ornamentation typical of the 1830s.

1. Nearly 100 pieces had been identified by the early 1990s, and that number is well over 100 by now. See Gregory R. Weidman and Jennifer Goldsborough, *Classical Maryland, 1815–1845: Fine and Decorative Arts from the Golden Age* (Baltimore: Maryland Historical Society, 1993), 115ff.
2. John Needles, "John Needles (1786–1878), An Autobiography," ed. Edward Needles Wright, *Journal of Quaker History* 58, no. 1 (Spring 1969): 18.
3. *Federal Gazette*, June 28, 1817, quoted in Gregory R. Weidman, *Furniture in Maryland, 1740–1940: The Collection of the Maryland Historical Society* (Baltimore: Maryland Historical Society, 1984), 85.
4. *Baltimore American & Commercial Daily Advertiser*, May 16, 1826, quoted in Weidman, *Furniture in Maryland, 1740–1940*, 86. By comparison, William Camp's 1822 probate inventory records just forty-nine pieces of "ready made" furniture, though also ninety-three unfinished pieces.
5. Ibid., 120.

75

Pier Table, 1820–1835

Attributed to John Needles (1786–1878)
Baltimore
Mahogany; pine; marble
35½ × 33¼ × 19 in.

INSCRIPTION: Signed in script on the back: "Joseph King."

PROVENANCE: Probable descent from Joseph King (inscription on table); Joseph King Jr. (1784–1865); By descent through his family. With Charles Clark, Woodbury, CT, by 2020; Purchased by Schrimshers, 2020.

This table is attributed to Baltimore cabinetmaker John Needles based on a nearly identical labeled table in the collection of Centre Hill Mansion in Petersburg, Virginia.[1] Another extremely similar example attributed to Needles, now in the collection of the Maryland Center for History and Culture, was likely originally owned by Kitty Etting (1799–1837) and Benjamin I. Cohen (1797–1845) at the elegant townhouse they built on the northwest corner of Charles and Saratoga Streets in 1828.[2] The principal difference between them is that the apron of the Schrimshers' table has five flat-molded panels, one in the center and one at each corner.[3]

Even without the strong attribution to Needles's shop, there would be no question about the Baltimore origin of this table. The overall form—open legs without mirrored back or platform base, block over ball feet, and, in particular, the heavily reeded legs—are definitive Baltimore characteristics. The pointed reeds are almost unique to the city. They have an ancient antecedent in the Roman fasces, a symbol of authority that featured an axe within a bundle of bound rods. The heavy reeding seen in Baltimore is partly inspired by George Smith's *A Collection of Designs for Household Furniture* (London, 1808). However, the element becomes truly idiosyncratic in pieces from Baltimore cabinet shops, whether on corner columns for sideboards or pedestal bases for card (cat. 79), pier, center, and worktables.[4]

On the inside back is a large signature in the script of Joseph King, the likely first owner. This almost certainly was English immigrant Joseph King Jr., a highly successful Quaker merchant well known to Needles.[5] By 1850, King's real estate and personal property were valued at the astonishing sums of $100,000 and $50,000, respectively.[6] He married Tacy Ellicott (1795–1872), a member of another prosperous Quaker family—for whom Ellicott City, Maryland, is named—in 1818. The couple had a large number of children, of whom the eldest (and only surviving son) was Francis Thompson King (1819–1891), who worked in Johns Hopkins's firm and was on the first Board of Trustees of the university and hospital.

1. Gregory R. Weidman and Jennifer Goldsborough, *Classical Maryland, 1815–1845: Fine and Decorative Arts from the Golden Age* (Baltimore: Maryland Historical Society, 1993), fig. 141.
2. Gregory R. Weidman, *Furniture in Maryland, 1740–1940: The Collection of the Maryland Historical Society* (Baltimore: Maryland Historical Society, 1984,, fig. 169. Another smaller example descended in the Carey family of Baltimore; see Edgar G. Miller Jr., *American Antique Furniture: A Book for Amateurs, Vol. II* (Baltimore: Lord Baltimore Press, 1937), fig. 1448. A pair of very similar tables, once in the collection of the Atwater Kent Museum, had provenance from the family of Baltimore merchant banker Alexander Brown (1784–1865). Those tables sold at Christie's, New York, October 3, 2007, lot 127.
3. These panels are now picked out with black paint or dark stain, which may not be original.
4. Weidman, *Furniture in Maryland 1740–1940*, figs. 120, 138, 152, 153, 159; Weidman and Goldsborough, *Classical Maryland, 1815–1845*, figs. 138, 156, 159.
5. Needles was active in the same Quaker meeting house where King was a prominent member.
6. Census for Baltimore City, in *Seventh Census of the United States, 1850* (Washington, D.C.: Bureau of the Census, 1850).

76

Cylinder Desk and Bookcase, 1820–1835

Attributed to John Needles (1786–1878)
Baltimore
Mahogany, mahogany veneer, satinwood, maple veneer; tulip poplar, Honduras mahogany, glass, brass, baize
95 × 39 × 23 in.

PROVENANCE: Purchased at auction, possibly Pook & Pook Auction, Downingtown, PA. Collection of Christopher T. Rebollo (1964–2021), PA, by c. 2012; Sale, Pook & Pook Auction, Downingtown, PA, Apr. 22, 2022, lot 493; Purchased by Schrimshers, 2022.

This desk is attributed to the cabinetmaker John Needles on the basis of a nearly identical labeled Needles piece in a private collection in Baltimore.[1] The principal difference between the Schrimsher desk and the labeled example is in the doors of the bookcase top. Here the slightly taller doors are divided into six panes of glass rather than four. There is also a slight difference in the turning of the finial on the broken-scroll pediment. Otherwise, the design and ornamentation of both cylinder desks, including the maple-veneered interiors, appear to be identical in all respects. In addition to the design elements, the details of the drawer construction—especially the distinctive dovetails, the use of "baywood" (Honduras mahogany) drawer sides, and the curfed runners (small blocks) on the drawer bottom—are identical to Needles's labeled work.

Although most of the individual elements (recessed broken-scroll pediment, contrasting wood interior with arched center section (fig. 76.1), quatrefoil panels over the columns and on cabinet doors of the desk, classical columns at the corners of the base, lion's-paw feet) are known on case pieces from other Baltimore shops, the specific combination here is a distinctive design of Needles. The diamonds with round bosses at the center of the mullions are an unusual feature seen on bookcases from Needles, who was especially fond of combining Gothic elements like the arched panels on the doors and small quatrefoil molded panels above classical columns.[2] Notably, the cabinetmaker even advertised case pieces with combinations of "Gothic," "French," and "Grecian" design features to appeal to his fashion-conscious clientele in the mid-1820s.[3]

Another feature that sets this desk and bookcase apart is the cylinder lid. Although this complicated mechanism became much more common later in the nineteenth century, it required skills that few cabinetmakers mastered. Both Needles's labeled work and his newspaper advertisements document his shop's ability to produce cylinder lids. Similarly, three desks with this feature were an expensive option listed in William Camp's 1822 estate inventory.[4] Other Baltimore Classical furniture makers may have also made desks or writing tables with cylinder lids, but specific documentation for this has not survived.[5]

1. Gregory R. Weidman and Jennifer Goldsborough, *Classical Maryland, 1815–1845: Fine and Decorative Arts from the Golden Age* (Baltimore: Maryland Historical Society, 1993), fig. 146.
2. See, for example, the labeled Needles sideboard and secretary and bookcase in Weidman and Goldsborough, *Classical Maryland*, figs. 143, 147.
3. *Baltimore American & Commercial Daily Advertiser*, April 21, 1825.
4. Quoted in Gregory R. Weidman, *Furniture in Maryland, 1740–1940: The Collection of the Maryland Historical Society* (Baltimore: Maryland Historical Society, 1984), 141. Gerrard Hopkins of Baltimore advertised desks with cylinder lids in the 1790s. Neoclassical cylinder desks were also likely made in the shop of Bankson & Lawson (active 1785–1792); see Sumpter Priddy III, J. Michael Flanigan, and Gregory R. Weidman, "The Genesis of Neoclassical Style in Baltimore Furniture," in *American Furniture 2000*, ed. Luke Beckerdite (Milwaukee: Chipstone Foundation, 2000), figs. 26, 28.
5. The Schrimshers' cylinder desk with "mummy" carving is probably not from Camp's or Needles's shop, so at least one other Baltimore craftsman could produce this form. See cat. 73.

Fig. 76.1. Detail of cat. 76 showing interior of desk

77

Secretary and Bookcase, 1820–1835

Possibly John Needles (1786–1878)
Baltimore
Mahogany, mahogany veneer, tulip poplar, satinwood; white pine, Spanish cedar (Cedrela), glass, baize
96½ × 53 × 22 in.

INSCRIPTION: Inscribed in chalk inside the case in a number of places: "Dr. Chatard."

PROVENANCE: By descent through the Chatard family of Baltimore: Dr. Ferdinand Edme Chatard (1805–1888), married 1830 to Eliza Marean; To Dr. Ferdinand E. Chatard Jr. (1838–1900) and Josephine Miles; To their son William Miles Chatard (1875–1953) and Josephine Lee (1879–1958); To her niece Elizabeth Williams Lee (1920–1999) and Edmund Nolley; Sale, Richard Opfer Auctioneers, Timonium, MD, Sept. 28, 1990, lot 241; With J. Michael Flanigan, American Antiques, Baltimore, 1990; Purchased by Schrimshers, 1993.

Although the design and ornamentation of the bookcase top of this piece is typical of Baltimore Classical furniture, the design of the desk section is not. A fall-front desk or *secretaire à abattant* without a bookcase top, such as the one made by William Camp for Jacob I. Cohen Jr. in 1818 or the one made for Governor Charles Carnan Ridgely of Hampton (see p. 231), are of the more typical form.[1] This type also has small interior cubby holes over satinwood- or maple-veneered drawers, all over wide-panel doors. The Schrimshers' desk was clearly a custom order, varying from the more typical design but with elements reflecting the local style. The only desks of similar overall composition are massive, three-part secretaries with central fall fronts in the German Biedermeier style. These European examples differ greatly, particularly in the designs and proportions of the top sections.

The tentative attribution to the shop of John Needles is based on several factors. Although no identical example bears Needles's label, individual elements are closely related to his documented work: boldly reeded pilasters with stylized acanthus capitals, stylized mullions of the glazed doors, corner columns with Ionic capitals, and paw feet. A closely related fall-front desk executed entirely in maple is known, and Needles is the only Baltimore cabinetmaker documented to have made large and stylish case pieces in maple, which was deemed by fellow Quakers to be less ostentatious than mahogany.[2] However, the square-paneled lower doors, the interior design, and use of Spanish cedar (Cedrela) rather than tulip poplar drawer bottoms are atypical of Needles's shop. The rest of the drawer construction, however, is very similar to his work.

The Chatards, the original owners of the desk, were a family of French descent who came to Baltimore as refugees from the slave revolt in Haiti in 1794. Multiple generations of the Chatard family, including the founder Dr. Pierre Chatard (1767–1847), were doctors, so the precise one referred to in the inscription on the piece cannot be definitely determined. However, the desk was likely made at the time of Dr. Ferdinand Edme Chatard Sr.'s marriage to Eliza Marean in 1830. By the mid-nineteenth century, the desk and bookcase would have been in the family home at 516 Park Avenue, in the same block as the Smith and Wilson houses (see cat. 65).

Fig. 77.1. Detail of cat. 77 showing Ionic column capital and egg and dart motif

1. See Gregory R. Weidman and Jennifer Goldsborough, *Classical Maryland, 1815–1845: Fine and Decorative Arts from the Golden Age* (Baltimore: Maryland Historical Society, 1993), figs. 137, 165.
2. The maple fall-front desk was recorded and photographed by J. Michael Flanigan when it was owned by antiques dealers James and Diane Stradling in the early 1990s.

78

Pair of Side Chairs, 1810–1830

Unknown maker
Baltimore
Mahogany; ash, tulip poplar; replacement upholstery
32 × 17¾ × 16¼ in.

PROVENANCE: Private collection, Baltimore, MD; With J. Michael Flanigan, American Antiques, Baltimore, by 2002; Purchased by Schrimshers, 2002.

Mahogany side chairs with similar design and ornament were truly ubiquitous in early-nineteenth-century Baltimore. Numerous examples have survived, and others come to light often.[1] Among the most notable sets are those purchased by Maryland Governor Charles Carnan Ridgely (1760–1829) around 1815, still on view at Hampton mansion, his country residence.[2] Unfortunately, no documented examples are known, and the chairs were probably made in several of the city's most prominent shops. Ridgely, for example, was known to patronize multiple leading craftsmen in the 1810s, including William Camp and Edward Priestley.

Neoclassical chairs of similar design with a reeded square back and bannisters forming four Gothic arches were described in *The New-York Book of Prices for Cabinet and Chair Work.*[3] New York and Philadelphia chairs of related design are known, but the Baltimore examples have different, more compact proportions and a greater emphasis on the reeded elements. The balloon-shaped seat upholstered half over the rail, a distinctive feature, reflects the design of earlier Neoclassical chairs made in Baltimore. The flared, paneled termination of the legs is known almost exclusively on chairs of this design. The popularity of these chairs in Baltimore plus the even greater popularity of "fancy" chairs limited the demand for chairs in the klismos design that were popular in the other cities featured in this book.

1. See Gregory R. Weidman, *Furniture in Maryland, 1740–1940: The Collection of the Maryland Historical Society* (Baltimore: Maryland Historical Society, 1984), fig. 63 for a list. Also, another extremely similar chair, differing from the Schrimshers' in a small detail on the legs, is illustrated in Gregory R. Weidman and Jennifer Goldsborough, *Classical Maryland, 1815–1845: Fine and Decorative Arts from the Golden Age* (Baltimore: Maryland Historical Society, 1993), fig. 151.
2. The chairs are in the Dining Room at Hampton mansion, Hampton National Historic Site, Towson, MD. Images at https://www.nps.gov/media/photo/gallery-item.htm https://www.nps.gov/hamp/learn/photosmultimedia/photogallery.htm.
3. Weidman, *Furniture in Maryland, 1740–1940*, fig. 63.

79

Card Table, 1815–1835

Unknown maker
Baltimore
Mahogany; tulip poplar, cherry, *ormolu* mounts, brass
29 × 37¾ × 18½ in.

PROVENANCE: Probably Sale, Neal Alford Company, Inc., Aug. 1988; With J. Michael Flanigan, American Antiques, Baltimore, 1988; Purchased by Schrimshers, 1999.

Like the pier table with boldly reeded legs attributed to John Needles (cat. 75), the design of this card table is quintessentially Baltimore. The heavily reeded pedestal vase, with pointed reeds, and the distinctively reeded saber legs are conclusive Baltimore characteristics.[1] There is a large variety of related tables and stands with similar reeded pedestals and saber legs, including center, work, and writing tables, candlestands, and even Grand Harmonicon cases.[2] As is seen on most card tables in the Classical style, the hinged top rotates on an interior pivot attached to the cross brace and then is opened to create the surface for gaming. A storage well for cards, counters, and score pads is housed within the apron.

In its overall appearance, stance, proportions, material, quality of construction, and details, the Schrimsher table is an especially fine example of this well-known Baltimore form. All these characteristics and the overall quality show that the table must have come from one of the best shops in Baltimore, but none are documented to a specific shop. The Schrimsher table, however, is closely related in several key features to a Baltimore Classical writing table in the collection of the Maryland Center for History and Culture.[3] Although perhaps not sufficiently strong evidence to make a definite attribution, William Camp's shop should certainly be considered a likely source.

---

1. A considerable number of Baltimore card tables of this basic design have been published or have appeared on the market in recent decades, so the type is well recognized. See Edgar G. Miller Jr., *American Antique Furniture: A Book for Amateurs, Vol. II* (Baltimore: Lord Baltimore Press, 1937), fig. 1551. Dealer J. Michael Flanigan also noted several examples in Baltimore private collections and owned by Baltimore and other antiques dealers, including Austin McDonnell, Woldman & Woldman, and F. J. Carey III. Other examples were sold at auction, including at Sloan's, Washington, D.C., in July 1991.
2. See Gregory R. Weidman, *Furniture in Maryland, 1740–1940: The Collection of the Maryland Historical Society* (Baltimore: Maryland Historical Society, 1984), figs. 114, 138, 159; Gregory R. Weidman and Jennifer Goldsborough, *Classical Maryland, 1815–1845: Fine and Decorative Arts from the Golden Age* (Baltimore: Maryland Historical Society, 1993), figs. 156, 159.
3. The table has a suggested attribution to leading Baltimore cabinetmaker William Camp (1773–1822) based on drawer and case construction and the provenance of an identical writing table to a family who are documented to have purchased furniture from Camp. See Weidman, *Furniture in Maryland 1740–1940*, fig. 159.

80

Worktable, 1815–1830

Unknown maker
Baltimore or Philadelphia
Mahogany, satinwood, maple; tulip poplar, Spanish cedar (Cedrela), brass
30⅝ × 22⅜ × 16 in.

INSCRIPTION: Inscribed in pencil on the bottom drawer: "O. S. Anderson / Melrose Ave / Govans."

PROVENANCE: Possibly Collection of Catherine (1848–1929) and Edwin A. Gorsuch (1846–1936), Baltimore County, MD. Possibly by descent to their daughter Mary Elizabeth Gorsuch (Mrs. Oliver Sellman Anderson, 1876–1971), Baltimore; By descent to her son Edwin A. Anderson (1902–1968), Maplewood, NJ; By descent to his wife Eleanor O. Anderson, Maplewood, NJ; Collection of the Baltimore Museum of Art, by 1979 and later deaccessioned. Sale, Northeast Auctions, Mar. 4–5, 2000, lot 736. Sale, Christie's, New York, Oct. 5, 2000, lot 168; Purchased by Schrimshers, 2000.

Lyre-base worktables were a widely popular form across the country in the early nineteenth century. Philadelphia cabinetmakers produced numerous stylish and beautiful examples. Not made as frequently in Baltimore, this example is one of three known that were likely produced in the city; one is in the collection of the Maryland Center for History and Culture (MCHC), and another is owned by an old Baltimore family.[1] This last table notably has distinctive Baltimore-style reeding on the legs, and all three feature drawer fronts boldly veneered in bird's-eye maple. Both the Schrimshers' table and the one at the MCHC have double-ring turning on the corner columns of the case. The drawer construction is very similar to John Needles's shop, another feature supporting a Baltimore origin. The use of Spanish cedar drawer bottoms is also sometimes seen on Baltimore pieces (cat. 77).

The inscription referencing Oliver S. Anderson (1873–1945) places the table unquestionably in the Govans neighborhood of north Baltimore in the twentieth century. Oliver and his wife lived on Melrose Avenue from the 1910s until their deaths. However, the possible history of the table prior to their ownership suggests that the table might have a Philadelphia provenance and possibly origin. Anderson's grandmother Catherine Ashbridge Gorsuch was born in Delaware, and both her parents were natives of Pennsylvania. Also, descriptions of an estate auction following Mary E. Gorsuch Anderson's death in 1971 and the financial background of the Gorsuch family both suggest she was an antiques collector rather than just an inheritor. These factors muddy the waters related to the table's origin.

---

1. William Voss Elder III and Jayne E. Stokes, *American Furniture, 1680–1880* (Baltimore: Baltimore Museum of Art, 1987), fig. 132; Gregory R. Weidman, *Furniture in Maryland, 1740–1940: The Collection of the Maryland Historical Society* (Baltimore: Maryland Historical Society, 1984), fig. 164; Edgar G. Miller Jr., *American Antique Furniture: A Book for Amateurs, Vol. II* (Baltimore: Lord Baltimore Press, 1937), fig. 1570. Miller shows four other lyre-base worktables (figs. 1566–69), two of which have provenance with local Baltimore families and two that were owned by collectors.

81

Wing Wardrobe, 1820–1835

Unknown maker
Baltimore or Philadelphia
Mahogany, mahogany veneer; tulip poplar, white pine; brass
73 × 84 × 20 in.

PROVENANCE: Collection of Judith Hollander, New York; Sale, Stair Galleries, Hudson, NY, Apr. 2, 2016, lot 24; Purchased by Schrimshers, 2016.

Wardrobes with a center compartment flanked by side sections were usually called "wing" wardrobes in the early nineteenth century. The earliest type to appear in Baltimore in about 1800 had tall doors with interior drawers at center and was flanked by side sections with tall doors opening to reveal space for hanging clothes. This format was based on Thomas Shearer's illustrations for *The Cabinet-Maker's London Book of Prices* (London, 1788, 1793). Later wing wardrobes such as this one, with elements deriving from ancient Greek architecture, are based on classical models such as plate 134 of George Smith's *A Collection of Designs for Household Furniture and Interior Decoration* (London, 1808). The pieces are nearly identical but the maker elected to construct a standard-sized wardrobe rather than a "Dwarf" one as shown by Smith. These large, elaborate, and expensive storage pieces were solely for the homes of the wealthy, as suggested by their rarity.[1]

A debate about where this wardrobe was made continues. The Schrimshers purchased it as an example of Philadelphia cabinetmaking. The wardrobe does have brass molding on the recessed panels of the doors and inset into the flanking fluting that is typical of that city. However, other examples of this form lack a Philadelphia provenance.[2] A number of similar examples from Baltimore, including two from Maryland's wealthiest and most prominent families, the Ridgelys of Hampton and the Lloyds of Wye House. The drawer construction is also typical of Baltimore work. Without provenance, the origin of the Schrimshers' wardrobe will likely remain up for discussion.

1. See *The New-York Book of Prices for Manufacturing Cabinet and Chair Work* (1817), in which wing wardrobes are the single most expensive piece, nearly twice that of a large sideboard.
2. Per Alexandra Alevizatos Kirtley, July 2023, with confirming searches of several publications.

Fig. 81.1. George Smith, "Dwarf Wardrobe," plate 134 in *A Collection of Designs for Household Furniture and Interior Decoration* (London, 1808), hand-colored engraving (Courtesy Clark Art Institute Library, Mary Ann Beinecke Decorative Art Collection)

82

Pier Table, 1840–1850

Unknown maker; marble supplied by Levi Taylor (c. 1795–1855)
Baltimore
Mahogany, mahogany veneer; marble, mirror glass
36⅝ × 39¾ × 20½ in.

LABEL: Stenciled on underside of marble top: "From / LEVI TAYLOR / Marble Worker / BALTIMORE." (See Appendix II)

PROVENANCE: Sale, Alex Cooper Auctioneers Inc., Towson, MD, Sept. 8, 1996, lot 435; With J. Michael Flanigan, American Antiques, Baltimore, by 1998; Purchased by Schrimshers, 1998.

This table and another of very similar design are among the latest pieces of furniture in the Schrimshers' collection. Known as the *Restauration* style in France, the style of this table in the United States has been variously referred to as Late Empire, Late Classical, Pillar and Scroll (for obvious reasons), or Grecian Plain. Every element of the table is composed of S- or C-scrolls and covered with mahogany veneers. New steam-powered veneering saws appeared in the 1830s and made these pieces more economical for cabinetmakers to manufacture and for consumers to purchase, helping the fashion to become widely popular.

Because pieces made in different cities in this mode tend to look quite similar, it can be difficult to determine their origin. Fortunately, we know the supplier of the marble top, Levi Taylor, whose stenciled label is on the underside. A longtime stonecutter, Taylor ran a large marble yard from about 1840 until his death in 1855, with a primary location on Charles Street "near the Depot of the Baltimore and Ohio Railroad."[1] Taylor noted in his advertisements that he supplied "Pier and Centre TABLE TOPS, for Cabinet Makers," as well as marble mantels, monuments, and gravestones.[2]

The assigning of this table to Baltimore is further confirmed by the details of its form, which is similar to plate 17 in John Hall's *The Cabinet Makers' Assistant* (Baltimore, 1840), the first furniture design book authored by an American.[3] The principal difference is that the out-turned S-scrolled front columns end at a block on this table, rather than at the base as in Hall's design. Also, the base of the Schrimshers' table is straight in front but concave on the Hall design. A similar pier table based on Hall's designs and with a marble top supplied by Taylor is in the collection of the Maryland Center for History and Culture.[4]

1. *Baltimore Sun*, August 19, 1841. Taylor was also one of Baltimore's "Old Defenders," who had helped to defend the city during the attack by the British in September 1814.
2. Ibid.
3. Gregory R. Weidman and Jennifer Goldsborough, *Classical Maryland, 1815–1845: Fine and Decorative Arts from the Golden Age* (Baltimore: Maryland Historical Society, 1993), fig. 173.
4. Gregory R. Weidman, *Furniture in Maryland, 1740–1940: The Collection of the Maryland Historical Society* (Baltimore: Maryland Historical Society, 1984), fig. 173; Weidman and Goldsborough, *Classical Maryland*, fig. 172. The MCHC table has Baltimore provenance.

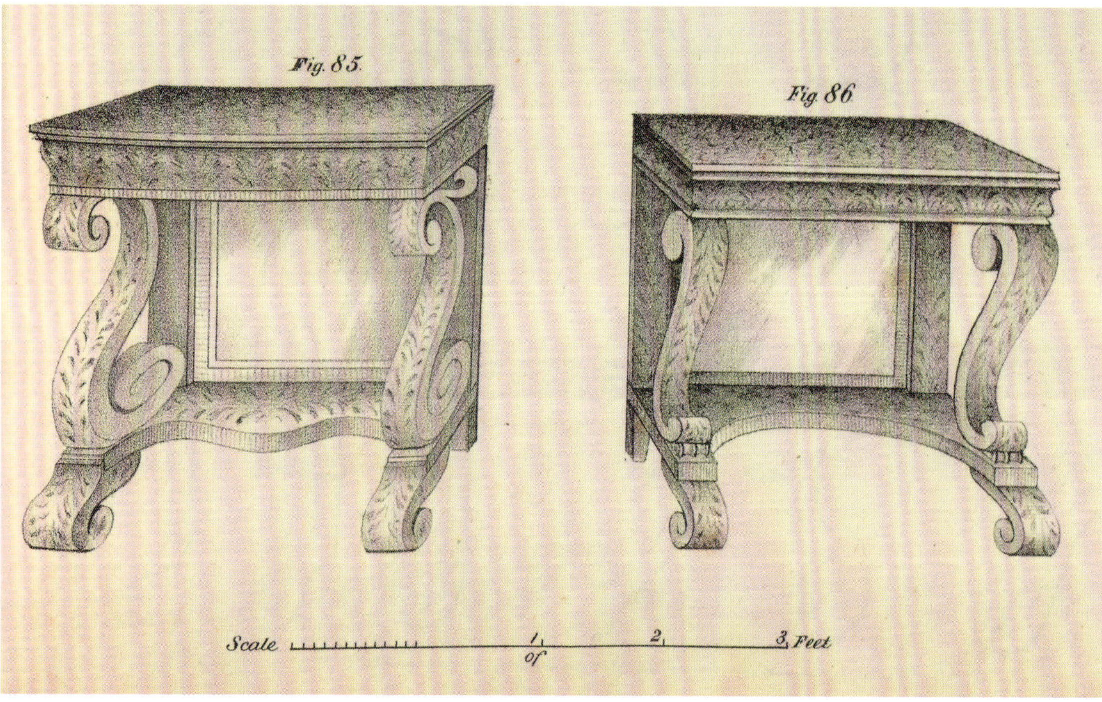

Fig. 82.1. "Pier Tables," plate 17 in John Hall, *The Cabinet Makers' Assistant* (Baltimore, 1840), lithograph (Courtesy Winterthur Museum, Garden & Library)

MORSE
1822

Seats of Democracy in Washington, D.C.: Chairs for the Nation's Capital

MATTHEW A. THURLOW

On August 24, 1814, British forces invaded Washington, D.C., resulting in the burning and destruction of several important government buildings, including the President's House (now known as the White House) and the Capitol.[1] The British targeted Washington for a variety of reasons, including a desire to retaliate against the burning of the Parliament buildings in York (now Toronto), Canada. Additionally, the British hoped that by capturing and burning the capital, they could weaken American morale and potentially force the United States into negotiations that would favor Britain.

When British forces under the command of Major General Robert Ross and Vice Admiral Alexander Cochrane advanced on Washington, they encountered a weak and ill-prepared American defense that generated little resistance. Upon entering the capital, British troops set fire to several government buildings. The President's House, which was then occupied by President James Madison and his wife Dolley Madison, was partially burned and the interiors heavily damaged. Dolley famously saved important documents and objects, including a Gilbert Stuart portrait of George Washington, before fleeing the residence.[2] Regrettably, the *de rigueur* Classical chairs produced in Baltimore by John (1777–1851) and Hugh (1780–1830) Finlay to designs provided by Benjamin Henry Latrobe (1764–1820) were lost in the conflagration.

The Capitol was also set ablaze. British soldiers reportedly stoked the fire with the combustible materials found within the building, including furniture and papers. The flames consumed the interior of both the House and Senate chambers, generating significant destruction (fig. 1). Although the British forces only remained in Washington for about twenty-six hours, the damage to other government buildings, including the Treasury Building and the War Department, was also extensive.

The burning of Washington had a profound impact on both the city and the nation. It was a symbolic blow to American pride and demonstrated the vulnerability of the young country. However, the destruction also galvanized the American spirit and fueled a renewed determination to defend its borders and, after a brief debate about relocating the capital elsewhere, solidified the resolve to rebuild and protect the capital.

During the years that followed, the federal government worked steadily to rebuild the prominent structures that had been injured.[3] On March 10, 1815, Madison appointed a three-person commission to administer the funds to repair public buildings, which in turn hired James Hoban (1755–1831) to

F. B. Morse (1791–1872), *The House of Representatives* (detail), 1822, probably reworked 1823, oil on canvas, Corcoran Collection, Museum Purchase, Gallery Fund, National Gallery of Art, Washington, D.C., 2014.79.27 (Courtesy National Gallery of Art)

Fig. 1. George Munger (1781–1825), *The Capitol in Ruins* (detail), 1814–15, ink and watercolor on paper, Library of Congress Prints and Photographs Division, Washington, D.C. DRWG/US - Munger, no. 1 (B size) (Cabinet B) (Courtesy Library of Congress)

restore the President's House (fig. 2) and Latrobe to tackle work at the Capitol. Latrobe, whose contributions to the built environments of Philadelphia and Baltimore were widely admired, had worked on the Capitol since 1804. The following year, the supervision and maintenance of the Capitol was transferred to a single commissioner of public buildings, Samuel Lane (1769–1845), a veteran officer of the War of 1812. Although Latrobe had enacted revised plans for both chambers of Congress and building was underway, the pace and cost did not meet the expectations of newly inaugurated President James Monroe or the expediency of Lane, an inveterate taskmaster.

Latrobe resigned toward the end of 1817 in response to his deteriorating relationship with Lane and the disappointment of Monroe. At the encouragement of Massachusetts Senator Harrison Gray Otis, Monroe encouraged Lane to fill the vacancy with the Boston architect Charles Bulfinch (1763–1844), whom the president had met twice in the past year and whose buildings in Boston Monroe praised. Bulfinch would bring the Capitol to completion, relying primarily on Latrobe's established plans for the chambers of the House and Senate, which Bulfinch described as "beautifully executed," with a design "in the boldest style."[4]

Meanwhile, the president and Congress were housed in temporary accommodations. The Monroes opted to remain in the Neoclassical Caldwell House at 2017 I Street NW, which they had occupied during his service as secretary of state, until returning to the as-yet-unfinished President's House in

Fig. 2. Benjamin Henry Latrobe (1764–1820), *The President's House, Washington, D.C., south front elevation*, 1817, watercolor, wash, and ink on paper, Library of Congress Prints and Photographs Division (ADE – Unit 2564, no. 3 (B size) (Cabinet B) (Courtesy Library of Congress)

Fig. 3. Unknown artist, *Southwest Grounds of the White House*, 1827, watercolor on paper, Private Collection (Courtesy The White House Historical Association)

fall 1817. Congress was housed in the so-called Brick Capitol, designed by Latrobe and completed by the end of 1815, before they returned to the Capitol on December 6, 1819. Amidst the grandeur of Congress's restored chambers, Washington remained largely undeveloped and sparsely populated (fig. 3).

As work progressed on the President's House and the Capitol, their respective occupants turned to the materials necessary to outfit the restored rooms. The decision of the president and Congress to look outside the District of Columbia for furnishings should not be considered an indication of the total absence of local cabinetmaking talent. Monroe turned to an in-town source, William King Jr. (1771–1854), for the East Room, intended to be one of the most important reception spaces in the President's House. Other craftsmen, including Henry Hill (active 1810s–1820s) and William Worthington (1775–1839), had received the patronage of the government for public buildings as well as private households.[5] Artisans such as Gustavus Beale (active c. 1800–1820) were introducing styles from Northern sources into the market as a less-expensive alternative to wares imported from those cities.[6] Furthermore, the constant stream of work at the Capitol for carpenters and carvers ensured that talented craftsmen were always on hand.[7]

What local cabinetmakers could not overcome, however, was the incessant claim from the District's style mavens that goods made there were inherently inferior. After moving to the capital from Richmond in 1817, United States Attorney General William Wirt informed his wife, Elizabeth, that Susan Wheeler Decatur "insists most strenuously that you should depend on the furniture you have for this winter, and get what you want from N. York in the Spring—She has tried it and you must not get your furniture here."[8] The extant elegant furniture ascribed to makers in Georgetown and Alexandria working in the late eighteenth and early nineteenth centuries belies this claim, but such was the ignorance of politicians moving to Washington.[9]

---

1. For a comprehensive history of the War of 1812 and attack on Washington, D.C., see Walter R. Borneman, *1812: The War That Forged a Nation* (New York: HarperCollins, 2004), 216–35.
2. Betty C. Monkman, *The White House: Its Historic Furnishings & First Families* (Washington, D.C.: White House Historical Association, 2000), 41.
3. For a comprehensive history of the oversight of the reconstruction of the Capitol following the War of 1812, see William C. Allen, *History of the United States Capitol: A Chronicle of Design, Construction, and Politics* (Washington, D.C.: U.S. Government Printing Office, 2001), 101–23.
4. Ibid., 128.
5. Anne Golovin, "Cabinetmakers and Chairmakers of Washington, D.C., 1791–1840," *The Magazine Antiques* 107, no. 5 (May 1975): 898–922.
6. Ibid., 901.
7. Allen, *Capitol*, 119–20; Sumpter T. Priddy III and Ann Steuart, "Seating Furniture from the District of Columbia, 1795–1820," in *American Furniture 2010*, ed. Luke Beckerdite (Milwaukee: Chipstone Foundation, 2010).
8. William Wirt to Elizabeth Wirt, December 3, 1817, William Wirt Papers, Virginia Historical Society, Richmond.
9. For example, see Priddy and Steuart, "Seating Furniture. . .," figs. 63, 90.

83

Armchair, 1818

William King Jr. (1771–1854)
Georgetown, Washington, D.C.
Mahogany, mahogany veneer; ash, tulip poplar; replacement brass castors, replacement upholstery
41¼ × 25½ × 25⅜ in.

PROVENANCE: President's House (later White House), 1818–82. A local Baltimore auction;[1] With J. Michael Flanigan, American Antiques, Baltimore, 1995; Purchased by Schrimshers, 1995.

In 1818, President James Monroe commissioned an extensive suite of seating furniture for the East Room from Georgetown cabinetmaker William King Jr. Elizabeth Kortright Monroe, of an affluent New York family, likely provided input on this purchase as well as on her husband's broader plans for outfitting the President's House. Remarkably, both the furniture and the room remained unfinished until Andrew Jackson moved into the executive residence more than a decade later.

This tale is one of simple economics. The Monroes were allocated $20,000 to furnish the President's House by an act of Congress passed on April 20, 1818. In their defense, they faced an insurmountable challenge in filling the entirety of the rebuilt public rooms with that sum. They certainly did not set out with the expectation that the East Room, intended as the primary reception room, would remain an unfulfilled vision. All but $284 of their allotment was spent on imported goods.[2] Monroe was an unabashed Francophile with extensive ties to France following his service as minister in the 1790s under George Washington and while assisting Robert Livingston with the acquisition of the Louisiana Territory under Thomas Jefferson. Upon turning his sights to the President's House in 1817, Monroe looked to connections abroad to procure a grand suite of gilt seating furniture for the Blue Room from Parisian maker Pierre-Antoine Bellangé (1757–1827) and an extensive French porcelain service.[3]

As with many furnishings acquired for the presidential household, an extensive paper trail provides a timeline for the unusual fate of the chairs and sofas provided by King. On May 30, 1818, Monroe wrote to Samuel Lane to suggest that their purchasing agents in France, Russell & La Farge, should acquire sufficient yardages of silk for the East Room window treatments and upholstery.[4] In this correspondence, Monroe refers to his wife's involvement, stating, "on these points Mrs. Monroe will decide." In discussing the furniture needed for the East Room, Monroe suggested that "King has a good model for the chairs." The balance of the furniture for the executive residence was procured from fellow Georgetown cabinetmaker William Worthington.

At some point in the ensuing months King must have received word that Monroe's kitty had run dry and the French silks would not arrive. In an undated invoice, he billed the President's House for the frames of the chairs and sofas, noting they remained unvarnished and unstuffed, reducing the cost accordingly from $33 per chair to $28, and $198 per sofa to $184.[5] On December 17, 1818, King received a $600 payment against the $1,408 bill; it is unknown whether he ever received the balance due.

The specific whereabouts of the King suite for the remainder of Monroe's presidency and ensuing tenure of John Quincy Adams remains unknown. After the arrival of Jackson, a widower, at the President's House, however, the set was sent to Philadelphia and entrusted to Louis Veron (1793–1853), a luxury-goods retailer of French extraction. Veron billed Jackson's aide, William B. Lewis, $600 on November 25, 1829, for the stuffing, covering, and varnishing of the chairs and sofas.[6] This amount was a fraction of the overall invoice of $9,358.27, which included expensive chandeliers, Brussels carpeting, and seven tables supplied by the renowned Philadelphia cabinetmaker Anthony Quervelle (1789–1856), whom the Monroes patronized shortly after leaving Washington in 1825 (cat. 54).

Once Veron's acquisitions were installed, the East Room was transformed from an unfinished disappointment into a majestic reception room, replete, as referenced in the invoice, with "ornamental rays over the door" and "7 doz Gilt Stars" that likely lined the cornice. King's seating furniture had finally received its due and remained in situ until an 1873 remodel during Ulysses S. Grant's administration. The set was likely sold during a local 1882 auction of furniture castoff from the White House.[7]

Scholars have previously suggested that the Classical design of the King chairs was influenced by Monroe's suite of imported Bellangé furniture, which had arrived by the time the first family moved into the unfinished President's House in the fall of 1817. Monroe's reference to King's "good model" suggests, however, other influences in the cabinetmaker's hand. The model could refer to a design of his own creation or to a chair or drawing he acquired from another source. A chair that mimics the East Room design descended through the King family and was referred to as the "sample chair."[8]

No other piece of extant furniture tied to King's shop equals this aspirational attempt at elegance and ornament. The maker blended a variety of stylistic influences, borrowing from the French strain of Classicism and beyond. The open armchair with upholstered back builds on the French *fauteuil* form but lacks the graceful scale and proportions of contemporary interpretations (see cat. 51). The juxtaposition of the turned vasiform stump, the floral carved corner blocks, and the reeded legs represents an intermingling of outside influences. More important, perhaps, than the chairs' appearance is their robust construction, which enabled them to weather more than forty years of active use in the President's House before their sale. The original set of furniture contained twenty-eight chairs and four sofas; the whereabouts of eleven chairs and one sofa are currently known.[9]

1. According to Flanigan, the chair had an anecdotal provenance from the Ford family of Washington, D.C., which had a branch in Baltimore. The White House recorded a King armchair owned by Lucy Sellers Wood (Mrs. Robert K. Wood) in Baltimore in 1980.
2. William Seale, *The President's House, Vol. 1* (Washington, D.C.: White House Historical Association, 2008), 154.
3. William Allman et al., *Official White House China, From the 18th to the 21st Centuries* (Washington, D.C.: White House Historical Association, 2016), 33–39.
4. James Monroe to Samuel Lane, May 30, 1818, James Monroe papers, Manuscripts and Archives Division, New York Public Library, courtesy of the Office of the Curator, The White House.
5. Invoice, William King Jr. to the President's House, undated, Miscellaneous Treasurers Accounts, RG217: MT43754-70, courtesy of the Office of the Curator, The White House.
6. Invoice, Louis Veron to William B. Lewis, November 25, 1829, courtesy of the Office of the Curator, The White House. The invoice does not reference the source of the upholstery work. According to Alexandra Alevizatos Kirtley, a significant number of upholsterers were working in Philadelphia at the time. John Rea (1774–1871), whose involvement in projects for the federal government extends back to at least 1807, is a tempting source. Joseph Barry (1757–1838), whose shop was near Veron's store, is another.
7. Duncanson Bros., Auctioneers, advertisement, *Evening Star* (Washington, D.C.), April 13, 1882, courtesy of the Office of the Curator, The White House. The advertisement references "Parlor suites, window hangings, arm chairs &c., from East Room."
8. Sold at Northeast Auctions, Portsmouth, NH, November 6–7, 2004, lot 706, purchased for a private client by dealer Milly McGehee.
9. The White House has five chairs in its collection. The Office of the Curator has also recorded two chairs at the Daughters of the American Revolution Museum and single examples at Ford's Theatre National Historic Site, the Baltimore Museum of Art, and James Monroe's Highland. In addition to the chair referenced in note 8 above, the White House documented an armchair owned by Mrs. Ford Richardson in 1991. The sofa is in the collection of the Smithsonian National Museum of American History.

84a

Armchair, 1819

Thomas Constantine & Co. (active 1815–1825)
New York
Mahogany, mahogany veneer; ash, white pine, maple; replacement brass castors, replacement horsehair upholstery
36½ × 22⅞ × 19½ in.

LABEL: "T. CONSTANTINE, & Co. / Cabinet Makers / 157 FULTON, Late PARTITION St. / Opposite St. Paul's Church Yard / NEW YORK." (See Appendix II)

PROVENANCE: United States House of Representatives, 1819–59. Sale, Sotheby's, New York, Jan. 24, 2014, lot 386; Purchased by Schrimshers, 2014.

84b

Armchair, 1819

Thomas Constantine & Co. (active 1815–1825)
New York
Mahogany, mahogany veneer; ash, white pine, maple; brass; replacement horsehair upholstery
37 × 22½ × 20 in.

LABEL: "T. CONSTANTINE, & Co. / Cabinet Makers / 157 FULTON, Late PARTITION St. / Opposite St. Paul's Church Yard / NEW YORK." (See Appendix II)

PROVENANCE: United States House of Representatives, 1819–59. Sale, Doyle, New York, Apr. 5, 2017, lot 344; Purchased by Schrimshers, 2017.

Upon receiving authorization on April 20, 1818, to spend $30,000 to outfit the not-quite-yet-restored House of Representatives chamber, Speaker of the House Henry Clay set out to swiftly locate the cabinetmaker who would furnish the desks and chairs. Although Clay maintained discretionary powers over all expenditures, he leaned on Thomas Claxton (d. 1821), longtime Doorkeeper of the House, to manage the process. Claxton had previously served Adams and Jefferson as a procurement agent to acquire furnishings for the President's House, as well as acting on Congress's behalf at the Capitol since the federal government's arrival in Washington.[1] His tenure began in Philadelphia, and he was well connected to craftsmen there.

Claxton's first step was to place an advertisement in newspapers between Washington and New York soliciting proposals to furnish the House.[2] The description of the furniture included therein relied on prototypes developed by Henry Hill (active 1810s–1820s), a local cabinetmaker who previously sold wares for the Capitol. The successful applicant would provide the House with 187 armchairs and 51 tables to fit the semicircular shape of the chamber. Furniture historians lament Claxton's decision to select the maker solely based on cost. For a modest sum more, Congress could have enjoyed the work of the august New York cabinetmaker Charles-Honoré Lannuier (1779–1819), rather than the relatively anonymous Thomas Constantine (1791–1849), who submitted the low bid. Although only twenty-seven at the time and with just a few years as an independent master craftsman under his belt, Constantine certainly did not lack confidence or moxie in proposing a flat rate of $30 per chair and drawer. The New Yorker beat out the Washington competition of Hill, William Worthington Jr., and Benjamin Belt (1785–1828), all of whom had previously supplied furniture to the federal government. Furthermore, Constantine bested Philadelphia upholsterer John Rea (1774–1871) who had worked with Benjamin Henry Latrobe on the Capitol's interiors since at least 1807 along with artist and decorator George Bridport (1783–1819). Rea supplied and installed the drapery and carpeting requisitioned for the restored chamber.

Constantine was born in Derbyshire, England, and immigrated to New York in 1793 at the age of two.[3] His father, John, was a blacksmith who died in 1799. Constantine apprenticed in the city with cabinetmaker John Hewitt (1777–1857) between 1806 and 1812 and remained as a journeyman until 1814.[4] Entries in Hewitt's account book testify to the range of Constantine's abilities, including payments for expensive and complex French sideboards. After starting out on his own in 1815, he operated under the guise of T. Constantine & Co., in close proximity to two of the city's leading makers of the day, Duncan Phyfe (1770–1854) and Michael Allison (1773–1855).

The effort to ramp up production for the House commission must have been staggering. Whether Constantine saw Hill's model in person is unknown, but the chairs do not align with New York seating furniture of the Classical period. The Neoclassical French *fauteuil* form of a square-back, open armchair with an upholstered seat and back and mahogany frame was previously adopted for the Capitol buildings in New York and Philadelphia.[5] The use of black upholstery was also a House tradition that extended back to New York. Constantine's chairs are simple and utilitarian, ideal qualities for seating that was to see tremendous wear in the coming decades. The streamlined design also facilitated the rapid production of parts to supply the massive quantity ordered by the House. The lack of padded arms, which are found on Congressional furniture in New York and Philadelphia, was an additional nod to economy and efficiency.

However inelegant and unfashionable the chairs may be considered today, Constantine's furniture was well received upon arrival in Washington for the quality of its construction. The *National Intelligencer* reported that the work "is said to be equal to anything of the kind for strength, solidity, and excellence of workmanship manufactured in the United States," and had "received the approbation of all who have seen it, and particularly that of the best judges of cabinet work."[6] Each chair was affixed with Constantine's paper label (see Appendix II).

The chairs were modified in the 1830s in response to a statute requiring that representatives remove their hats during sessions of Congress, which instigated the addition of stretchers and woven

84a

84b

racks (seen in cat. 84a).[8] When the House moved its new chamber following Thomas U. Walter's expansion of the Capitol, the decision to sell the Constantine furniture in favor of more decorative and conspicuously symbolic furniture designed by Walter scattered Constantine's wares on the wind.[7] Only seven chairs and eight desks are known today.[9]

---

1. Thomas Claxton to John Adams, November 3, 1800, Adams Papers, Massachusetts Historical Society; Thomas Claxton to Thomas Jefferson, May 13, 1808, Jefferson Papers, Coolidge Collection, Massachusetts Historical Society.
2. Advertisement, *National Intelligencer* (Washington, D.C.), May 12, 1818. The advertisement later appeared in the *Baltimore Patriot, Franklin Gazette* (Philadelphia), and *Mercantile Advertiser* (New York).
3. For a comprehensive history of Constantine's biography and career, see Matthew A. Thurlow, "Aesthetics, Politics, and Power in Early-Nineteenth-Century Washington: Thomas Constantine & Co.'s Furniture for the United States Capitol, 1818–1819," in *American Furniture 2006*, ed. Luke Beckerdite (Milwaukee: Chipstone Foundation, 2006), 185–90. The House commission is described at length in Margaret B. Klapthor, "Furniture in the Capitol: Desks and Chairs Used in the Chamber of the House of Representatives, 1819–1857," *Records of the Columbia Historical Society*, 69/70 (1969/1970): 190–211.
4. Manuscript Group 84, John Hewitt Records, 1800–1814, New Jersey Historical Society, Newark.
5. Alexandra Alevizatos Kirtley, *American Furniture, 1650–1840: Highlights from the Philadelphia Museum of Art* (Philadelphia: Philadelphia Museum of Art, 2020), 139. Reinforcing the continuity between the New York and Philadelphia seating furniture, Kirtley recounts how Thomas Affleck wrote that Congress "Engaged me to make the Furniture nearly of the same plan with that at N. York." See Thomas Affleck to Tench Coxe, September 16, 1790, in Charles Bangs Bickford et al., *Documentary History of the First Federal Congress, 1789–1791*, vol. 21, *Correspondence—Third Session* (Baltimore: Johns Hopkins University Press, 2015).
6. *National Intelligencer* (Washington, D.C.), October 29, 1819. Reprinted in the *New-York Daily Advertiser*, November 2, 1819.
7. Thurlow, "Aesthetics, Politics, and Power in Early-Nineteenth-Century Washington," 221.
8. Asher C. Hinds, *Hinds' Precedents of the House of Representatives of the United States: Including References to Provisions of the Constitution, the Laws, and Decisions of the United States Senate* (Washington, D.C.: United States Government Publishing Office, 1907), 2:750.
9. In addition to the Schrimshers' two examples, House chairs are owned by the Smithsonian National Museum of American History, a private collection in Maryland, the Curator of the House of Representatives, a private collection in Florida, and Clemson University. The desks, most of which are heavily modified, are in the collections of the National Museum of American History; National Women's Party, Sewell-Belmont Museum; the Curator of the House of Representatives; Quincy National Historic Site; Clemson University; Weymouth Center for the Arts and Humanities; and the Frederick Douglass National Historic Site.

85

Armchair, 1819

Thomas Constantine & Co. (active 1815–1825)
New York
Mahogany, mahogany veneer; maple; brass, replacement castors, replacement leather upholstery
38⅜ × 23¼ × 19½ in.

INSCRIPTIONS: Various chalk, pencil, and paper numbers on the seat frame, and slip seat frame.

PROVENANCE: United States Senate, Washington, D.C., 1819–81, Hannibal Hamlin (R-Maine, 1857–61, 1869–81); by descent through the Hamlin family; Sale, Cowan's Auctions, Inc., Cincinnati, OH, Dec. 10, 2010, lot 282; Purchased by Schrimshers, 2010.

Unlike the House of Representatives, who outfitted their restored chamber through a variety of sources, the Senate permitted Vice President Daniel D. Tompkins (1774–1825) the full purchasing power for the furnishings they required. Tompkins primarily resided in New York City in order to manage his personal affairs and troubled finances, which provided easy access to the expansive local market for household goods.[1] For unknown reasons, he waited until the fall of 1819 to start the process, ultimately turning the shopping list over to Thomas Constantine, who obtained everything from carpeting to drapery to lamps, in addition to manufacturing the desks and chairs required to seat the Senate.[2]

There is no extant documentation regarding the selection of the design of the Senate furniture. The chairs are almost directly modeled from a plate in Thomas Hope's *Household Furniture and Interior Decoration* (London, 1807), and the desk also appears to synthesize two table designs from that source.[3] The decision to opt for Hope's particular brand of Classicism represents a bold departure from the plain furniture provided for the House. It is tempting to credit Constantine for this choice, and Hope's book was available in New York in 1819, but the lasting influence of Benjamin Henry Latrobe and his Philadelphia team offer a persuasive alternative. The talented artist and designer George Bridport owned a copy of *Household Furniture*, and Constantine may have been asked to execute a design picked prior to Latrobe's departure from Washington in 1817.[4]

Regardless of the source, these elegant furnishings certainly sustained the Senate's tradition of outshining their colleagues in the House. The selection of red leather upholstery follows the Senatorial furnishings ordered in Philadelphia and for their pre-fire chamber in Washington.[5] In Constantine, Tompkins also had the benefit of easy access to an upholsterer, the cabinetmaker's twenty-three-year-old brother John. In addition to covering the Senate's chairs, Thomas Constantine's petition includes sums for "Making 1729 yds carpeting" and "Work at putting up monumental work in Senate Chamber."[6] These references imply that John Constantine traveled to Washington at least twice to install the materials procured in New York City. The "monumental work" likely references the draped canopy that stood above the desks used by the vice president (who served as the president of the Senate) and the secretary of the Senate.

Although Tompkins's poor management of the purchasing process put Constantine under undue pressure, the results were applauded. An 1822 guidebook described the grand effect of the cabinetmaker's provisions, remarking how "The whole room is showy, splendidly furnished."[7] The commercial failure of Morse's painting of the House's chamber (see p. 276) precluded his documentation of the Senate's room, but early prints reinforce this complimentary review.[8] Constantine was eager to ensure his firm's lasting connection to this auspicious commission. In addition to applying his paper label to the House chairs, the cabinetmaker also commissioned a set of bespoke wheels for the rear castors bearing his name and city (fig. 85.1).[9]

Although unseen in illustrations of the restored Senate chamber, Constantine's petition references the additional furniture he provided for the committee rooms, President's Room, and gallery. According to one guidebook, the back of "the last tier of Senators' seats is an enclosure, forming the bar of the Senate, outside of which is a lobby furnished with handsome sofas, for the accommodation of privileged persons."[10] The need to generate a broad swath of furniture forms in a short period of time had led Constantine to recruit twenty sofa makers for "immediate work either in or out of the shop."[11] Constantine provided eight curved sofas to sit within the pilasters on the back wall of the Senate chamber. These are seen in early floorplans of the room, and fragments remain in situ in the Capitol's restored Old Senate Chamber.[12] The other elements described in the petition are no longer extant.

The Senate retained all of Constantine's furniture during the relocation to the new chamber in 1859.[13] The original chairs and desks were supplemented to accommodate the growing body as the nineteenth century progressed, including a set of four in 1869 from New York cabinetmaker James Alexander, who was sent a Constantine-made desk and chair to serve as models.[14] A tradition emerged in the closing quarter of the nineteenth century, however, that permitted Senators to keep their chair upon retirement. This custom resulted in the need to gradually replace the original seats. The present example is one of only three known.[15] A fourth, owned by Jefferson Davis, the future president of the Confederacy, was destroyed during Hurricane Katrina.[16] All forty-eight desks remain in use on the Senate floor.

Fig. 85.1. Rear castor, marked "T. CONSTANTINE N. YORK" detail of cat. 85

1. Mark O. Hatfield, with the Senate Historical Office, *Vice Presidents of the United States, 1789–1993* (Washington, D.C.: United States Government Printing Office, 1997), 73–79.
2. Petition of Thomas Constantine of New York, December 21, 1826, RG46, SEN 20A-G4, National Archives and Records Administration. Constantine described how "toward the close of the year AD 1819 he was employed by the Hon. Daniel D. Tompkins . . . to provide at the expense and cost, and on account of the United States Senate, the necessary and proper articles of Furniture for the Chamber and Committee Rooms." Constantine received the bulk of the amount expended but was never fully compensated for the Senate commission.
3. Thomas Hope, *Household Furniture and Interior Decoration* (London: Longman, Hurst, Rees, and Orme, 1807; reprint, ed. Clifford Musgrave, London: Alec Trianti, 1970), pl. 59 (chair), pls. 20 and 26 (desk).
4. Alexandra Alevizatos Kirtley and Peggy A. Olley, *Classical Splendor: Painted Furniture for a Grand Philadelphia House* (Philadelphia: Philadelphia Museum of Art, 2016), 156.
5. Alexandra Alevizatos Kirtley, *American Furniture, 1650–1840: Highlights from the Philadelphia Museum of Art* (Philadelphia: Philadelphia Museum of Art, 2020), 139.
6. Petition of Thomas Constantine of New York, December 21, 1826.
7. George Watterston, *The L . . . Family at Washington, or, A Winter in the Metropolis* (Washington, D.C.: Davis and Force, 1822), 93, courtesy of the Office of the Senate Curator.
8. See, for example, Philip Haas, *Senate Chamber*, 1839–40, lithograph, U.S. Senate Collection, 38.01048.001.
9. In recognition of the brief turnaround time to complete the Senate commission, Constantine had the castors already in hand by the fall of 1819 or commissioned them locally. The latter is more likely given the need to shape the caps to fit the specific shape and size of the klismos legs. See Matthew A. Thurlow, "Aesthetics, Politics, and Power in Early-Nineteenth-Century Washington: Thomas Constantine & Co.'s Furniture for the United States Capitol, 1818–1819," in *American Furniture 2006*, ed. Luke Beckerdite (Milwaukee: Chipstone Foundation, 2006), 215.
10. Robert Mills, *Guide to the Capital of the United States: Embracing Every Information Useful to the Visiter, Whether on Business or Pleasure* (Washington, D.C., 1834), 42, courtesy of the Office of the Senate Curator.
11. *New-York Daily Advertiser*, November 2, 1819.
12. See, for example, Alexander Jackson Davis, Plan for the First Floor of the United States Capitol, Washington, D.C., 1832–34, drawing, Library of Congress.
13. Thurlow, "Aesthetics, Politics, and Power in Early-Nineteenth-Century Washington," 207, 218. The forty-eight desks he provided remain in use today. Shaped to fit a particular location on the risers in the chamber, the desks are an impressive illustration of cabinetmaking might.
14. Contingent Expenses of the Senate, 1869. On October 1, 1868, R. B. Griffin billed the Senate for crating a chair and desk to send to New York. On March 4, 1869, James Alexander billed the Senate for making four chairs and desks, as well as refinishing the desk and reupholstering the chair sent up from Washington. Courtesy of the Office of the Senate Curator.
15. In addition to the Schrimsher example, the Office of the Senate Curator owns a chair, and a third resides with the descendants of Senator Jonathan Chace (R-Rhode Island, 1885–89).
16. Thurlow, "Aesthetics, Politics, and Power in Early-Nineteenth-Century Washington," 220.

Form, Motif, and Ornament in Classical Furniture

CHRISTINE THOMSON AND WENDY A. COOPER

IN 1810 JOSEPH HOPKINSON, president of the Pennsylvania Academy of the Fine Arts, stated in his annual address to the members:

> It may surprise some to learn that most of the ornaments introduced to the persons and houses of the wealthy and the gay, under the irresistible recommendation of being "new fashions," are really some thousands years old; purloined from the relics of former ages . . . How various! How inexhaustible! is the profit and pleasure to be derived from the studies of antiquity.[1]

Hopkinson understood that almost every manner of form, motif, and ornament of this new Classical fashion was based on ancient models.

At the same time, fashion-minded Americans embraced a new vision of a cohesive, overall decorative scheme for their interiors, coordinating furniture, wall ornament, drapery, carpets, and upholstery. That, combined with the visual language of the ancients, provided an altogether new approach to interior furnishing and decoration. For example, in 1806, Rosalie Stier Calvert (1778–1821) of Maryland was contemplating the decoration of her new home and wrote to her father in Antwerp: "I am convinced that you would approve the way we are furnishing the house—everything will be as unified as possible but quite different from the style here. People talk about the [house] a lot." In a subsequent letter she commented to her father that "everything new [here] makes a big impression."[2] It is unknown whether Calvert used the skills of an architect or interior designer to create these unified interiors, like William and Mary Waln of Philadelphia who hired British architect Benjamin Henry Latrobe (1764–1820) to design a suite of Classical furniture for their new house. In turn, Latrobe hired London-trained theatrical set designer and decorative painter George Bridport (1783–1819) to paint the walls and decorate the furniture, creating a completely integrated system of interior design for their home (see p. 167).

The variety and drama derived from ancient objects and ornament were key to providing dazzling interior spaces. Stylish statements were made with bold new forms of furniture and contrasting surface ornamentation that was informed by the motifs of antique art and architecture. The mythological world of the ancients provided a variety of fantastic imagery that could be incorporated into the design of Classical furnishings. These included eagles, griffins, sphinxes, serpents, dolphins, and robed maidens called caryatids. These figures were used to support tabletops, as the arms and legs of sofas,

***Secretary Bookcase*, c. 1820–1830 (detail of cat. 23)**

Fig. 1. *Rod Tripod Stand*, Greek, 6th century BCE, bronze, Metropolitan Museum of Art, New York, Gift of Mr. and Mrs. Klaus G. Perls, 1997, 1997.145.1 (Courtesy Metropolitan Museum of Art / Art Resource, NY). Objects like this one were the inspiration for Classical furniture craftsmen to decorate elements with *vert antique*, a paint treatment imitating antique patinated bronze.

or as gilt bronze ornaments applied to extravagant mahogany, rosewood, or paint-decorated surfaces. Columns and pilasters were pervasive, whether as structural members or decorative additions to desks, sideboards, worktables, and many other forms. Besides mythical animals, other classical ornamental motifs included lyres, harps, festoons, scrolls, acanthus and lotus leaves, anthemion, paterae, and cornucopia.

The real brilliance of Classical furniture comes from the various surface techniques employed, many intended to create an impressive shimmer in the flickering light of Argand lamps at social gatherings (see p. 41). One of the most effective techniques for this purpose was the use of gleaming gold leaf, either left matte or burnished to a bright shine, creating rich sculptural effects on winged creatures, paw feet, carved foliage, and other three-dimensional elements. The skilled craftsman's arsenal of dramatic visual effects also included distinctive carving, richly figured veneers with French-polished surfaces, die-stamped brass and wood banding, cast or stamped metal mounts, composition ornaments, and decorative painting. Antique bronze objects unearthed by archaeologists and antiquarians were found to have aged to rich shades of blue and green (fig. 1). This "antique surface" inspired craftsmen to reproduce the look of the rich and varied patinas found on these long-buried objects to accentuate different elements of a piece of furniture, using a paint technique on wood often referred to as *vert antique*.

The Economics of Ornamentation

In the first quarter of the nineteenth century, the wealthier American populous embraced the new Classical style, paying exorbitant sums for top-of-the-line furniture. Much of that high cost was due to expensive ornamentation, which might include gilding, gilt brass and bronze ornaments, exotic wood veneers, and skilled painted decoration, such as the use of the *vert antique* treatments, all of which are labor-intensive processes. Meanwhile, the middle class was growing by leaps and bounds, and they too wanted to have stylish furniture in their homes. Fortunately, there were less expensive options available to create similar effects.

Plain veneered surfaces, simply polished to a reflective level, without any inlaid or painted decoration were most economical. English brass mounts, finished with tinted lacquer, were much less expensive than the French *ormolu* mounts—from *or moulu*, meaning "ground gold"—that were more finely chased and put through the fire-gilding process.[3] Modest carving without gilding or *vert antique* could still communicate some of the motifs from antiquity while keeping the costs down. Other cost-saving options included the use of molded composition (a putty-like material) instead of metal to create ornamental mounts, which were simply gilded and glued to the surfaces of furniture for a similarly dramatic statement. The molds for these could be reused, making composition mounts far less costly to produce than their cast metal counterparts.

Cabinetmakers could order from England cut brass or hardwood ornaments in various shapes—such as anthemions, bellflowers, *fleur-de-lis*, and paterae—to inlay into veneered surfaces. When ordered in quantity these could be very economical, as noted by London brass founder James Barron (active 1805–1839) in 1814.[4] Some of the most expensive and elaborate Classical furniture employed imported exotic hardwoods such as highly figured varieties of mahogany, rosewood, ebony, and satinwood. However, if these were too expensive, a skilled painter could utilize a *faux bois* or graining technique on less costly wood to imitate the exotic appearance of genuine veneers. Additional enhancements with freehand gilding and stenciling with bronze powders would further enrich this *trompe l'oeil* effect.

Regional Specialties

Classical furniture from the major urban centers of America has much in common—after all, each location was inspired by the same published drawings of the art and architecture from the ancient world and the variety of English and French pattern books. Affluent citizens were able to travel to Europe to see ancient monuments for themselves and observe the Neoclassical and Classical furniture produced in Britain and France. American cabinetmakers were crafting similar furniture forms, embracing new interpretations of seating and table designs, as well as those for secretaries, beds, cellarettes, and others.

Nonetheless, over time and geographic distance, each city developed its own distinctive preferences for particular designs, levels of elaboration and ornamentation, and materials. Unfortunately, there are few hard and fast guidelines for recognizing the Classical furniture from any one region. A combination of features must be closely examined to confirm an identification, and even then, the experts can be stumped. Some locales showed a greater preference for a certain form: for instance, Boston embraced sofa tables more than other major cities. Boston tables in the highest style are often elegantly restrained, supported by columns, while those produced in New York and Philadelphia can be more animated, sporting dolphins, caryatids, and various other winged creatures.

Some motifs were universally employed in all regions. The lyre, for example, was used in chair backs, card tables, other tabletop supports, and occasionally chair arms (see Appendix I). Beautifully carved cornucopia were also made in most regions, but more often in the mid-Atlantic. Boldly carved paw feet and acanthus leaves were employed throughout the Eastern seaboard, though sometimes the crispness and depth of exquisitely carved acanthus leaves can signal the work of a certain region or in some cases a particular known carver, as in Thomas Wightman's (1759–1827) work in Boston (see cats. 3, 8–10, 12, and 16).

Identifying the regional origin of American Classical furniture can be challenging, given the potential for overlapping forms, motifs, materials, and types of ornament and construction. Yet when considering a particular piece of furniture, assessing the type and combination of embellishments proves fruitful. What follows is a brief review of the various methods of decoration and enhancement found on Classical furniture, including a discussion of the materials available to craftsmen and a brief description of the techniques they likely used to create these remarkable effects.

TYPES AND METHODS OF ORNAMENTATION

Gilding

Gilt decoration as an enhancement of Classical furniture was universally embraced, though New York and Philadelphia craftsmen seemed to apply it in greater quantity and more expansively on both flat and carved elements. In Boston, with its preference for more austere furnishings, the use of gilt decoration is relatively rare. However, Bostonians still appreciated a gilded surface and favored extravagantly gilded looking glasses and picture frames to accompany their furnishings. With the exception of painted furniture Baltimore cabinetmakers rarely incorporated gilding.

Water gilding and oil gilding

Gilding is the application of gold in the form of thin sheets or "leaves" onto an object of a more mundane material to enhance its appearance and has long been a practice in many cultures throughout the world. Gold's relative scarcity, coupled with its unique resistance to tarnishing, has made it a seductive and irresistible metal throughout history. With its high level of malleability it can be easily pounded into thin sheets, only microns thick, which can then be manipulated with special brushes and laid onto the surface of an object of any material, transforming its appearance to look like it is made of solid gold.

There are two distinct traditional processes used for gilding with gold leaf: water gilding and oil gilding. Both methods were used regularly on Classical furniture, often in combination. Oil gilding is the more straightforward technique: an oil-based varnish (the mordant) is applied to a prepared surface; gold leaf is then placed onto the varnish just before it is completely dry, the slightly tacky surface allowing the gold leaf to adhere permanently. A wooden substrate is not required for oil gilding; any type of material—a painted surface, metal, plastic, or composition ornament—can be oil gilded. However, an object gilded in this manner is only as smooth as the surface underneath it and will not have the high reflectivity of solid gold unless the surface underneath is first polished to a high shine.

Water gilding, a process suitable only for application to wood, is a more intensive technique and requires careful preparation of the wood substrate. First, a sealing coating of glue is applied, followed by many layers of gesso—traditionally a mixture of chalk (calcium carbonate) and a collagen-based animal glue referred to in gilding as rabbitskin glue, which is the material derived from boiling the bones, hides, and connective tissue, not just of rabbits but of a variety of other animals. The multiple gesso layers hide wood grain and tool marks, creating a perfectly smooth bed for the application of gold leaf. On top of the gesso, additional preparatory layers are often applied, typically consisting of a clay mixture referred to as "bole," available in a range of colors which are ground in water and mixed with a binding medium such as rabbitskin glue. The flat plate-shaped particles of clay allow the bole to be aligned in a single smooth shiny plane by pressing into the surface with a burnishing tool. When the clay is burnished, either before or after the application of gold leaf, the gold leaf is given a consistent shiny gloss reminiscent of solid polished gold. Leaving the surface unburnished gives the gold a more matte appearance. A combination of matte and burnish gives a gilded surface more depth and interest, as the play of light on the surface enhances any carved details. The caryatid figures on many of Charles-Honoré Lannuier's card tables (see cat. 35a) were often gilded with this combination technique, giving details such as the tops of the wings and the band around the figure's chest the look of bright burnished gold.

The water gilding method does in fact use water to adhere the gold leaf to the prepared surface. Known as gilder's liquor, the water is modified slightly with alcohol (to break surface tension) and a drop or two of rabbitskin glue (to help with adhesion). When brushed onto the bole, the gilder's liquor reactivates the rabbitskin glue binding the bole and creates a sticky surface upon which leaf can then be gently laid with a special brush called a gilder's tip.

When applied to furniture or interior woodwork, gold leaf is always given a coating, either varnish or glue, as a last step in the gilding process to protect and modify the color of the gold. Tinted coatings, referred to as toners, use pigments and dyes to impart a richer, warmer appearance to the gold leaf. The term "sleepy" has been used to describe the color of gold leaf after toning, when it is no longer bright and raw-looking.

Fig. 2. Fine details in the wing of a gilded caryatid figure were recut with a *reparure* (detail of cat. 35a)

Toning varnishes can also compensate for the color of the leaf, which is produced in a variety of colors, determined by the addition of other metals to the gold mixture. Gilders had access to 24-karat gold leaf, but 22-karat leaf with additives of silver and copper was less expensive. The latter's color is lighter and less "golden," which was easily corrected with a toning varnish. Cost-conscious craftsmen could get the rich gold color they desired yet save money by using a lower-karat gold leaf, a common practice on furniture and frames.

The gilded elements found on nearly all Classical furniture use the less labor-intensive method of oil gilding, most likely because it is very inefficient to water gild a carved surface due to the difficulty of floating gold leaf into depressions and low spots. Some of the caryatid figures on Lannuier's pier tables are the exceptions. Entirely water gilded, details such as the tops of the wings were picked out in burnished water gilding. Interestingly, only oil gilding was identified on a Duncan Phyfe card table with similar caryatid figures (cat. 35b).

The gesso grounds on the caryatid figures on Lannuier's tables (fig. 2) have also been "recut," a French process of enhancing the detail of a gessoed surface using a variety of shaped cutting tools called *reparures* to sharpen and define edges—for example, on the feathers on the wings of the figures. Many of Lannuier's shop workers were French immigrants

Fig. 3. It is assumed that nineteenth-century decorators used transfer patterns to correctly place the ornament, but the application of varnish was done freehand by a skilled practitioner. An exceptional example of freehand gilding enhanced with shading and penwork can be seen on the front rail of this card table (detail of cat. 22, fig. 22.3).

Fig. 4. Gold powder was used to enhance the leaf details on the armrest whereas stencil gilding appears along the front rail of a couch (detail of cat. 24)

Fig. 5. Skilled examples of freehand gilding enhanced with shading and penwork can be seen on the pedestal base of this Philadelphia center table (detail of cat. 53)

well-versed in Parisian shop practices. Recutting has not been found on furniture with gilded surfaces made in cities other than New York.

Freehand gilding

Freehand gilding is a common form of embellishment on Classical furniture—particularly in New York and Philadelphia—the decoration often bearing a resemblance to actual metal mounts, and could have been a less expensive form of decoration or a substitute when metal mounts were not available. This technique relied on the skill of decorative painters to create the ornament freehand, often over a transferred design to guide them. Using a yellow-tinted oil varnish, the design is drawn freehand with a brush onto a flat surface; before the varnish is completely dry, gold leaf is laid over the design, adhering only to the varnished areas. Upon drying, the unadhered leaf is brushed away, leaving behind the painted design with its newly gilded surface. Freehand gilded decoration could be enhanced with tinted varnishes for shading, sgrafitto, or penwork—inked black lines—to give the decoration a sense of three-dimensionality (fig. 3).

Gilding with gold and metal powders

Other gilding methods do not involve gold leaf but rather gold in powder form. Roman gilding (also known as flash gilding) is a technique using a paint made of powdered gold or other metal powders suspended in a rabbitskin-glue binder. It can be applied like paint and lightly burnished when dry but does not produce the brilliant gleam of true gold leaf. Gold powder can also be brushed directly onto a varnished surface before it is completely dry. Powders are commonly found on picture frames and occasionally on furniture. A New York couch in the Schrimsher Collection features this technique (cat. 24). The wooden elements were first painted black, then varnished. Loose metal powder was applied to the almost-dry varnish with a dry brush or a bob (a piece of suede or fabric wadded into a ball or wrapped around a finger). By focusing on the protruding parts of the carving and giving them a metallic sheen, in contrast to the darker recessed areas, enhances the three-dimensional quality of the carving (fig. 4).

Stencil gilding

Stencil gilding is a technique that uses powdered gold or other metals such as brass and copper to create a design, particularly a repetitive one. The tradition developed in England as a way to decorate metal objects, such as tin canisters and trays, and was eventually adapted to furniture decoration. In America, stencil gilding was prevalent in New York and Philadelphia but less so in Boston and Baltimore. Stencils are cut from heavy paper, which is waxed on the back side. The surface to be decorated is first given a coating of oil varnish, which is allowed to dry nearly completely but still retains a slight tackiness. The stencil is gently placed waxed-side down onto the surface, and metal powders, often of different colors, are brushed over the stencil with a soft piece of leather or fabric formed into a bob. Three-dimensionality is achieved by applying powders unevenly–more thickly at the edges, and lighter at the centers, creating a shaded effect. A final clear coating of varnish is applied over the stenciled designs to seal and protect them (fig. 4).[5]

Paint

One distinctive specialty of the Classical period is highly sophisticated painted furniture. In the Schrimsher Collection there are several examples of furniture that utilize a variety of paint techniques, displaying an unending variety of Classical ornamentation. Pieces painted in strong colors and decorated with painted and gilded imagery were being made in all major cities, but it was in Baltimore and Philadelphia that this trend flourished and reached its apogee. A tradition of painted furniture that had long existed in England migrated to America with trained craftsmen.

Furniture to be painted is first given a coating of oil or resin-based varnish, or sometimes a thin coating of animal hide glue, to seal the wood and prevent the subsequent paint layers from soaking in too deeply. Traditional pigments are mixed with oils (linseed or walnut) or resins (shellac, mastic, copal, sandrac, etc.). Typically the paint treatments begin with a ground layer of primer, followed by one or more finish coats, sanded between layers to impart a smooth surface and even shine. Added ornament, which can include gold leaf, gold and

Fig. 6. The decorator of this chair, John Philip Fondé, first created a background of faux-wood graining, imitating a lighter wood such as tiger maple, and then applied gilded lines and decoration in imitation of inlaid brass (detail of cat. 42)

Fig. 7. An example of a pier table with a faux-rosewood-graining paint technique applied to the background. It was then decorated with Classical ornamentation in freehand gilding and applied penwork and shading (detail of cat. 66b).

metal powders, glazes, and penwork, is then applied on top of the prepared surface. The final step is to brush a clear varnish over all painted surfaces to protect the decoration and provide a consistent sheen to the finished piece.

Faux wood graining

This specialty decorative technique uses paints and glazes applied in a manner to imitate exotic woods. Found frequently on Classical furniture, this method was also applied to interior architectural elements such as doors, architraves, baseboards, stair risers, and raised paneling. Exotic woods of all varieties could be imitated by a skilled practitioner, sometimes so well that it can be difficult to discern the actual grain of a wood surface from a skillfully painted replica. A pair of Philadelphia klismos chairs in the Schrimsher Collection were painted by decorator John Philip Fondé to look more like maple, enhanced with gilded geometric designs that imitated inlaid brass (fig. 6).

The technique of faux wood graining involves first laying down a ground color in shades of pink or tannish yellow followed by a "glaze" of semi-translucent pigmented oil paint. The slow-drying oil paint can be manipulated by dragging brushes through it to simulate the grain patterns of wood. The realistic quality of the graining was often enhanced with a graining tool, an object that looks somewhat like a comb, which is dragged through the upper layer of paint to create thin parallel lines. Once dry, the treatment is sealed with a clear varnish to protect the graining and provide a consistent gloss. Skilled decorators could create painted surfaces nearly indistinguishable from true rosewood or other exotic veneers. The faux wood graining was then further decorated with mounts or stenciling and freehand gilding, just as actual veneered pieces would be (fig. 7).

Vert antique

The excavation of Greek and Roman bronze objects, such as tables with lion's-paw feet (fig. 1), provided a trove of new design possibilities for craftsmen, especially those in Philadelphia and New York, who strove to reproduce the look of the rich and varied patinas found on these long-buried antiquities. On Classical furniture these elements are generally carved of wood, then enhanced with gilding and painted components in imitation of antique bronze ornament. The term *vert antique* (also *verte antique* or *verd antique*) is used today to describe this particular paint treatment; earlier period descriptions of this method also refer to it as bronzage or bronzing, patina antiqua, or sea green.[6]

Chemically patinating metal surfaces to give them the appearance of age has a long tradition in craft practice, and many recipes exist to produce various colors and effects. However there is no known standard recipe for the creation of a *vert antique* paint treatment. This technique of layering paints and varnishes to create a metallic effect is believed to have been developed in France, but it is not mentioned in any extant French eighteenth- and early nineteenth-century craftsmen's guidebooks, and only a few descriptions of paint techniques to imitate bronze are found in later nineteenth-century publications.

A typical *vert antique* treatment usually begins with a base coating or primer, sometimes gesso or clay mixed with animal-hide glue or a layer of oil paint, followed by gray- or green-pigmented paint layers. There were not many stable green pigments available to craftsmen in the early nineteenth century; consequently, a number of examples have been identified with paint composed of a mixture of Prussian blue and chrome yellow.[7] The paints used to create *vert antique* could have either oil, spirit varnish (such as shellac in alcohol), or glue binders. Varnish layers, sometimes as many as four or five, are then laid on top, occasionally interspersed with thin layers of pigment, culminating in a transparent varnish topcoat. In technical studies, a variety of different resinous varnish components have been identified, including shellac, copal, and mastic. The layering varnishes are often tinted with pigments and can also contain gold, bronze, or copper powders. Occasionally, metallic powders were brushed onto the tacky surface of a nearly-dry varnish layer, leaving a thin, reflective film of metal to enhance the protruding areas of a carving, intended to imitate the look of bronze that has been rubbed through on the high spots, exposing the shiny unoxidized metal underneath the corrosion. However, a *vert antique* treatment, as we now understand it, is not always green, and it sometimes does not contain metal powders. The variety of execution in observed examples suggests many craftsmen were experimenting with the process and materials to achieve the desired effect (figs. 8–9).

Fig. 8. An example of *vert antique* paint technique on the carved lion's-paw foot of a French bedstead, with metallic highlights over a green background (detail of cat. 31)

Fig. 9. This pier table has modern re-creations of original gilded and *vert antique*–decorated carved surfaces that had been previously damaged or removed. Conservators Robert Mussey Associates of Boston re-created the appearance of the original decoration using microscopy and other methods of analysis to determine the original pigments and varnishes still extant in protected areas and consulted painter's guidebooks from the early nineteenth century to identify similar techniques. Having determined the specific stratigraphy of paints and varnishes on this particular piece, they reproduced the layering process using traditional materials with the intent of replicating the look of the original *vert antique* surface. It is surprisingly a much lighter green but nevertheless may be a more accurate example of *vert antique*'s original appearance, before becoming darkened by aging of materials and grime (detail of cat. 47).

Interpretation of these complex surfaces is problematic, as the materials used to create them change color and darken as they age and interact chemically with one another. Natural resin varnishes, oils, and certain green pigments oxidize. This could be an explanation for why many restorers over the years have reinterpreted *vert antique* elements by painting them black. It also suggests that there may be many other examples of this ephemeral paint decoration that were covered or removed in the course of modern restoration treatments.

Metal Mounts and Hardware

Ornamental metalwork on Classical furniture can include baguette moldings, consisting of quarter-round or half-round cores of wood with a thin sheet of brass wrapped around them; inlaid brass, consisting either of bands or singular elements; and three-dimensional ornaments, either die-stamped or cast brass or bronze, that when gilded are often referred to as *ormolu* mounts.

Metal mounts, either varnished or gilded, were typically available as imports, primarily from England and France. New York furniture makers, especially Charles-Honoré Lannuier, used superior-quality French gilded bronze *ormolu* mounts. To a much lesser degree, French and British *ormolu* can also be found on Boston pier tables and other forms. Baltimore examples rarely used *ormolu* or stamped brass mounts.

Brass trim and inlay

Brass, either inlaid into wood or as the covering on a baguette molding, appears on furniture from New York, Boston, and Philadelphia but is rarely seen in Baltimore. In New York, brass inlay is found frequently, especially on wares coming out of the Lannuier and Phyfe shops, both of which utilized this type of enhancement, in the form of small ornaments or long bands of die-stamped brass with wood (often rosewood or ebony) inlaid into the voids. These narrow aprons and bands were used most frequently to trim the edges of tabletops and plinths but are found on other furniture forms as well.

Lannuier's association with Denis-Michel and Pierre-Aurore Frichot, who were specialists in the fabrication of stamped brass ornaments, suggests that he imported die-stamped ornament rather than fabricating it himself, which required highly skilled craftsmen and specialized equipment.[8] It is also possible that Lannuier or Aurore Frichot imported the requisite devices from France, thereby making it possible to fabricate the trim in the New York studio. This question remains unresolved, but Lannuier undoubtedly did much to disseminate an appreciation for French style throughout New York and beyond through the importation of many types of brass metalwork from France. In 1803, for example, he advertised that he had brought with him from France "gilt and brass frames and borders of ornaments."[9]

Philadelphia makers also produced a variety of forms decorated with ornate metal inlays. The Schrimsher Collection contains a Philadelphia cylinder secretary desk (fig. 10a–b) that is embellished with elaborate brass and wood inlaid panels

Fig. 10a and b. *Cylinder Secretary Bookcase*, c. 1825–1850, Philadelphia, mahogany, rosewood, ebony, brass inlay, poplar, pine; mirror glass, Schrimsher Collection. The brass inlaid in ebony is reminiscent of French Boulle work.

reminiscent of French "Boulle work"— a technique that allows for brass to be inlaid into ebony or tortoiseshell and was perfected in France by cabinetmaker André-Charles Boulle (1642–1732).

Metal mounts

Metal mounts, either cast bronze or stamped from brass, are a trademark of Classical furniture, adorning many examples from all urban centers not only in America but also in Europe and England. They function a bit like jewelry, adding interest to a surface. Mounts are found on the flat vertical surfaces of tables, on columns as capitals and bases, and as "slippers" forming parts of casters for the feet of tables. They came in an endless variety, portraying an array of ancient images and designs. Lannuier and others imported extremely sophisticated mounts from France, displaying allegorical figures in various modes of activity, beautifully chased, polished, and gilded. English mounts were also imported by American cabinet-makers. A French mount can be difficult to distinguish from an English one unless they are marked by the maker on the back, which is not always the case. French *ormolu* mounts are often fire-gilded and are considered more finely chased than English mounts, but this is not a hard and fast rule. English cabinet furniture catalogues also listed "gilt ornaments for Chairs, Cornices, and Cabinet Furniture" (fig. 11).[10]

Mounts are created by one of two methods: sand casting, pouring melted brass or bronze into a sand mold, or die-stamping, forcing a brass sheet into a mold under pressure. Sand-cast hardware was smoothed and embellished by hand with specialty tools and then either fire-gilded or dipped in acid and coated with lacquer to imitate the look of gold. Cast mounts are made of brass (an alloy of copper and zinc) or bronze (an alloy of copper and tin). Bronze has a reddish copper-colored tone, whereas brass is more yellow and less expensive. Bronze is less malleable due to its tin component, so it cannot be pounded into thin sheets like brass and is therefore not used for die-stamping. Bronze is also less prone to corrosion, which is why it is preferred as a base metal for gilding. Die-stamped brass mounts can be either gilded or acid-dipped and lacquered. Die-stamping was a less labor-intensive process that did not require chasing, generating more mounts at a lower cost. Mounts created by both methods, however, lent themselves to selective burnishing, to heighten the appearance of the form and enhance the play on light on the surface.

Cast *ormolu* mounts and other bronze objects made in France, such as clock parts and lighting fixtures, were gilded using a method known as fire gilding. Gold dissolved into mercury using acid created a liquid (the amalgam) that was then brushed onto the surface of a base metal, such as brass or bronze. When the metal was heated to a specific temperature, the mercury vaporized, leaving behind the gold, now chemically bonded to the base metal. Mercury vapors are highly toxic and hastened the demise of many workers before the technique was eventually banned in France. With better ventilation and air-scrubbing systems available today, fire gilding is still carried out on a small scale.

There are examples of fire-gilded English mounts, but in most cases English hardware and mounts are coated with a varnish to give them a gold tone and protect them from tarnishing. The hardware was first dipped in a proprietary acid mixture that turned the surface a frosty yellow color. Details of the decoration could then be selectively burnished with a tool, providing a shiny contrast to the matte surface. They were then coated with a varnish made up of a variety of components including resins, pigments and dyes, which lent a more golden color to the metal.[11] This coating was referred to in the period as lacquer or changing varnish specifically when applied to metals. The metal was then heated to "bake on" the varnish, chemically cross-linking the molecules together, creating a stronger coating that was more impervious to solvents and oxidation.

Distinguishing whether a mount is fire gilded with gold or coated with lacquer is difficult. However, lacquers made of organic materials will start to break down, allowing the oxygen in the air to tarnish the base metal. The coatings that have survived are rare and are worthy of preservation.

More functional hardware, such as drawer pulls, handles, and hinges, can be just as decorative as metal mounts. They too are either sand cast or die stamped and can be either gilded or coated with lacquer.

Fig. 11. ***Metal Mounts*****, 1829–1830, gilt brass, Metropolitan Museum of Art, New York, Gift of Mrs. Edward Hunting Smith, 1968, Inst.68.8.31a, b (Courtesy Metropolitan Museum of Art / Art Resource, NY). Whether fire-gilded or coated with tinted varnish, these gilt brass and bronze mounts have the appearance of objects made of solid gold.**

Composition Ornament

More commonly seen as embellishment on nineteenth-century picture frames in place of carving, ornamentation cast in a material called composition, or "compo," can imitate the look of carved wood or metal mounts at a greatly reduced effort and cost. They are, of course, not as durable as metal mounts but can create the same visual effect. Traditional compo is made from animal hide glue, chalk (calcium carbonate), linseed oil, and pine rosin (with occasional other additives) mixed together in specific proportions to a putty-like consistency, which is then pressed into a mold created from a carved-wood or cast-metal model. Once the compo ornament is taken from the mold and allowed to dry, it can be gilded with gold leaf so that it bears a nearly identical resemblance to gilt wood or metal (fig. 12).

Compo mounts have been regularly identified on furniture from the Lannuier and Phyfe shops but are scarce otherwise. Perhaps Lannuier, who trimmed many of his game tables with rows of compo rosettes, found it more cost effective to simply make copies of a stamped brass mount. Some of his tables have a combination of metal mounts with compo replicas and compo ornamentation, suggesting that he augmented metal mounts to create his vision.[12]

Exotic Wood Veneers

As in furniture from earlier eras, choice wood was critical to achieve an elegant piece of Classical furniture. Mahogany veneers, often book matched, continued to be an integral material. Therefore, procurement of high-quality mahogany was essential for the success of any cabinetmaking business. Duncan Phyfe, for example, had sufficient capital to acquire the highest quality wood coming from the Caribbean, and occasionally even brought his own shipments to New York, bypassing local lumber merchants.[13]

Fig. 12. This fine example of gilded composition ornament is actually a replica. The original compo masque was lost but it left an image of its shape on the wood. By great fortune and assistance from Peter M. Kenny and Carswell Rush Berlin, an almost exact masque was identified on a bed canopy by Charles-Honoré Lannuier at the Bartow-Pell Mansion in the Bronx, New York. The museum generously allowed a mold to be taken from an original masque, and from the mold two replicas were made for this table (detail of cat. 30).

Fig. 13. Both metal and wood were used for inlay on Classical furniture, yet examples utilizing wood are more unusual. Here the wood inlay is either ebony or another fine-grained wood stained black (detail of cat. 28).

Other exotic imports feature prominently in Classical furniture. A pair of New York card tables display satinwood veneers exceptionally embellished with ebony inlaid designs (fig. 13). More commonly used, however, was rosewood veneer, with its rich array of grain patterns in various shades of brown that contrasted well with gilded decoration. Rosewood was a more expensive alternative to mahogany and was typically allocated to furniture destined for the most elegant domestic spaces.[14] In 1841, when Phyfe's Fulton Street firm was dissolved, they sold off "Mahogany, Rosewood and Ambina Boards Planks and Veneers."[15]

When utilizing veneers to decorate furniture, cabinetmakers could build a case with lesser-quality woods that would then be covered by veneers applied with animal-hide glue, giving the impression that the object was made solely of exotic woods. To show off veneers to their best advantage, they were given several coats of a resinous varnish, filling all wood pores and polishing the surface to a high gloss. This technique is commonly referred to as French polish, a method of wood finishing whereby thin coats of shellac varnish are applied with a pad rather than a brush. The use of the pad allows for burnishing the surface to a high shine between each application—an ideal treatment for achieving a glossy reflective surface that further enriches the beauty of the wood grain and complements other decorative elements to create a complete and integrated artistic vision.

1. Joseph Hopkinson, *Annual Discourse Delivered before the Pennsylvania Academy of the Fine Arts on the 13th of November 1810* (Philadelphia: Bradford and Inskeep).
2. Margaret Law Callcot, *The Plantation Letters of Rosalie Stier Calvert, 1795–1821* (Baltimore: Johns Hopkins University Press, 1992), 146, 148.
3. Wendy A. Cooper, *Classical Taste in America, 1800–1840* (New York: Abbeville Press; Baltimore: Baltimore Museum of Art, 1993), 184–85.
4. James Barron, *Modern and Elegant Designs of Cabinet and Upholstery Furniture* (London: W.M. Thistleton, 1814).
5. An in-depth description of bronze powder stencil gilding, along with step-by-step videos of the process, can be found on the website of the Historical Society of Early American Decoration at https://hsead.org/decorative-arts/. This organization, started by the well-known teacher and practitioner of early American decorative techniques Esther Stevens Brazer, has documented many lost or misunderstood techniques and methods of decoration. Their website provides fascinating in-depth videos of the processes of stenciling and depicts many other early American craft techniques, including some of the gilding techniques discussed here.
6. The term *vert antique* has many different spellings including *verte*, and *verd*, all of which are regularly used when describing this technique. *Verd antique* also describes a specific type of dark green serpentine stone similar to marble but harder and less porous. This material was used to ornament small items such as boxes and tabletops. See Robert D. Mussey Jr., "Verte Antique Decoration on American Furniture: History, Materials, Techniques, Technical Investigations," in *Painted Wood: History and Conservation*, ed. Valerie Dorge and F. Carey Howlett (Los Angeles: Getty Conservation Institute, 1998), 242–54.
7. The green color on the feet of cat. 47 is actually a mixture of chrome yellow and a carbon black. We are grateful to conservator and paint analyst Susan Buck of Williamsburg, VA, who confirmed the pigments using polarized light microscopy (PLM), referring to the color as "optical green"—that is, not containing any actual green pigments.
8. Peter M. Kenny, Frances F. Bretter, and Ulrich Leben, *Honoré Lannuier, Cabinetmaker from Paris: The Life and Work of a French Ébéniste in Federal New York* (New York: Metropolitan Museum of Art, 1998), 22.
9. Ibid., 164.
10. Alexandra Alevizatos Kirtley, *American Furniture, 1650–1840: Highlights from the Philadelphia Museum of Art* (Philadelphia: Philadelphia Museum of Art, 2020), 176.
11. Christine Thomson, "Last but Not Least: Examination and Interpretation of Coatings on Brass Hardware," in *Papers Presented at the Wooden Artifacts Group, June 6, 1991, AIC Annual Meeting, Albuquerque, New Mexico* (Washington, D.C.: American Institute for Conservation, 1991), 1–15.
12. Kenny et al., *Honoré Lannuier*, 158.
13. Peter M. Kenny, Michael K. Brown, Frances F. Bretter, and Matthew A. Thurlow, *Duncan Phyfe: Master Cabinetmaker in New York* (New York: Metropolitan Museum of Art, 2011), 48–49.
14. Ibid., 148–51.
15. Ibid., 49.

APPENDIX I
Furniture

French Secretaries

Cat. 6, Boston

Cat. 29, New York

Cat. 55, Philadelphia

Cat. 77, Baltimore

Cat. 5, Boston

Cat. 20, New York

Cat. 47, Philadelphia

Cat. 67, Baltimore

Cat. 8, Boston

Cat. 37, New York

Cat. 50, Philadelphia

Cat. 66a, Baltimore

Cat. 4, Boston

Cat. 27, New York

Cat. 58, Philadelphia

Cat. 65, Baltimore

Chairs

Cat. 12, Boston

Cat. 26, New York

Cat. 41, Philadelphia

Cat. 78, Baltimore

Paw Feet

Cat. 17, Boston

Cat. 23, New York

Cat. 47, Philadelphia

Cat. 77, Baltimore

Pad and Bun Feet

Cat. 14, Boston

Cat. 24, New York

Cat. 58, Philadelphia

Cat. 70, Baltimore

Lyres

Cat. 1, Boston

Cat. 26, New York

Cat. 41, Philadelphia

Cat. 80, Baltimore

Ionic Columns

Cat. 14, Boston

Cat. 25, New York

Cat. 62, Philadelphia

Cat. 74, Baltimore

Cat. 5, Boston

Cat. 29, New York

Cat. 59, Philadelphia

Cat. 66b, Baltimore

Cat. 5, Boston

Cat. 35b, New York

Cat. 55, Philadelphia

Cat. 68, Baltimore

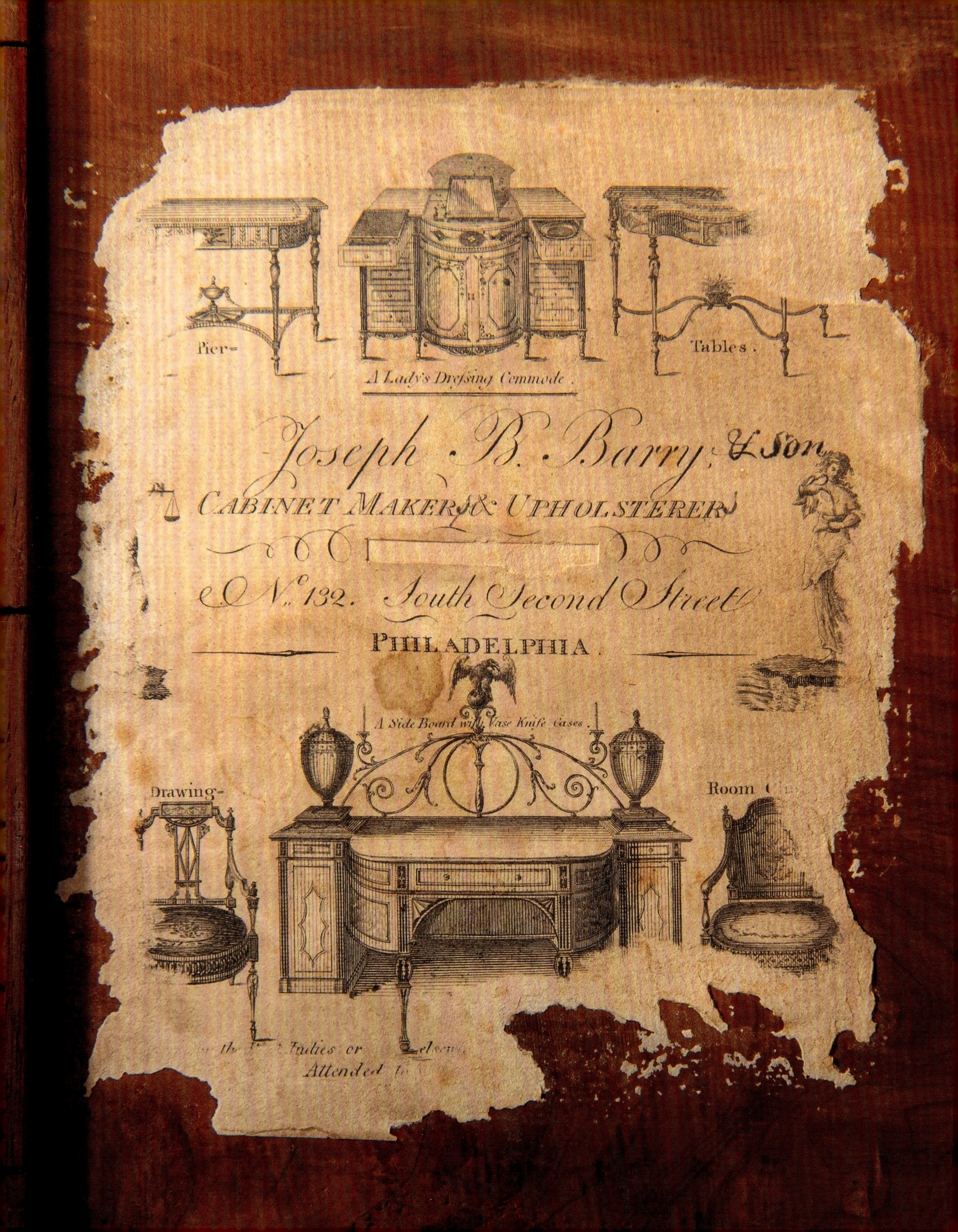
Pier-
A Lady's Dressing Commode.
Tables.
Joseph B. Barry, & Son
CABINET MAKER & UPHOLSTERER
No. 132. South Second Street
PHILADELPHIA.
A Side Board with Vase Knife Cases.
Drawing-
Room

APPENDIX II
Labels, Inscriptions, and Stamps

Boston

Cat. 4: William Hancock sofa

Cat. 9: T. Hunt & Co. card table

Cat. 5: Emmons & Archbald pier table

Cat. 6: Emmons & Archbald French secretary

Cat. 37: Duncan Phyfe card table

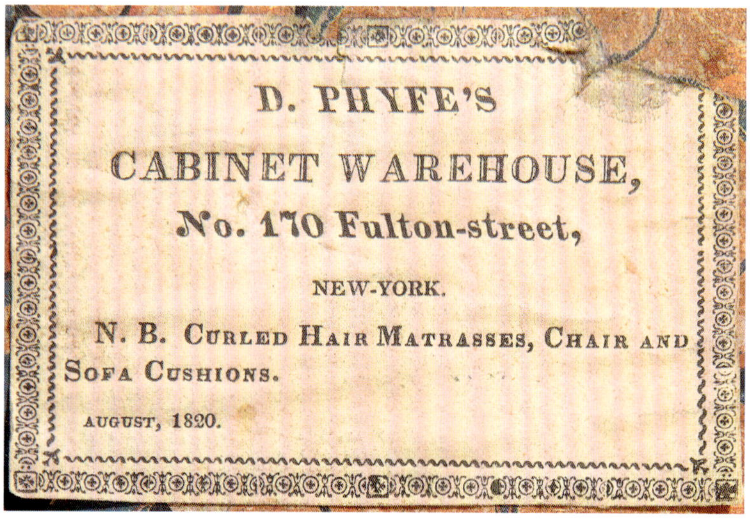

Cat. 30: Charles-Honoré Lannuier console or side table

Cat. 39: Joseph Meeks & Sons pier table (partial label)

Cat. 30: Lannuier console or side table

Cat. 58: David Fleetwood sofa

Cat. 59: Cook & Parkin pier table

Cat. 46a: Anthony Gabriel Quervelle card table

Cat. 49c: Charles Haight and John Ferris White worktable

Cat. 49a–b: Anthony Gabriel Quervelle worktables

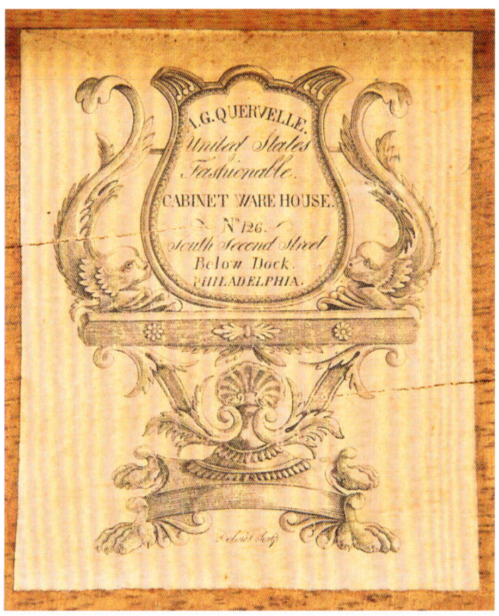

Cat. 40: Joseph B. Barry & Son wing wardrobe

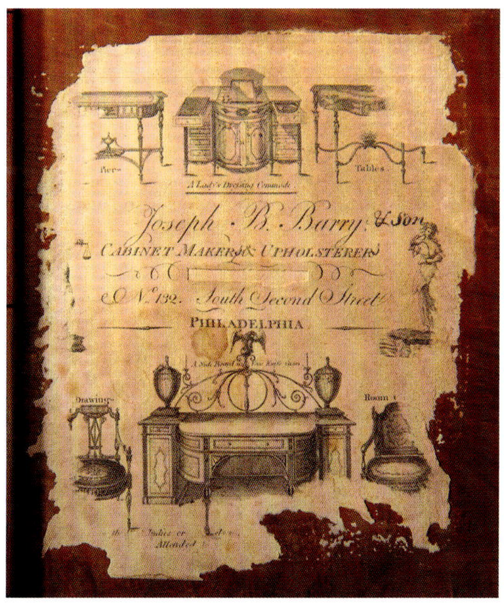

Baltimore

Cat. 71: Anthony H. Jenkins wardrobe

Cat. 82: Pier table, marble supplied by Levi Taylor

Cat. 74: John Needles pier table

Washington D.C.

Cat. 84a and b: Thomas Constantine & Co. armchair

BIBLIOGRAPHY

PRIMARY SOURCES

Newspapers

American Daily Advertiser (Philadelphia), November 4, 1794.

Baltimore American, September 25, 1832.

Baltimore American & Commercial Daily Advertiser, April 21, 1825; May 16, 1826; September 25, 1832.

Baltimore Evening Post, December 1, 1806.

Baltimore Sun, August 19, 1841; February 26, 1884; June 5, 1979.

Charleston Courier, December 28, 1818.

City Gazette and Commercial Daily Advertiser (Charleston), April 11, 1820; November 20, 1820.

Columbian Centinel (Boston), February 18, 1824.

Columbian Museum and Savannah Advertiser, October 5, 1798.

Evening Post (New York), September 18, 1818.

Evening Star (Washington, D.C.), April 13, 1882.

Federal Gazette (Philadelphia), June 10, 1790; June 28, 1817.

National Gazette (Philadelphia), April 25, 1826; May 28, 1839.

National Intelligencer (Washington, D.C.), May 12, 1818; October 29, 1819.

New-York Daily Advertiser, November 2, 1819.

New-York Evening Post, February 28, 1815.

New-York Gazette, March 9, 1814.

New-York Gazette & General Advertiser, May 1816.

New York Mercantile, December 3, 1810.

New York Times, June 23, 1878.

Pennsylvania Mercury (Philadelphia), July 10, 1788.

Philadelphia Inquirer, May 28, 1832; October 26, 1833; March 12, 1834; July 21, 1834; March 9, 1836; April 29, 1836; December 21, 1836; January 25, 1837; May 9–15, 1837; September 17, 1838; January 10, 1839.

Philadelphia Public Ledger, October 30, 1848.

Poulson's American Daily Advertiser (Philadelphia), September 11, 1824.

Republican and Savannah Evening Ledger, May 2, 1815.

United States Gazette (Philadelphia), June 8, 1830.

Archival Sources

Adams Papers. Massachusetts Historical Society, Boston.

Baltimore City Inventories. Maryland State Archives.

Baltimore County Register of Wills. Maryland State Archives.

Census for Baltimore City. Bureau of the Census, Washington, D.C.

Chester County Archives, West Chester, Pennsylvania.

Gordon Family Papers. Clements Library, University of Michigan, Ann Arbor.

Harriot Appleton Curtis Photographic Collection. Historic New England.

Jefferson Papers. Coolidge Collection. Massachusetts Historical Society, Boston.

McComb, John, Junr., Misc. Mss. Manuscript Department, New-York Historical Society.

Monroe, James, Papers. Manuscripts and Archives Division, New York Public Library.

National Archives and Records Administration.

New Jersey Historical Society, Newark.

New-York Historical Society.

Office of the Curator, White House, Washington, D.C.

Passano-O'Neill file. Maryland Center for History and Culture.

Philadelphia City Archives.

Philadelphia Wills and Inventories. Joseph Downs Collection of Manuscripts and Printed Ephemera, Winterthur Library, Delaware.

Ravenel, Harriott Horry, Family Papers, 1694–1935. South Carolina Historical Society, Charleston.

United States Federal Census. Available online through Ancestry.com.

Wirt, William, Papers. Virginia Historical Society, Richmond.

Pattern and Design Books

1737–38: Jean-François Blondel (1705–1774). *De la distribution des maisons de plaisance, et de la décoration des edifices en general* (The distribution of pleasure houses and the decoration of buildings in general). 2 vols. Paris: Charles-Antoine Jombert, 1737–38 (vol. 1, 1737; vol. 2, 1738).

1754, 1755, 1762: Thomas Chippendale (1718–1779). *The Gentleman and Cabinet-Maker's Director: Being a Large Collection of the Most Elegant and Useful Designs of Household Furniture in the Gothic, Chinese, and Modern Taste.* London, 1754; 2nd edition, 1755; 3rd enlarged and revised edition, 1762.

1755, 1765: Johann Joachim Winckelmann (1717–1768). *Gedanken über die Nachahmung der griechischen Werke in der Malerei und Bildhauerkunst.* Dresden and Leipzig, 1755. English translation by Henry Fusseli, *Reflections on the Painting and Sculpture of the Greeks*, published in London in 1765.

1758, 1770: Julien-David LeRoy (1724–1803). *Les Ruines des plus beaux monuments de la Grèce* (Ruins of the most beautiful monuments of Greece). Paris, 1758; expanded edition, 1770.

1762–96: James Stuart (1713–1788) and Nicholas Revett (1720–1804). *The Antiquities of Athens.* 4 vols. London, 1762–96 (vol. 1, 1762; vol. 2, 1787; vol. 3, 1794; vol. 4, 1796).

1762: William Ince (1737–1804) and John Mayhew (1736–1811). *Universal System of Household Furniture.* London, 1762.

1764: Johann Joachim Winckelmann (1717–1768). *Geschichte der Kunst des Alterthums* (The history of art in antiquity). Dresden, 1764.

1764: Robert Adam (1728–1792). *The Ruins of the Palace of the Emperor Diocletian at Spalatro in Dalmatia.* London, 1764.

1765: Robert Manwaring (active 1760–c. 1770). *The Cabinet and Chair-Maker's Real Friend and Companion, or, the Whole System of Chair-Making Made Plain and Easy.* London, 1765.

1766–76: Pierre-François d'Hancarville (1719–1805). *Collection of Etruscan, Greek, and Roman Antiquities from the Cabinet of the Honble. Wm. Hamilton, His Britannick Maiesty's Envoy Extraordinary at the Court of Naples.* 4 vols. Naples, 1766–76.

1767: Johann Joachim Winckelmann (1717–1768). *Monumenti antichi inediti* (Unpublished ancient monuments). Rome, 1767.

1773–79, 1786: Robert Adam (1728–1792) and James Adam (1732–1794). *The Works in Architecture of Robert and James Adam.* Vol. 1, 5 parts. London, 1773–78 (vol. 1, 5 parts, 1773–78; vol. 2, 1779). Reissued as two volumes in 1786.

1786: Nicolas Ponce (1746–1831). *Description des bains de Titus, ou collection des peintures trouvées dans les ruines des thermes de cet empereur* (Description of the baths of Titus, or collection of paintings found in the ruins of the baths of this emperor). Paris: Barbou, 1786.

1788: A. Hepplewhite & Co. *The Cabinet-Maker and Upholsterer's Guide, or, Repository of Designs for Every Article of Household Furniture, in the Newest and Most Approved Taste.* London, 1788. Published by Alice Hepplewhite, widow of George Hepplewhite (1727–1786).

1791–93: Thomas Sheraton (1751–1806). *The Cabinet-Maker and Upholsterer's Drawing-Book.* London, 1791–93. Published in forty-two biweekly installments; first complete edition issued in two volumes in 1793.

1798: Charles Percier (1764–1838) and Pierre-François-Léonard Fontaine (1762–1853). *Palais, maisons, et autres édifices modernes, dessinés à Rome* (Palaces, houses, and other modern buildings, drawn in Rome). Paris, 1798.

1799: Charles Heathcote Tatham (1772–1842). *Etchings, Representing the Best Examples of Ancient Ornamental Architecture; Drawn from the Originals in Rome, and Other Parts of Italy, during the Years 1794, 1795 and 1796.* London, 1799.

1799–1831: Pierre de La Mésangère (1761–1831). *Collection de meubles et objets de goût* (Collection of furniture and objects of taste). Paris, 1799–1831. Published serially.

1800, 1805: Jean-Nicolas-Louis Durand (1760–1834). *Recueil et parallèle des édifices de tout genre anciens et modernes.* Paris: Gillé Fils, 1800. Revised version with plates published in Brussels by Durand in 1805.

1802: Dominique Vivant, Baron Denon (1747–1825). *Voyage dans la Basse et la Haute Égypte, pendant les campagnes du Bonaparte, en 1798 et 1799* (Journey in Lower and Upper Egypt during Bonaparte's campaigns in 1798 and 1799). Paris, 1802.

1803: Thomas Sheraton (1751–1806). *The Cabinet Dictionary, Containing an Explanation of All the Terms Used in the Cabinet, Chair and Upholstery Branches.* 2 vols. London, 1803.

1804–7: Thomas Sheraton (1751–1806). *The Cabinet-Maker, Upholsterer and General Artist's Encyclopaedia*. London, 1804–7.

1805: Nicolas Ponce (1746–1831). *Collection des tableaux et arabesques antiques, trouvés a Rome, dans les ruines des Thermes de Titus* (Collection of ancient paintings and arabesques, found in Rome, in the ruins of the Baths of Titus). Paris, Brussels, and Lyon, 1805.

1807: Thomas Hope (1769–1831). *Household Furniture and Interior Decoration, Executed from Designs by Thomas Hope.* London: Longman, Hurst, Rees, and Orme, 1807.

1808: George Smith (1786–1826). *A Collection of Designs for Household Furniture and Interior Decoration, in the Most Approved and Elegant Taste.* London: J. Taylor, 1808.

1809–29: Rudolph Ackermann (1764–1834). *Repository of Arts, Literature, Commerce, Manufactures, Fashions, and Politics.* London, 1809–29. Monthly magazine.

1810: Aiken, Edmond. *An Essay on the Doric Order of Architecture: Containing a Historical View of Its Rise and Progress among the Ancients.* London: T. Bensley, 1810.

1812: Charles Percier (1764–1838) and Pierre-François-Léonard Fontaine (1762–1853). *Recueil de décorations intérieures, comprenant tout ce qui a rapport à l'ameublement comme vases, trépieds, candélabres, cassolettes, lustres, girandoles, lampes, chandeliers, cheminées, feux, poêles, pendules, tables, secrétaires, lits canapés, fauteuils, chaises, tabourets, miroirs, ecrans, &, &, &.* (Collection of interior decorations, including everything related to furnishing such as vases, tripods, candelabra, cassolettes, chandeliers, girandoles, lamps, candlesticks, fireplaces, fires, stoves, clocks, tables, secretaries, sofa beds, armchairs, chairs, stools, mirrors, screens, etc., etc., etc.). Paris, 1812. Issued as six loose, engraved plates in a series of twelve installments between 1801 and 1812, then published in Paris in a single bound edition under the same title in 1812.

1812–19, 1835: Peter Nicholson (1765–1844). *An Architectural Dictionary, Containing a Correct Nomenclature and Derivation of the Terms Employed by Architects, Builders, and Workmen. Exhibiting, in a Perspicuous Point of View, the Theory and Practice of the Various Branches of Architecture, in Carpentry, Joinery, Masonry, Bricklaying, and Their Dependence on Each Other; The Sciences Necessary to be Understood; and The Lives of the Principal Architects. The Whole Forming a Complete Guide to the Science of Architecture and the Art of Building.* London: J. Barfield, 1812–19. Published in twenty-six parts between 1812 and 1819; published in two volumes under the same title in 1819. Revised and reprinted in 1835 in three volumes.

1814: James Barron (active 1805–1839). *Modern and Elegant Designs of Cabinet and Upholstery Furniture.* London, 1814.

1817: The Society of the Dilettanti. *The Unedited Antiquities of Attica: Comprising the Architecture Remains of Eleusis, Rhamnus, Sunium, and Thoricus.* London: Longman, Hurst, Rees, Orme, Brown, and John Murray, 1817.

1826: George Smith (1786–1826). *The Cabinet-Maker and Upholsterer's Guide.* London: Jones & Co., 1826.

1826: Peter Nicholson (1765–1844) and Michael Angelo Nicholson (1794–1841). *The Practical Cabinet-Maker, Upholsterer, and Complete Decorator.* London: H. Fisher, Son & Co., 1826.

1828: George Smith (1786–1826). *The Cabinet-Maker and Upholsterer's Guide.* London: J. Haddon, 1828. Smith's second book of designs.

1829: Thomas King (c. 1790–1842). *The Modern Style of Cabinet Work Exemplified.* London, 1829.

1839–1935: Désiré Guilmard (1810–1885). *Le Garde-meuble, ancien et modern* (Furniture repository, ancient and modern). Paris, 1839–1935. Published bimonthly comprising up to nine loose plates.

1840: John Hall (1804–c. 1855). *The Cabinet Makers' Assistant.* Baltimore: John Murphy, 1840.

Price Books

1772, 1795, 1811, 1828: *Prices of Cabinet and Chair Work.* Philadelphia: James Humphreys, 1772. Revised 2nd and 3rd editions, 1795 and 1811, by Ormrod and Conrad, Philadelphia, published as *The Journeymen Cabinet and Chair-Makers Philadelphia Book of Prices.* Revised 1828 and published by W. Stavely in Philadelphia.

1788, 1793: *The Cabinet-Makers' London Book of Prices.* London: London Society of Cabinet Makers, 1788; revised edition, 1793.

1801: *Articles of the Salem Cabinetmaker Society, Associated June 26, 1801.* Salem, 1801.

1807, 1808: *London Chair-Makers' and Carvers' Book of Prices for Workmanship.* London: Committee of Chair-Manufacturers, 1807. See also the 1808 *Supplement.*

1802, 1810, 1815, 1817, 1834: *The New-York Book of Prices for Cabinet & Chair Work.* New York: Southwick and Crooker, 1802. Revised 2nd edition, 1810, and its 1815 supplement published by Southwick and Pelsue as *The New-York Revised Prices: for Manufacturing Cabinet and Chair Work.* Revised in 1817 under the same title by J. Seymour. Revised again in 1834 under the same title by Harper & Brothers.

City Guides and Directories

Goodrich, A. T. *The Picture of New-York and Stranger's Guide to the Commercial Metropolis of the United States.* New York, 1828.

Milbert, Jacques-Gérard. *Picturesque Itinerary of the Hudson River and the Peripheral Parts of North America,* translated and annotated by Constance D. Sherman. Ridgewood, NJ: Gregg Press 1968.

Mills, Robert. *Guide to the Capital of the United States: Embracing Every Information Useful to the Visiter, Whether on Business or Pleasure.* Washington, D.C., 1834.

Stafford, Cornelius William. *The Philadelphia Directory for 1798.* Philadelphia: William W. Woodward, 1798.

Published Journals, Letters, and Papers

Eliot, William Havard, and Isaiah Rogers. *A Description of Tremont House with Architectural Illustrations.* Boston: Gray and Bowen, 1830.

Fearon, Henry Bradshaw. *Sketches of America: A Narrative of a Journey of Five Thousand Miles through the Eastern and Western States of America.* 2nd edition. London: Longman, Hurst, Rees, Orme, and Brown, 1818.

Franklin, Benjamin. "Benjamin Franklin, Journal of a Voyage from England to Philadelphia 1726." *American History from the Revolution to Reconstruction and Beyond.* Last modified 2012. http://www.let.rug.nl/usa/documents/1701-1750/benjamin-franklin-journal-of-a-voyage-from-england-to-philadelphia-1726.php.

Franklin, Benjamin. *The Papers of Benjamin Franklin,* edited by Leonard W. Labaree. Vol. 1. New Haven: Yale University Press, 1959.

The L ... Family at Washington, or, A Winter in the Metropolis. Washington, D.C.: Davis and Force, 1822.

Latrobe, Benjamin Henry. *The Papers of Benjamin Henry Latrobe: The Microtext Edition,* edited by Edward C. Carter II. Clifton, NJ: James T. White & Co., 1976.

Latrobe, Benjamin Henry. *The Papers of Benjamin Henry Latrobe.* Vol. 3, *Correspondence and Miscellaneous Papers,* edited by John C. Van Horne and Lee W. Formwalt. New Haven: Yale University Press for the Maryland Historical Society, 1984.

Needles, John. "John Needles, An Autobiography," edited by Edward Needles Wright. *Journal of Quaker History* 58, no. 1 (Spring 1969): 3–21.

Powel, Samuel. *American Travelers to Italy in the Eighteenth Century: A Journal of Samuel Powel* (Rome, 1764), edited by Sarah Jackson. Florence: Studio per Edizione Scelte, 2001.

Royall, Anne. *Sketches of History, Life and Manners in the United States.* New Haven, 1826.

Smith, Margaret Bayard. *The First Forty Years of Washington Society Portrayed by the Family Letters of Mrs. Samuel Harrison Smith (Margaret Bayard) from the Collection of Her Grandson, J. Henley Smith,* edited by Gaillard Hunt. New York: Charles Scribner's Sons, 1906.

Wansey, Henry. *The Journal of an Excursion to the United States of North America in the Summer of 1794.* 2nd ed. London, 1798.

SECONDARY SOURCES

Agius, Pauline. *Ackermann's Regency Furniture & Interiors.* Ramsbury, Marlborough, Wiltshire: Crowood Press, 1984.

Albion, Robert Greenhalgh. *The Rise of New York Port, 1815–1860.* New York: C. Scribner's Sons, 1939.

Albion, Robert Greenhalgh. *Square-Riggers on Schedule: The New York Sailing Packets to England, France, and the Cotton Ports.* Princeton: Princeton University Press, 1938.

Alexander, Forsyth M. "Cabinet Warehousing in Southern Atlantic Ports, 1783–1820." *Journal of Early Southern Decorative Arts* 15, no. 2 (November 1989), 1–42.

Allen, William C. *History of the United States Capitol: A Chronicle of Design, Construction, and Politics.* Washington, D.C.: United States Government Printing Office, 2001.

Allman, William G., et al. *Official White House China: From the 18th to the 21st Centuries.* Washington, D.C.: White House Historical Association, 2016.

Armstrong, Tom. *An American Odyssey: The Warner Collection of American Fine and Decorative Arts.* New York: Monacelli Press, 2002.

Aymonino, Adriano. "'The True Style of Antique Decoration': Agostino Brunias and the Birth of the Adam Style at Kedleston Hall and Syon House." In *Robert Adam and His Brothers: New Light on Britain's Leading Architectural Family,* edited by Colin Thom, 104–22. Swindon: Historic England, 2019.

Baltimore Museum of Art. *Baltimore Furniture: The Work of Baltimore and Annapolis Cabinetmakers, 1760–1810.* Baltimore: Baltimore Museum of Art, 1947.

"Barron, James (1805–1839)." British and Irish Furniture Makers Online, Furniture History Society. Last updated April 20, 2023. https://bifmo.furniturehistorysociety.org/entry/barron-james-1814.

Bergdoll, Barry. "Introduction." In *The Complete Works of Percier and Fontaine.* Translated by Yolanda Stern Broad. Hudson: Princeton Architectural Press, 2018.

Berlin, Carswell Rush. "'A Shadow of a Magnitude': The Furniture of Thomas Cook and Richard Parkin." In *American Furniture 2013,* edited by Luke Beckerdite, 156–95. Milwaukee: Chipstone Foundation, 2013.

Berlin, Carswell Rush. "Presidential Appointments: Andrew Jackson and Three Philadelphia Cabinetmakers." *The Magazine Antiques* 184, no. 2 (March–April 2017): 74–83.

Bickford, Charles Bangs, et al. *Documentary History of the First Federal Congress, 1789–1791*. Vol. 21, *Correspondence—Third Session*. Baltimore: Johns Hopkins University Press, 2015.

Boor, Allison, John William Boor, and Andrew Steven Harris. *Philadelphia Empire Furniture*. West Chester, PA: University Press of New England, 2006.

Borneman, Walter R. *1812: The War That Forged a Nation*. New York: HarperCollins, 2004.

Bremer-David, Charissa. *French Tapestries & Textiles in the J. Paul Getty Museum*. Los Angeles: J. Paul Getty Museum, 1997.

Burleigh, Nina. *Mirage: Napoleon's Scientists and the Unveiling of Egypt*. New York: Harper, 2007.

Butcher, Samuel Henry. *Aristotle's Theory of Poetry and Fine Art*. New York: Macmillan, 1932.

Catalano, Kathleen M. "Abraham Kimball (1798–1890), Salem Cabinetmaker." *American Art Journal* 11, no. 2 (April 1979): 62–70.

Catalano, Kathleen, and Richard C. Nylander. "New Attributions to Adam Hains, Philadelphia Furniture Maker." *The Magazine Antiques* 117, no. 5 (May 1980): 1112–16.

Cheney, Robert C. "Roxbury Eight-Day Movements and the English Connection, 1785–1825." *The Magazine Antiques* 157, no. 4 (April 2000): 606–15.

Chicirda, Tara Gleason. "The Bowie Brothers of Port Royal Virginia and the Bernard Family Marble Chess Table." *Journal of Early Southern Decorative Arts* 38 (2017). https://www.mesdajournal.org/2018/the-bowie-brothers-of-port-royal-virginia-and-the-bernard-family-marble-chess-table/.

Conradsen, David H. "Ease and Economy: The Hancocks and the Development of Spring-Seat Upholstery in America." Master's thesis, University of Delaware, 1998.

Cooper, Wendy A. *In Praise of America: American Decorative Arts, 1650–1830*. New York: Knopf, 1980.

Cooper, Wendy A. *Classical Taste in America, 1800–1840*. New York: Abbeville Press; Baltimore: Baltimore Museum of Art, 1993.

Cornelius, Charles Over. *Furniture Masterpieces of Duncan Phyfe*. New York: Metropolitan Museum of Art, 1922.

"Denon, Jean-Dominique Vivant." Dictionary of Art Historians. Accessed June 4, 2024. https://arthistorians.info/denonv/.

de Tocqueville, Alexis. *Democracy in America*, edited by J. P. Mayer. Translated by George Lawrence. New York: Harper & Row, 1969.

Di Mauro, Damon. "Edmund Currier Revisited." *Journal of the National Association of Watch & Clock Collectors, Inc.* 65/1, no. 461 (January–February 2023): 29–38.

Earman, Cynthia. "An Uncommon Scold: Treasure-Talk Describes Life of Anne Royall." *Library of Congress Information Bulletin* 59, no. 1 (January 2000). https://www.loc.gov/loc/lcib/0001/.royall.html.

Elder, William Voss, III. *Baltimore Painted Furniture, 1800–1840*. Baltimore: Baltimore Museum of Art, 1972.

Elder, William Voss, III, and Jayne E. Stokes. *American Furniture, 1680–1880*. Baltimore: Baltimore Museum of Art, 1987.

Fairbanks, Jonathan L., and Elizabeth Bidwell Bates. *American Furniture 1620 to the Present*. New York: Richard Marek Publishers, 1981.

Feld, Elizabeth, and Stuart P. Feld. *Very Rich and Handsome: American Neo-Classical Decorative Arts*. New York: Hirschl & Adler Galleries, 2014.

Feld, Elizabeth, and Stuart P. Feld. *Augmenting the Canon: Recent Acquisitions of American Neo-Classical Decorative Arts*. New York: Hirschl & Adler Galleries, 2019.

Feld, Stuart P. *Boston in the Age of Neo-Classicism, 1810–1840*. New York: Hirschl & Adler Galleries, 1999.

Feld, Stuart P., and Wendell Garrett. *Neo-Classicism in America: Inspiration and Innovation, 1810–1840*. New York: Hirschl & Adler Galleries, 1991.

Fennimore, Donald L., and Robert T. Trump. "Joseph B. Barry, Philadelphia Cabinetmaker." *The Magazine Antiques* 135, no. 5 (May 1989): 1212–25.

Fitzgerald, Michelle. "The Furniture of John Needles." Lecture. The Beltway and Beyond: Neoclassical Furniture of Washington, D.C., Baltimore, and the Coastal Mid-Atlantic. Winterthur Museum Virtual Conference, October 8–9, 2020.

Flanigan, J. Michael. *American Furniture from the Kaufman Collection*. Washington, D.C.: National Gallery of Art, 1986.

Foley, Paul J. *Willard's Patent Time Pieces: A History of the Weight-Driven Banjo Clock, 1800–1900*. Norwell, MA: Roxbury Village Publishing, 2002.

Ford, John. "Rudolph Ackermann." Oxford Art Online. Last modified 2003. https://www.oxfordartonline.com/.

Fultz, Tamara. "A Passion for Antiquity: Sir William Hamilton and His Vase Collection." Metropolitan Museum of Art. October 17, 2018. https://www.metmuseum.org/articles/sir-william-hamilton.

Garrett, Jane. "Philadelphia and Baltimore, 1790–1840: A Study of Intra-Regional Unity." *Maryland Historical Magazine* 56, no. 1 (1960): 1–13.

Garton, Christina. "The Truth about Togas." PieceWork. March 13, 2020. https://pieceworkmagazine.com/the-truth-about-togas/.

Garvan, Beatrice B. *Federal Philadelphia, 1785–1825: The Athens of the Western World*. Philadelphia: Philadelphia Museum of Art, 1987.

Gerdts, William H., and Berry B. Tracy. *Classical America 1815–1845*. Newark, NJ: Newark Museum, 1963.

Glaeser, Edward L. "Reinventing Boston: 1630–2003." *Journal of Economic Geography* 5, no. 2 (April 2015): 119–53.

Gleason, Tara. "The Bayly Suite of Painted Furniture." *Antiques and Fine Art Magazine* (Spring 2003). https://www.antiquesandfineart.com/articles/article.cfm?request=385.

Golovin, Anne. "Cabinetmakers and Chairmakers of Washington, D.C., 1791–1840." *The Magazine Antiques* 107, no. 5 (May 1975): 898–922.

Gomme, Andor, and Gavin Stamp. "An American Forerunner? Minard Lafever and Alexander Thomson." In *'Greek' Thomson*, edited by Gavin Stamp and Sam McKinstry, 199–206. Edinburgh: Edinburgh University Press, 1994.

Green, James. N. "The First Colorplate Books Acquired by The Library Company, 1763–1772." Living Color: Collecting Color Plate Books at the Library Company of Philadelphia. Library Company of Philadelphia. Last modified 2007. https://www.librarycompany.org/color/index.htm.

Grout, James. "Stuart and Revett—And LeRoy." Encyclopedia Romana. Last modified 2024. https://penelope.uchicago.edu/~grout/encyclopaedia_romana/greece/architecture/classicism.html.

Harloe, Katherine. *Winckelmann and the Invention of Antiquity: Aesthetics and History in the Age of Altertumswissenschaft*. Oxford: Oxford University Press, 2013.

Hatfield, Mark O., with the Senate Historical Office. *Vice Presidents of the United States, 1789–1993*. Washington, D.C.: United States Government Printing Office, 1997.

Hawley, Henry. "Philadelphia Tables with Lyre Supports." *Bulletin of the Cleveland Museum of Art* 75, no. 1 (January 1988): 2–27.

Heckscher, Morrison H. "Philadelphia Chippendale: The Influence of the 'Director' in America." *Furniture History* 21 (1985): 283–95.

Heckscher, Morrison H. "Chippendale's Director: A Manifesto of Furniture Design." *Metropolitan Museum of Art Bulletin* 75, no. 4 (Spring 2018): 5–48.

Heckscher, Morrison H. "English Furniture Pattern Books in Eighteenth-Century America." In *American Furniture 1994*, edited by Luke Beckerdite. Milwaukee: Chipstone Foundation, 1994. https://chipstone.org/article.php/48/American-Furniture-1994/English-Furniture-Pattern-Books-in-Eighteenth-Century-America.

Heckscher, Morrison H. "Benjamin Bass and Boston Sideboards: A Question of Attribution." In *Boston Furniture, 1700–1900*, edited by Brock Jobe and Gerald W. R. Ward, 239–49. Boston: Colonial Society of Massachusetts, 2016.

"Hepplewhite, George (1786)." British and Irish Furniture Makers Online. Last modified 2019. https://bifmo.furniturehistorysociety.org/entry/hepplewhite-george-1786.

Hinds, Asher C., and Clarence Cannon. *Hinds' Precedents of the House of Representatives of the United States, Including References to Provisions of the Constitution, the Laws, and Decisions of the United States Senate*. Washington, D.C.: United States Government Printing Office, 1907.

The Historical Society of Early American Decoration. https://hsead.org/decorative-arts/.

Holden, Jack D., H. Parrot Bacot, and Cybèle Gontar. *Furnishing Louisiana: Creole and Acadian Furniture, 1735–1835*. New Orleans: Historic New Orleans Collection, 2009.

Humphries, Lance. "Provenance, Patronage and Perception: The Morris Suite of Baltimore Painted Furniture." In *American Furniture 2003*, edited by Luke Beckerdite. Milwaukee: Chipstone Foundation, 2003. https://chipstone.org/article.php/671/American-Furniture-2003/Provenance,-Patronage,-and-Perception:-The-Morris-Suite-of-Baltimore-Painted-Furniture.

Hunt, Tristram. *The Radical Potter: The Life and Times of Josiah Wedgwood*. New York: Metropolitan Books, 2021.

Hurst, Ronald L., and Jonathan Prown. *Southern Furniture 1680–1830: The Colonial Williamsburg Collection*. Williamsburg, VA: Colonial Williamsburg Foundation, 1997.

Jennings, J. L. Sibley. *Dolphin Tales: The Discovery of Related Southern Furniture of Exceptional Quality and Northern Mis-Attribution, or Move Over, Lannuier*. Washington, D.C.: J. L. Sibley Jennings, 1990.

Jenrette, Richard Hampton, *Adventures with Old Houses*. Charleston, SC: Wyrick & Co., 2000.

Jervis, Simon Swynfen. "John Stafford of Bath and His Interior Decorations." *Furniture History* 45 (2009): 143–92.

Jobe, Brock, and Gerald W. R. Ward, eds. *Boston Furniture, 1700–1900*. Charlottesville: University of Virginia Press, 2017.

Jones, Tom Devonshire. "Ackermann's 'Repository' 1809–28." *The British Art Journal* 11, no. 1 (2010): 69–74.

Jones, Robin D. "King, Thomas (fl. 1829–c. 1840)." In *Encyclopedia of Interior Design, Vol. 1*, edited by Joanna Banham. London: Routledge, 1997.

Kenny, Peter M. "Opulence Abroad: Charles-Honoré Lannuier's Gilded Furniture in Trinidad de Cuba." In *American Furniture 2004*, edited by Luke Beckerdite. Milwaukee: Chipstone Foundation, 2004. https://chipstone.org/article.php/177/American-Furniture-2004/Opulence-Abroad:-Charles-Honor%C3%A9-Lannuier%E2%80%99s-Gilded-Furniture-in-Trinidad-de-Cuba.

Kenny, Peter M. "From Bedford to New York to Rio and Back: The Life and Times of Elisha Blossom, Jr., Artisan of the New Republic." In *American Furniture 2003*, edited by Luke Beckerdite. Milwaukee: Chipstone Foundation, 2003. https://chipstone.org/article.php/278/American-Furniture-2003/From-New-Bedford-to-New-York-to-Rio-and-Back:-The-Life-and-Times-of-Elisha-Blossom,-Jr.,-Artisan-of-the-New-Republic-

Kenny, Peter M., Michael K. Brown, Frances F. Bretter, and Matthew A. Thurlow. *Duncan Phyfe: Master Cabinetmaker in New York*. New York: Metropolitan Museum of Art, 2011.

Kenny, Peter M., Frances F. Bretter, and Ulrich Leben. *Honoré Lannuier, Cabinetmaker from Paris: The Life and Work of a French Ébéniste in Federal New York*. New York: Metropolitan Museum of Art, 1998.

Keno, Leigh, Leslie Keno, and Joan Barzily Freund. *Hidden Treasures: Searching for Masterpieces of American Furniture*. New York: Warner Books, 2000.

Kimball, Marie. "The Original Furnishings of the White House." *The Magazine Antiques* 16, no. 1 (January 1929): 36.

Kirtley, Alexandra Alevizatos. "A New Suspect: Baltimore Cabinetmaker Edward Priestley." In *American Furniture 2000*, edited by Luke Beckerdite, 100–51. Milwaukee: Chipstone Foundation, 2000.

Kirtley, Alexandra Alevizatos. *The 1772 Philadelphia Furniture Price Book: An Introduction and Guide*. Philadelphia: Philadelphia Museum of Art, 2005.

Kirtley, Alexandra Alevizatos. "The Painted Furniture of Philadelphia: A Reappraisal." *The Magazine Antiques* 169, no. 5 (May 2006): 134–45.

Kirtley, Alexandra Alevizatos. "Benjamin Henry Latrobe and the Furniture of John and Hugh Finlay." *The Magazine Antiques* (December 9, 2009). https://www.themagazineantiques. com/article/benjamin-henry-latrobeand-the-furniture-of-john-and-hughfinlay/.

Kirtley, Alexandra Alevizatos. "Contriving the Madisons' Drawing Room: Benjamin Henry Latrobe and the Furniture of John and Hugh Finlay." *The Magazine Antiques* 178, no. 12 (December 2009): 56–63.

Kirtley, Alexandra Alevizatos. *American Furniture, 1650–1840: Highlights from the Philadelphia Museum of Art*. Philadelphia: Philadelphia Museum of Art, 2020.

Kirtley, Alexandra Alevizatos. "Athens of America." *The Encyclopedia of Greater Philadelphia*. Accessed March 17, 2024. https://philadelphiaencyclopedia.org/themes/athens-of-america/.

Kirtley, Alexandra Alevizatos, and Peggy A. Olley. *Classical Splendor: Painted Furniture for a Grand Philadelphia House*. Philadelphia: Philadelphia Museum of Art, 2016.

Klapthor, Margaret B. "Furniture in the Capitol: Desks and Chairs Used in the Chamber of the House of Representatives, 1819–1857." *Records of the Columbia Historical Society* 69/70 (1969/1970): 190–211.

Kuronen, Darcy. "Early Pianomaking in Boston, 1790–1830." In *Boston Furniture, 1700–1900*, edited by Brock Jobe and Gerald W. R. Ward, 315–34. Boston: Colonial Society of Massachusetts, 2016.

Lahikainen, Dean Thomas. "A Salem Cabinetmakers' Price Book." *American Furniture 2001*, edited by Luke Beckerdite, 152–219. Milwaukee: Chipstone Foundation, 2001.

Leben, Ulrich. *Molitor: Ébéniste from the Ancien Régime to the Bourbon Restoration*. London: P. Wilson, 1992.

Lee, Jean Gordon, and Philip Chadwick Foster Smith. *Philadelphians and the China Trade, 1784–1844*. Philadelphia: Philadelphia Museum of Art, 1984.

Lomax, James. "Chippendale, Thomas snr (1718–1779)." British and Irish Furniture Makers Online, Furniture History Society. Last modified February 15, 2024. https://bifmo.furniturehistorysociety.org/entry/chippendale-thomas-snr-1718-79.

Loth, Calder. "Notes on Moldings, the Change from Roman to Greek." Institute of Classical Architecture and Art. February 10, 2015. https://www.classicist.org/articles/notes-on-moldings-the-change-from-roman-to-greek/.

Lloyd, E. Keith. "Mr. Peter Nicholson, the Practical Builder and Mathematician." *Mathematical Gazette* 66, no. 437 (October 1982): 203–7.

Macaulay-Lewis, Elizabeth, and Matthew M. McGowan, eds. "Classical New York." In *Classical New York: Discovering Greece and Rome in Gotham*, 1–114. New York: Fordham University Press, 2018.

"Mary Osgood (Deland) Hodges (1808–1903)." Wikitree. Last modified January 5, 2023. https://www.wikitree.com/wiki/Deland-213.

McClelland, Nancy. *Duncan Phyfe and the English Regency, 1795–1830*. New York: Dover Publications, 1939.

McGlyn, Bethany. "Who Built the City on the Severn? Slavery, Material Culture, and Landscapes of Labor in Early Annapolis." Master's thesis, University of Delaware, 2020.

McInnis, Maurie D. *The Politics of Taste in Antebellum Charleston*. Chapel Hill: University of North Carolina Press, 2005.

McInnis, Maurie D., and Robert A. Leath. "Beautiful Specimens, Elegant Patterns: New York Furniture for the Charleston Market, 1810–1840." In *American Furniture 1996*, edited by Luke Beckerdite, 137–74. Milwaukee: Chipstone Foundation, 1996.

Mershon, Peggy. "Rhea Knittle Made a Name in Antiques." *Mansfield News Journal*, September 5, 2015. https://www.mansfieldnewsjournal.com/story/news/history/2015/09/05/rhea-mansfield-knittle-made-name-antiques/71772860/.

Miller, Edgar G., Jr. *American Antique Furniture: A Book for Amateurs, Vol. II*. Baltimore: Lord Baltimore Press, 1937.

Momon, Tiffany, and Torren Gatson. Black Craftspeople Digital Archive. Last modified 2024. https://blackcraftspeople.org/.

Monkman, Betty C. *The White House: Its Historic Furnishings and First Families*. Washington, D.C.: White House Historical Association, 2000.

Montgomery, Charles F. *American Furniture: The Federal Period in the Henry Francis du Pont Winterthur Museum*. New York: Viking Press, 1966.

Morley, John. *Regency Design, 1790–1840: Gardens, Buildings, Interiors, Furniture*. New York: H. N. Abrams, 1993.

Moss, Roger W. "Hall, John G. (1804–c. 1855)." Philadelphia Architects and Buildings. Accessed June 4, 2024. https://www.philadelphiabuildings.org/pab/app/ar_display.cfm/24997.

Mussey, Robert D., Jr. "Verte Antique Decoration on American Furniture: History, Materials, Techniques and Technical Investigations." In *Painted Wood: History and Conservation*, edited by Valerie Dorge and F. Carey Howlett. Los Angeles: Getty Conservation Institute, 1994.

Mussey, Robert D., Jr. *The Furniture Masterworks of John and Thomas Seymour*. Salem, MA: Peabody Essex Museum, 2003.

Mussey, Robert D., Jr., and Clark Pearce. "Classical Excellence in Boston: The Furniture of Isaac Vose, 1789–1825." In *Boston Furniture, 1700–1900*, edited by Brock Jobe and Gerald W. R. Ward, 252–90. Boston: Colonial Society of Massachusetts, 2016.

Mussey, Robert D., Jr., and Clark Pearce. *Rather Elegant Than Showy: The Classical Furniture of Isaac Vose*. Jaffrey, NH: Massachusetts Historical Society in association with David R. Godine, 2018.

Nouvel-Kammerer, Odile. "Discourse on Ornament under the Empire." In *Symbols of Power: Napoleon and the Art of the Empire Style 1800–1815*, edited by Odile Nouvel-Kammerer. Paris: American Federation of the Arts and Musée des Arts Décoratifs, 2007.

Ormsbee, Thomas Hamilton. *Early American Furniture Makers: A Social and Biographical Study*. New York: Archer House, 1930.

Pearce, Lorraine W. "Lannuier in the President's House." *The Magazine Antiques* 81, no. 5 (May 1962): 515–20.

Pearce, Clark, Catherine Ebert, and Alexandra Alevizatos Kirtley. "From Apprentice to Master: The Life and Career of Philadelphia Cabinetmaker George C. Wright." In *American Furniture 2007*, edited by Luke Beckerdite, 110–31. Milwaukee: Chipstone Foundation, 2007.

Pearce, Susan, and Frank Salmon. "Charles Heathcote Tatham in Italy, 1794–96: Letters, Drawings and Fragments, and Part of an Autobiography." *The Volume of the Walpole Society* 67 (2005): 1–91.

Podmaniczky, Michael S. "Samuel Gragg and the Elastic Chair." In *Boston Furniture, 1700–1900*, edited by Brock Jobe and Gerald W. R. Ward, 195–207. Boston: Colonial Society of Massachusetts, 2016.

Pollack, Jodi A. "Three Generations of Meeks Craftsmen, 1797–1869: A History of Their Business and Furniture." Master's thesis, Parsons School of Design, New York, 1998.

Potts, Alex. *Flesh and the Ideal: Winckelmann and the Origins of Art History*. New Haven: Yale University Press, 1994.

"Presidential Appointments." *The Magazine Antiques* (March 21, 2017). http://www.themagazineantiques.com/article/presidential-appointments/.

Priddy, Sumpter T., III, and Ann Steuart. "Seating Furniture from the District of Columbia, 1795–1820." In *American Furniture 2010*, edited by Luke Beckerdite, 121–26. Milwaukee: Chipstone Foundation, 2010.

Priddy, Sumpter, III, J. Michael Flanigan, and Gregory R. Weidman. "The Genesis of Neoclassical Style in Baltimore Furniture." In *American Furniture 2000*, edited by Luke Beckerdite. Milwaukee: Chipstone Foundation, 2000. https://chipstone.org/article.php/402/American-Furniture-2000/The-Genesis-of-Neoclassical-Style-in-Baltimore-Furniture.

"Privateer History." Pride of Baltimore II (website). Accessed March 17, 2024. https://pride2.org/education/privateer-history/.

Randall, Richard H., Jr. "Sources of the Empire Style." *The Magazine Antiques* 83, no. 4 (April 1963): 452–53.

"The Rhinelander family: An Old Colonial Fortune." *The New York Times*. June 23, 1878. https://www.nytimes.com/1878/06/23/archives/the-rhinelander-family-an-old-colonial-fortune-scraps-from-the.html.

"Robert Adam: Neoclassical Architect and Designer." Victoria and Albert Museum. Accessed May 4, 2024. https://www.vam.ac.uk/articles/robert-adam-neoclassical-architect-and-designer.

Schwarz, Robert D. *The Stephen Girard Collection: A Selective Catalog*. Philadelphia: Girard College, 1980.

Seale, William. *The President's House, Vol. 1*. Washington, D.C.: White House Historical Association, 2008.

Semmes, Raphael. *Baltimore as Seen by Visitors, 1783–1860*. Baltimore: Maryland Historical Society, 1953.

Smith, Thomas Gordon. *Thomas King Neoclassical Furniture Designs: A Reprint of Thomas King's "Modern Style of Cabinet Work Exemplified." 1829*. New York: Dover Publications, 1995.

Smith, Thomas Gordon. "Quervelle Furniture at Rosedown, in Louisiana." *The Magazine Antiques* 159, no. 5 (May 2001): 770–79.

Smith, Robert C. "The Furniture of Anthony G. Quervelle, Part I: The Pier Tables." *The Magazine Antiques* 103, no. 5 (May 1973): 984–94.

Symonds, R. W. "English Eagle and Dolphin Console Tables." *The Magazine Antiques* 18, no. 10 (October 1930): 304–7.

Talbott, Page. "Classical Conservatism: Card Tables and English Regency Style in Boston, 1810–35." *Maine Antique Digest* (December 1989): 10c–16c.

Talbott, Page. "Seating Furniture in Boston, 1810–1835." *The Magazine Antiques*, 140, no. 5 (May 1991): 956–969.

Talbott, Page. "The Furniture Trade in Boston, 1810–1835: Check List." *The Magazine Antiques* 141, no. 5 (May 1992): 842–55.

Tétart-Vittu, Françoise. "Biographie de Pierre de La Mésangère (1761–1831)." Encyclopaedia Universalis. Last modified February 10, 2009. https://www.universalis.fr/encyclopedie/pierre-de-lamesangere/.

"Thomas Hope and the Regency style." Victoria and Albert Museum. Accessed June 4, 2024. https://www.vam.ac.uk/articles/thomas-hope-and-the-regencystyle.

Thomson, Christine. "Last but Not Least: Examination and Interpretation of Coatings on Brass Hardware." In *Wooden Artifacts Group of the American Institute for Conservation*. Washington, D.C.: American Institute for Conservation, 1991.

Thurlow, Matthew A. "Thomas Constantine: Cabinetmaker and Mahogany Merchant in Early Nineteenth-Century New York." Master's thesis, University of Delaware, Winterthur, 2004.

Thurlow, Matthew A. "Aesthetics, Politics, and Power in Early-Nineteenth-Century Washington: Thomas Constantine & Co.'s Furniture for the United States Capitol, 1818–1819." In *American Furniture 2006*, edited by Luke Beckerdite, 184–228. Milwaukee: Chipstone Foundation, 2006.

Thurlow, Matthew A. "American Federal-Era Period Rooms." In *Heilbrunn Timeline of Art History*. November 2009. https://www.metmuseum.org/toah/hd/fede/hd_fede.htm.

Tracy, Berry B., Marilynn Johnson, Marvin D. Schwartz, and Suzanne Boorsch. *19th-Century America: Furniture and Other Decorative Arts*. New York: Metropolitan Museum of Art, 1970.

Tucker, Alicia. "Evenings at Home: Family Life in Southside Virginia, 1760–1836." Master's thesis, College of William and Mary, Arts and Sciences, 1988.

Valentiner, Wilhelm Reinhold, Henry Watson Kent, and Florence Nightingale Levy. *The Hudson-Fulton Celebration. Catalogue of an exhibition held in the Metropolitan Museum of Art commemorative of the tercentenary of the discovery of the Hudson River by Henry Hudson in the year 1609, and the centenary of the first use of steam in the navigation of said river by Robert Fulton in the year* 1807. 2 vols. New York: Metropolitan Museum of Art, 1909.

Venable, Charles L. "Germanic Craftsmen and Furniture Design in Philadelphia, 1820–1850." In *American Furniture 1998*, edited by Luke Beckerdite, 41–80. Lebanon, NH: University Press of New England for the Chipstone Foundation, 1998.

Vincent, Nicholas C. "American Furniture, 1730–1790: Queen Anne and Chippendale Styles." In *Heilbrunn Timeline of Art History*. December 2009. https://www.metmuseum.org/toah/hd/chip/hd_chip.htm.

Voorsanger, Catherine Hoover. "'Gorgeous Articles of Furniture': Cabinetmaking in the Empire City." In *Art and the Empire City: New York, 1825–1861*, edited by Catherine Hoover Voorsanger and John K. Howat, 287–325. New York: Metropolitan Museum of Art; New Haven: Yale University Press, 2000.

Willard, John Ware. *Simon Willard and His Clocks*. New York: Dover, 1968.

Wilentz, Sean. *Chants Democratic: New York City and the Rise of the American Working Class, 1788–1850*. Oxford: Oxford University Press, 1984.

Weidman, Gregory R. *Furniture in Maryland, 1740–1940: The Collection of the Maryland Historical Society*. Baltimore: Maryland Historical Society, 1984.

Weidman, Gregory R., and Jennifer Goldsborough. *Classical Maryland, 1815–1845: Fine and Decorative Arts from the Golden Age*. Baltimore: Maryland Historical Society, 1993.

Whitman, Walt. *Leaves of Grass*. Boston: Thayer and Eldridge, 1860.

Zimmerman, Philip D. "The American Sofa Table." *The Magazine Antiques* 155, no. 5 (May 1999): 744–53.

Zimmerman, Philip D. "Early American Furniture Makers' Marks." *American Furniture 2007*, edited by Luke Beckerdite, 132–67. Milwaukee: Chipstone Foundation, 2007.

INDEX